79 FURNITURE PROJECTS
PROJECTS
FOR EVERY ROOM

79 FURNITURE PROJECTS
FOR EVERY ROOM

PERCY W. BLANDFORD

TAB BOOKS Inc.

Blue Ridge Summit, PA 17214

FIRST EDITION
FIRST PRINTING

Copyright © 1986 by TAB BOOKS Inc.
Printed in the United States of America

Library of Congress Cataloging in Publication Data

Blandford, Percy W.
79 furniture projects for every room.

Includes index.
1. Furniture making—Amateur's manuals. I. Title.
II. Title: Seventy-nine furniture projects for every
room.
TT195.B587 1986   684.1'042   86-5866
ISBN 0-8306-0704-8
ISBN 0-8306-2704-9 (pbk.)

Contents

Introduction

The title, *79 Furniture Projects for Every Room*, is an all-embracing one that needs clarifying. It could mean how to take an empty house and make every piece of furniture needed to fill it. That is not impossible, but it would be a vast undertaking and require an instruction book much bigger than this.

This book offers suggestions for furniture that an amateur woodworker can make for every room. Perhaps these are basic items you want to make for an unfinished room. More likely you have the basic furniture, but want to add some luxuries or personal pieces to fill a particular need. These might be items you think desirable, but would not buy, or one-of-a-kind pieces. If you want it, you must make it. Many times standard, store-bought furniture is not the size you want. If you make it yourself, it can be designed to fit any space. More important to many of us is the satisfaction of making and owning something that no one else owns—something unique.

Many types of furniture can be used in several rooms. You are unlikely to move a bed out of a bedroom or a dining table out of the dining room, but such things as small tables, hanging shelves, stools, and bookcases could be used in any room. For convenience this book is divided into chapters devoted to particular rooms, though there are a few items that could have been in any chapter. Consult the book as a whole to find furniture to suit your needs, even if you want to use it in a room different from the one in which we have included it. Use the table of contents and the index to find what you want.

Suggestions for woods are not specific because supplies vary, not only in different parts of the country, but at different times. Furniture woods are imported from many parts of the world and supplies are not constant. Your supplier may have wood with a strange name now and its place will be taken by another with a different name in a few months. Your supplier should be able to advise you on the relative characteristics of the wood he offers compared with something more familiar. In general, good-quality furniture for important use should be made of hardwood, although for some things softwood is acceptable. We are all using more manufactured boards, particularly plywood and veneered particleboard. These have many advantages, particularly in availability and price. Providing the limitations in possible designs are considered, satisfactory results can be obtained, although care is needed to avoid merely making copies of mass-produced furniture.

We are used to measuring in feet and inches. Elsewhere, the metric system is used. Some imported wood might be already cut to metric sizes. You can get a close conversion with 1 inch to 25 millimeters (mm) and 39 inches to 1 meter (m). All sizes in this book are in inches, unless marked otherwise. Nearly all materials lists give exact widths and thicknesses, but lengths might be full.

Chapter 1

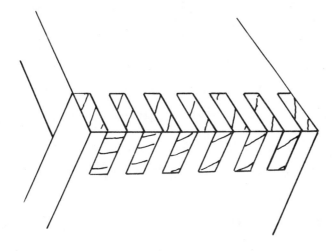

Furniture-Making Techniques

Any woodworker with a few basic tools, whether hand or power, and the ability to use them should be able to make a large range of furniture, even if previous experience has been with more general carpentry. Many items of furniture only involve the application of simple carpentry techniques, taken step-by-step. This experience can then be followed confidently with more ambitious projects.

Furniture making may be called cabinetmaking or cabinetry, and can be regarded as an extension of carpentry. The wood is usually better and more expensive than woods in general use. It is often hardwood, which needs different techniques than everyday softwoods. You must keep in mind the finished product. With structural carpentry, such as the framing of a building or merely making shelves, it does not usually matter if you put the wood on something that marks the surface. Grit or a stray nail denting the surface might not matter. The quality of the surface might not be important. When making furniture you have to remember that the finished exposed surfaces should be as un-blemished as possible. Bench tops should be smooth and uncluttered, while working surfaces of machines should be kept smooth and free from the chips and dust from previous cuts. A hand brush is an important part of your equipment. Because you might have to spend some time and skill in bringing a surface to the state you want, do not risk damaging it during other working.

Some hardwoods can be worked as easily as softwoods. Others have grain that tends to tear up or cannot be planed to a good surface in any direction. The beauty of many of these woods is in grain pattern, so the complications this brings have to be accepted. In general carpentry you may manage with tools that are not as sharp as they should be, but for furniture making you should keep all cutting tools as sharp as you can make them. A skilled cabinetmaker uses an oilstone much more frequently than the beginner who wants to get on with the job and not waste time sharpening. The need for sharpening applies to the cutters of power tools as well as to hand tools.

It is modern practice to use power tools as

much as possible, and that is perfectly good technique. For the best finish on furniture, however, it is often advisable to follow with hand tools. In particular, power planing can be finished by hand planing using a very sharp smoothing plane. No amount of sanding over the surface left by power planing can equal that obtained by hand planing. Where the grain is difficult, a finely-set, sharp hand plane used diagonally or directly across the grain could be the answer. With some surfaces the only way to smooth convoluted grain is with a scraper. Many woodworkers are unfamiliar with this tool, but if you are going to work on choice hardwoods, you will be glad for it.

SCRAPING

Some scrapers are mounted in handles and are used with a pulling and pressing action. Others are mounted in bodies similar to a plane. Both are quite good, but equally effective is what is sold as a "cabinet scraper." This is a rectangle of steel usually 3 inches by 6 inches. Thickness is about the same as a handsaw. Actual sizes are not important, and you can make your own from any piece of tool steel. It should not be tempered excessively hard—you must be able to file it.

File an edge straight and finish it by draw filing. With the scraper held in a vise, hold a fine file square across and move it along the edge (Fig. 1-1A) until it has removed all file marks across. It is possible to use a scraper at this stage for coarser work, but for the better finish, follow with an oilstone. Hold the scraper upright on the stone and rub it until the file marks are removed (Fig. 1-B). Next, rub its surface on the stone (Fig. 1-1C). Do this from both sides to finish to an exactly squared edge with smooth surfaces. A medium grit stone should be satisfactory, although some users continue with a fine one.

That is not sharpening. It is preparation of the edge. You might not have to return to those stages very often, although much depends on the wood being worked on. Sharpening consists of turning the edge over, shown exaggerated in Fig. 1-1D. The amount turned over is not usually visible, unless you look closely with a lens. Turning over is done

with a piece of hard steel. You can buy handled burnishers, which are just pieces of round steel. As long as the steel is harder than the scraper, you can use almost anything. The back of a chisel or gouge will do. An experienced user will turn the edge in his hands, but for first attempts it is better to have the scraper in a vise. Rub the burnisher along the edge, using plenty of pressure and a slight tilt (Fig. 1-1E). Do this several times tilted both ways to produce two turned edges, which you can feel even if you cannot see them.

To use the scraper, hold it so the fingers pull back and the thumbs press forward to curve the steel slightly (Fig. 1-2). Tilt the steel forward and push it over the wood, regulating the angle so the turned edge cuts (Fig. 1-1F). The wood should come away as very fine shavings. If all you get is dust, the scraper is at the wrong angle or has not been sharpened properly. Scraping can be done in any direction in relation to grain lines. Over the twisted grain of some woods it might be the only tool that will produce a good surface. Scraping follows planing with the finest plane you have.

After some use the tiny edge will wear and turn back. It is best then to rub it entirely back with the burnisher flat on the surface (Fig. 1-1G) before turning it again (Fig. 1-1E). You will be able to do this several times before having to use an oilstone again or go right back to filing. All four edges can be sharpened to cut both sides to give you four wide and four narrow cutting edges. There are curved scrapers for special moldings and similar shapes, but on modern furniture there is little use for them.

SQUARING

Unless a piece of furniture is an unusual item, it should be square in all directions or sometimes symmetrical. This is important for practical reasons, such as the fit of drawers, but more important for the sake of appearance. A leg out of true or a side that does not match the opposite side is very obvious to even the most casual observer. This means that careful squaring during construction and assembly is very important. If the corner of a room is slightly out of square, as it often is, no one notices. If you make something for the yard and it

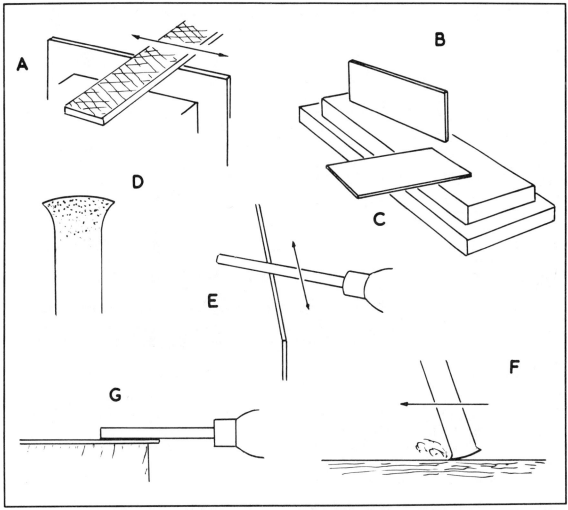

Fig. 1-1. A scraper is sharpened with a file and oilstone, then the edge is turned over to form the burr which does the cutting.

does not finish exactly square, it might not matter. If you make a table, sideboard, bookcase, or other piece of furniture and a part is out of true, you will certainly notice it and many other people will notice it as well.

There are means of squaring on many power tools, and you can use a try square for work on the bench, but all these devices are limited to 12 inches, or not much more. If you want to mark out a table to 36 inches wide, it is no use marking 12 inches and extending the line. It could be upwards of 1/4 inch out at the far end. Some other method has to be used to achieve accuracy. The edges of a sheet

of plywood should be square to each other, but you ought to test a corner before assuming that it is so.

To mark 90 degrees up to any size, the geometric *3:4:5* method is best. This uses the fact that a triangle with sides in this proportion has an angle between the two shorter sides of 90 degrees. Suppose you want to draw a line 36 inches long square to a longer edge. Mark where the line will come on the edge and mark four units along the edge from it. In this case 12-inch units are appropriate (Fig. 1-3A). Measure three units (36 inches) from the first mark and swing a short arc that will obviously cross a square line (Fig. 1-3B). That is

3

Fig. 1-2. A scraper is bent to a slight curve and pushed forward so it removes very fine shavings.

most easily done with the hooked end of an expanding rule on the edge at the first mark and a pencil against 36 inches. From the second mark on the edge measure five units (60 inches) to a point on the arc (Fig. 1-3C). If a line is drawn through that point and the first mark, it will be square to the edge (Fig. 1-3D).

If you expect to make much furniture that needs squaring to larger sizes than your ordinary squares, it is worthwhile making a large plywood triangle with a square corner. Some workers set out two permanent lines at 90 degrees on the shop floor and use them for squaring large assemblies.

During assembly, squareness can be tested by measuring diagonals. If you are putting together something that should be rectangular, the measurements across opposite corners should be the same. You can measure with a rule or tape, but it is generally more accurate to use a strip of wood on edge and make pencil *peck marks* (Fig. 1-4A). Variations are more easily seen than by reading graduations on a rule.

This method also checks symmetry. Suppose legs taper to the top on a stand. Checks of diagonals will show if the angles on each side are the same and, just as important, that the top is level (Fig. 1-4B).

Most furniture is a framed structure. It is possible to assemble all at once, but there is less risk of error if assembly is in stages. Opposite sides can be assembled and tested for squareness and that they match when put over each other (Fig. 1-5A). When the glue has set, other parts are added and checked for squareness (Fig. 1-5B), not only in side view, but when viewed from above.

It is possible to get everything apparently square, yet the assembly is twisted. You look across diagonally and find that, for instance, the near leg is sloping in relation to the rear one. This is what is called "being in winding" and calls for additional tests. When you assemble a frame, check that it is square, then sight across two surfaces or edges that should be flat in relation to each other, two legs for example (Fig. 1-5C). Within reason, the further

4

back you can get your eye, the easier it is to see any error. Do this also when you assemble the other way and again from above, when the top framing should match any lower down.

You might find you have to force frames the other way so they spring back true. Make sure an assembly is on a flat surface. It might have to be left with a weight on top to keep it in shape.

SCREWING

Nails are not often seen in furniture, except in places where finishing nails or fine pins are used; but where cut joints are not made, parts may be screwed. Plain steel screws are not generally favored, partly because oak and some other hard-

woods attack the steel and corrosion is rapid. Screws may be plated, but brass screws are the usual choice of a furniture maker.

In hardwoods, drilling suitable holes is important. Do not attempt to drive screws without a hole in the lower piece, as might be done successfully in softwoods. There is a risk of splitting, and in many cases you would find driving completely impossible. The hole in the upper piece should just clear the neck of the screw, and the hole in the lower piece should go as deep as the screw and be about the diameter of the core of the screw thread (Fig. 1-6A). How much you countersink depends on the wood. The head will usually pull in slightly, so if you want it to finish level with the surface, do not countersink too much (Fig. 1-6B).

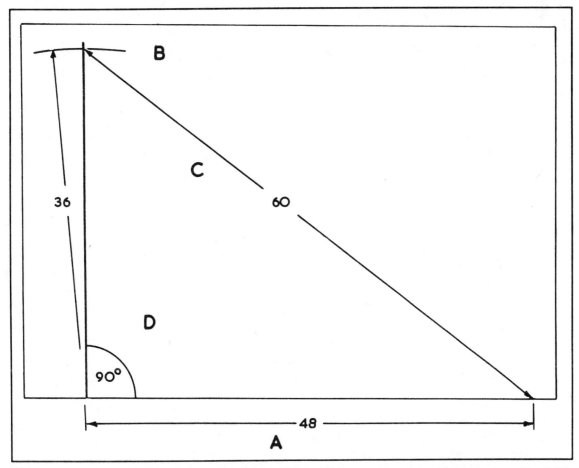

Fig. 1-3. A line square to an edge can be drawn to any size by using a triangle with its sides in the proportion 3:4:5.

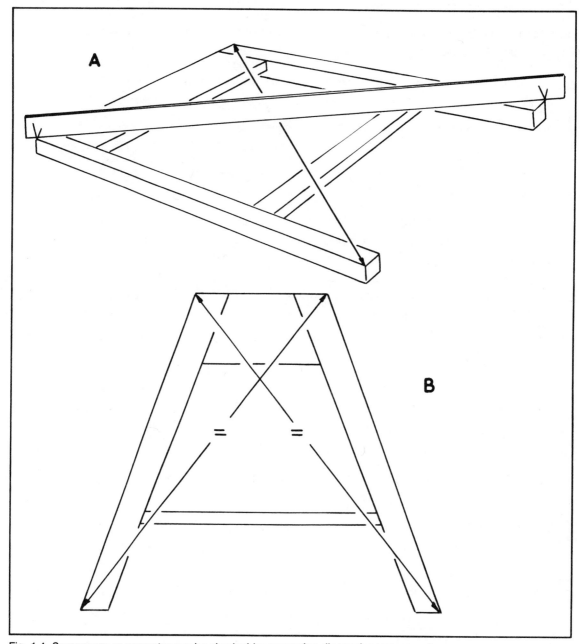

Fig. 1-4. Squareness or symmetry can be checked by comparing diagonal measurements.

End grain does not offer a very good grip to a screw thread. If you have to drive into end grain, use a longer screw. A better way to get a good grip is to provide some cross grain by letting in a piece of dowel (Fig. 1-6C). Position it so the screw thread goes right through it. The dowel need not go right through the wood. You can make the hole from the least important side. As long as it goes past the screw, it is deep enough.

If screws have to be used from a visible sur-

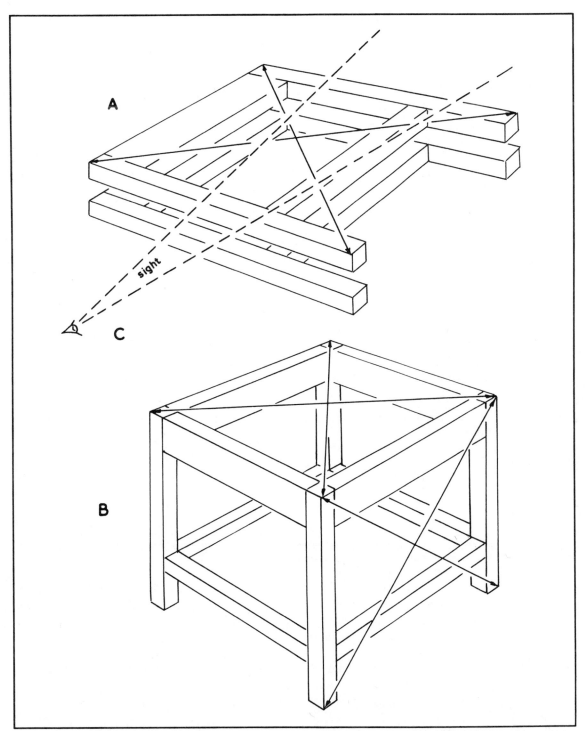

Fig. 1-5. Parts of a framed assembly should be checked for squareness in all directions and for freedom from twist by sighting across.

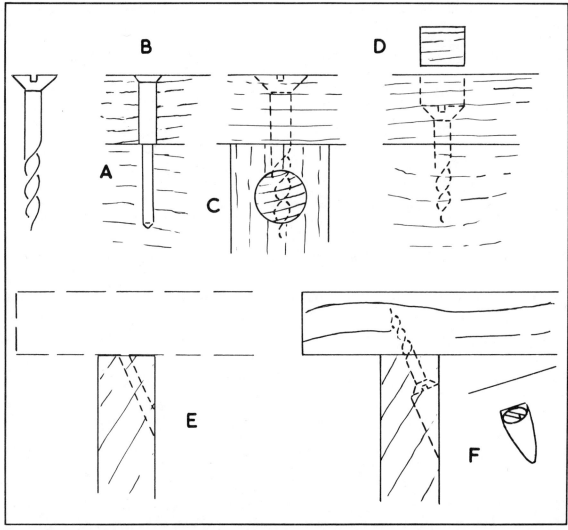

Fig. 1-6. Screw holes should be drilled (A, B); a dowel across strengthens the grip in end grain (C); heads may be sunk and plugged (D). A tabletop may be held with pocket screws from below (E, F).

face, and you want to hide them, they can be counterbored. Drill a hole bigger than the screw head and of a size that will suit a plug, then drive the screw in that (Fig. 1-6D). The plug could be a dowel, but that would show end grain on the surface. It is better to use a plug cutter in a drill press (Fig. 1-7) to cut cross-grain plugs from scrap wood of the same type as that drilled. One of these plugs, with its grain the same way as the surrounding wood, can be glued in and planed off so it is almost invisible.

Pocket screws are useful for attaching something like a tabletop to a rail when the rail is too deep to drill through and screw heads are not wanted on top. Plan for the screw to go diagonally and pass through the top surface of the rail near its center (Fig. 1-6E). Drill downwards, then cut out a pocket for the screw head to have a flat surface to pull against (Fig. 1-6F).

DOWELLED JOINTS

At one time dowels were made by driving scraps

of wood through holes in a steel plate. Now they are obtainable in long lengths and increasing use is made of them. In furniture making there is often a choice between dowelled joints and mortise and tenon joints. It can be argued that dowelled joints are appropriate to quantity production and mortise and tenon joints should be used by the individual craftsman. Dowelling can be done with mechanical aids, and there is little risk of errors. Although there are mechanical ways of making mortises and tenons, these devices are not usually available to the individual worker. Consequently there is more hand work and individual skill in making mortise and tenon joints.

Apart from considerations of convenience, there are places where one method of jointing is preferable to the other. In assemblies where there is much load, mortises and tenons should be stronger than dowels. Both methods of jointing are done to impart mechanical strength and to give side-grain-to-side-grain gluing surfaces. Gluing on end grain does not have much strength, but modern glues are very strong where side grain surfaces meet. Unless there are a very large number of dowels in a joint, the mortise and tenon joint usually gives a better expanse of glue surfaces. If absolute maximum strength is unnecessary, dowel joints can be used instead of mortise and tenon joints. These alternatives are indicated in many projects in this book.

With the availability of prepared dowel rods, the only considerations are the need to drill holes of the right size, in the right places, and square to the surface on surfaces that meet closely. It is possible to mark carefully and drill squarely freehand (Fig. 1-8A), but it is better to have a guide to squareness, if not to location. There are several dowelling jigs available that can be adjusted to position the holes correctly and hold the drill squarely as they are used. If a lot of dowelling is to be done, one of these tools may be worth having.

You might prefer to mark by hand. A dot at each position can be made with a center punch to guide the drill point. If drilling is done with a drill

Fig. 1-7. Plugs for counterbored screws may be cut from scrap wood with a cutter in a drill, then broken out with a chisel.

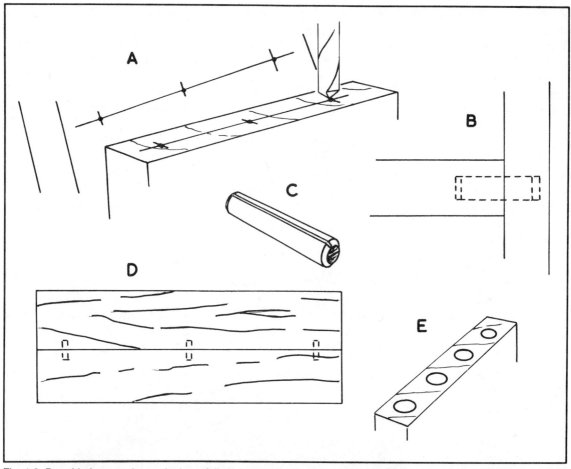

Fig. 1-8. Dowel holes must be marked carefully in both parts (A), drilled slightly too deep (B), and spaced closer in end than in side grain (D, E). A groove along the dowel allows air and surplus glue to escape (C).

press or an electric hand drill mounted in a stand, squareness is maintained and a depth stop can be used.

Holes should always be slightly deeper than the dowels (Fig. 1-8B). A dowel going into a hole is like a piston compressing air in a cylinder, particularly if it is coated with glue. In some cases the compression could be enough to burst out the fibers of the wood. Some excess depth in the hole helps to reduce this risk, but it is also a help to bevel the ends of a dowel and cut a shallow sawn groove along it (Fig. 1-8C) to let the compressed air and excess glue escape.

The size and number of dowels depends on several factors. On a long edge joint they only have to supplement glue and do little more than keep the edges in line while the glue sets, so they can be far apart (Fig. 1-8D). In a **T** shaped joint they are the main gluing area, so must be plentiful. Usually the dowel diameter should be a little more than half the thickness of the wood and the dowels spaced so the gaps between them are only a little more than the dowel diameter (Fig. 1-8E). There is a choice between more thinner dowels and fewer thicker ones. Usually the thicker dowels are better. Take the dowels as deep as possible into the thinner wood and about the same, or a little more, into the end grain of the other piece. The strength of a dowelled joint then comes from using adequate glue and tight clamping.

MORTISE AND TENON JOINTS

Mortise and tenon joints are the traditional way of joining parts in many types of woodworking as well as furniture construction. They provided strength when glues could not be trusted. Now that much better glues are available, the joints have the advantage of providing good areas of side grain for the glue to grip.

In the basic joint there is a tenon 1/3 of the thickness of the wood on which it is cut, going into and through the other piece (Fig. 1-9A), which can be the same thickness or greater. At one time the mortise was chopped out with a chisel and the width of tenon and mortise was made to suit this. Today it is more usual to remove the waste in the mortise with a drill or router cutter and only use a chisel to square the ends. The tenon can be cut by hand or it can be done accurately on a table saw.

If the tenon does not go through the other piece, it is a *stub tenon* and a *blind mortise* (Fig. 1-9B). In furniture, joints often come between rails and a leg. To get the maximum penetration and glue area, the tenon ends are mitered (Fig. 1-9C).

A *through tenon* can be tightened by wedging— sometimes with the wedges outside the tenon (Fig. 1-9D), but more securely by driving the wedge into a saw cut in the tenon. In a wide tenon there could be two wedges (Fig. 1-9E). It is also possible to wedge a stub tenon. This is called *foxtail wedging* (Fig. 1-9F). One or more saw cuts hold short wedges, which hit the bottom of the mortise and spread the tenon as it is driven in. The mortise should have a widened bottom to allow the tenon to spread.

For a deep rail it is unwise to make a full-depth tenon as that means a mortise so long that it might weaken the wood. It is better to cut two or more tenons with a space between and even better to allow a small piece in the space to go into the mortise (Fig. 1-9G).

If the joint is at a corner, it could be made open, and this is called a *bridle joint* (Fig. 1-10A). With the open outer parts, this is not as strong. To avoid the open form and obtain more strength, the tenon could be cut back (Fig. 1-10B), but it is stronger to make it haunched (Fig. 1-10C) with the short haunch showing at the end. If that ought to be hidden, the haunch can taper (Fig. 1-10D).

In some traditional furniture a tenon goes through far enough to be held with a wedge. These *tusk tenons* date from the days when substantial furniture had to be taken apart to accompany an important person on his journeys, but they have a decorative use in newer furniture. The tenon projects and a slot is cut to take a wedge (Fig. 1-10E), undercut enough so as the wedge is driven, it presses against the mortised part and pulls the tenoned part tight (Fig. 1-10F). The end of the tenon and the ends of the wedge may be shaped to provide decoration.

Draw pinning is a useful way of tightening a mortise and tenon joint without the use of a clamp. Drill through the mortised part towards the joining side (Fig. 1-10G), then mark another hole on the tenon slightly nearer its shoulder (Fig. 1-10H). Taper the end of a suitable dowel rod and drive it through (Fig. 1-10J). This pulls the tenon further in. Cut off the surplus dowel ends and plane them level.

If the end of a wide board meets another across its grain, the tenoned end should not make a wide mortise across the other piece as that would weaken it. It is better to have several short tenons (Fig. 1-11A). If they are wedged, the wedges could be driven into diagonal cuts (Fig. 1-11B).

If mortise and tenon joints have to be made between parts that have rabbets, as in frames, it is best to arrange sizes so the mortise comes entirely within the rabbet, then the tenoned part has shoulders of different lengths to fit in (Fig. 1-11C). At the corner of a frame the joint could be haunched in the usual way (Fig. 1-11D). If the parts are grooved to take a panel, as in many doors, a mortise and tenon joint is normal, except that the tenon should be thicker than the width of the groove. If it is at a corner, there will be a haunch that will reach the bottom of the plowed groove (Fig. 1-11E).

There are a great many variations on the mortise and tenon joint, some of which are described where they occur in projects. A craftsman can adapt the basic forms to suit connections in his own designs.

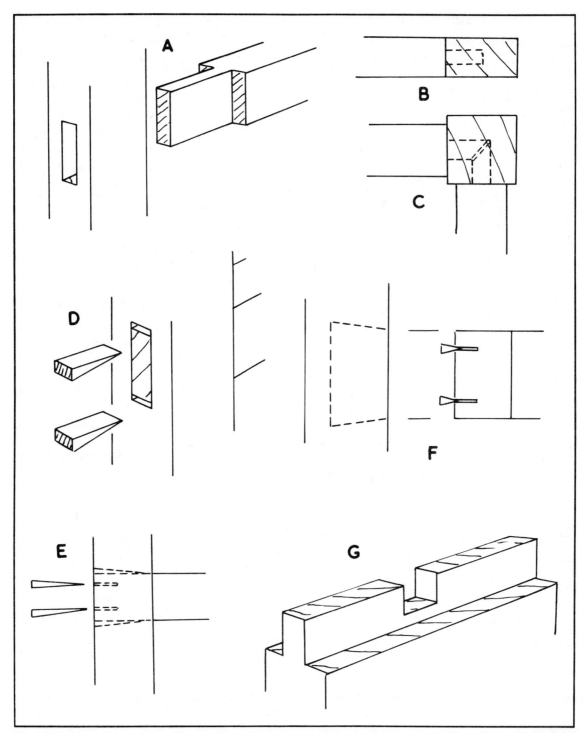

Fig. 1-9. Mortise and tenon joints take many forms. The tenon may go through (A), be stopped (B), or mitered (C). Wedges will tighten (D-F). Wide tenons should be separated (G).

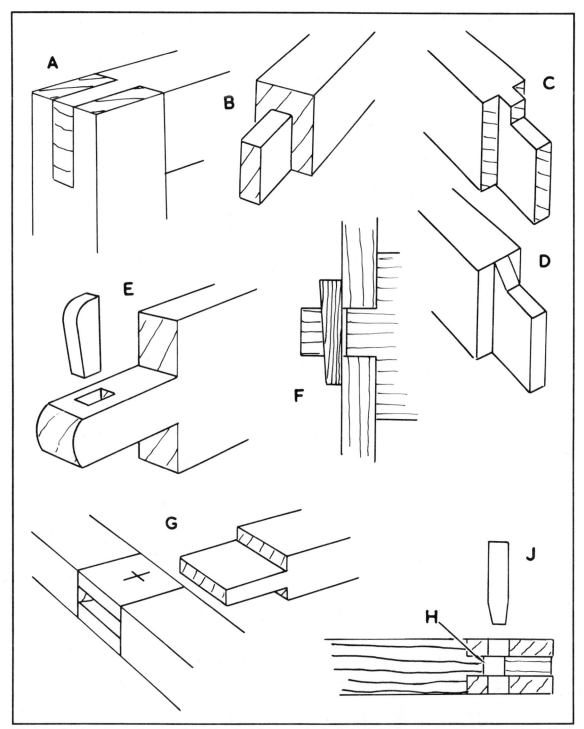

Fig. 1-10. At a corner an open mortise and tenon joint may also be called a bridle joint (A). It may be cut back (B-D). A tusk tenon extends through and may be wedged (E, F). A tenon may be pulled tight with a dowel (G-J).

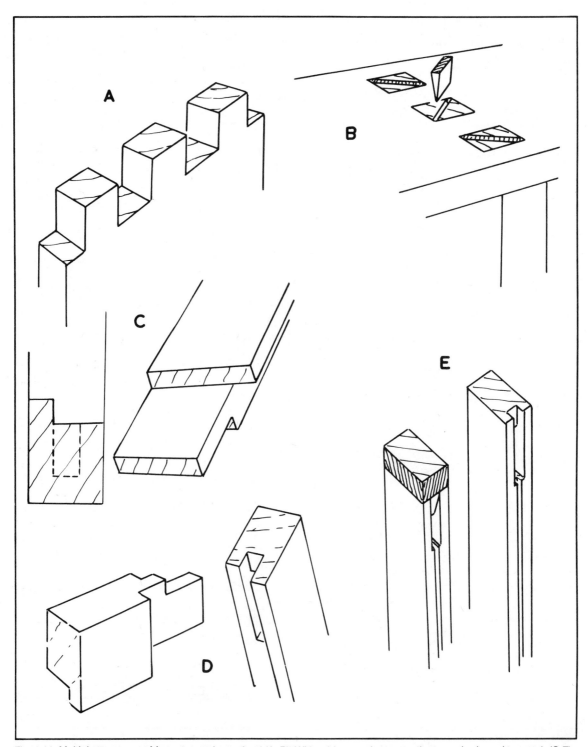

Fig. 1-11. Multiple tenons on wide parts may be wedged (A, B). With rabbets and grooves, the tenon is shaped to match (C-E).

CORNER JOINTS

One piece lapped over the other and nailed may be acceptable in some forms of woodworking, but it is not the corner joint to use anywhere in furniture making. In some constructions there may be a rabbet, with the other part fitting in and pins or finishing nails driven both ways (Fig. 1-12A). If the nails are set below the surface and covered with wood filler, their presence will not be very obvious.

Another joint of this type also has a tongue (Fig. 1-12B). It needs careful cutting if the short-grained piece is not to break away. If the overlap in either of these joints is to be hidden, there can be a miter (Fig. 1-12C), but this further complicates cutting.

Finger or *comb joints* (Fig. 1-12D) are strong because they give a good glue area. They are often machine-cut in quantity production, however, and individual craftsmen tend to avoid them.

Narrower pieces may be mitered (Fig. 1-12E). For picture frames and similar assemblies they are glued and held with pins driven one or both ways, but that does not provide much strength. There could be dowels arranged diagonally, either right through (Fig. 1-12F), in from one side only, or hidden between the two parts.

If there is sufficient depth, pieces of veneer can be glued into saw cuts across a joint (Fig. 1-12G). A common use of a miter is at the corner of a plinth under a cabinet. In that case strength can be provided by a block glued inside (Fig. 1-12H).

A miter is generally considered to be 45 degrees, but there are places where parts meet at other than 90 degrees, then the miter is arranged to bisect the angle. If one part is wider than the other, the miter cut goes from the meeting inner and outer surfaces, whatever the overall angle.

The corner joint that has stood the test of time is the *dovetail*. There can be a single tail in a narrow joint or a series of them across wide boards. The shape of the tail prevents withdrawal one way (Fig. 1-13A). In hardwoods the slope of the side of a dovetail is usually 1 in 8. For softwoods it can be broadened to 1 in 6 (Fig. 1-13B).

The oldtime cabinetmaker took pride in making the pins between tails very narrow, but there is no need to go too narrow. How many tails to put in the width of a board is a matter of personal choice, but having the tails about twice as wide as the thickness of the board is about right (Fig. 1-13C).

There are ways of cutting dovetails by machine. Otherwise they must be sawn and chiselled, with one part cut and used to mark the other piece.

Stopped, or *half-blind*, dovetails are hidden one way. This is a common form on traditional drawer fronts (Figs. 1-13D and 1-14). This is the only form a common type of machine can cut, but the results can be recognized because the pins and tails will be the same size (Fig. 1-13E).

Further forms are the *blind-lapped* dovetail, where the dovetail form is hidden both ways, but there is a narrow lap of one piece over the other. A further step is the *secret-mitered dovetail*, in which the whole dovetail construction, including the ends, is hidden by mitered laps.

GROOVED JOINTS

Tongue and grooved joints (Fig. 1-15A) were more common before the days of strong glues and plywood. They give more glue area than a plain butt together of the edges. Without glue they allow for expansion and contraction without leaving spaces. Before plywood, they were used for boards forming the backs of cabinets.

Grooves are used in furniture to make *halving joints* where two pieces, usually rails, cross at the same level (Fig. 1-15B). Cutting away half the thickness of each piece weakens the wood, but if they need only go partly into each other or one is thicker and cut away more than the other, that would be stronger.

A variation on this comes at a T junction where the end may be cut in dovetail form for greater length (Fig. 1-15C). A rail could be let into the top of a leg in the similar way (Fig. 1-15D).

A common grooved joint is the *dado* or *housing* joint (Fig. 1-16A). If its front is to be hidden it could become a *stopped dado* (Fig. 1-16B). There is not much strength in this form of the joint, although it is satisfactory for book shelves and similar applications. It can be strengthened with nails or screws driven diagonally upwards (Fig. 1-16C).

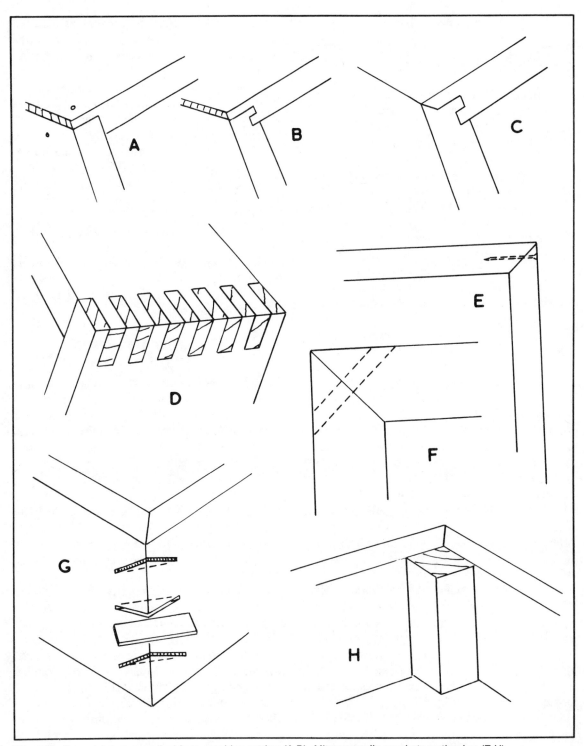

Fig. 1-12. Some joints are applicable to machine-cutting (A-D). Miters usually need strengthening (E-H).

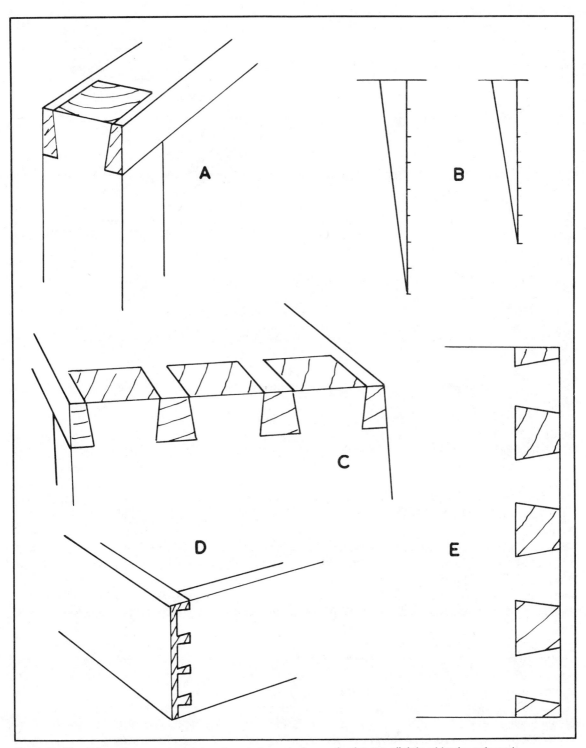

Fig. 1-13. Dovetails make a strong joint and come in many forms. Angles are slightly wider for softwoods.

Fig. 1-14. A stopped dovetail joint makes a good connection between the sides and front of a drawer.

Another way is to cut it with a dovetail form (Fig. 1-16D). Even if screws from outside are unacceptable, the appearance of tenon ends may not. The dado can be combined with tenons going through (Fig. 1-16E), where they can be wedged.

UPHOLSTERY

Many woodworkers think that adding padding to seats is something they could not do. Advanced upholstery is work for a specialist, but with modern materials it is possible for anyone to satisfactorily pad stools, chairs, and divans. Today, a block of plastic or rubber foam can provide all the stuffing needed.

A simple example is a lift-out seat for a chair or stool (Fig. 1-17). Cut a piece of plywood to size, with a little clearance all round to allow for the turned-under cloth. Drill a few holes in the wood (Fig. 1-18A) to allow air in and out as the foam is compressed or expands.

Cut a piece of foam (2-inch thickness will do)

a little bigger all round. A long broad-bladed knife, such as a carving knife, will cut it. Wetting the blade can help. Also cut about 45 degrees around the underside for about half the thickness (Fig. 1-18B). Cutting the oversized foam in this way allows the edge to compress to a rounded shape without exposing the hard edge of the plywood.

If a plastic-coated fabric or a fairly stout cloth is to be used for covering, it can be put directly on the foam. If the covering is a lighter or more loosely woven cloth, it is better to first cover the foam with a soft, flexible plain cloth to get the shape. The outer cloth then goes on with little strain applied to it.

Use tacks to attach the covering to the underside of the plywood. Have the assembly inverted on a padded surface that cannot damage the covering. Pull the cloth across the centers each way (Fig. 1-18C) tight enough to draw the foam to equally-curved edges. Tack about 1 inch in from the edge. You might have to experiment with tensions and

18

be prepared to remove and replace tacks occasionally. Work from the center towards the corner. The tack spacing depends on the cloth, but about 1 1/2-inch spacing should give a reasonable shape on top. At the corners fold the cloth under to give a good shape on top and cut and tack through the folds (Fig. 1-18D).

If there are two thicknesses of cloth, do the same with the outer covering, placing the tacks inside the others so the edges and tacks of the first layer are hidden. Cut the cloth edges evenly inside the line of tacks (Fig. 1-18E). That will probably

be sufficient, but you could cover underneath with another piece of cloth with its edges turned under (Fig. 1-18F).

For increased comfort the seat should be over webbing instead of the unyielding piece of plywood. Make a frame (open mortise and tenon joints are suitable). Webbing is about 2 inches wide and may be fabric or rubber. With it you need a strainer. There are several types that can be bought, but a simple one is a slotted strip of wood with a peg. The important thing is that the webbing pass through the slot. Other sizes are unimportant (Fig. 1-19A).

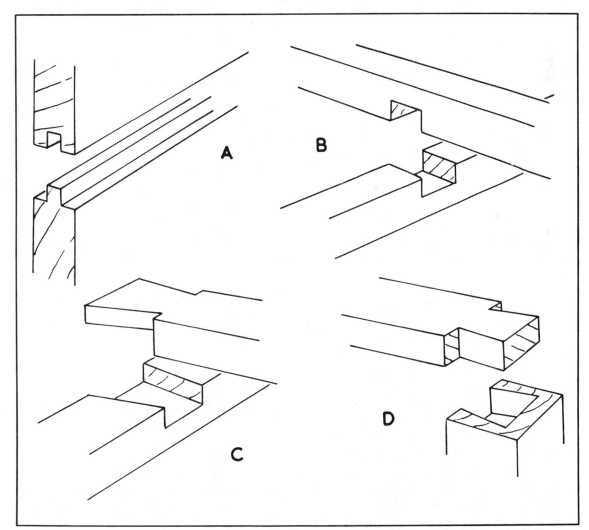

Fig. 1-15. Tongue and groove is a strong edge joint (A). There are several variations on the halving joint (B-D).

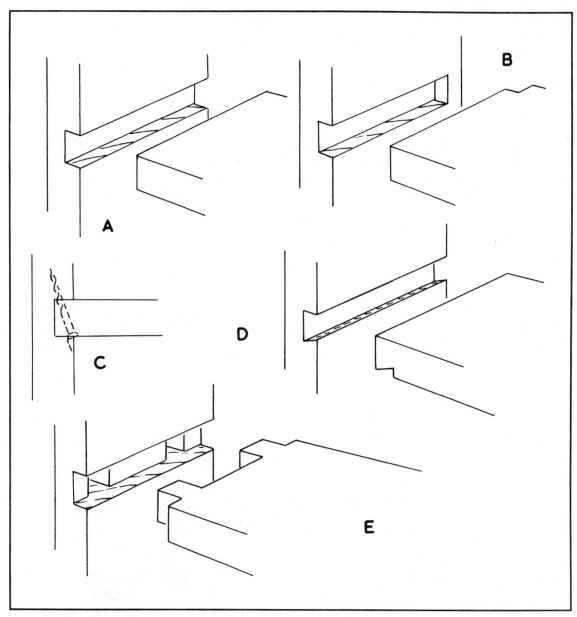

Fig. 1-16. The dado or housing joint may go through (A) or be stopped (B). It can be strengthened with screws, dovetailing, or tenons (C-E).

Webbing spacing should show gaps of about 2 inches or a little more. Turn over the end of a piece of webbing and tack it near the edge of the frame (Fig. 1-19B) with at least three tacks. At the other side use the strainer to get a moderate tension. Drive in two tacks while you hold the tension (Fig. 1-19C). Cut the webbing and fold over to drive two more tacks (Fig. 1-19D). Complete tacking webbing that way, then change to the other direction and do the same, with the webbing interwoven through the first pieces (Fig. 1-19E).

Further steps are the same as for covering the

plywood base; tack the cloth to the underside of the frame.

Although rubber webbing can be used in the same way as fabric webbing, there are metal fittings that attach to its ends. There are several forms, but a useful one is intended to press into a slot plowed in the wood frame. Strips of rubber webbing can then be tensioned fairly close together under loose cushions to provide comfortable seating or back supports. This arrangement can be seen in store-bought furniture. When using rubber webbing in this way, the frame parts have to be grooved, either square to the surface or at a slight angle, before assembly. It is important that the rubber webbing is tensioned by the same amount. One piece should be made up with its ends to give the right tension, then the others assembled to the same untensioned size.

Traditional upholstery is buttoned. This was necessary with some forms of stuffing; threading through prevented the stuffing from moving to form lumps in one part and hollows in another. That cannot happen with foam in one piece, but buttoning has become accepted as part of upholstery and buttons on the surface are expected. Besides their appearance, they still help to hold the covering to the foam and give an even effect to the whole thing. For buttoning you need a needle longer than the thickness of the seat or back. Upholsterer's thread is fairly stout. Carpet thread is suitable. Buttons can be obtained to match many coverings, and an upholsterer's supplier can cover buttons with your own material.

Decide on the pattern of buttons before cover-

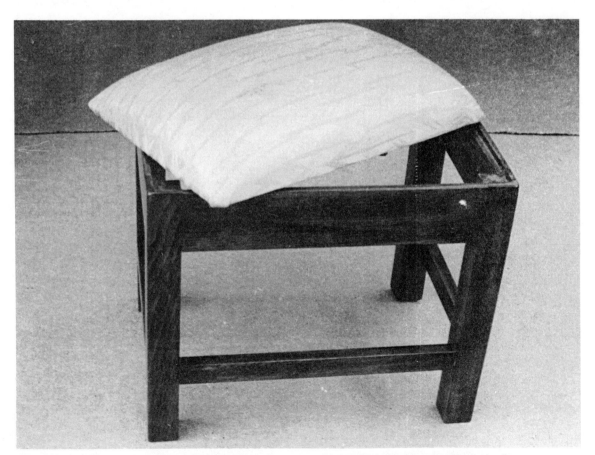

Fig. 1-17. An upholstered top for a stool can be made on a panel that fits into rabbets in the stool rails.

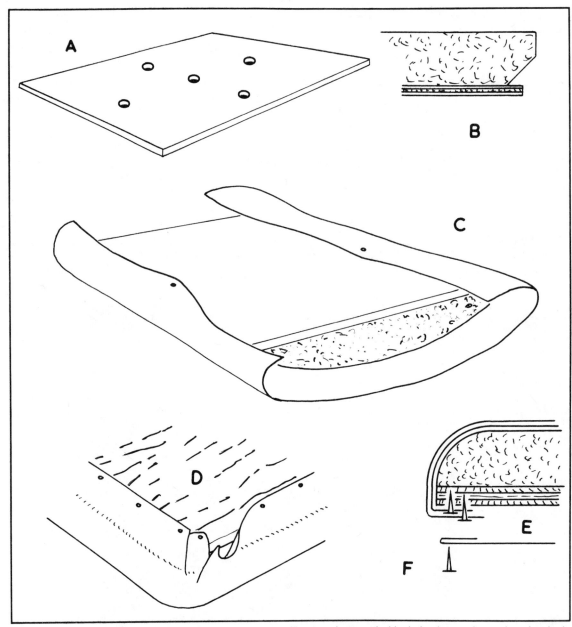

Fig. 1-18. Plastic or rubber foam may be fitted over a plywood base and covered with cloth taken underneath and tacked.

ing the plywood and drill small holes (1/4 inch will do) in the right places. Cover the foam in the way already described. Thread the needle and push it up through the plywood and the covering. Put on the button and push the needle down close to where it came up (Fig. 1-20A). Underneath you can use

a piece of thin dowel rod with a hole across it, or you can have a plain button. Pass the thread through the dowel or button (Fig. 1-20B). Tie the thread with a slip knot, such as the one shown (Fig. 1-20C).

Thread all the buttons in the same way. You

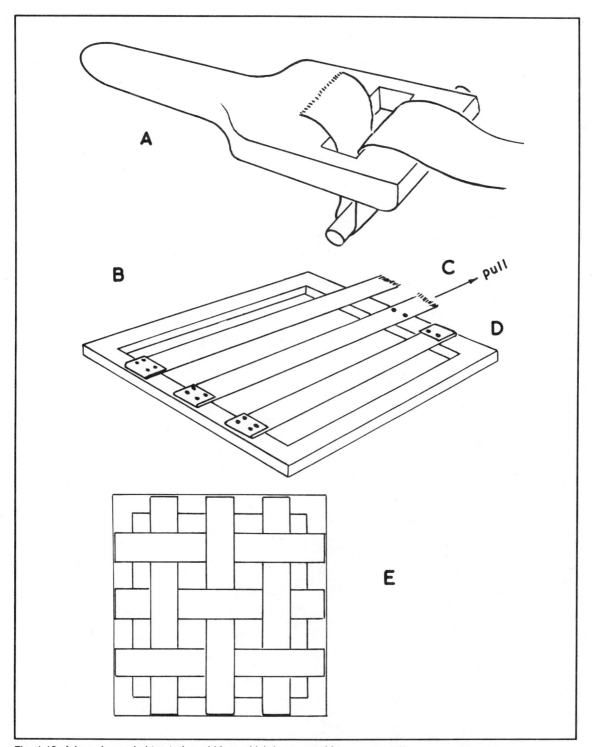

Fig. 1-19. A lever is needed to strain webbing, which is arranged in a woven pattern on a seat.

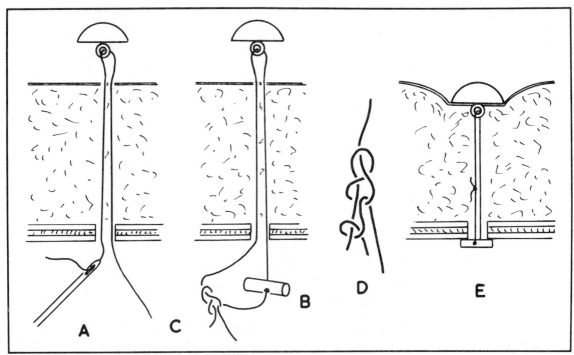

Fig. 1-20. A button is threaded through the upholstery, then it is pulled and knotted to come below the surface.

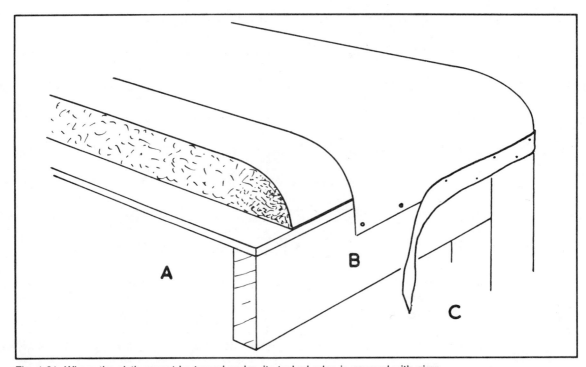

Fig. 1-21. Where the cloth cannot be turned under, its tacked edge is covered with gimp.

now have to adjust the lengths of the thread so the buttons pull in on the surface by the same amount. Try adjusting the slip knots until you have the tension you want. Lock the knots with a half hitch (Fig. 1-20D) and cut off the thread. Compress the padding to slacken the threads and push the knot inside the foam (Fig. 1-20E).

Upholsterers have a useful material called *gimp* which is used to cover exposed tacks and cut cloth edges. Gimp is a stout decorative form of tape in many colors and patterns, from 1/2-inch wide upwards. An example of its use is a stool with rails flush to the legs, where the covering cannot be taken underneath for tacking.

The covering material is brought down and tacked to the rails and tops of the legs (Fig. 1-21A). Keep the line of tacks straight, as the gimp will not cover tack heads that wander out of line very much. Trim the edges of the cloth fairly close to the tacks (Fig. 1-21B).

Gimp pins are fine black nails used to attach the gimp. Pin one end of the gimp, then go round the stool with a moderate tension and zig-zag the pins so they are near the edges of the gimp (Fig. 1-21C). Overlap the ends and cut off.

Further information on upholstery will be found in the instruction for particular projects that have stuffed coverings.

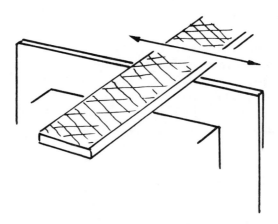

Chapter 2

Finishes

Not many things you make will be left untreated. The pores of bare wood will absorb dirt and moisture. A few items for kitchen or laundry may be left bare and scrubbed occasionally, but most pieces of furniture need a coating of something to seal the grain. A finish is usually also applied for the sake of appearance as a surface with some degree of gloss improves looks by enhancing the grain pattern. You may also change the color of the wood by staining, again for the sake of appearance. In some cases the wood may be treated with paint, so the opaque coat hides any details in the wood as well as seals it.

There are a great many types of finish, some of traditional natural form, but an increasing number with synthetic ingredients. Because some need special treatment or particular methods of application, read the instructions carefully. In general you can expect a better and more durable finish from something that needs several coats than from a one-coat quick finish.

PREPARATIONS

The quality of finish starts with the preparation of the surface. Time spent on planing, scraping, and sanding will be reflected in the final results. Consider the finish quite early in your work. Avoid too much glue escaping from a joint, sand surfaces that will be difficult to get at before assembly, deal thoroughly with any awkward grain, and avoid damage to a prepared surface by keeping the bench clean.

Power planing with cutters that are not absolutely sharp tends to pound the wood fibers and bend some of them instead of cutting them off. Sanding can continue to bend them, and they do not become apparent until they stand up as the finish is applied. Hand planing after power planing will usually cut off these fibers. Scraping will deal with them, particularly in places where the grain is uneven. Wiping the surface with a damp cloth will lift stray fiber ends and allow you to cut or sand them off.

The amount of sanding and how it is done depends on the wood. You might be able to apply a finish directly after planing some woods, but usually you have to do some sanding. It may be sufficient to follow planing with a fine abrasive paper, but usually you have to use two or more grades to get the best surface. After using a coarser grade, wipe or brush the surface to remove particles of the coarse grit that might be picked up by the finer paper. Sand with the grain. End grain might need more sanding to get it to the same quality as the side grain. Be careful that edges and corners do not become rounded, particularly if using a power sander. Hand sanding with the paper wrapped around a flat block is preferable for the final work. Use shaped pieces of wood if you have to sand moldings.

FILLING

Some woods have very open grain, and the spaces are so wide that they remain open after applying a polish or varnish. Some oaks are very open. There are fillers in the form of pastes for use on these woods. Use a cloth and wipe them across the grain so the gaps are filled. Let dry, then sand off carefully so as not to lift the filler out of the grain. Fillers are available in colors to match woods.

Other woods are not so open, but they still show smaller spaces and absorb much of the finish if untreated. There are liquid fillers to brush on and leave to dry before sanding. Shellac dissolved in alcohol is sometimes used for this purpose, but not if the wood is to be stained.

Many woods do not need filling in any way because the grain is close and the pores or cracks not obvious. If your chosen wood looks smooth, the finish will probably be enough to serve as its own filler.

STAINING

The color of wood can be changed. Sometimes this is done to produce unnatural shades, but in general it is better to regard staining as a means of emphasizing the natural color. In some cases a deepening of the color has become expected. Most mahogany furniture is redder than the natural wood, and most people expect oak furniture to be a richer brown than the bare wood would be.

There are chemical ways of changing the color of woods. Permanganate of potash wiped on will deepen the brown shade of oak. Fumed oak has been a popular finish for oak, and has a characteristic appearance that was achieved by exposing the wood to ammonia fumes in an enclosed cabinet. This is not a method for single pieces of furniture.

Staining is more commonly composed of a dye in a solvent that is brushed or wiped on. Water stains are cheapest and simplest. They are bought as powders or crystals to dissolve in water to the depth of color you want. Because they tend to raise the grain, before their use it is advisable to wipe water over the work and let it dry, then sand again before staining. It is difficult to get an even finish with water stain if it is too dark. It is better to get a dark color by applying several coats of lighter stain.

Oil stain comes as a liquid in a naptha or similar base and is available in a great many wood colors. It is the simplest stain to use because it can be applied liberally and will dry evenly. It also penetrates the wood more than water stain, so if the furniture later suffers much abrasion, the worn wood will still keep its stained color. Rubbing with a cloth while wet allows you to graduate color, which is sometimes effective when a panel is lighter at the center than at the edges.

Spirit stain uses alcohol as a base and is very quick-drying. This becomes a problem if you use it over a large area as there will be streaks where a fresh brush stroke adjoins a part that has already dried. Spirit stain can be used on narrow parts, such as moldings, or for touching up damaged work. It is not advised for general staining. In addition to the wood colors, spirit stains can be obtained in brighter colors not usually associated with wood, such as green and blue. If you want to try special effects, this is the stain to use.

Varnish stains are not really craftsman finishes. The color is in the varnish, so it does not penetrate the wood. If the varnish becomes worn or chipped, the natural color of the wood will show through. It is much better to apply stain as one operation and follow with varnish or other finish.

RUBBED FINISHES

At one time furniture was finished by rubbing with waxes or oils. To get a good effect is a very slow process. The result is characteristic. An old table with a beautiful gloss might have had many coats of oil or wax applied, but much of its appearance is due to the patina of age.

Linseed oil can be used. Enough is rubbed on with a cloth to get it into the grain and to leave some on the surface. It is then left for maybe two weeks and treated again, and so on. The final gloss is obtained by rubbing with a coarse, dry cloth. If you are attempting to reproduce antique furniture, this may be the finish to use; otherwise it is too slow and laborious a process.

Many waxes are available, and the best results are obtained with commercially prepared mixtures. Treating bare wood with wax is very similar to using linseed oil, although the time between coats may be shorter. Early coats fill the grain, then further coats, with hard rubbing, will produce a gloss.

If you want the appearance of this finish, it is better to start with one or two coats of varnish. Sand them enough to remove the gloss, then follow with linseed oil or wax polishing. You will still have to rub hard and, with linseed oil, wait a long time between coats. You have to finish the furniture to a usable condition, then polish again at long intervals. When you have a hard wax finish you can touch up occasionally with a modern silicone spray polish. It may not be traditional, but it gets results.

Another rubbed finish is french polishing, which was used for much Victorian and later furniture. It produces a smooth gloss, but it is vulnerable to heat and moisture. The technique requires practice. The material is shellac dissolved in alcohol. Buy it as polish because some other shellac will be inferior. You apply it using a pad of cotton batting enclosed in a piece of soft, smooth cloth.

The wood should have been filled, if necessary. Early strokes are done with the pad wiped along the grain to build up a shellac surface. Always load the pad by soaking the batting from the bottle and wrapping the cloth around it tight enough to force the polish through.

Further polishing is done with less polish on the pad and a circular action, never stopping on the surface and completing by lifting off over an edge. Allow a few hours between coats. Lightly sand if there is any roughness, but make sure all dust is removed. This should build up a reasonable gloss and a thickness of shellac. The final polish is done with the polish on the pad diluted with a little alcohol. There are several finer points to master to get the best results, and instruction from an expert or a book with more space available to the subject is advisable.

VARNISHES

A gloss finish to brush on can be called a varnish. At one time these were made of many natural lacs, but are now usually synthetic, and without some of the problems of earlier varnishes. Use a brush uncontaminated with anything else. Work in reasonably warm conditions. It will help to stand a can of cold varnish in a bowl of hot water. So far as possible use the minimum number of brush strokes and always lift off over a part already done.

A varnish finish is satisfactory on most furniture and is difficult to distinguish from other gloss finishes. If you are doubtful about your ability to get good results with other finishes, this is a safe choice. Of the various varnishes, any described as *boat* varnishes may be expected to be the best quality and most easily applied so brush marks flow out.

The first coat of varnish tends to soak in. The second builds up a moderate gloss. It is the third coat, however, that gives a smooth gloss. Allow time between coats as advised by the manufacturers. With some varnishes there should be light sanding between coats, though there are some types where subsequent coats are advised at intervals too close for a coat to be hard enough for sanding. Some high-quality work has many more than three coats and has been carefully sanded between coats to produce a finish as good as french polishing, but with a surface immune to moderate heat, moisture, and many chemicals.

LACQUERS

There are several finishes intended primarily for spraying, but some of them can be brushed. They are quicker drying than varnishes, but give a very similar appearance. The solvents evaporate quickly. Some that are sprayed dry almost instantaneously. This means that care is needed in spraying to get an even spread, avoiding excesses where surplus can run and set unevenly. Lacquer intended for brushing takes longer to dry, but it is still difficult to get a good surface.

Spraying needs special equipment that must be cleaned after use. This might not be much extra work after a day of mass production, but it could be a nuisance with a one-of-a-kind project.

Spraying is particularly suitable for quantity production. As the craftsman making an individual piece of furniture will want it to keep its individuality, it is usually preferable to employ a different finish from that favored by the makers of mass-produced furniture.

PAINTING

If good-quality wood is used to make furniture, it would be a pity to hide its grain under paint. However, there are some items, such as those used by children, for which a painted finish would be the best choice. In this case the wood can be less expensive and may be of different types because the paint will make it all the same color.

For furniture that is to be painted, the quality of finish is not as important. You may be able to leave surfaces from the power planer or use knotty wood that does not finish so smoothly. Places where the grain has torn out may be filled to bring the surface level. If the painted finish is to be the best quality, however, the surface of the wood should be prepared to as good a standard as for varnish or other clear finish. Gloss paint tends to emphasize imperfections underneath. Ridges from power planing will show through the paint. Open grain should be filled or the paint coats might not bridge over gaps.

Like varnishes, modern paints are nearly all synthetic. This gives smoother spreading and quicker drying to the dust-free stage. There are three stages in painting: priming, undercoat, and top coat. In some systems the same paint may be used for the first two stages. Priming paint makes a bond with the wood and forms a base for the other coats. Two coats of primer might be necessary to get adequate coverage. This is without gloss, as is the undercoat. The top coat may be gloss, matt, or anywhere between.

The undercoat is more important than some users expect. It is this that makes the smooth surface on which the top coat merely adds the exterior appearance. More than one coat of undercoat paint might be necessary, possibly with sanding between the coats. Allow the drying time the manufacturers specify, then apply one layer of top coat. It is unwise to use two top coats, particularly if it is a gloss finish, because they might not bond well and the second coat might run.

Use the paint system of one manufacturer and follow the instructions. Modern paints are not all used the same way. Clean brushes in the solvents recommended by the manufacturers. It is possible to change a varnish brush to paint, but never the other way around, because there will be residue of paint no matter how careful the cleaning. There are special paints for metal and plastics and others for special effects. Make sure the specification of the paint you get says it suits wood. There are interior and exterior paints and varnishes. Even if your furniture will never be taken outside, it is usually best to have an exterior finish, because that should be a better quality.

Chapter 3

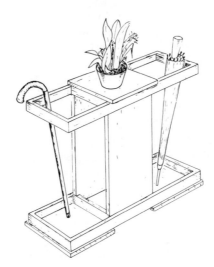

Entrance

There might not be a special room directly inside all your exterior doors, but there is usually an enclosed porch, vestibule, or other area where you change from outdoor to indoor clothes or prepare yourself to go out. Several items of furniture have a place there. The projects that follow can make the area more useful and convenient, as well as personalize it in the eyes of visitors who will see the first examples of your craftsmanship.

COAT RACK

A free-standing rack for coats, hats, and other clothing has the advantage of portability, although for much of the time it stays in one place. If you need to hang many wet coats, it can be taken outside. This design (Fig. 3-1) has four long and four short hooks at heights that keep long coats off the floor. There could be more hooks at a lower level for children's clothing or short jackets. The feet of the rack spread far enough to provide stability.

It would be possible to make the rack of softwood and paint it, but it would look better if made of a good furniture hardwood, finished with stain and polish. In any case, the main pillar should have reasonably straight grain to reduce any risk of warping. Because the other parts have their grain in the direction shown, there is no short grain across parts that might break under load.

The suggested sizes should suit most situations. If you alter them, make sure the feet spread several inches more than the hooks each way. Dowelled and mortise and tenon joints are equally suitable, but make sure they are all pulled tight when glued.

1. Mark out the pillar (Fig. 3-2A), leaving a little extra at the ends until after the the joints have been cut. Show the positions of the hooks and feet so they are ready for the joints to be marked and cut when the other parts have been prepared.

2. If dowels are used, they should be 1/2-inch diameter. Tenons should be 1/2 inch thick. Allow for the type of joint when marking out the hooks and feet.

3. Draw the outlines of the hooks (Fig. 3-3A and B). Note the grain directions. They meet and are glued together when being attached to the pil-

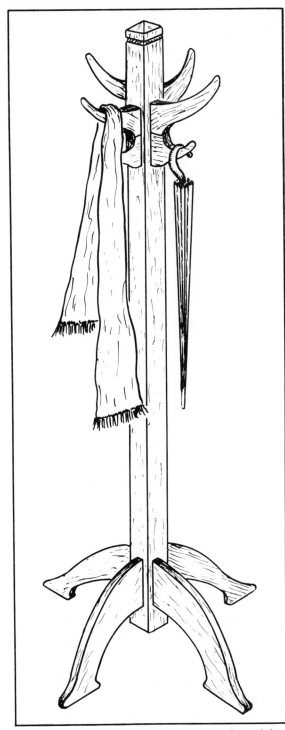

Fig. 3-1. This coat rack stands independently and has hooks all around.

lar. It will help us to use a card or hardboard template, although one hook could be used to mark the others.

4. Cut the parts that will come against the pillar, but do not cut the curved outlines yet. Mark and drill for dowels in the hook parts (Fig. 3-3C) and the pillar. If tenons are used, mark and cut them (Fig. 3-3D) and their mortises. In both cases go almost deep enough for the joints to meet in the pillar.

5. When these joints have been prepared, cut the outlines of the hooks. Round the projecting parts of the hooks, particularly at the tips, but the cross section can blend into square edges nearer the pillar.

6. Do the feet (Fig. 3-3E) in a similar way, preparing the joints before shaping the curves. To use clamps to draw opposite joints close, leave projections (Fig. 3-3F) that can be cut off after assembly is complete. The feet need not be rounded as much as the hooks, but take sharpness off edges. In all of these shaped parts make sure saw and other tool marks are removed from the curves, as they will become more obvious under polish and spoil the appearance of your work.

7. Mark and cut the top and bottom of the pillar. The top is shown with a V groove (Fig. 3-2B), which can be sawn and smoothed with a file or abrasive paper around a strip of wood. Taper the top to a shallow cone (Fig. 3-2C). The bottom could be cut square across or made into a similar shape.

8. Assemble opposite sides, whether dowels or tenons. Clamps can be put across the top hooks on their inner flat parts. Use thin scrap wood pads to avoid damage to the surfaces. The shorter hooks can be clamped over their ends.

9. Draw opposite legs tight by clamping over the pieces left on for this purpose. Cut off the pieces after clamping and smooth the surfaces to match those adjoining.

10. Check that the parts are square across. In particular, measure between the tips of the 4 feet. These distances should be the same and the bottoms should be level, although the wood can be trimmed slightly if necessary to make the feet stand level and the pillar upright.

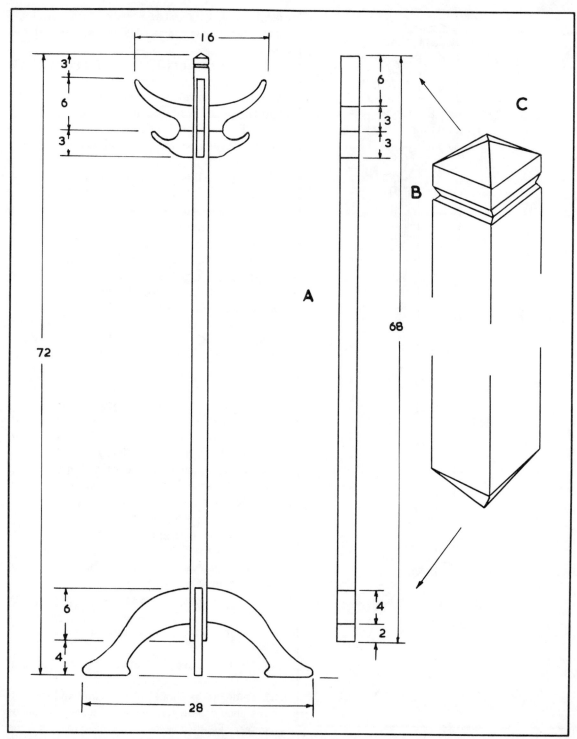

Fig. 3-2. Sizes of the coat rack and suggested decoration of the top.

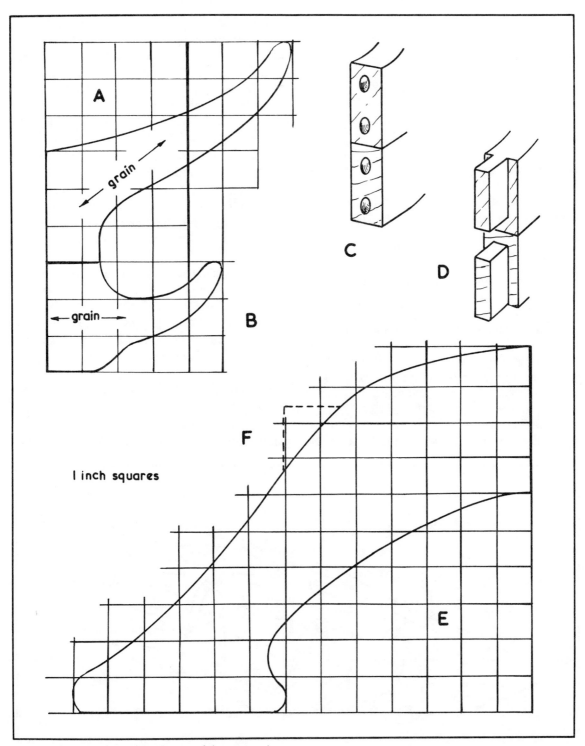

Fig. 3-3. Outlines of the shaped parts of the coat rack.

Materials List for Coat Rack	
1 pillar	2 × 2 × 68
4 hooks	1 × 4 × 11
4 hooks	1 × 4 × 7
4 feet	1 × 6 × 18

COAT HANGER

A wall-mounted coat hanger with several hooks can be used in any convenient space and has the advantage of not using any part of the floor. It could come above a table or be in a corner or an alcove. It might go on the back of a door.

The shape could be just a rectangle, but this coat hanger (Fig. 3-4) is fashioned after the horns of a steer in a rather stylized form. The back and four hooks in two sizes are horn-shaped.

The hanger could be made of hard or softwood and given a painted finish. If you want to carry the horn effect as far as possible, paint all the tips of the horns white for a few inches and the rest of the wood brown, red, or black. Alternatively, use a good hardwood, then stain and polish it to match other furniture.

Screwed construction is suggested, because the screw heads will be hidden at the back of the hanger, but dowels could be used in place of screws.

1. Make sure the main board is flat on both sides. Make a paper or card template of half the shape (Fig. 3-5A). Turn this over on the centerline to mark the shape, including the position of the hooks. Drill the screw holes and countersink at the back. With a 3/4-inch back, screws 10 gauge and 1 1/2 inches or 2 inches long should be satisfactory.

2. Cut the shape of the back. True the edges and round their fronts.

3. Mark out the hooks (Fig. 3-5B and C) and cut them to shape. Pay particular attention to the flatness and squareness of the rear surfaces, which will control the accurate fitting against the backboard.

4. Round the outer ends of the hooks and continue the rounding to blend into squareness towards the back.

5. Put each hook in place and mark through the screw positions. Drill undersize holes, then glue and screw the hooks through the back.

6. If dowels are used, locate them in similar positions to the screws—3/8-inch diameter should be satisfactory.

7. Drill for widely spaced fixing screws or at suitable spacing to suit strong points in the wall.

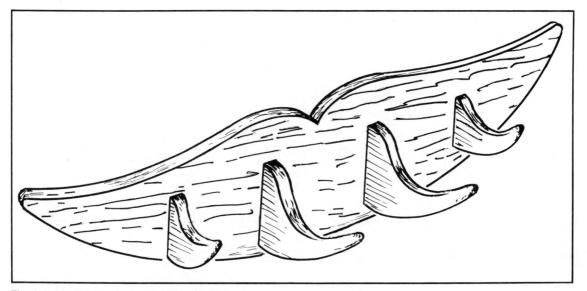

Fig. 3-4. A wall coat hanger based on cattle horns.

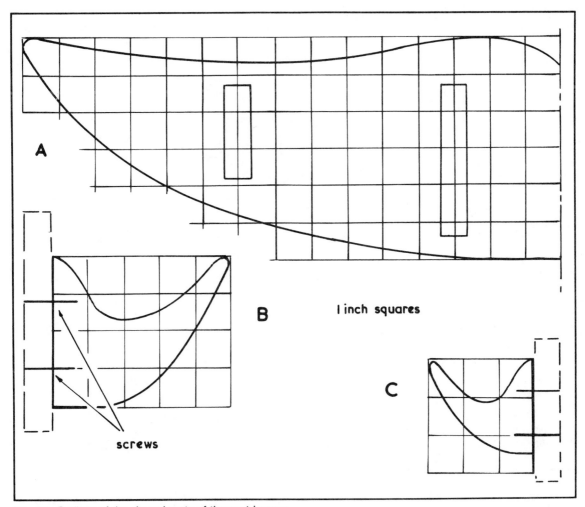

Fig. 3-5. Outlines of the shaped parts of the coat hanger.

A

B

I inch squares

C

screws

Materials List for Coat Hanger	
1 back	3/4 × 6 × 30
2 hooks	3/4 × 4 × 5
2 hooks	3/4 × 2 1/2 × 3

UMBRELLA STAND

It helps to have somewhere to put umbrellas, canes, and long items such as fishing poles; so they can be found next time they are needed and so they can be kept tidy. There are very many forms of umbrella stands, those with single and double compart-ments, or those forming parts of other furniture. The one in Fig. 3-6 is intended to stand alone. It has a small center tabletop and spaces on each side, which should be large enough for all the umbrellas in the average home.

The stand is intended to be made of solid wood and could be a hardwood to match other furniture. It might be made of softwood and finished with paint. The stand is shown with its ends flat on the floor, but it could have small square or turned feet with glides or casters so you can move the stand, if only to clean the floor. The two uprights are prob-ably best left plain, particularly if they have an at-tractive grain. There could be a fretted pattern in

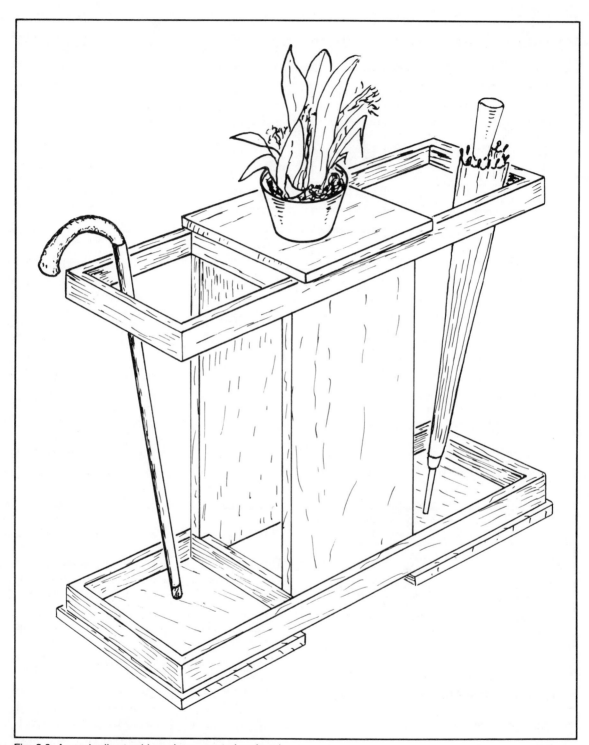

Fig. 3-6. An umbrella stand based on a central pedestal.

one or both of them, however. This could also be a place for a carved overlay or some other added decoration.

Top and bottom are similar frames, and should be made first. They are held by the two uprights, then the top and bottom pieces close parts of the frames. The suggested sizes may be altered. Measure what you wish to put in the stand, in case you want to make alterations. The proposed construction is suitable for any reasonable size.

1. Cut the wood for the top and bottom frames (Fig. 3-8A and B), which will be the same.

2. In the simplest construction, corners could overlap and be nailed or screwed. The best corner joints are dovetails (Fig. 3-7A), but finger joints are just as strong (Fig. 3-7B). Both can be regarded as decorative features if well made, with their exposed alternating side and end grains.

3. The intermediate joints could be stub tenons (Fig. 3-7C) or dowels (Fig. 3-7D).

4. Mark out the frame parts together so that matching parts will be the same. Assemble the frames, checking that they are square and the same as each other.

5. Make the two uprights (Fig. 3-7E). The width of each piece should fit across the rails in the frames and be cut away to fit between them (Fig. 3-8C).

6. Take the sharpness off all edges and round the frame corners that will be exposed in the finished stand. Assemble the uprights to the frames with glue and screws driven from inside the uprights. Sight downwards over the frames to see that there is no twist.

7. Cut the top (Fig. 3-8D) to overlap the parts of the frame it covers 1/4 inch all around (Fig. 3-7F).

8. Attach the top with screws driven from below in counterbored holes in the crosswise rails (Fig. 3-8E). The holes could be plugged afterwards, but as they will normally be out of sight, that does not matter.

9. Make the two bottoms (Fig. 3-8F) level with the inner crosswise rails, but overlapping outside 1/4 inch to match the top. Screw to the rails from below. The edges of the wide pieces are shown square, but they could be molded. They

might be made of a different wood to contrast in color with the other parts, if the stand is to be given a clear finish.

Materials List for Umbrella Stand

4 frame sides	5/8 × 2 × 24
4 frame ends	5/8 × 2 × 9
4 frame rails	5/8 × 2 × 9
2 uprights	5/8 × 8 × 22
1 top	5/8 × 8 1/2 × 9 1/2
2 bottoms	5/8 × 9 × 9 1/2

ENTRANCE MIRROR

A wall mirror is useful anywhere, but it is particularly appropriate near your entrance door. You can see yourself as you enter or leave and check if your clothes and hair are in order.

The mirror in Fig. 3-9 is designed in three parts. The mirror itself is a fairly plain wood frame. Beneath it is a shelf to hold brush and comb and other small items. Clothes brushes can be hung underneath it. At the top of the mirror is a canopy enclosing a strip light. Its top can also be used as a shelf. The mirror could be made and used without either of the other parts or with one or both of them.

Sizes will depend on where the mirror is to be hung or on an available mirror, but the sizes suggested in Fig. 3-10 give a good reflection if hung at eye level. The general construction is fairly light. Decoration is provided by plenty of curves, but straight edges could be used if the decor and other furniture nearby is more severe.

The wood could be any furniture-quality hardwood. It is possible to cut joints between some parts, but there will be only light loads. Screws through parts connected to the mirror frame and pins or glue in other parts should be sufficient. Because the glass mirror will be heavy, its frame should be strong. The canopy and shelf look better if kept light, however.

1. Prepare the molding for the frame. It is 1 1/4-inch square (Fig. 3-10A) with a wide rabbet for the plywood back and a deeper one for the glass and its retaining fillet. The front of the frame is

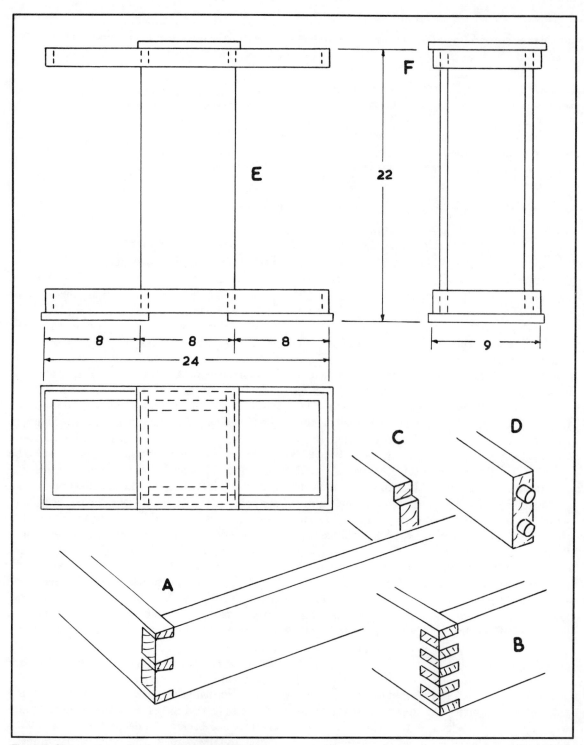

Fig. 3-7. Sizes and construction of the umbrella stand.

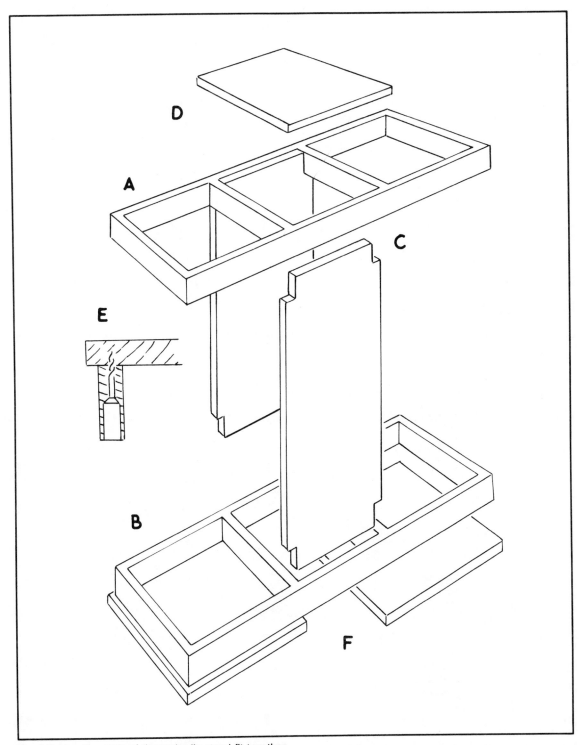

Fig. 3-8. How the parts of the umbrella stand fit together.

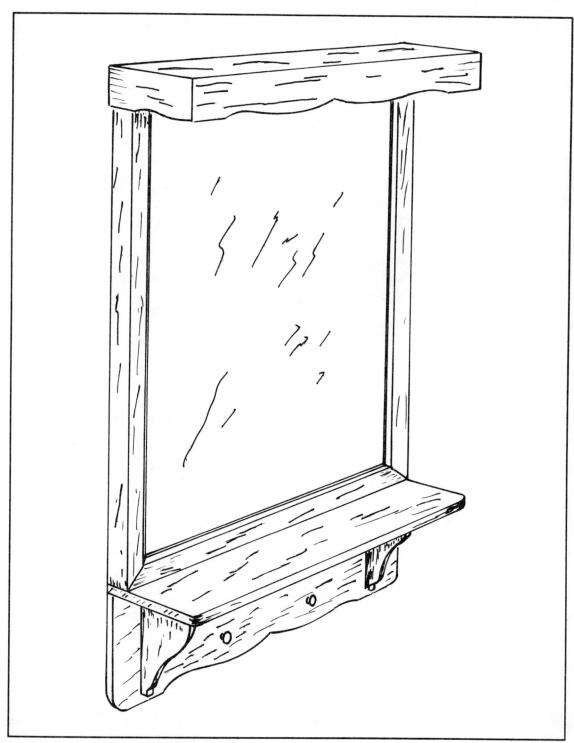

Fig. 3-9. A hall mirror with shelf and covered light.

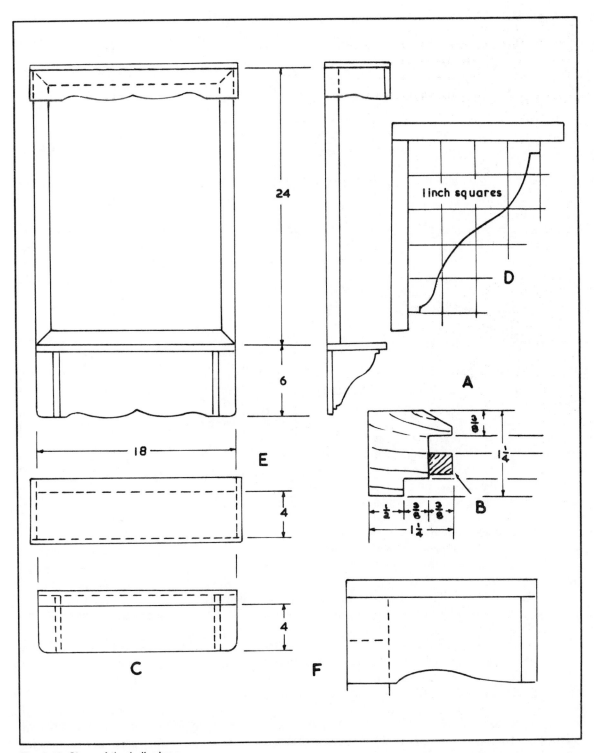

Fig. 3-10. Sizes of the hall mirror.

shown with a simple bevel, but you could work a molding if you have suitable equipment. Adjust the sizes of the rabbets to suit the thickness of the glass and the plywood back. The drawing assumes both are 1/4 inch thick.

2. Miter the corners. The plywood back will provide some strength in the joints, but pieces of veneer in saw cuts or a dowel across each corner (Fig. 3-11A) may be used for added strength.

3. Use black paint inside the glass rabbet to cut down unwanted reflection around the glass edges.

4. The glass is held in with fillets (Fig. 3-10B) pinned to the frame. Make them thin enough so when the back is fitted it will not bear down on them against the back of the mirror, risking damage to its silvering. Also prepare the back plywood, but delay fitting it and the mirror until the other parts are made and a finish applied.

5. The shelf is a piece of wood with rounded outer corners (Fig. 3-10C) that screws upwards into the mirror frame. Below it comes a vertical piece (Fig. 3-11B), also with rounded corners, but with a pattern worked on its edge (Fig. 3-11C). Because the same pattern is used on the canopy, make a card template of half the width.

6. The brackets (Fig. 3-10D) have curves to match the bottom profile. Sand and round all exposed edges. Screw and glue the horizontal and vertical parts together and screw from the back into the brackets, but use a few pins downwards through the shelf into the brackets.

7. There could be two or more hooks in the upright part for hanging brushes or keys. With a lathe you can turn knobs (Fig. 3-11D) to fit into holes to hold cords from brushes.

8. The canopy sizes might have to be adjusted to suit your strip light, but the lighting assembly used need not be very big. It should fit into the canopy shown.

9. There are two canopy sides that come outside the mirror frame, and these support the front and top (Fig. 3-11E). The canopy extends about the same amount as the shelf (Fig. 3-10E).

10. Make the two sides (Fig. 3-10F), with the lower edges curved in a similar way to the shelf bottom.

11. Make the front to fit over the sides and the top to fit over all (Fig. 3-11F). Shape the front to match the shelf bottom (Fig. 3-11C).

12. Pin and glue the parts together, making sure they will fit over the mirror frame.

13. Finish the three parts as separate units. Fit the mirror and its back.

14. Decide how the assembly will be attached to the wall. Two screws through the top of the mirror frame and one centrally below the shelf will be inconspicuous. Screw the shelf upwards into the bottom of the frame. Attach the frame and shelf to the wall. Add the light fittings to the canopy. If necessary, drill some ventilating holes in the top. Lower the canopy on to the mirror frame and screw it without glue. You can then remove it if you want to get at the screws to take the mirror from the wall.

Materials List for Entrance Mirror					
2 mirror frames	1 1/4	×	1 1/4	× 24	
2 mirror frames	1 1/4	×	1 1/4	× 18	
2 mirror fillets	3/8	×	3/8	× 23	
2 mirror fillets	3/8	×	3/8	× 17	
1 mirror back	17	×	23	× 1/4	plywood
1 shelf	1/2	×	5 1/4	× 18	
1 shelf support	1/2	×	5 1/2	× 18	
2 shelf brackets	1/2	×	4	× 5	
2 canopy sides	1/2	×	3	× 51/2	
1 canopy front	1/2	×	3	× 19	
1 canopy top	1/2	×	6	× 19	

BOOT JACK

Removing boots can be a tricky performance, balancing on one leg. The process can be even more complicated if they are muddy and you want to avoid spreading dirt around. A boot jack (Figs. 3-12 and 3-13) is a simple device which takes all the bending and other contortions out of removing boots, however stubborn they are, and it limits the spread of mud. One foot holds down the rear end while the forked end grips the heel of the boot being removed.

This boot jack (Fig. 3-14A) is made of hardwood. It can be stained and varnished so it has an acceptable appearance when hanging on a hook inside the door.

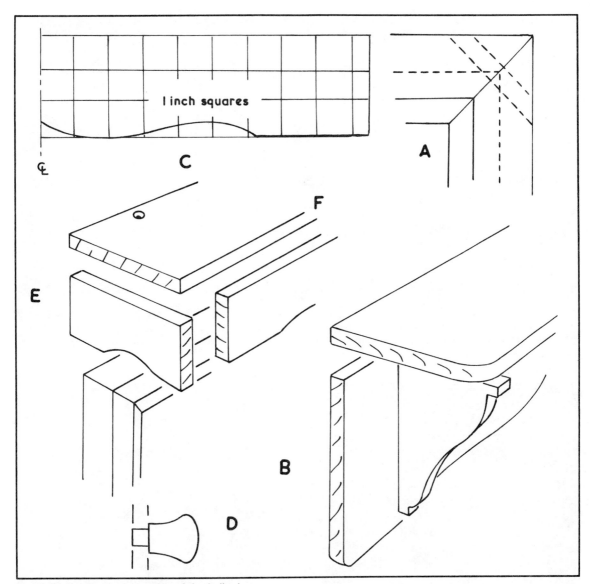

Fig. 3-11. Details of construction of the hall mirror.

1. Cut the wood to size and shape the fork (Fig. 3-14B). Take sharpness off the ends, but do not round the edges of the V excessively.

2. At the other end round the corners and edges and drill a hole for hanging.

3. The sides can be hollowed for the sake of appearance, but this is not essential.

4. Screw on a piece of 1 1/2-inch square wood under the center (Fig. 3-14C). Round the underside, including its ends, so it does not harm floor coverings.

Materials List for Boot Jack					
1 piece	5/8	×	5	×	18
1 piece	1 1/2	×	1 1/2	×	5

Fig. 3-12. A boot jack is made with a pivot block across the center.

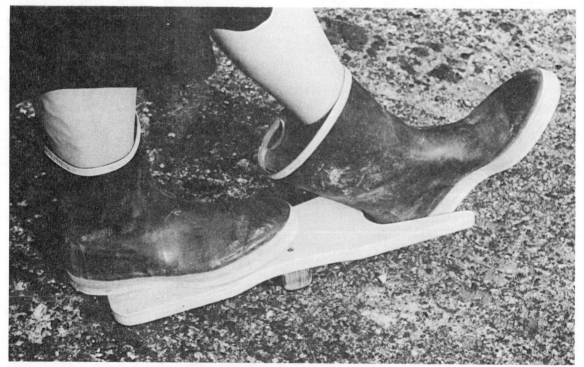

Fig. 3-13. In use, one foot holds down the back of the jack while the boot to be removed is gripped in the forked end.

44

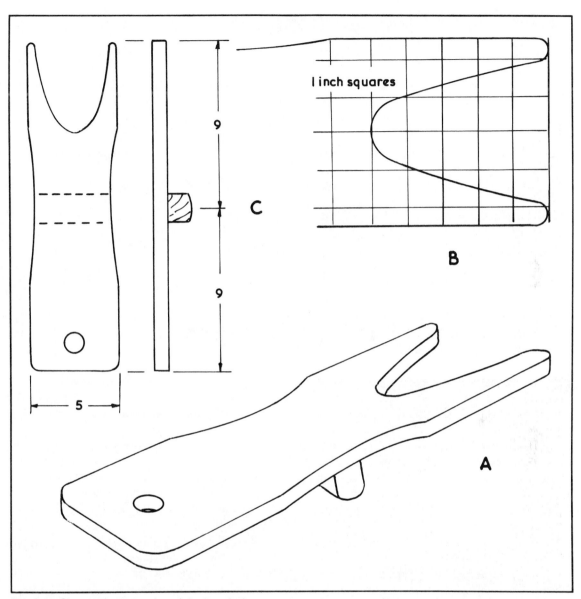

1 inch squares

9

C

9

5

B

A

Fig. 3-14. Sizes and construction of the boot jack.

Chapter 4

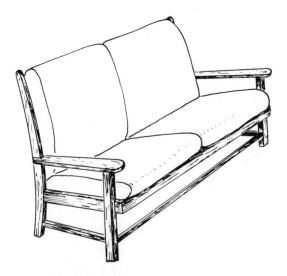

Living Room

There is one room in the home where most people gather, where we greet visitors, and where we relax. It is not usually a place for hobbies, meals, or other activities, unless yours is a small house and the one room has to double for many other purposes. In this case you might have to include furniture more correctly put in a dining room, den, or study. For the purpose of this book it is assumed that this is a living or family room only, where we read, watch television, listen to music—and the mood is relaxed. Anything very active takes place elsewhere.

You might already have lounge chairs, side tables, and shelving. If not, there are ideas here and in other chapters. The projects that follow are mostly complementary to the basic furniture. They add to your comfort and convenience as well as help to create an attractive, lived-in appearance to the room.

FOLD-DOWN COFFEE TABLE WITH ROUND TOP

Although most coffee tables do not occupy much space, it can be an advantage to reduce the size when a table is not in use. The table in Fig. 4-1 has a 24-inch diameter top when opened (shown dotted in Fig. 4-2), but it reduces to about 9 by 24 inches when not in use. Folding is arranged by having the top in three parts, with the center piece pivoted at its center. When closed, the two outer parts hang down, but when they are lifted and the top turned through 90 degrees, the tabletop holds rigidly in the circular shape.

The table looks best if made of good hardwood, such as oak or mahogany. The legs are shown turned, but they could be left square. The sizes given will suit most needs. If they are altered, make sure the top supporting board comes only just within the circle of the top and is wide enough to give good support to the opening top.

1. Mark out the legs (Fig. 4-2A). They are shown dowelled to the top and bottom boards (Fig. 4-3A). These dowels could be turned on the legs at the same time as the central parts. Holes might be drilled and loose dowels used, whether the legs are turned or left square. Alternatively, tenons might be cut.

Fig. 4-1. A fold-down coffee table has a round, swivelling top.

2. Make the top and bottom boards (Fig. 4-3B and C). They could be the same, although the bottom looks better with the ends extended and curved. Drill for the dowels.

3. Make the feet to fit around the bottom boards (Fig. 4-3D). Shape the ends and cut away underneath.

4. Cut the wood for the top and mark out the circle while the parts are held close together to get an accurate circle in the assembly. A square top is possible, but its corners should be well rounded.

5. So the top will turn smoothly, its parts must be joined with backflap hinges, which fold back further than normal hinges, and the knuckle can be buried (Fig. 4-2B). Make sure they are let in flush with the surface so they cannot foul the board below when the top is turned.

6. The pivot is a stout screw (Fig. 4-2C). A

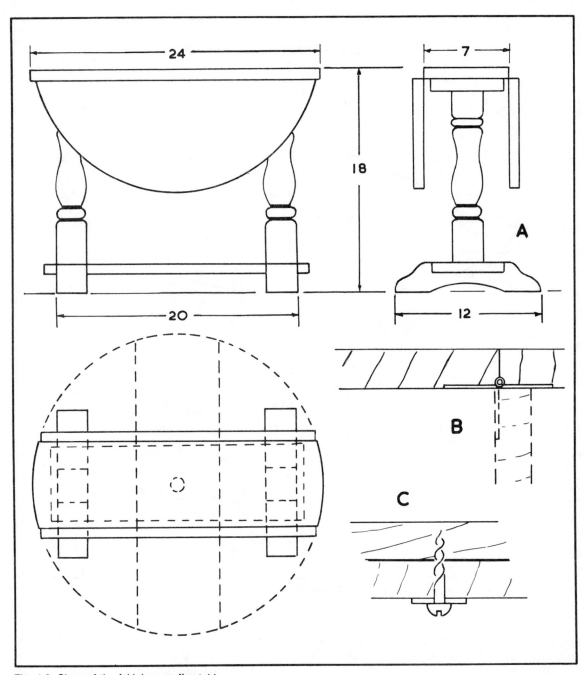

Fig. 4-2. Sizes of the fold-down coffee table.

thickness of at least 14 gauge is advisable and its length through the washer must go as deeply as possible into the top without breaking through the surface. Drill the parts for the screw and screw on the backflap hinges.

7. Assemble the legs to the top and bottom boards. Check that the assembly is free from twist as well as square. Add the feet and check that the

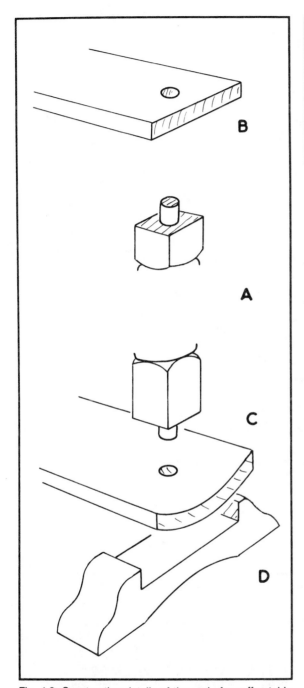

B

A

C

D

Fig. 4-3. Construction details of the end of a coffee table.

2 legs	2 1/2 × 2 1/2 × 17
1 top board	3/4 × 6 × 22
1 bottom board	3/4 × 6 × 24
2 feet	2 1/2 × 2 1/2 × 12
1 top	3/4 × 7 × 24
2 tops	3/4 × 9 × 24

MAGAZINE TABLE

A coffee table with a rack underneath will keep magazines tidy and provide a top to spread them on. Because most magazines will fit into a 15-inch space, that should be the minimum size for the width of a rack under a table. The little table in Fig. 4-4 is shown 30 inches long, but it could be adapted to suit needs or available space. The top might be solid wood or manufactured board or, as suggested, made of plywood faced with an attractive veneer and surrounded by a solid wood frame. The legs could be square or turned. The magazine rack is made with spaces between slats, so it is easily cleaned.

1. Mark out the four legs (Fig. 4-5A), leaving a little extra at the ends until after the joints have been cut. These could be tenons (Fig. 4-6A) or dowels (Fig. 4-6B).

2. If you wish to turn the legs (Fig. 4-5B), mark the limits of the square parts before mounting the wood in the lathe.

3. The legs could be left square and the same size throughout. They look better, though, with a slight taper below the lower rails (Fig. 4-5C).

4. Prepare the wood for the top rails. The lower edges may be cut away (Fig. 4-5D) to give easier access to the magazines.

5. Make the bottom rails. They could be dowelled, but with the smaller section the joints are better tenoned (Fig. 4-6C). Plow grooves 1/4 inch wide and deep on the long rails to take the ends of the slats.

6. Reduce the ends of the four slats to fit the rail grooves (Fig. 4-6E).

7. Assemble the table ends first, checking for squareness and match against each other.

table will stand level and upright.

8. Check the action of the hinged top parts, then mount them with the pivot screw.

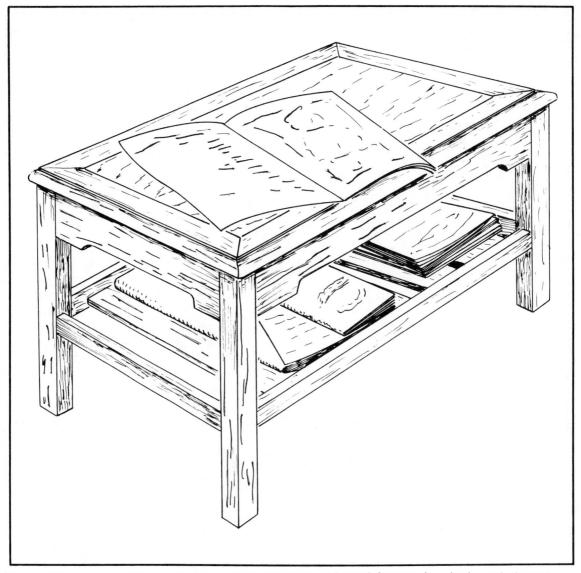

Fig. 4-4. This magazine table has a framed top and a slatted rack underneath for magazines, books, and other papers.

8. Have the long parts and the slats ready, then assemble completely. Check for squareness and lack of twist. See that the legs stand level.

9. Make the top so it is 1 inch outside the legs all around. Prepare the border strips (Fig. 4-5E) with rabbets to suit the plywood. Make them 3/4 inch wide to give a broad glue area.

10. Cut the miters so the length of the inner edges of these pieces come over the inner surfaces of the legs.

11. If the edges of the top are to be left square or rounded, dowels diagonally across the joints can be used (Fig. 4-6F). If the edges are molded, it would be better to use short dowels square to the miter (Fig. 4-6G) or parallel with one side (Fig. 4-6H).

12. Assemble the top frame, then cut the plywood to fit. For the closest fit give the plywood

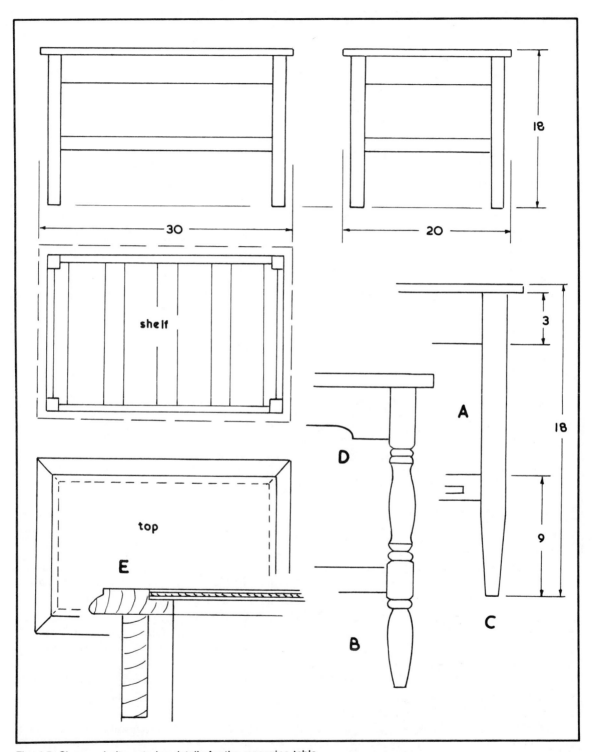

Fig. 4-5. Sizes and alternate leg details for the magazine table.

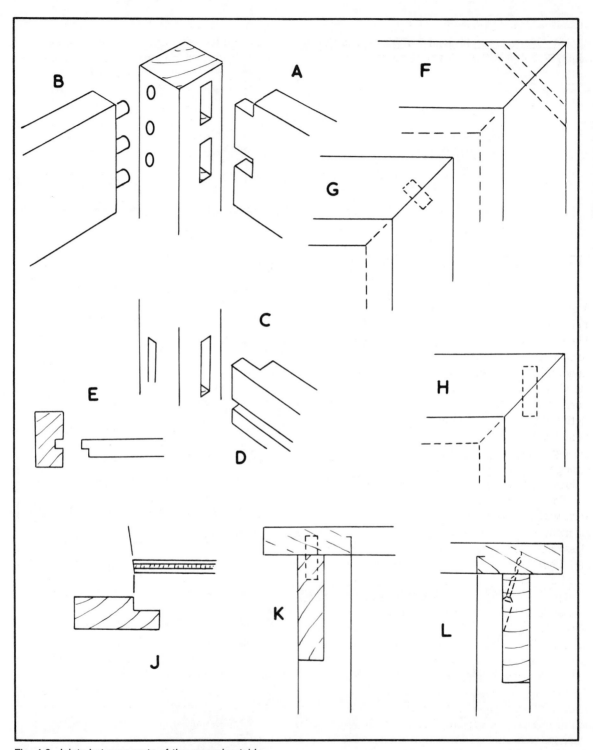

Fig. 4-6. Joints between parts of the magazine table.

edge a very slight taper (Fig. 4-6J).

13. The top may be held with dowels in the rails (Fig. 4-6K) or with pocket screws (Fig. 4-6L).

Materials List for Magazine Table	
4 legs	1 1/2 × 1 1/2 × 18
2 rails	3/4 × 3 × 28
2 rails	3/4 × 3 × 18
2 rails	3/4 × 1 1/2 × 28
2 rails	3/4 × 1 1/2 × 18
4 slats	1/2 × 4 × 18
2 top frames	7/8 × 2 1/2 × 30
2 top frames	7/8 × 2 1/2 × 20
1 top	3/8 × 18 × 28 plywood

GLASS-TOPPED TABLE

A glass top makes an attractive table, but forming it completely of glass involves structural problems. The fact that the underframing shows through can detract from its appearance, unless the glass is clouded or obscured. It is usually better to frame the glass panel with wood, then the construction work may be similar to that of a table with a completely wood top. The wooden border can be designed to hide details of the rails and the tops of the legs. Building in this way makes the whole thing stronger, and the glass edge will be protected so it does not have to be as thick or polished.

This small table (Fig. 4-7) has a modern appearance, with a broad frame around the glass and each leg made with two pieces in an angular section. The glass rests in position and can be lifted out for cleaning. There is a lip around the outer edge, which could be level or raised slightly. The main structural part of the top is thick plywood. As not much of it shows, it does not have to be of any special wood. Above it comes the mitered border around the glass. This could be veneered plywood or solid pieces of an attractive hardwood, the same thickness as the glass or slightly thicker. The legs may then be the same wood. The narrow lips on the edges of the top could be the same wood as the top or a different color to provide contrast. A dark top and legs, with a lighter color lip looks good, or the color combination could be reversed.

The glass panel should be 1/4 inch or more thick. It could be clear, tinted, or smoky glass. It will probably have smooth surfaces, but there are glasses with slightly uneven surface patterns that produce interesting effects. It is advisable to get your glass first; it will be easier to get a good fit, because you can make the frame to suit the glass. It would be difficult to alter slightly inaccurate glass to fit an existing frame.

The suggested construction uses dowels. You could use tongues and grooves between the leg parts, if you have the means of cutting them, to produce a strong leg assembly. The rail ends could be tenoned into mortises in the legs.

1. Decide on sizes (Fig. 4-8). Changes in overall sizes need not affect the details unless you want to make the table much bigger, when leg and rail sections should be increased.

2. Make the plywood square to form the top (Fig. 4-9A). Finishing the outside to size can be left until after the frames have been added. Cut the opening carefully to size now and finish its edges smoothly. Underneath the opening the plywood edges can be rounded slightly, but leave the top angles square.

3. Make the frame strips (Fig. 4-9B). Their corners are mitered and their inner edges should match the glass sizes. If there are any slight inequalities in the glass sizes, allow for them and mark where each strip comes. Glue the frame strips to the plywood base (Fig. 4-9C). Plane the table edges true.

4. Plain lips (Fig. 4-9D), which may be carried above the table surface if you wish, are rounded before fitting (Fig. 4-9E). Attach with glue and a few pins, which should be set below the surface and filled.

5. If you have suitable router bits or other tools to make the joint, you can get an increased glue area and therefore a stronger joint by cutting tongues and grooves (Fig. 4-9F).

6. Make the lips slightly too wide and plane them level with the tabletop after the glue has set, if you are not using the raised lips. Round the exposed edges and corners.

7. The legs are each made of two overlapping

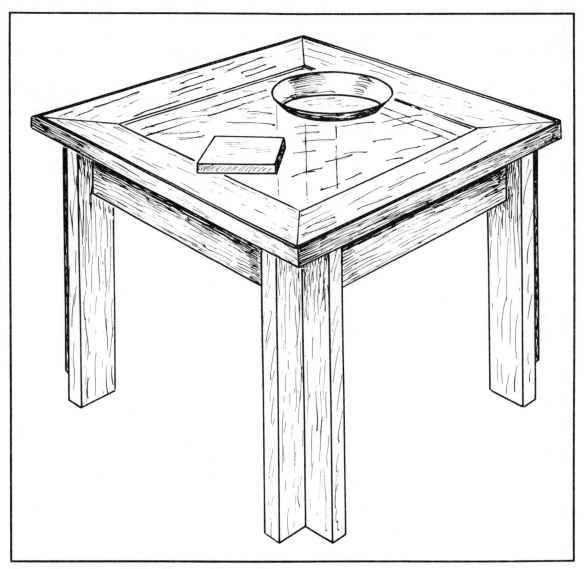

Fig. 4-7. A glass-topped table with unusual legs.

pieces (Figs. 4-8C and 4-9G). If they are not joined with tongue and groove joints, include a few dowels to supplement glue. Choose wood with reasonably straight grain, although the method of construction will limit any tendency to warp. Make the parts for the legs and drill holes for the dowels that join them.

8. Prepare the four rails (Fig. 4-8D). Mark and drill them and the legs for the dowels (Fig. 4-9H) so the rail ends are centered in the 3-inch width of a leg.

9. Join the parts to make the four legs. Plane the joints level, if necessary. Take the sharpness off all edges.

10. Join the two pairs of legs with their rails first. See that they are square and without twist and that opposite assemblies match, then join in the rails the other way. Measure diagonals and try the assembly on the inverted top to check squareness.

11. Remove surplus glue, sand the parts, and prepare the wood for finishing.

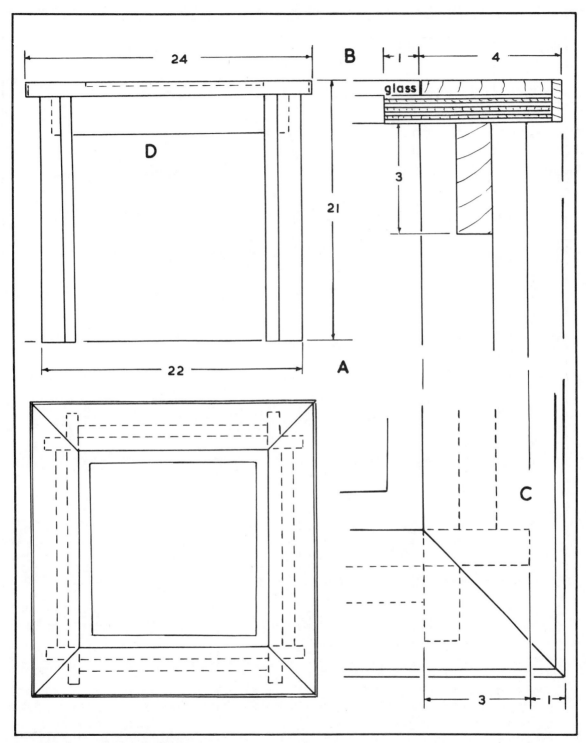

Fig. 4-8. Sizes of the glass-topped table.

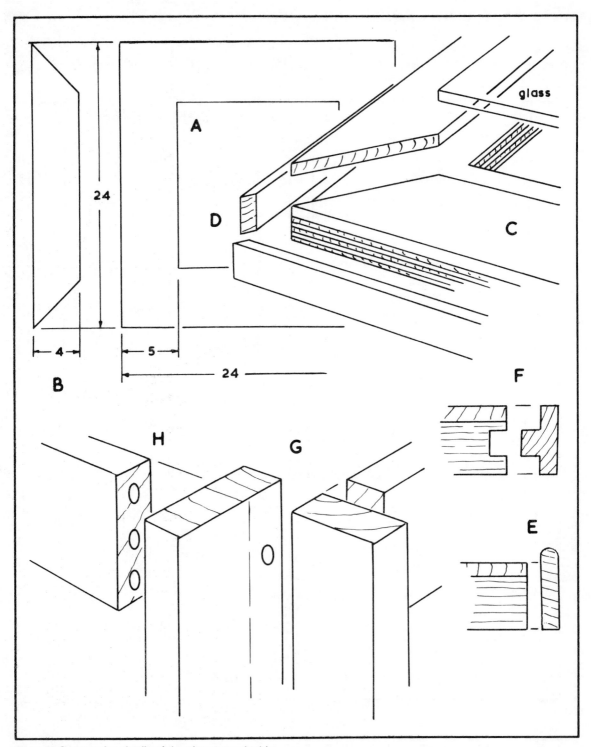

Fig. 4-9. Construction details of the glass-topped table.

12. Dowels can be used to join the rails to the top. It should be sufficient to have three 1/2-inch dowels spread out in each rail. You might find it easier to finish the wood with stain and polish or varnish at this stage and not join the top to the other parts until that has been done.

Materials List for Glass-Topped Table	
1 top	24 × 24 × 3/4 plywood
4 frames	3/8 × 5 × 24
4 lips	1/4 × 1 1/4 × 25
or for T and G	
joints	1/2 × 1 1/4 × 25
4 legs	1 × 2 × 21
4 legs	1 × 3 × 21
4 rails	1 × 3 × 17
1 piece glass	16 × 16 × 1/4 minimum

SOLID WOOD NESTING TABLES

Broad boards of solid hardwood always look attractive under stain and polish, particularly if there is a distinctive grain. Some woods, such as oak, have their appearance enhanced by exposed joints. This set of three tables (Fig. 4-10) is intended to be made with 3/4-inch boards, which might have to be glued to make up widths. The severity of the appearance is broken by curved cutouts for feet, rails, and handholes.

If you want to demonstrate your skill with hand tools, dovetails are the choice (Fig. 4-12A), but machine-made comb or tongue joints (Fig. 4-12B) would be just as strong. In both cases the pattern of alternate side and end grain provides decoration. A final demonstration of skill is to miter the meeting boards at the edges.

When tables have to fit into each other there

Fig. 4-10. A nest of three solid wood tables.

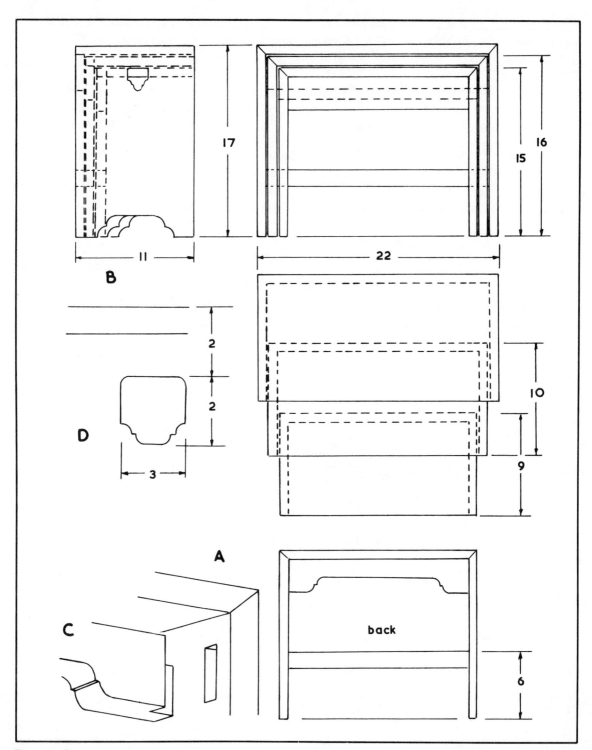

Fig. 4-11. Sizes of the solid wood nesting tables.

cannot be front rails, at least for the two large tables. The corner joints provide considerable strength. Each table also has a lower rail and an upper one under the top to resist any tendency to distort the tables and to act as stops when they are pushed together.

Each table is 1 inch smaller all around than the next larger one (Fig.4-11). With 3/4-inch stock, this gives a 1/4-inch clearance. If your wood is a different thickness, make suitable allowances.

All three tables are made in the same way. Stock for all may be marked out at the same time. When you reach the stage of cutting joints and trial assemblies, make the largest table first, then check the size of the second one against it, followed by fitting the smallest table into that. The following instructions apply to making one table.

1. Cut the wood for the top and ends. Allow about 1/16 inch extra at each end for planing level after joints are assembled. Mark out the dovetail or comb joints, choosing widths that will space evenly.

2. Prepare the wood for the two rails. The top rail has a short tenon at each end cut back from the top (Fig. 4-11A). The lower rail has similar tenons. Cut the tenons and the mortises to take them.

3. Make templates for the curved work from thin plywood or stout card. Because the one for the feet (Fig. 4-12C) is used from each side of an end, the cutout will become narrower on the inner tables. The other template (Fig. 4-12D) gives the shapes under the top rail and at the corners of the handholes in the ends.

4. Mark and cut the feet in the end (Fig. 4-11B). Cut away the bottom edge of the top rail (Fig. 4-11C). Mark the outline of the handhole (Fig. 4-11D) in each end. Use the template to mark the lower corners. Round the top corners. The hole may be cut right through, but suitable router cutters could be used to make it only about 1/2 inch

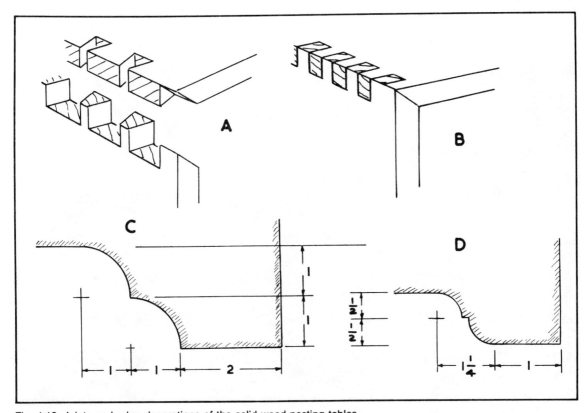

Fig. 4-12. Joints and edge decorations of the solid wood nesting tables.

deep for fingertip gripping.

5. Cut the corner joints. Glue the rails to the ends. Bring the top down onto this assembly and glue to the top rail as well as into the corner joints. When the glue has set, clean off the joints and lightly round them. Excessive rounding might take off enough wood to weaken them. Elsewhere, rounding will not affect strength.

Materials List for Solid Wood Nesting Tables			
(All wood 3/4 inch thick)			
1 top	11	×	23
2 ends	11	×	18
1 top	10	×	21
2 ends	10	×	17
1 top	9	×	19
2 ends	9	×	16
1 rail	3	×	22
1 rail	3	×	20
1 rail	3	×	18
1 rail	1 1/2	×	22
1 rail	1 1/2	×	20
1 rail	1 1/2	×	18

CHAIRSIDE MAGAZINE RACK

This is a unit with space for magazines and books or other items and a flat top to form a small table. The unit stands beside a chair and is either on casters so it can be moved or given a plinth (Fig. 4-13). The main parts might be solid wood, veneered particleboard, or plywood (for a painted finish). The slats could be in a contrasting color—varnished light hardwood looks good when the other parts are given a dark finish.

The sizes shown (Fig. 4-14) will suit most magazines, but if you have particular books or magazines to accommodate, alter the sizes. Dowelled construction can be used for the main parts. The slats are screwed on.

1. Make the ends and divider (Fig. 4-15A, B, and C) all the same height, but the magazine end is rounded to slat level.

2. Make the lengthwise divider (Fig. 4-15D). Mark and drill it and the adjoining parts for dowels.

3. The bottom (Fig. 4-15E) projects 1/2 inch all around and may have its corners rounded.

4. The top (Fig. 4-15F) should have its edge

Fig. 4-13. This chairside magazine rack has space for books as well as magazines and newspapers and a small tabletop.

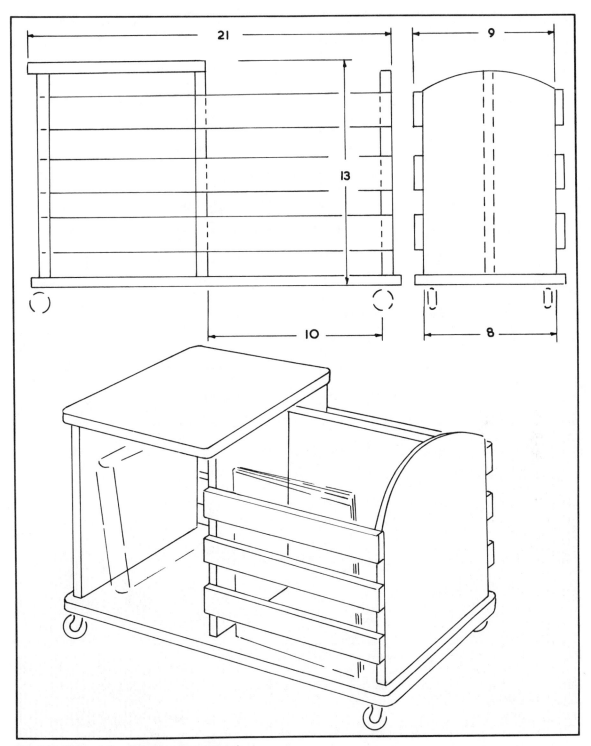

Fig. 4-14. Sizes of the chairside magazine rack.

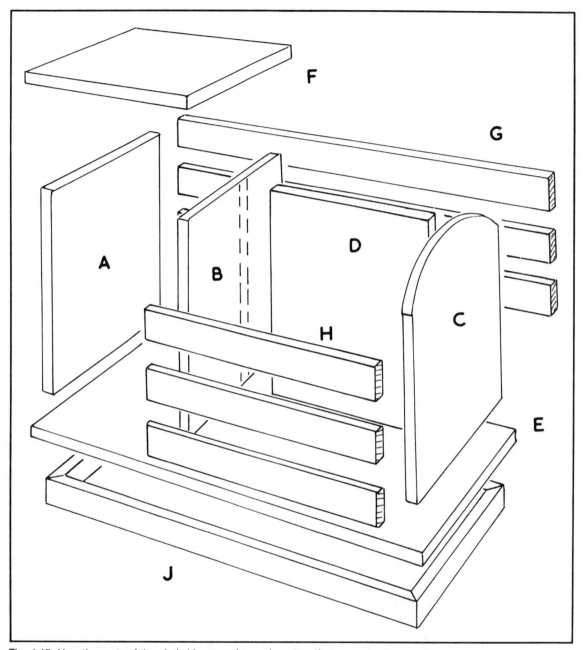

Fig. 4-15. How the parts of the chairside magazine rack go together.

level with the divider, but project 1/2 inch on the other three sides. Round the corners to match the bottom.

5. Mark and drill all the main parts for dowels (1/4-inch dowels at about 3-inch intervals should be satisfactory). Assemble these parts tightly and squarely.

6. The laths extend the full length of the back (Fig. 4-15G), but only over the magazine rack at the front (Fig. 4-15H). Round all the exposed edges. Fit

the slats with two screws at each crossing. They could be made a design feature by using plated round-head screws.

7. If casters are to be used, choose the type with a drilled plate fitting to screw on.

8. If a plinth is to be used (Fig. 4-15J) make it from strips mitered at the corners.

Materials List for Chairside Magazine Rack	
2 ends	5/8 × 8 × 12
1 divider	5/8 × 8 × 12
1 divider	5/8 × 10 × 12
1 bottom	5/8 × 9 × 21
1 top	5/8 × 9 × 12
3 slats	3/8 × 2 × 20
3 slats	3/8 × 2 × 12
2 plinths	3/4 × 1 1/2 × 20
2 plinths	3/4 × 1 1/2 × 8

DOWEL MAGAZINE RACK

Chairside magazine and newspaper racks take many forms. Keeping these publications and other papers together can be arranged in many ways. In this case, the rack is a simple assembly of dowel rods between a frame and a base (Fig. 4-16).

Although plywood could be used, with the top frame cut from one piece, the rack will look better if the top frame is jointed solid wood and the base is one piece of solid wood. Softwood or hardwood could be used, preferably to match the wood from which the dowel rods are made. The completed rack could be given a clear finish over the natural wood, or it might be stained first to match other furniture.

1. Settle on sizes (Fig. 4-17), which could be varied to suit available wood or an economical way of cutting stock lengths of dowel rod.

2. Mark out the parts of the top frame with

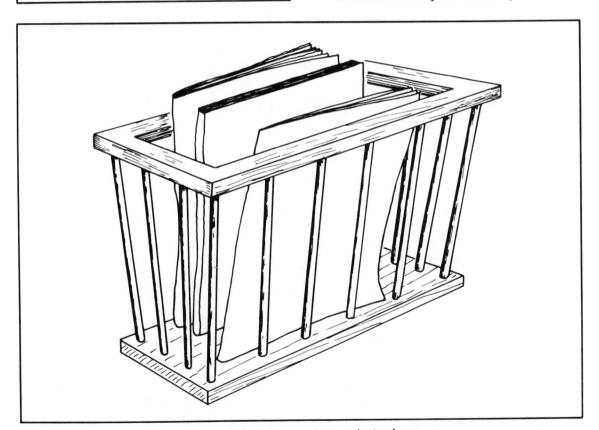

Fig. 4-16. This dowel magazine rack has spindles between a base and a top frame.

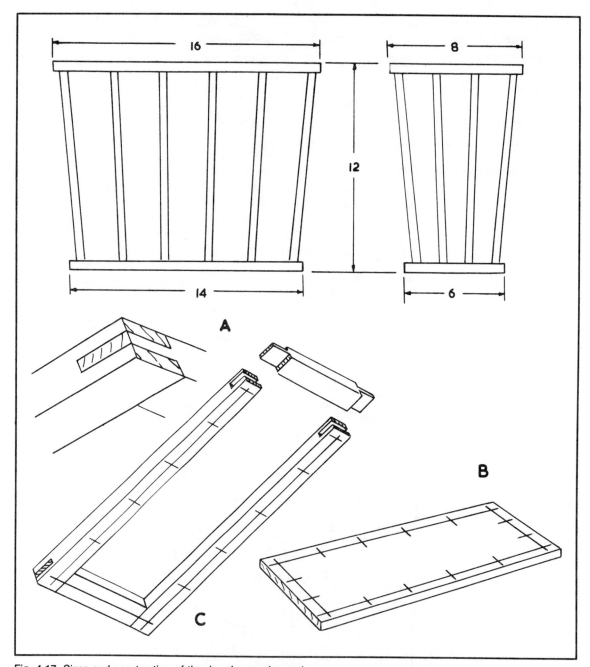

Fig. 4-17. Sizes and construction of the dowel magazine rack.

open mortise and tenon, or bridle, joints at the corners (Fig. 4-17A). Make the parts slightly too long so the ends can be trimmed level after the joints have been glued together.

3. Cut the base to size and draw the lines for the holes (Fig. 4-17B). Allow for a hole coming where the lines cross at the corners, then space the others evenly.

4. Do the same under the frame, with centerlines and the same number of holes spaced evenly (Fig. 4-17C).

5. Although the rods splay outwards, this is at such a small angle that it is not enough to affect drilling. Drill the top and bottom as deep as possible without the drill point breaking through the other side. Use a stop on the drill or drill press so all holes are the same depth.

6. Cut the dowel rods to the same length and remove any raggedness from the ends.

7. Glue all the rods into the top or bottom, then bring the other part into place. Check that the amount of flare is the same at opposite sides and ends. Instead of clamps, weights could be put on the rack while the glue sets.

Materials List for Dowel Magazine Rack	
2 tops	5/8 × 1 1/4 × 17
2 tops	5/8 × 1 1/4 × 9
1 bottom	5/8 × 6 × 14
24 dowel rods	12 × 12 1/2 diameter

DIVAN

A divan or day bed is a piece of furniture with many uses. It can be a long seat or sofa. If it is long enough and some cushions are added, it makes a comfortable place for reclining during the day and becomes an extra bed for guests. It might be made into a couch by adding a back and ends, but the basic divan is just a padded seat or bed that may be put against a wall or fitted into a corner.

This divan holds three store-bought cushions, each about 25 by 30 inches and 4 inches or more thick. Besides the springing provided by the cushion interiors, there is more from the webbing base of the divan.

The sizes of cushions available may govern overall sizes, but it is best to make the divan a little more than 72 inches long (Fig. 4-17). Almost anyone will be able to lie full length on it without their legs overhanging so it is big enough to use as an occasional bed. The drawings are for the suggested size obtained by cushions to make up 30 inches by 75 inches (Fig. 4-19A).

The divan consists of a supported frame with

Fig. 4-18. This divan has three cushions supported on interwoven webbing.

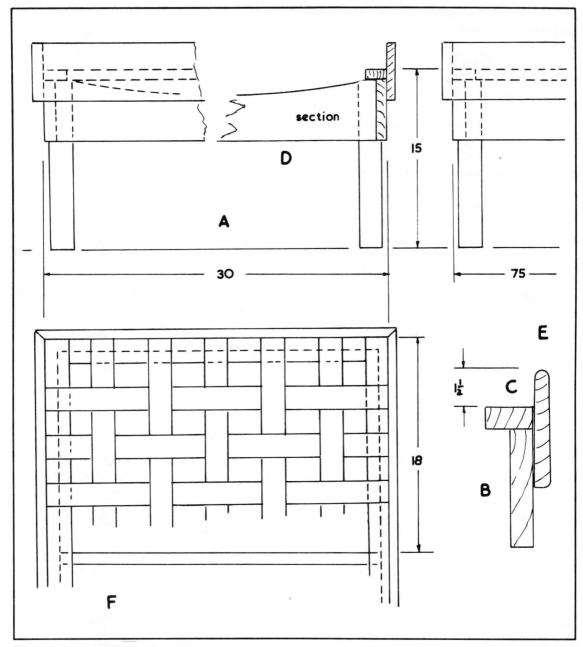

Fig. 4-19. Sizes and details of the divan.

interlaced webbing to fit under the cushions. It has border strips to retain the cushions and legs to raise the seat to a comfortable height.

1. Measure the cushions together. Make the main frame to this size. It will be best to have the cushions fitting closely so there are no gaps between or around them. Cut the main frame sides and ends to size (Figs. 4-19B and 4-20A and B).

2. The corner joints could be overlapped and screwed or nailed, rabetted and nailed both ways,

or dovetailed. The webbing frame and the legs with their glue and screws provide more strength in the corners, and the leg tops also help to hold the corners together.

3. Cut the webbing frame strips (Figs. 4-19C and 4-20C and D) to fit on top of the main frame. There is no need for cut joints between them at the corners, but one piece may overlap the other (Fig. 4-20E). Glue and nail the webbing frame to the main frame. If necessary, plane the outer surface level.

4. The legs should be notched to half the thickness of the frame at their tops, so the down-ward load is taken on their shoulders (Fig. 4-20F).

5. The lower parts of the legs could be left parallel and square or they could be shaped. Another form is shown (Fig. 4-20G). Mark the end of a leg as an octagon, then taper the corners to it from points just below the frame level.

6. Fit the legs to the frame and see that the assembly stands square and level.

7. Divide the length into four and make three stiffeners to fit into these three marked positions. Their purpose is to prevent the long sides from bowing inward under the pull of the webbing and

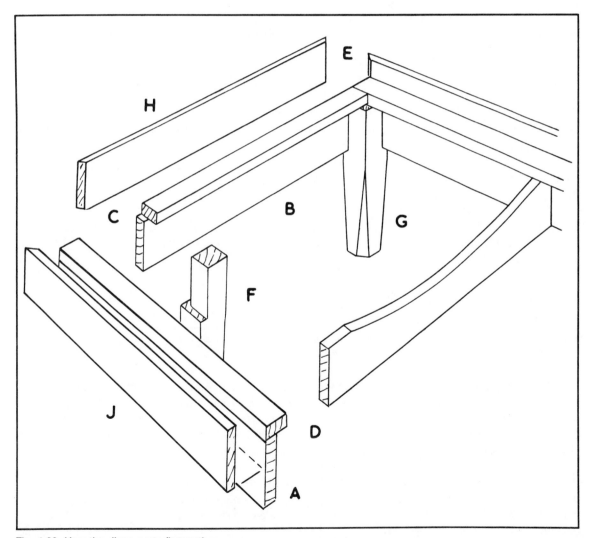

Fig. 4-20. How the divan parts fit together.

the weight of the users. Each stiffener fits between the side frames (Fig. 4-19D). Hollow the top between the edges of the webbing frames to provide clearance if the seat sags. How much hollowing depends on the weight and tension of the webbing, but a curve 1 inch deep should be enough. The stiffeners can be glued in and screwed down through the webbing frame and through the main frame high enough for the screws to be hidden by the border strips.

8. Make the border strips (Figs. 4-19E and 4-20H and J). They stand above the webbing frame to retain the cushions. Miter the corners. Round all over the top edges and round the outer corners at the bottom. Have these parts cut to size and drilled ready to screw on, but do not fit them yet.

9. The webbing could be the plain fabric type, which has little stretch, or rubber-reinforced, which is more elastic. Most webbing is about 2 inches wide. Get enough to cover in both directions with 2-inch to 3-inch gaps (Fig. 4-19F). The crosswise pieces mainly determine the amount of support provided, with the lengthwise pieces reinforcing them. Deal with the webbing the narrow way first. Fix with 3/8-inch or 1/2-inch tacks.

10. Mark where the webbing will come to get an even spacing. Start near the middle of the divan on a long side and fix one piece of webbing to serve as a guide to the fitting and tension of the other pieces. Turn back the end and attach it firmly to the webbing frame strips with tacks—five will probably be needed (Fig. 4-21A). Have the fold in the webbing close to the frame edge, but do not let it overlap. Keep all webbing folds within the line of the edge so they do not interfere with the fit of the border pieces.

11. Bring the strip across the near side with no more tension than is needed to keep it level, then pencil where the wood edge comes (Fig. 4-21B). Stretch the webbing to what you judge to be a suitable tension and pencil on the new edge position (Fig. 4-21C). How much stretch depends on the webbing. It may be little more than 1/2 inch with fabric webbing, but could be 2 inches with rubber webbing. Note the distance between the pencil marks and tension other bands in that direction by the same

amount. This will give even support for the cushions.

12. With the webbing pulled to the second mark, drive in three tacks. Cut off the webbing, leaving enough to turn back (Fig.4-21D). Turn over the end and drive two more tacks through the double thickness (Fig. 4-21E).

13. Do this with all the crosswise bands of webbing, then add the lengthwise bands starting with the center one. Tack one end and tension the interwoven band, marking with pencil, in the same way as when working across. Fit all the lengthwise bands in the same way.

14. Be sure the border strips fit outside the webbing. It will probably be easier to finish the wood with stain and polish or varnish before the border strips are finally fitted. It is advisable to attach the borders without glue. Then if the webbing ever has to be repaired, it can be taken off for easier working.

15. Add the cushions and the divan is ready for use.

Materials List for Divan				
2 main frames	1	× 5	× 76
2 main frames	1	× 5	× 31
2 webbing frames	1	× 2	× 76
2 webbing frames	1	× 2	× 31
3 stiffeners	1	× 5	× 30
2 borders	3/4	× 5	× 78
2 borders	3/4	× 5	× 33
4 legs	2	× 2	× 15

SOFA

A two-place sofa or love seat is a useful addition to the seating of a room. It is only a little more complicated to make than a chair and does not involve the extra strengthening like a longer seat. Some similar furniture is fully upholstered, and only the feet may show the wooden construction. An alternative is to make a wooden sofa where most of the wood is exposed and padding is with loose cushions.

This project (Fig. 4-22) is of this type and is intended to be used with four, 20-inch square cushions about 4 inches thick. The cushions could

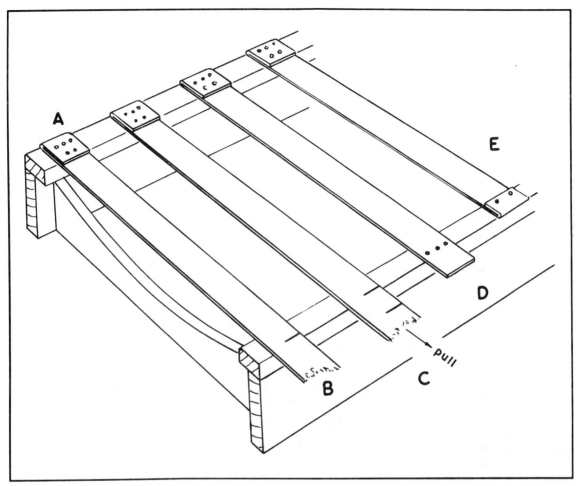

Fig. 4-21. How to fit the crosswise webbing on the divan.

be made or bought as a standard size. Get the cushions first in case measurements of the sofa have to be altered to suit the exact sizes of available cushions.

The seating is sprung with rubber webbing (taken from the sides to the center, not interwoven as in the divan), but the back cushions rest against vertical dowel rods. Construction has been simplified as far as possible, without sacrificing comfort or appearance. Although the complete assembly appears complicated, the work is straightforward if tackled one step at a time.

The sofa is heavier and more stable than a chair and not likely to be abused by tilting in use, but it should still be strongly made, preferably with a good hardwood. The design allows for dowelled joints, except for tenons on the bottom rails where there is insufficient space for two dowels, and there could be tenons in place of dowels elsewhere.

The design can be used to make a matching lounge chair, if the lengthwise parts are shortened to suit a single cushion width. All other construction is the same.

1. Set out the rear legs (Fig. 4-24). Cut them to shape and mark on them the positions of other parts. Draw a full-size end view of the sofa, marking the rear leg shape around the one you have cut (Fig. 4-23A). This drawing will give you the sizes

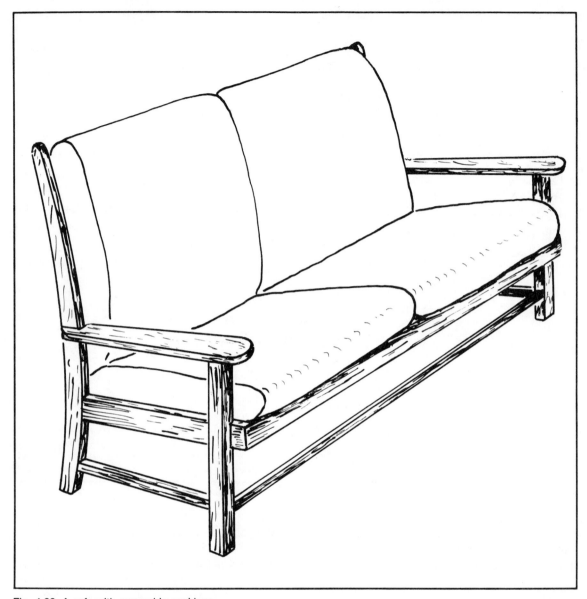

Fig. 4-22. A sofa with removable cushions.

and angles of other parts.

2. The seat ends and center rail have to be grooved to take the metal ends of the rubber webbing (Fig. 4-24A). Obtain the clips and webbing and squeeze one clip on to the end of a strip of webbing. Measure this for the size of groove needed, with enough depth for the lip on the clip to come level with the surface. Put a single groove in each

seat end (Fig. 4-24B) and double grooves in the center rail (Fig. 4-24C). Round the edges of the wood where the rubber will cross.

3. Make the seat frame (Fig. 4-25A). The ends extend at the angle shown on the full-size drawing to attach to the rear legs (Fig. 4-24D). The long rails can be attached to the end rails with dowels, comb joints, or dovetails. Dowel the cen-

ter rail in place. Drill for the dowels into the rear legs—three, 1/2-inch diameters should be enough.

4. Make the two front legs (Figs. 4-23B and 4-25B), using your full-size drawing to get the positions and angles of the other parts.

5. Allow for mortises for the bottom rails. Make shallow notches for the seat frame. When you

assemble you may screw into these joints from inside the seat frame. At the top there could be four dowels or two stub tenons (Fig. 4-24E). These joints should be strong as users tend to pull up on the arms.

6. Make the bottom rails (Fig. 4-25C) to fit all around with tenons into the legs. Use the seat

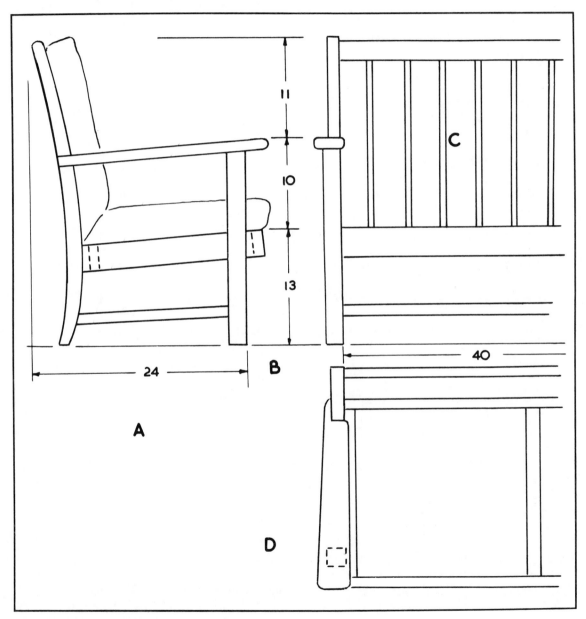

Fig. 4-23. Sizes of the wood parts of the sofa.

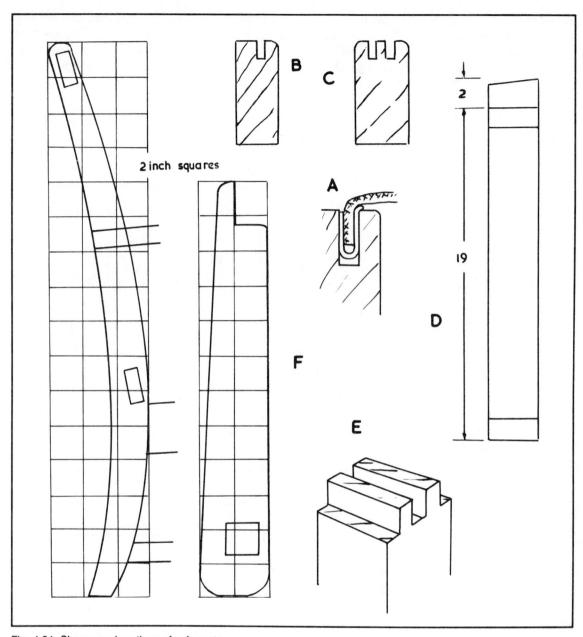

Fig. 4-24. Shapes and sections of sofa parts.

frame, with an allowance for the front leg notches, as a guide to length between the shoulders of the long rails. The full-size drawing gives you the size of the end rails.

7. Make the two back rails (Fig. 4-25D) and prepare the ends for mortise and tenon joints or dowels. Drill the rails for the upright spindles (Fig. 4-23C) at about 3 1/2-inch spacing.

8. Mark out the two arms (Fig. 4-24F). Their inner edges come square to the front, but the other edge flares outwards (Fig. 4-23D). Delay completely cutting to size until after the other parts have been

assembled, in case there are slight discrepancies. The front ends could be prepared for the joints to the front legs, but leave the notch to be cut at the other end as you fit each arm.

9. Fit the dowel spindles between the back rails, but check that the spacing between the rails suits their positions on the rear legs.

10. Join the back rails and the long bottom rails

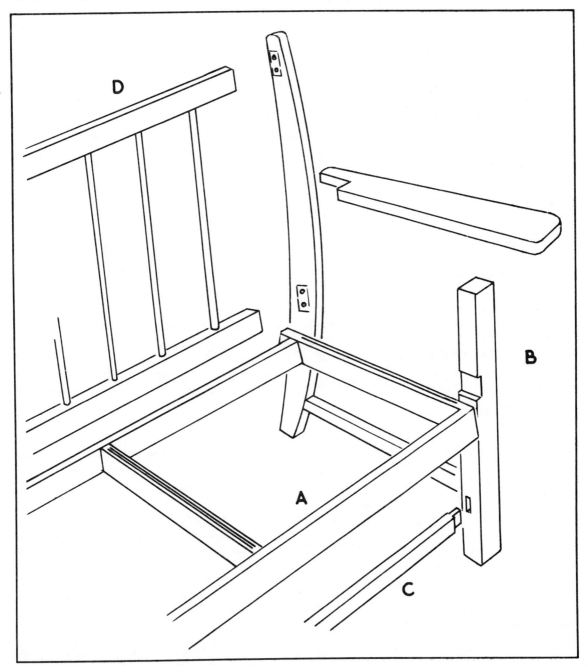

Fig. 4-25. An end of the sofa showing how the parts fit together.

between the rear legs. See that the assembly is square so far and matches the length of the seat frame.

11. Join the front legs to the seat frame and the front bottom rail. Put in the end bottom rails. Check that the assembly is square and stands level.

12. Try the arms in position and cut the notches. Round the forward parts of the arms. Use dowels between the notched parts and the rear legs.

13. The 2-inch rubber webbing should be used with spaces about 1 1/2 inches. That means five or six strips each side for a total length of about 20 feet plus 24 clips to squeeze on the ends. If you do not have a special tool, the clips can be squeezed to close them and make their teeth penetrate the webbing in a vise. Make a trial strip. Put a clip on one end and press that in the rail groove. Stretch the webbing across until you judge there is a suitable tension to give adequate springing under a cushion. Mark that length, with an allowance for the clip. Let this spring back and use it as a guide to make all the other pieces the same length.

14. Fit all the rubber webbing strips, evenly spaced in their sections, and try the seating with all the cushions in position. If it is satisfactory, remove the webbing and cushions and give the woodwork a final sanding before applying its finish.

Materials List for Sofa

2 rear legs	1 1/4	× 5 × 32
2 front legs	2	× 2 × 23
2 arms	1	× 4 × 24
2 seat ends	1 1/4	× 3 × 24
2 seat rails	1 1/4	× 3 × 44
1 seat center rail	1 1/2	× 3 × 24
2 bottom rails	1 1/4	× 1 1/4 × 23
2 bottom rails	1 1/4	× 1 1/4 × 44
2 back rails	1 1/4	× 2 × 44
10 back spindles	20	× 1/2 diameter dowel rods

CORNER CUPBOARD

To make the best use of the corner of a room, a piece of furniture has to be arranged so access is diagonal to the corner, otherwise, a square shape will cut off a triangle which cannot be used. A simple triangular unit does not provide much top area or shelf space, but squaring away from the walls before making the cut across increases the available area considerably.

If the top is arranged at table height, it can be used as a sideboard or side table. It could make a corner dresser in a small bedroom. It could serve as a television stand. The angle does not have to be 45 degrees. The shape could be arranged longer along one wall than the other, but unless there is a need to fit a space or other good reason for a different shape, equal sides look better.

This corner cupboard (Fig. 4-26) is shown at table height and with one shelf and a door. Other sizes could be made in the same way, with one or more open shelves.

The exposed parts may be a good hardwood to match other furniture. Hidden parts could be softwood. Softwood could be used for everything if a painted finish is used. Wall panels are shown, and they could be hardboard or thin plywood. They might be omitted and the house walls exposed as inside surfaces instead. The door panel should be plywood veneered to match the wood around it. For economy, the bottom might be plywood or softwood, with hardboard about 2 inches wide glued on where it will show under the sides and door. The shelf could be solid wood or plywood with a lip across the front.

1. Check the squareness of the room corner. If it is not square, make a template of the actual angle from scrap plywood or hardboard. Use that instead of a square when marking shapes that have to fit against walls.

2. Make the two wall frames (Fig. 4-28A) first. At the room corner one overlaps the other (Fig. 4-27A); keep one frame narrower by the thickness of the wood. Because the bottom is 3 inches above the floor, the framing extends below the bottom rail (Fig. 4-28B).

3. The corners of the wall frames could be cut as halving joints, particularly if you are not having wall panels. With a panel it should be sufficient to cut the parts to fit closely (Fig. 4-28C) and glue and nail the panels to them. The panels need not ex-

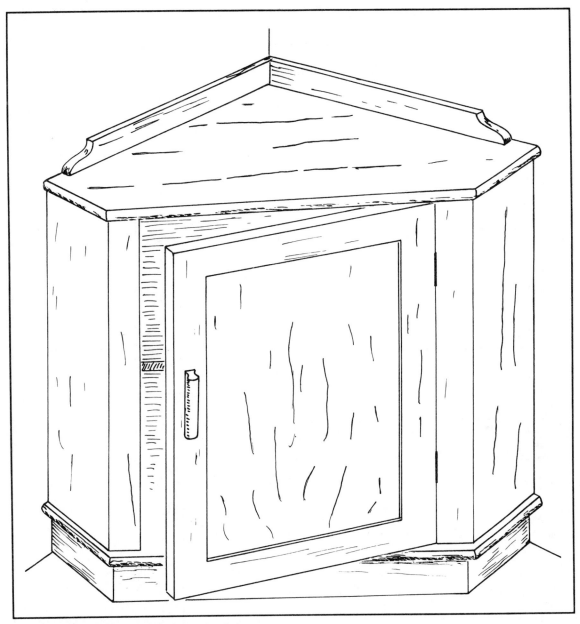

Fig. 4-26. This triangular cupboard fits closely into a corner.

tend below the bottom rails.

4. Set out the bottom (Fig. 4-28D) to get the sizes and positions of the other parts (Fig. 4-27B). If the bottom is to be softwood with hardwood edges, glue those on before completing setting out (Fig. 4-28E).

5. Make the top to match the bottom, fitting over instead of around other parts. Both will have rounded or molded edges, but final shaping can be left until other parts have been made and assembly tested. In this way overhangs can be adjusted evenly.

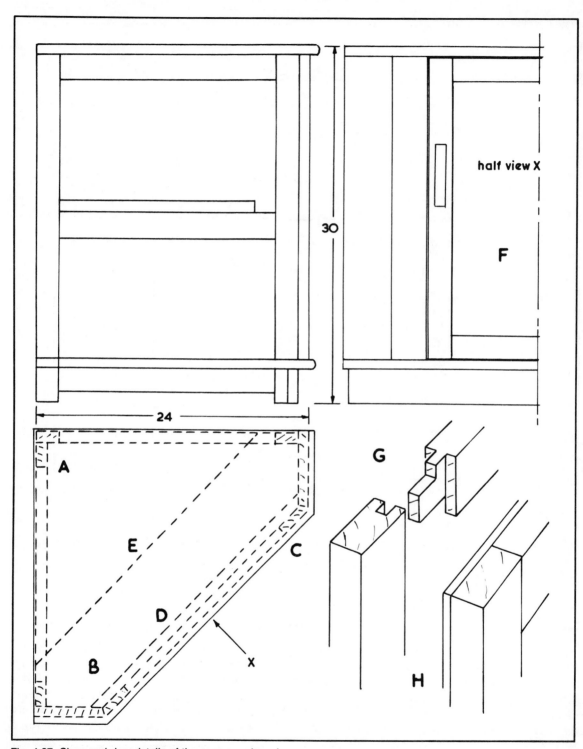

Fig. 4-27. Sizes and door details of the corner cupboard.

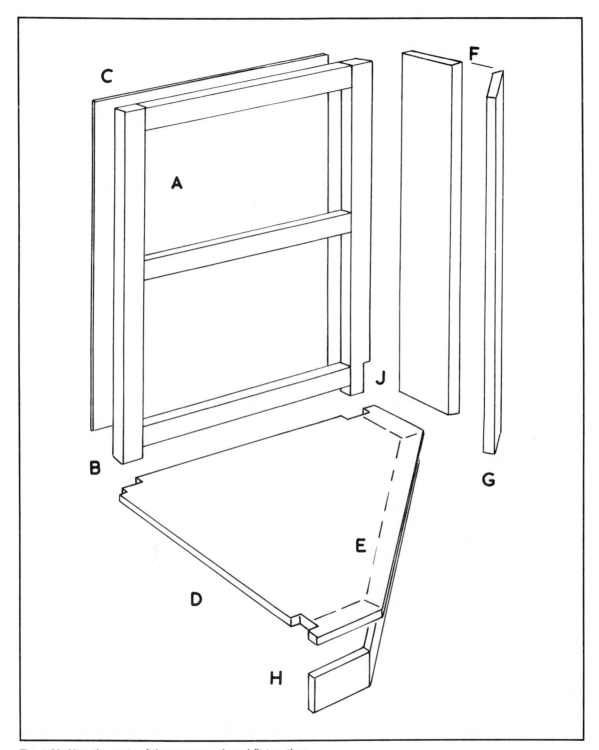

Fig. 4-28. How the parts of the corner cupboard fit together.

6. The fronts are built up and fit between the top and bottom, to which they are dowelled. The wide part fits against the wall (Fig. 4-28F) and covers the edges of its wall panel and frame. The narrow part (Fig. 4-28G) has a square edge towards the door, but the two pieces are mitered together (Fig. 4-27C). The angle to plane is 67 1/2 degrees. Test the parts together in position and make any adjustment necessary.

7. It should be sufficient to glue the front parts together. There could be a few thin dowels to keep them in the correct relation to each other. Assemble the two fronts before joining to the other parts.

8. The plinth (Fig. 4-28H) is set back under the bottom about 1 inch. It touches the walls, and the frames will have to be notched to clear its ends (Fig. 4-28J). The plinth parts have to be mitered together in the same way as the front parts. Once the plinth is in position, however, there is no load on the joint. Glue and dowel the plinth to the bottom.

9. Join the frames together and assemble the bottom to them. Mount the front pieces in position. Glue alone may be sufficient along the edges to the frames, although a few dowels could be used there and should be put in the end grain to the bottom.

10. Put the top in place with dowels upwards from the other parts. Round or mold the outer edges of the top and bottom to give a matching, even overlap on the fronts.

11. Put a strip across under the top to act as a door stop (Fig. 4-27D).

12. Check that the external surfaces that will meet the walls are level. Try the cupboard in position. It is a help when fitting to leave the edges of the top and front oversize for any slight adjustment needed.

13. The shelf rests on its rails and is a simple triangle, kept narrow enough to pass through the frame edges (Fig. 4-27E). It can then be pulled forward and twisted to pull it through the doorway if you want to remove it for cleaning.

14. There are several ways to make the door. Here it is framed (Figs. 4-26 and 4-27F). The bet-

ter quality door has grooved framing for the panel and the corner joints are mortises and tenons (Fig. 4-27G). For a simpler assembly the panel goes behind the frame, which could be dowelled (Fig. 4-27H), and is glued and held with pins or thin nails.

15. Let in hinges and arrange a spring or magnetic catch. The handle could be any type you wish, but one made from the same wood as the door is appropriate.

16. If another unit is to be stood on top (see next project), the cupboard top must be left without projections. If it is to stand alone, add strips to the top (Fig. 4-26). They improve appearance and protect the walls. Attach these strips with glue and dowels. You could make this unit and use it as it is for some time, then add an upper unit later. In this case press the dowels into dry holes in the top, so the strips can be lifted out without causing any damage later.

Materials List for Corner Cupboard

4 uprights	1 × 2 × 30
6 rails	1 × 2 × 24
2 wall panels	24 × 29 × 1/8 hardboard
1 top	3/4 × 22 × 36
1 bottom	3/4 × 22 × 36
1 shelf	3/4 × 13 × 30
2 fronts	3/4 × 7 × 26
2 fronts	3/4 × 3 × 26
1 plinth	3/4 × 3 × 27
2 plinths	3/4 × 3 × 7
2 door parts	3/4 × 2 × 26
2 door parts	3/4 × 2 × 20
1 door panel	20 × 26 × 1/4 plywood
2 top strips	1 × 2 × 22

CORNER DISPLAY CABINET

The corner of a room is a good place to display valuable or interesting items, such as crockery and trophies which will look better behind glass. They can be in a case that hangs on the wall or stands on another piece of furniture. Various sizes are possible, but if the items to be displayed are few and not very large, a compact cabinet looks neat and will fill a space that otherwise would be vacant.

This cabinet (Fig. 4-29) has storage on three levels and has a glass door. It could be screwed to the wall so the contents are at eye level, or it could stand on the corner cabinet (see previous project) to make an attractive piece of combined furniture.

Sizes can be varied to suit the intended contents. The door opening, as drawn, is about 11 inches wide, and the greatest height that can be accommodated is about 10 inches. The best appearance is when the cabinet is tall in relation to its width. Some edge molding is suggested. All of the profiles can be made with one router cutter, or square edges could be combined with simple rounding.

The cabinet is made of solid wood. The wider parts can be made up by glueing narrower pieces. Particleboard may be used for the backs and shelves, with lips or veneers on the edges that show. The glass in the door is fitted so it can be removed, if necessary.

1. Check the squareness of the corner of the room. If it is out of square, make a template at least as large as the cabinet bottom out of scrap hardboard or plywood and use that instead of a square for parts that have to fit into the corner.

2. Set out the bottom (Figs. 4-30A and 4-31A), allowing the extension for molded edges. Mark on it where the other parts will come. Use this as a guide when preparing parts that connect to it.

3. Make the two backs (Fig. 4-31B). One is narrower than the other by the thickness of the wood, so projections along the walls will be the same when they overlap. Make dado grooves for the shelves (Fig. 4-31C). Prepare both ends for dowels. Overlap the backs and glue and screw them together.

4. Make the two shelves (Fig. 4-31D). They extend the full width of the back. The front piece will fit against them. Check with the marked bottom that the shelves follow the correct outline. If necessary, veneer or put a lip on the edge of each

shelf that shows inside the door. The shelf edges act as door stops.

5. Make the top to the same outline as the bottom. Mold both parts on the exposed edges (Fig. 4-30B).

6. Prepare the fronts the same height as the backs. The wider pieces (Figs. 4-30C and 4-31E) cover the edges of the backs and fit against the walls. The narrow pieces (Figs. 4-30D and 4-31F) have their square edges forming the door opening. Miter the two sets of parts to fit against each other, then glue and dowel them.

7. When the cabinet has been assembled there is little strain on most joints. To help locate the parts correctly during assembly, however, set a few thin dowels into top and bottom (Fig. 4-31G) and between the fronts and the shelves. At the top of the door opening include a strip across (Fig. 4-30E and F) with dowels to the fronts.

8. Fit the shelves to the backs, then the fronts to them, followed by the top and bottom.

9. The top overhang can be further decorated with a narrow strip carried around and cut with a similar molding (Fig. 4-30G).

10. Prepare the door parts with a rabbet. Its size depends on the thickness of the glass, but leaving about 3/16 inch at the front will usually be satisfactory.

11. Make the door with mortise and tenon joints. Let in hinges. There can be a spring or magnetic catch and handle of your choice. The handle might be the type with a shaft through to operate a catch inside.

12. To fit the glass make narrow beads with mitered corners to go inside the rabbet. The strips could be square, but they look better if the inner surface is rounded (Fig. 4-30H). Fix them with pins; but before you do that, stain and polish the wood so you do not risk marking the glass.

13. If the cabinet is to stand on the corner cabinet, screw into each wall near the top to prevent tilting. If the cabinet is to hang without other support, fasten four or six screws into the walls through the backs.

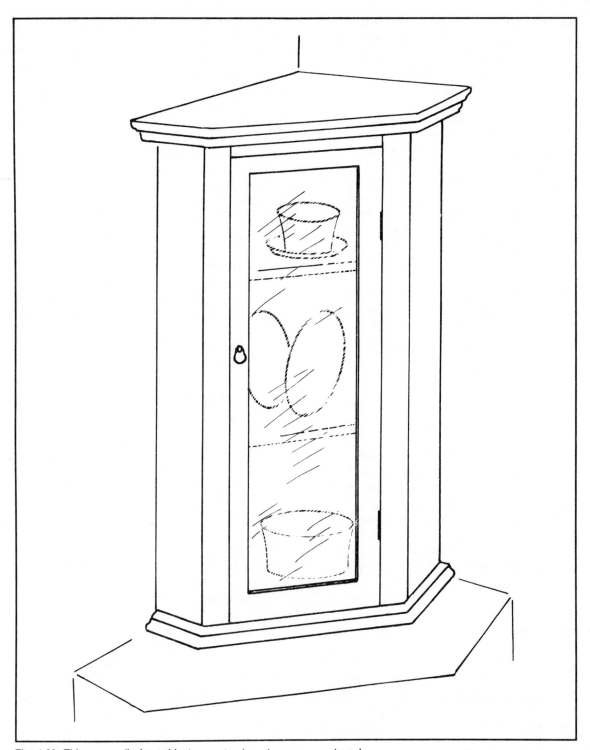

Fig. 4-29. This corner display cabinet may stand on the corner cupboard.

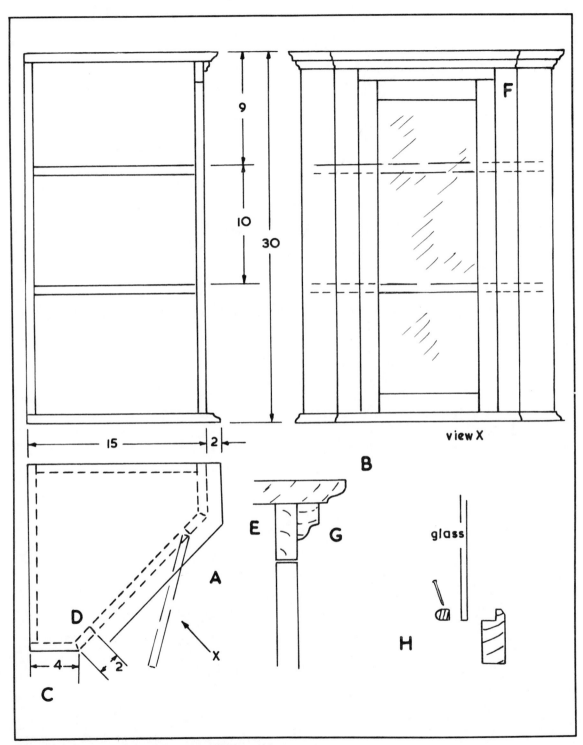

Fig. 4-30. Sizes and details of the corner display cabinet.

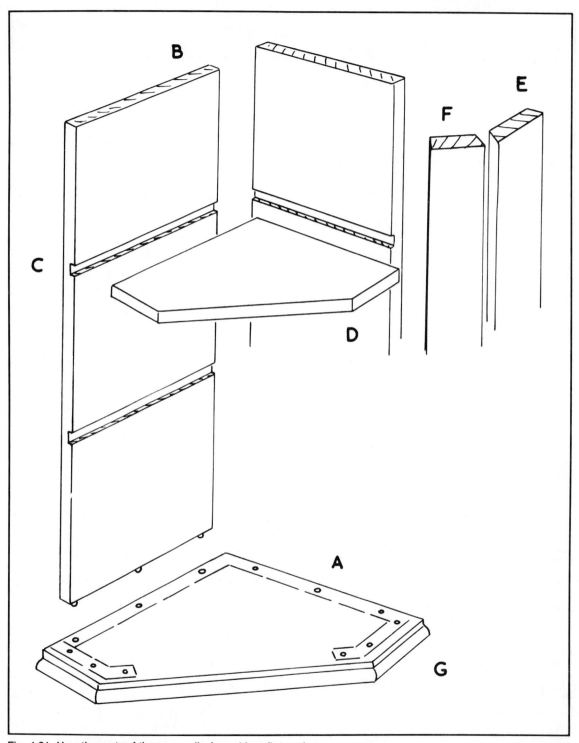

Fig. 4-31. How the parts of the corner display cabinet fit together.

Materials List for Corner Display Cabinet

1 top	5/8 × 15 × 27
1 bottom	5/8 × 15 × 27
2 sides	5/8 × 14 1/2 × 29
2 shelves	5/8 × 12 × 20
2 fronts	3/4 × 4 × 29
2 fronts	3/4 × 2 × 29
1 front above door	3/4 × 1 1/2 × 12
1 molding	5/8 × 1 × 17
2 moldings	5/8 × 1 × 6
2 door parts	3/4 × 1 1/2 × 28
2 door parts	3/4 × 1 1/2 × 12
2 beads	5/16 × 3/8 × 25
2 beads	5/16 × 3/8 × 9

FLOWERPOT TROUGH

Potted plants and flowers will make an attractive show if brought together in a trough. The trough can be part of the indoor furniture, to stand under a window all year or just during the winter, then it can be moved outside for the summer.

This trough (Fig. 4-32) is shown on a stand, from which it can be lifted. In some situations, as when the plants are very tall, it could be put on the floor and made without legs.

If it is to be indoor furniture, the trough and its stand could be made of hardwood and finished with stain and polish. For outdoors, or to match other furniture, it might be made of softwood and finished with paint.

1. Decide on the pots to be used and make the trough to match. The sizes shown (Fig. 4-33) suit three containers about 10 inches in diameter and height.

2. Set out the trough end (Fig. 4-33A) and a stand end with its top slightly wider than the trough (Fig. 4-33B). Let the legs spread to about the same width as the top.

3. Cut the two ends and the bottom. There are several possible ways of joining these parts. A simple way is to rabbet the bottom so nails can be driven both ways (Fig. 4-33C). Prepare these joints, but do not nail until the other parts are ready.

4. The ends could be decorated. The shamrock design (Fig. 4-33D) might go right through or stop about halfway by drilling and working with a router or chisel.

5. Prepare the lengthwise slats (Figs. 4-33E and 4-34A). Round the outer edges (Fig. 4-34B). Drill four screws into the ends. Assemble the trough.

6. The stand is shown dowelled. The rails and legs could have mortise and tenon joints. When marking out, arrange the dowel holes to miss each other (Fig. 4-33F).

7. Use the full-size drawing to obtain the angles of the legs and end rails.

8. Make up the stand end assemblies first (Fig. 4-34C). Check that they match. Let the glue set before adding the parts the other way.

9. Cut the rim strips (Figs. 4-33G and 4-34D) with miters at the corners. Round the outer edges. Screw or nail them on.

Materials List for Flowerpot Trough

2 ends	1 × 12 × 12
1 bottom	1 × 9 × 36
6 slats	3/4 × 2 1/2 × 36
4 legs	1 1/2 × 1 1/2 × 13
2 rails	1 × 3 × 8
2 rails	1 × 3 × 36
2 rims	1/2 × 2 × 13
2 rims	1/2 × 2 × 38

KNICK-KNACK SHELVES

A block of small shelves hanging on the wall can display the small souvenirs brought back from trips and vacations. A pattern of squares will frame some items and provide open places for taller items. If it is possible to rearrange the shelves into different patterns, you can have a variety of displays or change shelves around to alter the appearance with different shelf patterns as well as different items on them.

This rack can be made of a collection of strips that slot together (Fig. 4-35). The strips could be glued if you want a permanent design, but if the slots fit each other tightly, the parts will hold together when hung, yet they can be separated and rearranged (Fig. 4-36).

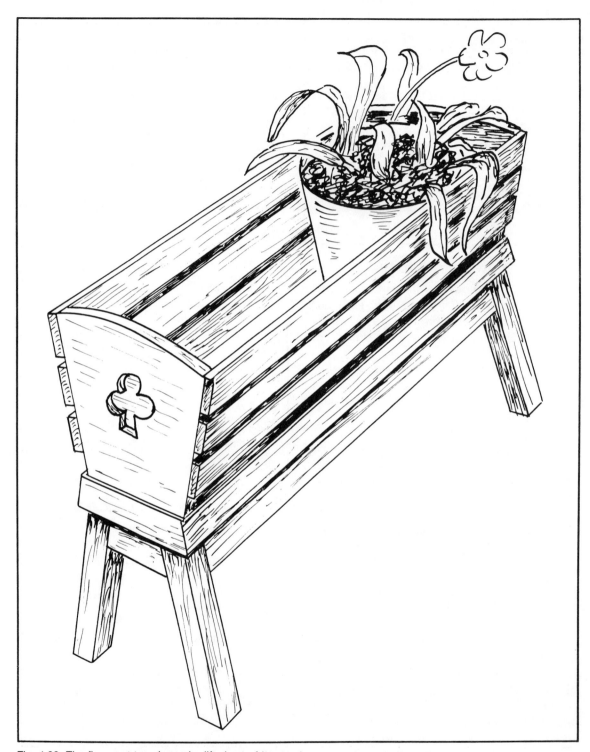

Fig. 4-32. The flowerpot trough can be lifted out of its stand.

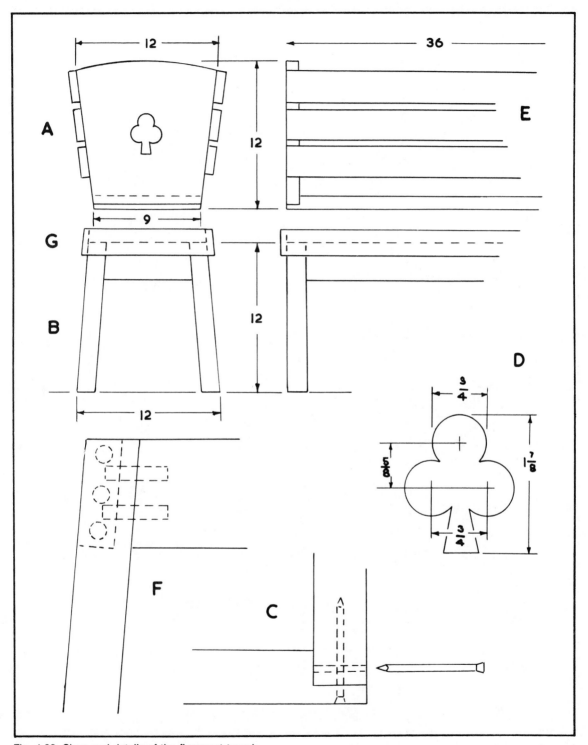

Fig. 4-33. Sizes and details of the flowerpot trough.

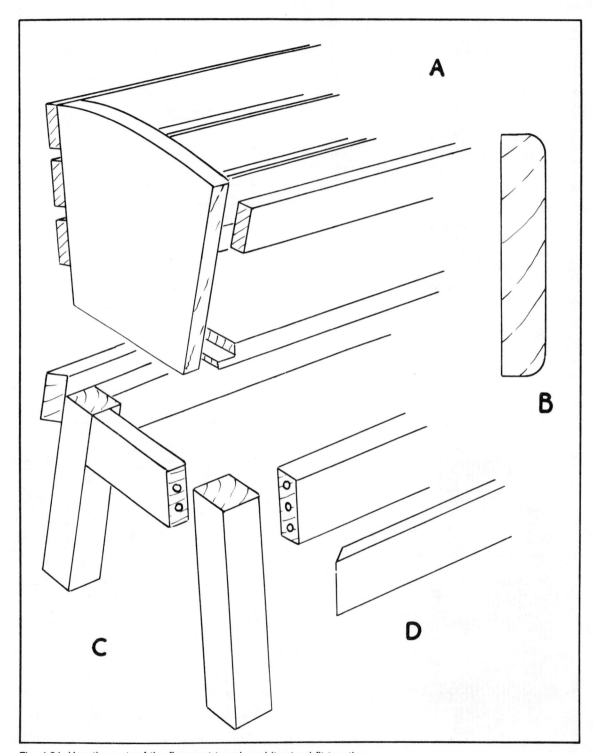

Fig. 4-34. How the parts of the flowerpot trough and its stand fit together.

Fig. 4-35. The knick-knack shelves lock together to provide displays for small items.

The size suggested has the parts linked so there are 4-inch squares and the shelves are 2 inches wide (Fig. 4-37). For many small items this is ample, although the squares could be bigger or you could make the sizes different in each direction, but that limits the variations possible. The method of slotting suits shelves 2 inches or a little wider. With very wide shelves there would be a danger of warping as half the shelf width is unsupported at each joint.

Almost any wood could be used, but if you anticipate taking the shelves apart and rearranging them very often, a close-grained hardwood is best: you can make accurately-fitting joints more easily, and they are stronger and more durable than those of softwood or coarser hardwood.

1. The shelf sections may have two, three, or four notches (Fig. 4-38A). You must decide how many of each you need, depending on the patterns you wish to make (Figs. 4-37 and 4-38B, C, D). Other arrangements are possible. You could turn the patterns through 90 or 180 degrees for different effects. You could make shelves with five or

Fig. 4-36. Each shelf has its slots sawn and the waste cut out with a chisel.

Fig. 4-37. A crossed form of assembly is only one of several ways the shelves can be assembled in the knick-knack rack.

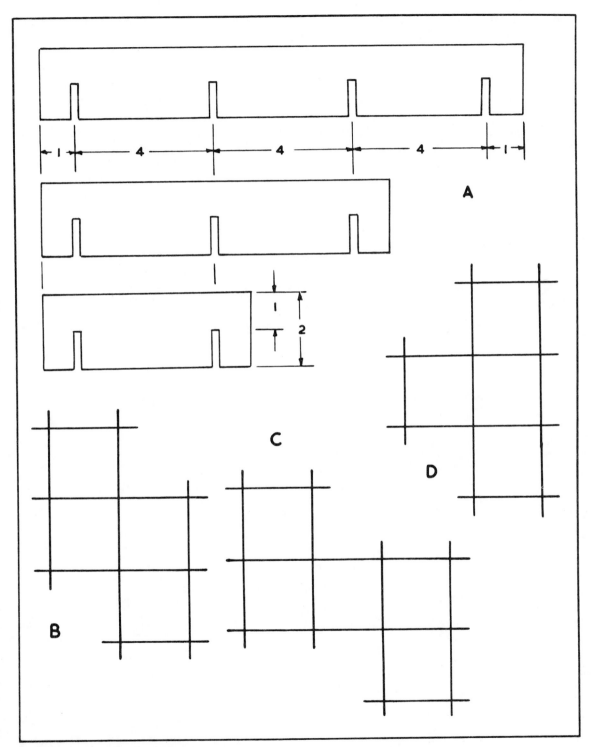

Fig. 4-38. Shelf sizes and possible arrangements.

more notches, if the space on the wall you want to fill is very wide or tall. If you are undecided or intend altering patterns occasionally, extra pieces could be made at the start.

2. If you are making one block of shelves that will be glued and remain unaltered, extreme accuracy in the joints is not so important. If the parts are to be interchangeable, however, widths, thicknesses, and slot sizes must be consistent. Prepare more than enough wood; sawing, planing, and sanding all at the same time so sections do not vary.

3. Make as many parts together as possible to match slot spacing and lengths. Use the actual wood to get the widths of slots. Gauge or set a stop on the machine exactly at the center of the wood.

4. Cut the slots so they push together tight enough to grip, yet you can separate them. Allow for varnish or other finish increasing thicknesses slightly. If you are using a power saw or router, it is advisable to make a pair of slots in offcuts of the same wood to check that the slots fit and edges come level when the joints are tight.

5. Cut the ends squarely. Although the final appearance of the shelves is with square edges, sand them enough to take off sharpness on all edges and corners, but avoid rounding the ends of slots.

6. There are several ways of hanging the shelves. Support should be arranged towards the ends of high shelves. There could be a strip of 1/2-inch square wood under a shelf, for screws into the wall. Little pieces of thin sheet metal could be nailed to the back of a shelf, projecting enough for screws through holes in them into the wall.

Materials List for Knick-Knack Shelves

Pieces 1/4 × 2 × 6 or 10 or 14 as required

Chapter 5

Dining Room

There has to be somewhere to eat in every home. Ideally it is a separate dining room. Even if the room also has to be used for other purposes as well, the requirements are the same. The most important requirement is a table. Dining tables take many forms, depending on if they can be kept full size or if they have to fold. With the table go chairs, and you usually need a side table or some sort of storage place with a serving top. Some dining furniture can be shared with the kitchen and be wheeled in.

What you make may depend on what you have. Even if you feel that small light furniture is really your normal choice of project, there is great satisfaction in making something bigger. The dining table may not be beyond your woodworking skills. Many woodworkers shirk chairmaking. Some chairs are certainly complicated, but a set of dining chairs can be made by anyone with moderate skill and suitable equipment.

DINING CHAIR

A dining or side chair usually has angles other than square, and has some curves if it is to provide reasonable comfort. The sections of wood must be kept fairly light, rely on joints that are not very large. This means chairmaking involves a slightly different working scheme than other furniture projects where the corners are square and the joints do not have to stand up to such abuse as sitters tilting back on two legs. Despite this, the making of a chair is only a little more difficult than many other projects.

Side chairs are not usually needed singly. The design in Fig. 5-1 might be made in a batch of four or six. Maybe one could be made to learn the techniques, then the others made as a short series, with parts and joints for all made at the same time. The design is intended to match the table described in the next project.

The wood chosen should be a strong hardwood that will make secure joints. The sizes in the materials list are a guide, but it would not be wise to increase them much because of added weight, or reduce them much because of weakened joints.

Before cutting any wood, familiarize yourself

Fig. 5-1. A dining chair with a pierced back slat.

with the chair proportions (Fig. 5-2). At the front the legs are upright and parallel (Fig. 5-2A) with the seat rail square to them. The back legs are closer together and parallel with each other. Their curves are arranged so the top comes directly over the bottom (Fig. 5-2B). The seat and the lower rails slope downwards towards the back. Between the seat rails there are corner brackets set down far enough for the lift-out seat to rest on them (Fig. 5-2C). The back has two rails and three splats (Fig. 5-2D), with the center splat decorated with a fretted design if you wish (Fig. 5-2E). If making a table as well, choose a fretted design you can repeat on that.

1. Make the two front legs (Fig. 5-3A). Leave a little extra at the top until after the joints have been cut. Mark the positions of the top rails and their mortises (Fig. 5-4A). There will be a cutout 1/2 inch deep in the leg corner to take the seat. Cut down the tenons by the same amount. Mark the positions of the bottom rails. The legs could be left plain, but they may be decorated by stopped chamfers (Fig. 5-3B). Do not cut the mortises yet.

2. Mark out and cut the rear legs (Fig. 5-3C). Where the seat joints come should be upright and straight, but the outline curves from there. Mark the positions of the rear seat rail (Fig. 5-3D) upright both ways. Mark the back rails at an angle so their line continued down will meet the seat rail (Fig. 5-3E). Mark the positions of all parts that meet the legs, but do not cut mortises yet.

3. Draw the seat shape full-size symmetrically around a centerline to get the angles and lengths of the rails in relation to the legs.

4. Make the front seat rail (Figs. 5-2F and 5-4B) and cut its tenons 1/2 inch down from the top of the leg.

5. Make the rear seat rail (Figs. 5-2G and 5-4C) and cut its tenons the full depth of the rail.

6. Make the pair of side seat rails (Fig. 5-2H) allowing for the angles at the ends. The front tenons are cut back (Fig. 5-4D) in the same way as the front rail. The rear tenons are cut to the full depth (Fig. 5-4E).

7. Cut the mortises in the legs. Miter the tenons where necessary.

8. The side bottom rails have plain tenons into the legs, but allow for the angles when cutting their shoulders. The crosswise bottom rails should have square stub tenons into the side rails (Fig. 5-4F). When assembling, these joints can be reinforced by thin nails driven upwards from below where their heads will not show.

9. The two back rails have plain stub tenons into the rear legs. The splats are thinner, so cut them with barefaced tenons (Fig. 5-4G), then their rear surfaces will come level with the rear of the rail and the fronts will be set back slightly. At the bottoms of the splats they meet the seat rail at a slight angle. Cut the mortise and tenon joints there with a taper so the front of a joint is upright (Fig. 5-4H).

10. Use the actual thickness of the rails that meet the front legs as guides to the sizes of the cutouts for the seat (Fig. 5-4J). Make the corner brackets, but leave final trimming of the angles until the chair is being assembled. Note that the rear brackets fit into the corners (Fig. 5-4K), but the front ones fit around the legs (Fig. 5-4L).

11. Cut the design in the center of the splat (Fig. 5-2E).

12. Round all exposed edges, particularly outer edges of seat rails, the tops of all legs, and the edges of back parts. Do as much of the rounding as possible before assembly. Clean up all the parts and sand everything thoroughly.

13. Assemble the front legs and the front seat rail. Fit the rails and splats between the rear legs. Check squareness.

14. Join the bottom crosswise rails to their side rails. Join the seat rails and bottom rails to the back and front leg assemblies. Have the chair on a level surface and check that it is symmetrical when viewed from above, that the legs stand upright when viewed from the front, and there is no twist when you sight across the legs. Use clamps to get all joints tight and leave them on while the glue sets.

15. Trim the corner brackets to fit closely and fit them with glue and screws into the rails, keeping them parallel with the top edges of the rails and 1/2 inch down.

16. The seat base is a piece of 1/2-inch

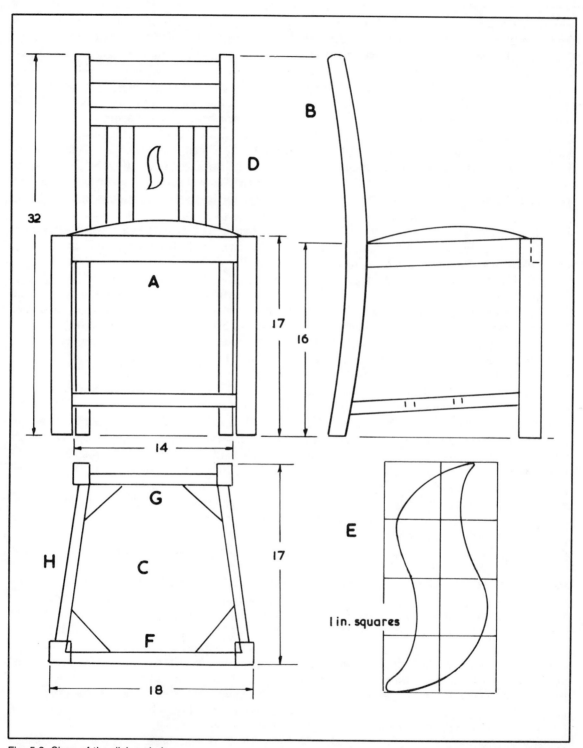

Fig. 5-2. Sizes of the dining chair.

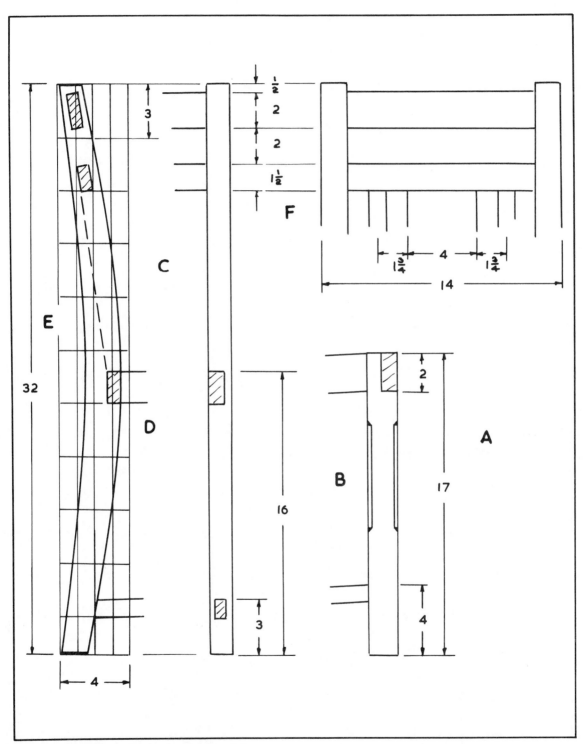

Fig. 5-3. Leg and back details of the dining chair.

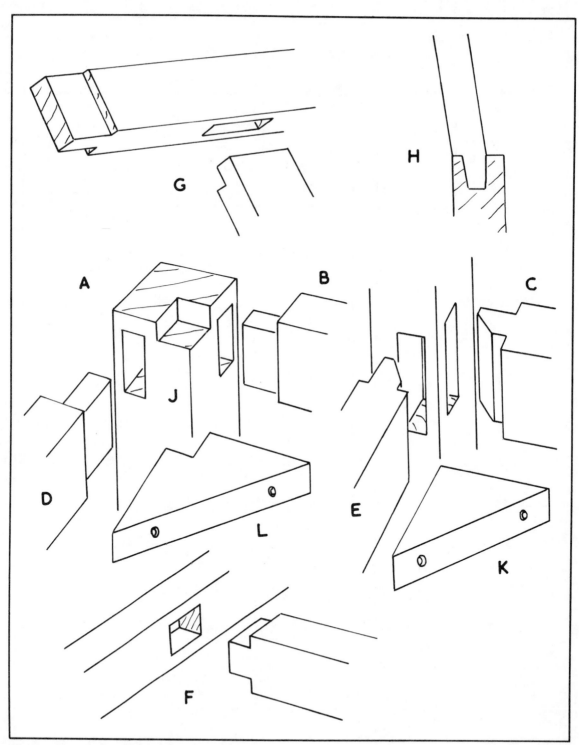

Fig. 5-4. Joints for the dining chair.

plywood cut to fit into the frame seat rails with enough clearance to allow upholstering, but not so slack that it will move about when covered. Drill a pattern of holes and upholster the seat as described in Chapter 1 (Fig. 1-18).

Materials List for Dining Chair

2 rear legs	1 1/2 × 3 1/2 × 32
2 front legs	1 3/4 × 1 3/4 × 17
1 front rail	1 × 2 × 16
1 rear rail	1 × 2 × 13
2 side rails	1 × 2 × 16
4 bottom rails	3/4 × 1 × 17
1 splat	1/2 × 4 × 11
2 splats	1/2 × 1 × 11
1 back rail	3/4 × 2 × 13
1 back rail	3/4 × 1 1/2 × 13
4 corner brackets	3/4 × 3 × 6
1 seat	17 × 17 × 1/2 plywood

DINING TABLE

A table intended to be mainly used for meals should have a top large enough at a height which suits the chairs to be used with it. Its area depends on the number of diners and will usually be more spacious in a home than in a restaurant. This table (Fig. 5-5) has space for four with plenty of room for six or even eight, if tighter spacing is accepted. The design is intended to match the chairs in Fig. 5-1, with the arrangement of legs in the same proportion as the splats on the chair back and a similar pierced decoration on the main legs.

Hardwood similar to that used for the chairs is best for the main parts. The central portion of the tabletop could be veneered particleboard or thick plywood.

1. Make the top first because variations in its final size could affect sizes of some of the parts of the underframing. In the top it is advisable to make

Fig. 5-5. A dining table with panelled top and pierced legs.

the veneered particleboard insert first as there might be slight differences in the finished size due to preparing the edges of it true. This does not matter if the framing is then made to fit it.

2. The overall size of the tabletop is 32 inches by 60 inches (Fig. 5-6). The framing occupies 3 inches all around, so the size of the particleboard is 26 inches by 54 inches. There could be variations to suit stock sizes. Square and true the edges of the particleboard.

3. Make the top framing. Cut a rabbet 1 1/2 inches wide and deep enough to match the particleboard (Fig. 5-7A). Miter the corners (Fig. 5-8A). Dowels across the miters will add strength.

4. The outer edge of the top could be left square, but several other treatments are possible. Do not mold too far in or dishes can be tipped over the edge. There can be minimum shaping (Fig. 5-8B and F). The other moldings are related to the shaping of the feet, so they are appropriate. The small squared lip on them (Fig. 5-8C-E) serve to mark a limit and discourage users from pulling a plate over the edge.

5. Attach the top framing to the particleboard with glue and a few screws driven from below (Fig. 5-7B).

6. Make the two end leg assemblies with the same top and bottom parts, except the bottom parts are longer (Fig. 5-7C). Mark out the four pieces together so the mortise positions match. The lengthwise rails will come between the uprights. The shapes of the ends of these pieces are all the same. Make a card template (Fig. 5-7D) so they are all marked to match.

7. Mark out the six leg pieces together. If the other parts are as specified, they will be 20 1/2 inches between the tenon shoulders. Check that this will give the table height you want, possibly by comparing it with the heights of other tables you have. The stub tenons may be 3/4 inch thick and 1 1/4 inches long. Cut the tenons and their mortises. The broad piece has divided tenons (Fig. 5-7E).

8. Mark out and cut the fretted decoration on the broad legs. This can be larger than on the chairs and could be drawn on a grid of 1 1/2-inch or 2-inch squares instead of 1 inch.

9. Make and fit the blocks under the ends of the feet (Fig. 5-7F).

10. Make up the two leg assemblies (Fig. 5-6A). See that they are square and match each other.

11. The legs should be 9 inches from the ends of the top (Fig. 5-6B). Make the four lengthwise rails the same and to a length to suit this (Fig. 5-7G). The double tenons should go about 1 1/4 inches into the mortises.

12. Assemble the rails to the legs so the framing is square and upright. Squareness can be checked on the inverted top.

13. At the top attaching is done in two stages. Use filler strips to go across under the top and within its frame (Figs. 5-7H and 5-8G). First glue and screw these downwards into the top pieces of the legs, then drive screws upwards into the top. Make and attach strips to the legs, then attach similar strips to the top rails.

14. Invert the top and position the assembly on it. There need not be a very large number of screws into the top. Position screws near the ends of the filler strips. Others at 9-inch or greater intervals should be enough.

Materials List for Dining Table	
1 top	26 × 54 × 3/4 veneered particleboard
2 top frames	1 1/2 × 4 1/2 × 60
2 top frames	1 1/2 × 4 1/2 × 32
2 top filler strips	1/2 × 4 × 56
2 top filler strips	1/2 × 4 × 28
2 crosspieces	2 × 3 × 28
2 crosspieces	2 × 3 × 25
2 uprights	1 1/2 × 6 × 25
4 uprights	1 1/2 × 2 × 25
4 feet	1 × 3 × 5
4 rails	1 1/2 × 3 × 42

MODERN REFECTORY TABLE

The name *refectory table* comes from the type of table used for meals in medieval monasteries. It had a top supported on pedestals with broad feet instead of a leg at each corner. Some of the tables were very

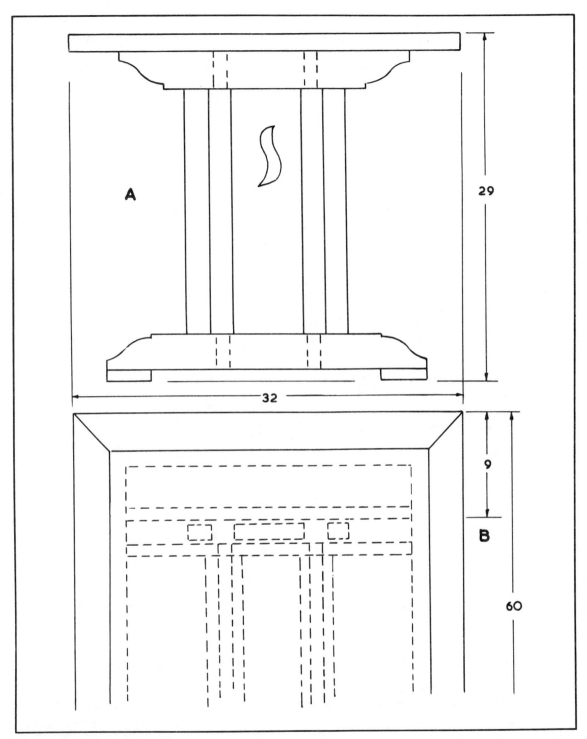

Fig. 5-6. Sizes of the dining table.

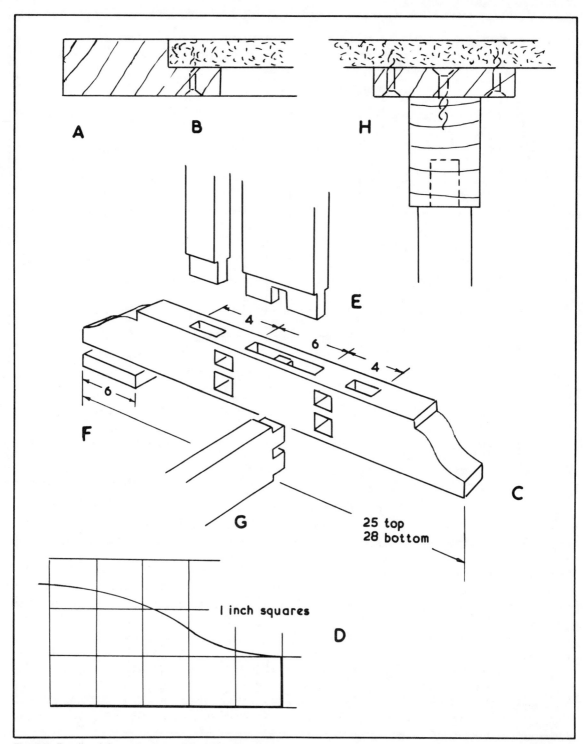

A   B   H

E

4

6

4

6

F

C

G

25 top
28 bottom

1 inch squares

D

Fig. 5-7. Details of the main parts of the dining table.

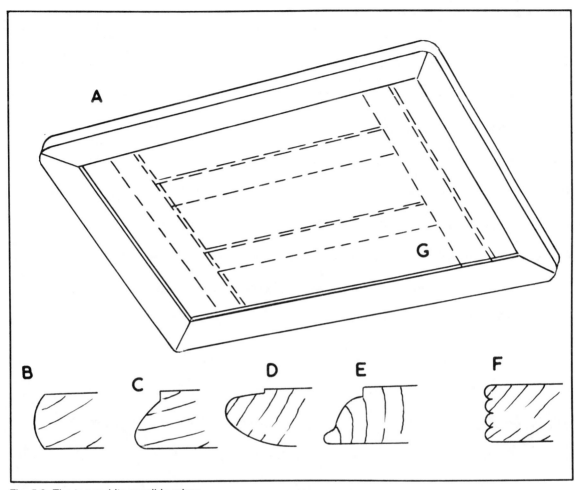

Fig. 5-8. The top and its possible edges.

long and the pedestals very ornate. This version (Fig. 5-9) is brought down to a size more suitable for a modern home with pedestals that are more in keeping with present-day ideas of design. The table should fit in with the usual home surroundings.

The size of table suggested (Fig. 5-10) should not be too cramped for six or possibly eight people. It should pass through most room doorways, either upright or on edge.

The top is shown as veneered plywood framed with solid wood. A top made of solid boards glued together would be attractive and more like a traditional refectory table, but suitable wood might be difficult to obtain and expensive. You could use veneered particleboard with solid wood lipping.

The structure of the table should be all solid wood, 2-inch-by-3-inch sections. An attractive hardwood that can be stained and polished may be chosen. For a less important table, use a softwood and paint it. The whole softwood table could be given a clear polish for the fashionable "knotty pine" finish, if other furniture is of that type.

Joints as shown are mortise and tenon. A table has to stand up to many knocks and jolts. Strains have to be resisted by the joints, and double mortise and tenon joints give greater strength than would be possible with any arrangement of dowels.

Obtain all the wood before starting construction and work to the actual sizes when laying out. It does not matter if widths and thicknesses are a little under size, providing you allow for that. The sequence of work suggested is: prepare all the pedestal parts, followed by the lengthwise parts, then assemble the structure, and finally make and fit the top.

1. Cut the wood for the feet (Figs. 5-10A and 5-12A). Glue the blocks together.

2. Cut the wood for the pedestal tops (Figs. 5-10B and 5-12B) the same length as the feet. Mark the positions of the legs and rails.

3. Cut the legs (Figs. 5-10C and 5-12C), allowing sufficient length at the ends for the tenons. Plow grooves for the plywood (Figs. 5-10D and 5-12D). Mark out the mortise and tenon joints (Fig. 5-11A) and cut them. The gap between the tenons should clear the thickness of the plywood and its groove.

Cut the plywood panels to size. If possible, veneer each side to match the wood of the legs.

4. Make a template of the shape of the ends of the pedestal top (Fig. 5-11B). Mark and shape the ends.

5. Make a template of the ends of the feet (Fig. 5-11C). Mark and shape the ends. Make sure saw marks are removed and the curves are finished smoothly as these ends are very obvious in the completed table.

6. The five lengthwise rails are similar. Make sure the top rails (Fig. 5-12E) come level with the tops of the pedestals. The bottom rail (Fig. 5-12F) will be used as a foot rail. The main purpose of the other two (Fig. 5-12G), which are longer to reach the legs, is to provide lengthwise rigidity. Prepare standard tenons (Fig. 5-11A) on all rails. Cut the mortises in the pedestal parts.

Fig. 5-9. A modern-style refectory table.

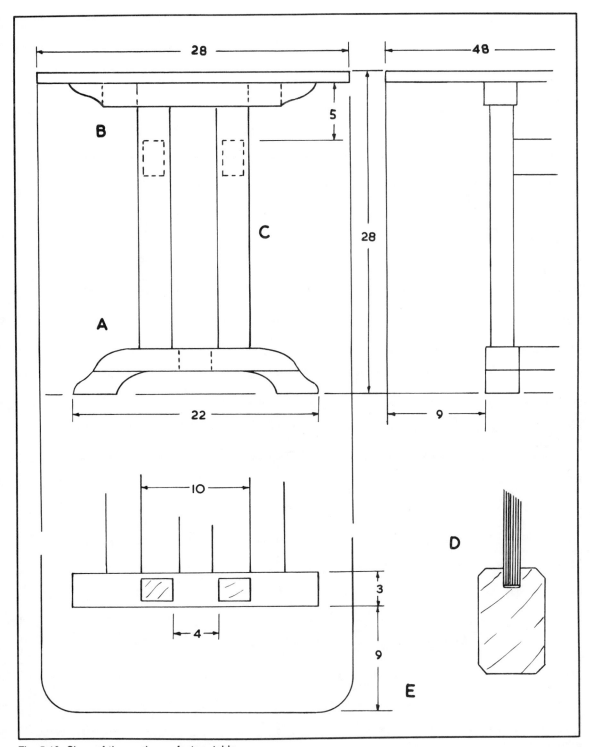

Fig. 5-10. Sizes of the modern refectory table.

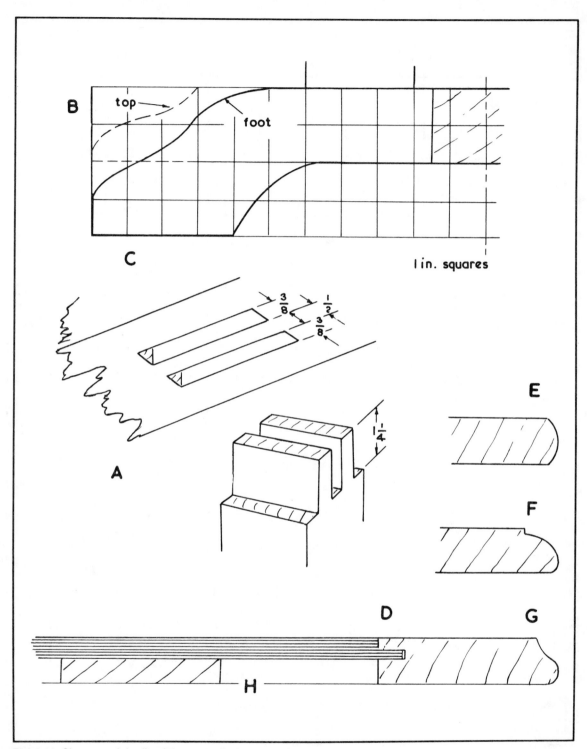

Fig. 5-11. Shapes and details of the modern refectory table.

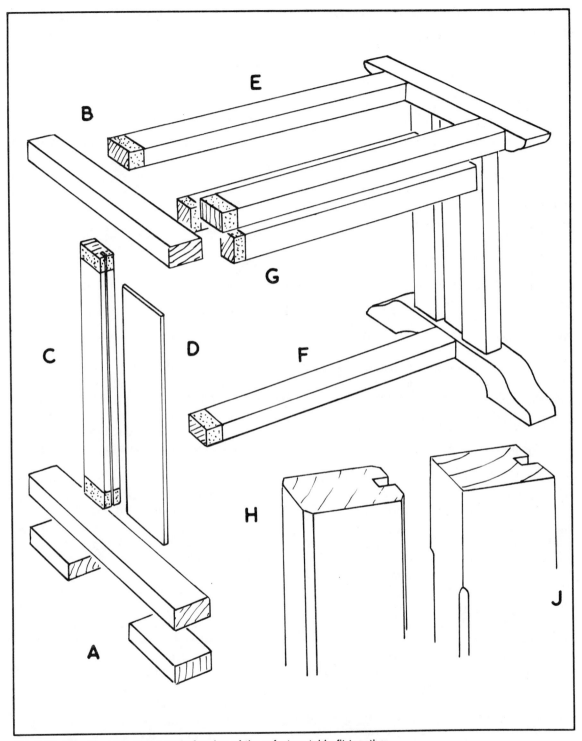

Fig. 5-12. How the parts of the underframing of the refectory table fit together.

105

7. The legs and rails may be left with square edges. The legs could have small chamfers the full length of all edges (Figs. 5-10D and 5-12H), or stopped chamfers (Fig. 5-12J),leaving about 4 inches with square edges on all four corners or only on the outer ones. Lengthwise rails might be treated in a similar way. Even if the other rails are left square, the bottom one (Fig. 5-12F) should be chamfered to reduce wear from shoes.

8. When all the parts have been made and sanded, assemble the pedestals. It will help to secure joints tightly, particularly if you have to move clamps before glue has set, to drill across a joint and drive a glued dowel through the tenons. Check that the pedestals match each other.

9. The plywood panels fit into grooves in the legs, but their top and bottom edges rest against wood surfaces. Hide these meetings with pieces of quarter-round molding glued and pinned on.

10. Join the pedestals with the rails. See that the framework is square and stands level.

11. The plywood top panel is joined to its frame with a tongue and groove joint (Fig. 5-11D). Prepare the wood for the frame and cut the groove and the tongue to match so the surfaces will be level. Make the groove slightly deeper than the tongue; the visible surfaces meet tightly and cannot be held open by the tongue pressing into the bottom of the groove.

12. The edges of the top could be left square or be molded in one of many ways. A curve (Fig. 5-11E) is fairly easily made with ordinary tools, but other shapes (Fig. 5-11F and G) will depend on available router or other cutters. The top corners should be rounded and the molding must be carried around them. Allow for this when choosing the edge treatment.

13. Complete preparation of the plywood and its frame, then join these parts. The corner miters may be dowelled.

14. Underneath the plywood make up the thickness between the frames with glued packings (Fig. 5-11H) in positions that will come above the rails and pedestals.

15. There are several ways of attaching the top to the framework. Counterbored screws could be driven upwards into the thickening pieces. An arrangement of dowels could be used. Metal plates extending over the edges could be let into the rails so screws could be driven upwards. Assemble with the table inverted so the top and framework can be checked square to each other.

Materials List for Modern Refectory Table	
4 legs	2 × 3 × 24
2 feet	2 × 3 × 22
4 feet	2 × 3 × 8
2 pedestal tops	2 × 3 × 22
5 rails	2 × 3 × 30
2 panels	6 × 24 × 1/2 plywood
8 fillets	1/2 × 1/2 × 5 quarter round
1 top	24 × 44 × 1/2 plywood
2 top frames	1 × 3 × 48
2 top frames	1 × 3 × 28
2 top packings	1/2 × 3 × 43
2 top packings	1/2 × 3 × 23

GATELEG TABLE

A gateleg table has the advantage of folding to a small size, while still retaining a flat top which can be used, yet opening to give a rigid top of considerable area. This one (Fig. 5-13) reduces to a top size of 7 by 27 inches, but it opens to make a table 27 by 49 by 30 inches high.

The main assembly and the gates should be made of hardwood. The three-part top can also be hardwood, with boards glued to make up the widths. It could be stout plywood with a veneered top surface and a lip around the edges. It could be veneered particleboard.

Dowelled construction is shown, but mortise and tenon joints could be used on the gates and the feet. The top shelf could be dovetailed to the legs.

If sizes are modified, choose a central length sufficient for gates long enough to support the flaps to fold. Arrange the lower shelf at a height where it will be hidden when the flaps are down.

1. Mark out the legs (Figs. 5-14A and 5-15A).

2. Make and drill the feet (Fig. 5-15B) and dowel them to the legs.

3. Cut the two shelves to length (Fig. 5-15C

Fig. 5-13. A simple-to-make, minimum-space gateleg table.

and D). Cut the stiffener (Figs. 5-14B and 5-15E) to the same length. It will be dowelled at the center of the top shelf and into the legs.

4. Cut the gatelegs (Fig. 5-14C) to the same height as a leg with its foot.

5. Make the other parts of the gate framing for both sides (Fig. 5-15F). The top and bottom parts are spaced to fit between the shelves, with sufficient gaps to allow washers where the pivot screws will be driven. They should allow the top of each leg to project to the same level as the top shelf.

6. Assemble the gates and use them to mark the cutouts on the shelves (Fig. 5-15G). The legs should close level with the shelf edges.

7. Dowel together the shelves, stiffeners, and

legs. Squareness is important if the open and closed top parts are to look right.

8. The gates pivot on screws driven into the shelves. Long screws can be avoided if the holes are counterbored so the screw heads are sunk to about half the wood thickness. Drill the gate parts first, then fit them in the closed position and mark through.

9. Assemble the gates to the central part and test their action. Leave them in position until the top has been fitted, then they can be removed for the table to be given a polish or other finish.

10. The central member of the top (Figs. 5-14D and 5-15H) is the same width as the legs.

11. Make the flaps to match it and round their outer corners (Fig. 5-14E).

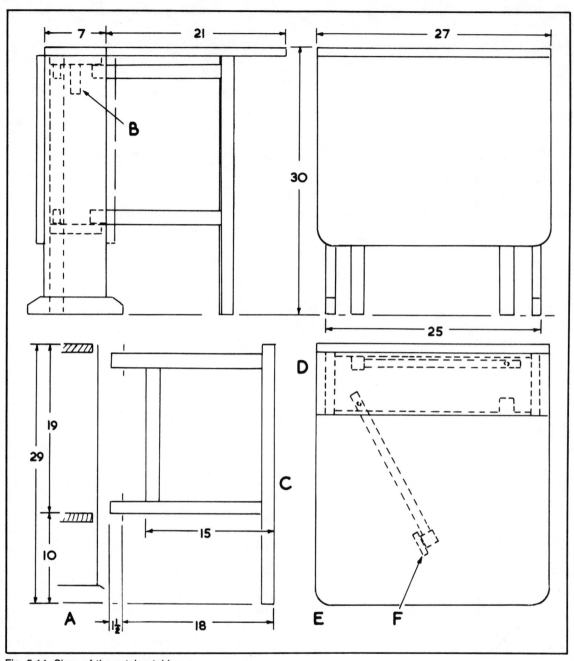

Fig. 5-14. Sizes of the gateleg table.

12. Join the three parts of the top with hinges (Fig. 5-15J), but space them out of the way of the gates when closed or being opened.

13. Try the assembled top temporarily in position and test its action. If it is satisfactory, screw upwards through the top shelf into it.

14. When a flap is raised and its gate swung out, the leg top should finish halfway across the

flap. Mark this position in the first test and put a small stop block there (Fig. 5-14F).

Materials List for Gateleg Table	
2 legs	1 × 7 × 28
2 feet	1 × 2 × 11
2 shelves	1 × 6 × 23
1 stiffener	1 × 3 × 23
2 gate legs	1 1/2 × 1 1/2 × 29
2 gate struts	1 × 1 1/2 × 16
4 gate rails	1 × 1 1/2 × 20
1 top	1 × 7 × 27
2 tops	1 × 21 × 27

SIDE TABLE

A narrow table that does not project far from the wall and does not take up much space is convenient for holding food and dishes not yet ready to be served on the dining table. Drawers in it can hold cutlery, napkins, and other small items. Various sizes are possible, and the design suggested (Fig. 5-16) can be adapted to suit needs and available space.

The main parts should be hardwood. Because the legs do not have lower rails to control them, the wood used to make them should be reasonably straight-grained to minimize the risk of warping.

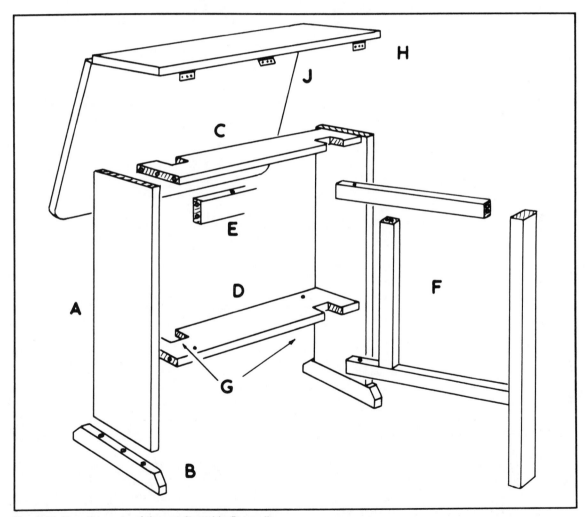

Fig. 5-15. How the parts of the gateleg table fit together.

Fig. 5-16. A side table with drawers for cutlery.

The top could be solid wood, with boards glued to make up the width, or veneered particleboard.

Construction is shown with mortise and tenon joints between the rails and legs, which is the traditional way, but dowels could be used. The drawers are shown with screwed joints, but the corners could be dovetailed or made with interlocking joints if you have suitable equipment to cut them.

1. Prepare the wood for the legs and mark the joints (Fig. 5-17A). The front rails may have full tenons (Fig. 5-17B), but the other wider rails are better cut away (Fig. 5-17C). Let the mortises go as deep as possible and miter the ends of the tenons (Fig. 5-17D).

2. Make all the rails. Check that the lengths of those on opposite sides match.

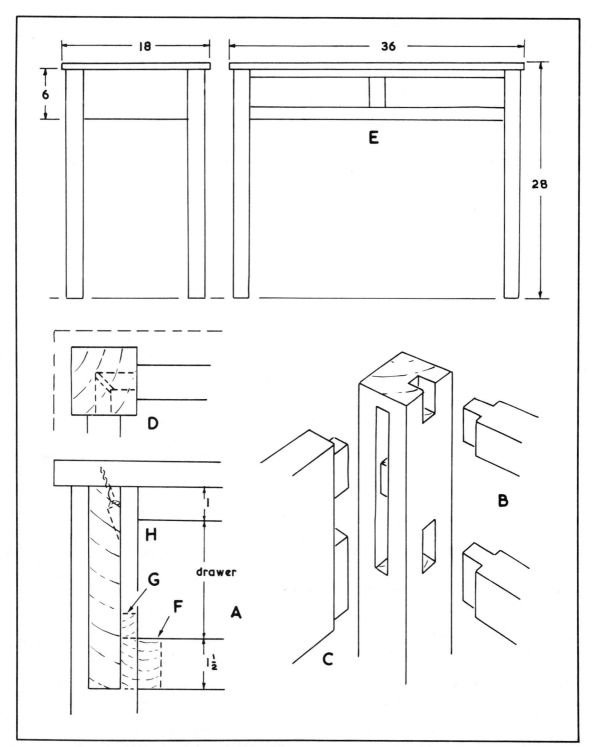

Fig. 5-17. Sizes and construction details of the side table.

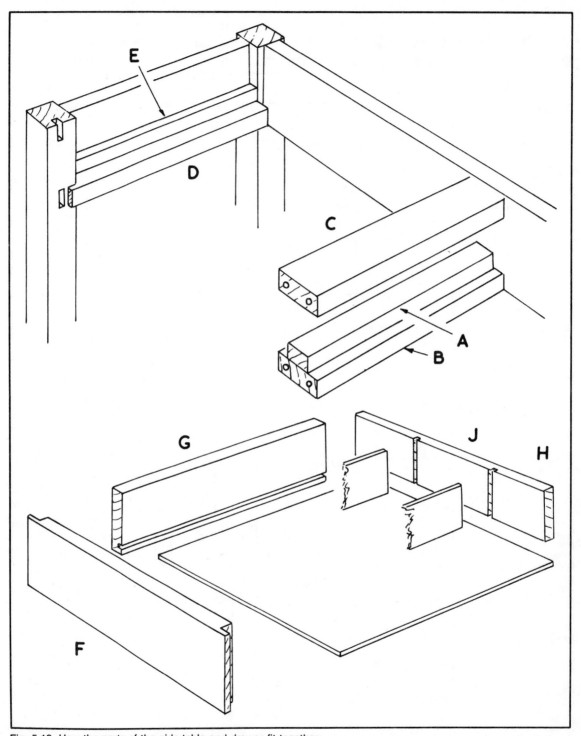

Fig. 5-18. How the parts of the side table and drawer fit together.

3. The two drawers are separated by a 2-inch wide strip (Fig. 5-17E). Dowel or tenon it to the rails. Behind and connected to the back rail is another 2-inch strip (Fig. 5-18A) to act as a drawer guide. This is supported on a wider strip (Fig. 5-18B) to serve as a drawer bearer. Another piece (Fig. 5-18C) goes under the tabletop to act as a kicker and prevent the drawers from tilting as they are pulled out. The joints could have dowels or tenons.

4. To match these pieces there are strips between the legs on each side. One strip (Figs. 5-17F and 5-18D) projects to form a drawer bearer. Another piece above it (Fig. 5-17G and 18E) is level with the leg surfaces to form a drawer guide.

5. Assemble the back and front legs and rails first, checking for squareness and that the parts match.

6. Add the end rails and other parts to join these assemblies, checking for squareness in all directions and that the legs stand level.

7. The two drawers should be the same, but it is wise to make each fit its own space to allow for minor differences.

8. Make the drawer fronts (Fig. 5-18F) an easy fit in their openings.

9. Cut the sides (Fig. 5-18G) to width and check that they will slide easily. Groove them and the fronts for the bottoms.

10. Make the backs (Fig. 5-18H) to fit above the bottoms.

11. Rabbet the ends of the front so the sides can be screwed in. Allow the sides to project beyond the back at first so they can be trimmed to hit the back rail when the drawer front is level with its rails.

12. If required, make divisions for one or both drawers, notched into the back and front (Fig. 5-18J).

13. Assemble the drawers and fit wood or metal handles.

14. Make the tabletop to overlap the legs by 1/2 inch all around. The edges could be left square or molded to match other tables.

15. The top can be held by screws driven upwards through the top front rail. If there are kickers at the ends, screws can go through them. Pocket screws (Fig. 5-17H) can be driven through rail edges. A screw spacing about 9 inches all around should be satisfactory. There could also be glue between the rails and a particleboard top, but with a solid wood top it would be better to rely on screws only to allow for slight expansion and contraction in the wood width.

Materials List for Side Table	
4 legs	2 × 2 × 28
2 rails	1 × 6 × 16
1 rail	1 × 6 × 34
1 rail	1 × 1 × 34
1 rail	1 × 1 1/2 × 34
1 top	3/4 × 18 × 36
1 drawer spacer	1 × 2 × 6
2 drawer runners	1 1/2 × 4 × 16
2 drawer runners	1/2 × 1 × 16
1 drawer kicker	1 × 4 × 16
1 drawer guide	1 × 2 × 16
2 drawer guides	1/4 × 3/4 × 16
2 drawer fronts	7/8 × 3 1/2 × 16
4 drawer sides	5/8 × 3 1/2 × 16
2 drawer backs	5/8 × 3 × 16
2 drawer bottoms	1/8 × 16 × 16 hardboard
2 drawer divisions	3/8 × 3 × 16

SLIDING-DOOR CUPBOARD

This piece of furniture provides storage for many things (Fig. 5-19). These could be books, hobby materials, crockery, or any of the many things that accumulate in a home. The sliding doors are plywood; when they are shut the appearance is tidy, even if there is a muddle inside. Glass panels could be substituted for plywood if you wish to make it a dining room display cabinet. The sloping front improves access and has a better appearance than a vertical front. Sliding doors only expose up to half the contents at a time, but these doors lift out easily if you need to get at everything inside.

Solid wood construction is suggested, except for plywood for doors and back. Most of the joints are dadoes. If veneered particleboard is used, these joints would be difficult to make and dowels might have to be used.

1. The key parts are the sides. Mark out the

Fig. 5-19. A cupboard with sloping sliding doors.

114

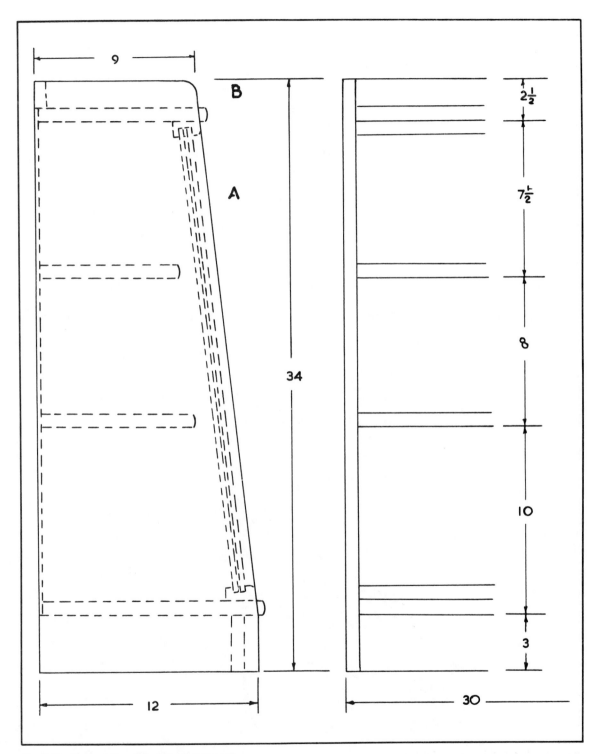

Fig. 5-20. Sizes of the sliding-door cupboard.

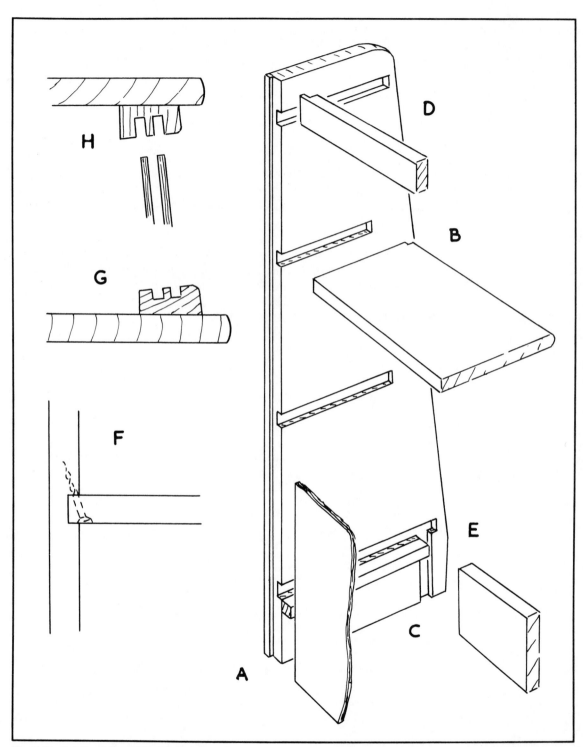

Fig. 5-21. Details of the sliding-door cupboard.

pair (Fig. 5-20A) with the shelf positions. Cut rabbets for the back plywood (Fig. 5-21A). Allow for the widths of the shelves, then mark back a short distance for notching the shelf ends (Fig. 5-21B).

2. Mark out all the shelf lengths the same. Round their front edges. Top and bottom shelves should project forward of the sides (Fig. 5-20B).

3. The plinth fits close under the bottom shelf and will be glued to it. Its ends could be dowelled to the sides, but a dado is shown here (Fig. 5-21C).

4. Make a piece at the top to notch into the rabbets (Fig. 5-21D). This fits above the top shelf, and the plywood back is stopped on the shelf edge below it.

5. Assemble all the lengthwise parts to the ends. Under the bottom shelf there may be strips glued in (Fig. 5-21E) and screwed each way as well, if thought necessary. Provide extra strength at the top shelf with two screws driven diagonally from below at each end (Fig. 5-21F).

6. Add the plywood back to hold the assembly square. It need not continue below the bottom shelf.

7. Make the door guides. In both cases grooves should fit the plywood doors easily. The grooves are about 5/16 inch wide and 3/16 inch apart for 1/4-inch plywood. The bottom guide (Fig. 5-21G) may have grooves 1/4 inch deep. The top guide has grooves about twice as deep (Fig. 5-21H), but the doors only go in about 1/4 inch. Plow the grooves square to the surface, then bevel the other face so the grooves will be parallel in section with the sloping front. Use abrasive paper to smooth the insides of the grooves.

8. Glue the guides to the top and bottom shelves level with the edges of the ends.

9. Cut the plywood for both doors, making the heights suitable to go fully into the top grooves while just clearing the bottom guides. This allows the doors to rest in the bottom guides and be retained in the top ones by their weight, but if you lift a door fully into the top groove, it can be swung out at the bottom and removed.

10. Use sunk handles near the outer edges of the doors. When the wood has a finish applied, wax in the grooves or on the door edges will make action smooth.

Materials List for Sliding-Door Cupboard

2 ends	3/4 × 12 × 31
1 shelf	3/4 × 12 1/2 × 30
1 shelf	3/4 × 9 × 30
1 shelf	3/4 × 8 × 30
1 shelf	3/4 × 9 1/2 × 30
1 plinth	3/4 × 3 × 30
1 top back	3/4 × 2 1/2 × 30
1 back	28 × 30 × 1/4 plywood
2 doors	16 × 26 × 1/4 plywood
2 door guides	1 × 2 × 30

Chapter 6

Kitchen

Increasingly, kitchens tend to be equipped with built-in furniture, with cookers and other operational equipment fitted into banks of working surfaces, closets, and often ingenious storage arrangements. Despite all this fairly standardized equipment, however, there is plenty of scope for the amateur woodworker to make furniture and other items that will help the cook with kitchen tasks.

Much depends on the size of the kitchen and the space left amid all the existing items. The cook will be glad of somewhere to sit, a way to reach high storage areas, and despite all that is provided already, more working surfaces. The tables and other furniture described in other chapters could be brought into the kitchen, but the items in this chapter are particularly appropriate.

TALL STOOL

A chair gives comfort when sitting at a table, but when you want to rest from standing, yet need to have the same reach, your seating has to be higher.

That is when a tall stool has its place. It is also useful when sitting at any counter or bar made at a height primarily for use when standing. The stool shown in Fig. 6-1 is made extra high and with a broader base for stability when operating a machine in a shop, but the sizes given (Fig. 6-2) should suit a stool for use in a kitchen or den.

The stool here was made of hardwood with mortise and tenon joints. It is possible to use dowelled joints in the top rails and substantial dowel rods in place of the lower rectangular rails. The top is a piece of plywood upholstered with a pad of plastic foam covered with plastic-coated fabric or leathercloth.

1. Make a full-size drawing of the main lines (Fig. 6-2A), either the full width or just one side of the centerline. This tells you the rail lengths and angles of joints. The stool has the same appearance both ways. When an assembly has legs at a considerable splay, the joint angle when viewed from above needs special setting out. In this stool with only a slight splay, the angle across each joint can be regarded as square.

Fig. 6-1. A tall stool in a workshop.

with partial miters (Fig. 6-2F). Trim the ends of the dowels in the top rails in the same way.

6. Assemble two opposite sides. Check that they are symmetrical by measuring diagonals and see that they match each other.

7. Let the glue set before adding the rails the other way. Check that the new sides are also symmetrical, the legs stand level, and the stool is square at the top and when tested at a lower rail level.

8. Cut the plywood for the top (Fig. 6-3A). Round its corners and drill a few holes to let air in and out of the plastic foam as it is compressed and expands.

9. Level the top rails and legs, then screw the plywood to the rails.

10. Cut the plastic foam slightly too large. Very soft foam may be 1/2 inch oversize, but harder foam may be less (Fig. 6-3B). Cutting oversize allows the foam to compress and avoids a hard edge on the plywood.

11. Cut the underside of the foam at an angle to about half thickness (Fig. 6-3C) all around.

12. Have the covering material slightly too large. Use 3/8-inch tacks to fix it. Start at the center of each side, stretching across and tacking underneath (Fig. 6-3D). See that the foam is compressed evenly and with neat rounded edges above the tacks. Continue tacking outwards toward the corners. Tack spacing will depend on the material and what is needed for a satisfactory result, but 1 inch between tacks will probably be about right. At the corners, pull diagonally and tack underneath. Trim the surplus material all around inside the line of tacks. Fix gimp (trim), if you wish, around the edge to improve appearance.

2. Mark out the legs (Fig. 6-2B) with the angles of the ends and joints marked. Leave trimming to length until after the joints have been cut.

3. Mark the rails sizes and angles from your drawing. Check that all rails at each level are the same length between shoulders.

4. If tenons are to be used, allow their lengths to almost meet with miters in the legs (Fig. 6-2C). The tenons can be the full depth of the lower rails, but at the top rails, the joint will be stronger if they are divided (Fig. 6-2D).

5. If dowels are to be used, cut the top rails to the length between shoulders and use two dowels at each end (Fig. 6-2E). If dowel rods are to be used as lower rails, allow for them meeting in the legs

Materials List for Tall Stool	
4 legs	1 1/4 × 1 1/4 × 24
4 rails	5/8 × 1 1/4 × 13 or 5/8 dowel rods
4 rails	5/8 × 1 1/4 × 12 or 5/8 dowel rods
4 rails	5/8 × 2 1/2 × 10
1 top	12 × 12 × 1/2 plywood
1 piece plastic foam about 1 1/2 thick × 13 × 13	
1 piece plastic-coated fabric 18 × 18	

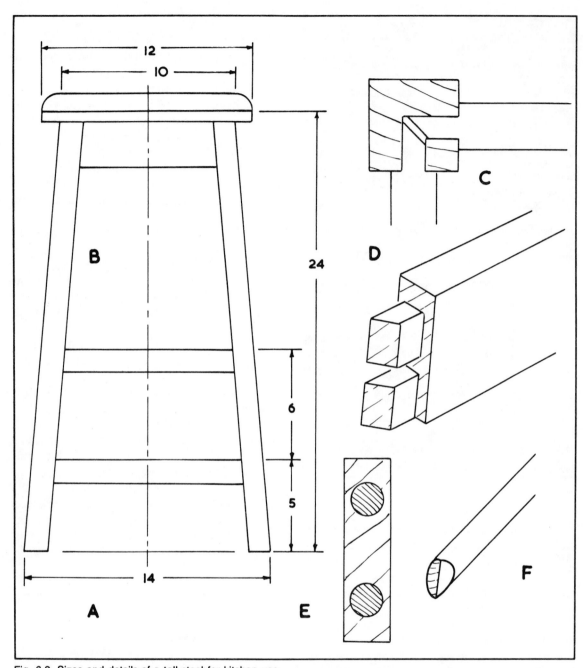

Fig. 6-2. Sizes and details of a tall stool for kitchen use.

STEP STOOL

The cook might be glad of a seat higher than a normal chair, but not as high as the tall stool in Fig. 6-1. This may also have steps to reach high shelves.

There is an advantage in combining the two functions in one piece of furniture, particularly if the kitchen is compact.

This step stool (Fig. 6-4) provides a seat 10

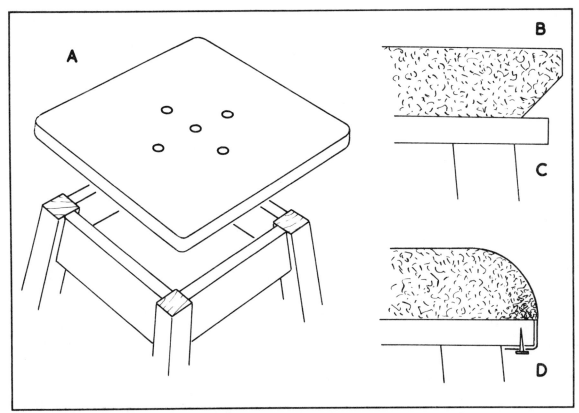

Fig. 6-3. Details of the upholstered top of a tall stool.

inches by 16 inches and 18 inches above the floor, with a step that swings out at half that height. Climbing to the top is safer when the steps are equally spaced. The stool is substantially framed and should withstand hard use. The folding step stows upside-down wholly within the stool. It swings out to rest on the floor, but if the stool is lifted with it out, it does not drop further.

Stool construction is straightforward. Position the rails accurately to pivot the step as shown in Fig. 6-5A so it will swing in and out without touching other parts.

Parts could be made of hardwood or softwood. The seat and tread sides and top are plywood. Joints could be dowelled or mortised and tenoned. Tenons are stronger in all joints, although dowels are adequate for most of them, but the rails are better tenoned into the plywood sides of the step.

1. Set out a full-size end view of the stool (Fig. 6-5B) symmetrically about a centerline. Mark on it the positions of the top and bottom crosswise rails (Fig. 6-6A and B). These are upright, although the legs slope. Also mark the top and bottom end rails (Fig. 6-6C and D).

2. Join the top and bottom rails to the legs. There can be two, 1/2-inch dowels in each bottom joint and three at the top. Otherwise use stub tenons (Fig. 6-6E).

3. Check that opposite ends match. Make the four crosswise rails and join these with dowels or tenons to the legs (Fig. 6-6F).

4. Level the top of the framing and make the plywood top to fit (Fig. 6-5C). Round the edges and corners. For this stool it might be satisfactory to glue and screw down through the top into the rails. If you do not want screw heads showing, however, drive them upwards from pockets inside the rails.

5. Make the two sides for the step (Figs. 6-5D

Fig. 6-4. The lower part of this step stool folds into the main part.

and 6-6G). The pivot allows the side to swing to rest against a stool rail in the open position when the step top is horizontal. Mark the positions of the three step rails and the pivot hole. Cut the step sides to shape. Smooth all edges and around those that will be exposed.

6. Drill small holes to take nails at the pivot positions in the side. Use these as guides to check

the pivot positions on the legs. Try the action of the step sides when swung fully in and out on nails.

7. Make the step rails a suitable length to allow the step sides to fit easily between the stool legs. They could be screwed through the plywood. Dowel joints in plywood would not be satisfactory, but tenons could be taken through and wedged (Fig. 6-6H). Put short strips between the ends of the top rails to take screws into the tread (Fig. 6-6J). Make

the tread (Fig. 6-6K) ends level with the plywood sides. Round the long edges. Glue and screw it in place.

8. The pivots may be 1/4-inch coach bolts. Enlarge the holes to suit. Include a washer at each side between the wood parts (Fig. 6-5E). Some form of locking nut is advisable to prevent the pivot loosening.

9. A painted finish is appropriate; or the lower

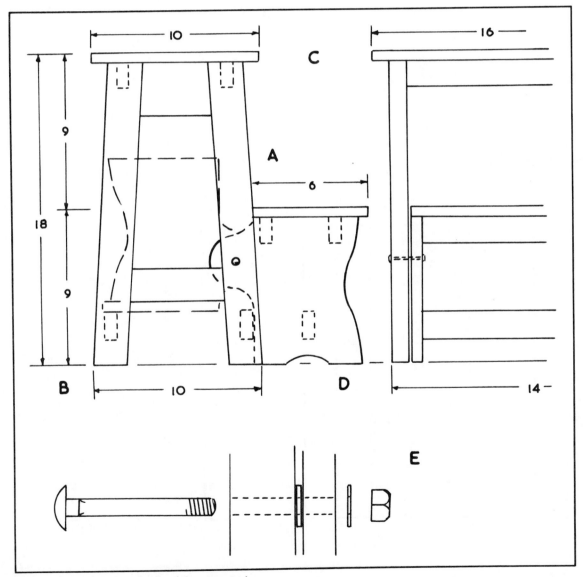

Fig. 6-5. Sizes and pivot details of the step stool.

123

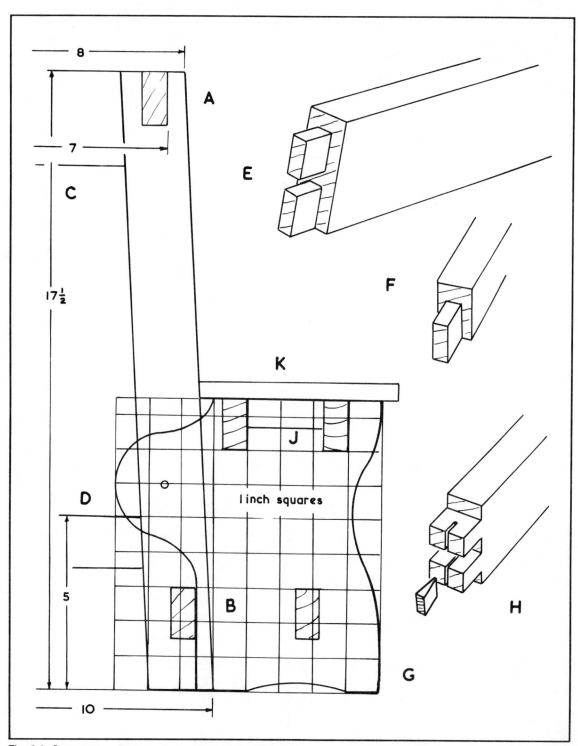

Fig. 6-6. Construction details and step sizes of the step stool.

parts can be varnished or polished, if a suitable wood has been used, and only the tread and top painted. The top and tread might also be covered, both for comfort and to reduce the risk of slipping. Upholstery is inappropriate, but plastic-coated fabric, pieces of carpet, or vinyl floor covering may be attached.

Materials List for Step Stool	
1 top	10 × 16 × 1/2 plywood
1 step	6 × 12 × 1/2 plywood
2 step sides	8 × 9 × 1/2 plywood
4 legs	1 × 2 × 18
2 top rails	1 × 3 × 8
4 stool rails	3/4 × 1 1/2 × 14
3 step rails	3/4 × 1 1/2 × 12

FOLDING FOOD TROLLEY

A trolley to carry food from the kitchen to the dining table or patio saves a lot of steps. It can also be a serving table or a food preparation surface. When not in use, however, most food trolleys take up precious space. This food trolley (Fig. 6-7) has two lift-out trays. When they are removed, the trolley folds to a few inches thick. The lift-out trays increase the usefulness of the trolley.

The whole trolley is best made of a good hardwood, but if lightness is important the trays could be of softwood. Rigidity of the frame depends on the strength of the joints, and this will be greater with hardwoods. Exact sizes are not important, but those shown will make a trolley of useful proportions.

The wheels are casters with plastic or rubber-tired wheels suitable for use on carpet. Wheel diameters of 2 or 3 inches are suitable. Get the type with a stem that pushes into a hole in the bottom of its leg. Obtain the casters first because their size controls the lengths of the legs.

1. Mark out the four legs (Fig. 6-8A) with the positions of the rails. Prepare the long rails (Fig. 6-8B). The joints are shown with tenons (Fig. 6-9A), but there could be dowels. The inner surfaces of

the legs and rails should be level.

2. Cut the joints, then shape the tops of the legs. These will be prominent in the finished trolley and should be shaped neatly. Three possible shapes are shown: simple bevels (Fig. 6-9B), a shallow cone (Fig. 6-9C), or rounded (Fig. 6-9D).

3. Drill the bottoms of the legs for the casters, then assemble the legs and long rails making sure the assemblies match as a pair.

4. Cut all the end rails, which are divided at the middle (Fig. 6-8C). Use hinges the full depth of the rails. At the center, screw on hinges with the rails flat and tight together. At the corners the screws have to go into the end grain in the rails. To increase their grip, 1/4-inch dowels can be let in for the threads to penetrate cross grain (Fig. 6-9E). They need not go right through to show on the outside.

5. The trays have to fit between the rails. Make them with enough clearance to lift in and out easily. Since projecting handles would be a nuisance, the ends of the trays are given finger slots. Several types of corner joints are possible, but a simple rabbet is shown (Fig. 6-9F) with the sides screwed into the ends.

6. Make the tray sides. Plow grooves for the plywood bottoms and put strips outside to rest on the rails (Figs. 6-8D and 6-9G). These could be full length or just short pieces near the corners.

7. Cut the ends to shape (Fig. 6-9H) with grooves to match those in the sides. Round the top edges and finger slots.

8. Check the tray sizes against the trolley frame, then assemble them. Check that the trays lock the trolley in shape and that the ends hinge correctly for the trolley to fold flat.

9. Polish or varnish the wood and add casters.

Materials List for Folding Food Trolley		
4 legs	1 1/4	× 1 1/4 × 27
4 rails	3/4	× 2 × 28
8 rails	3/4	× 2 × 7
4 tray sides	5/8	× 2 × 26
4 tray side strips	1/2	× 1/2 × 24
4 tray ends	5/8	× 4 × 13
2 tray bottoms	13	× 26 × 1/4 plywood

Fig. 6-7. This trolley folds flat after the trays are lifted out.

BUTCHER BLOCK TABLE

A small table that can be moved around in the kitchen has many uses. If it has a substantial top on which chopping and other heavy work can be done, it becomes a preparation table as well as an extra surface for dishes and other items. If it is a suitable size, it can also serve as somewhere to eat a hasty meal or take a coffee break.

This table (Fig. 6-10) has a butcher block top that looks the part and will stand up to the heaviest treatment that a cook is likely to give it. Underneath is a trough with two sides that are square

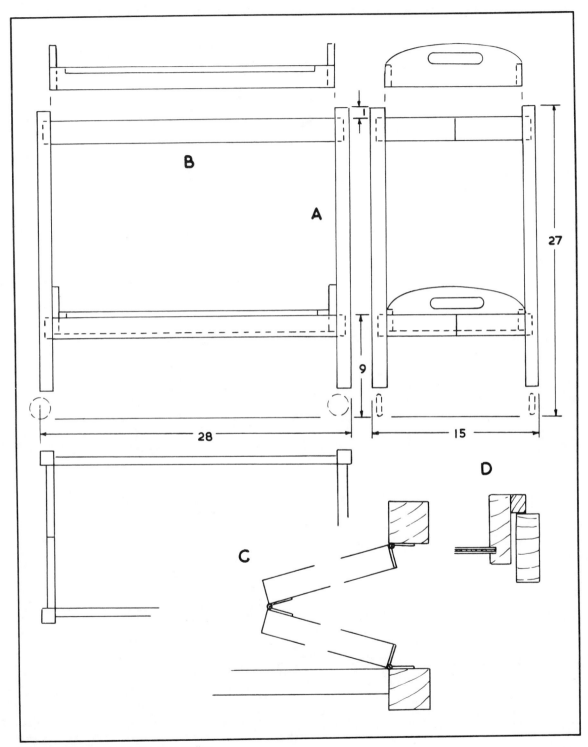

Fig. 6-8. Sizes of the folding food trolley.

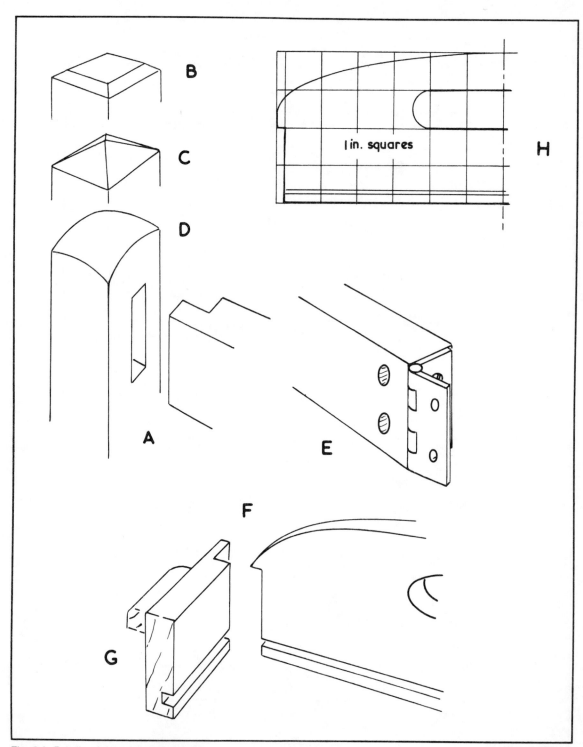

Fig. 6-9. Details of the folding food trolley.

Fig. 6-10. A movable butcher block table with storage underneath.

to each other. This could be a rack for cookbooks or can hold equipment. The trough takes the place of rails to stiffen the table lengthways. The table is shown with casters so it can be moved about. For a stationary table, make the legs a little longer.

Use a good hardwood. The lower parts may be polished or varnished, but you might prefer to leave the top plain so it can be scrubbed.

There are three steps in construction: the two leg assemblies that determine several other sizes; the trough that controls length; and the top to fit overall.

1. The leg assembly has a top rail 2 inches less in width than the width of the tabletop (Figs. 6-11A and 6-12A). The two feet are made in a similar way, but are as long as the width of the top (Figs. 6-11B and 6-12B). The legs (Figs. 6-11C and 6-12C)

are shown tenoned (Fig. 6-12D), but they could be dowelled. Make these parts for the two ends and assemble them. If the table is to be used without casters, blocks under the feet (Fig. 6-12E) will make the table stand better on a surface that might be slightly uneven.

2. The trough (Fig. 6-11D and E) is made with two boards having their edges overlapped and glued and screwed. Triangular pieces (Fig. 6-12F) then

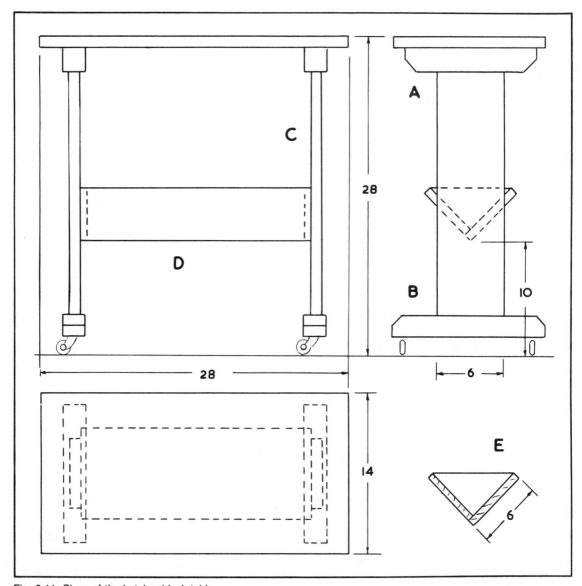

Fig. 6-11. Sizes of the butcher block table.

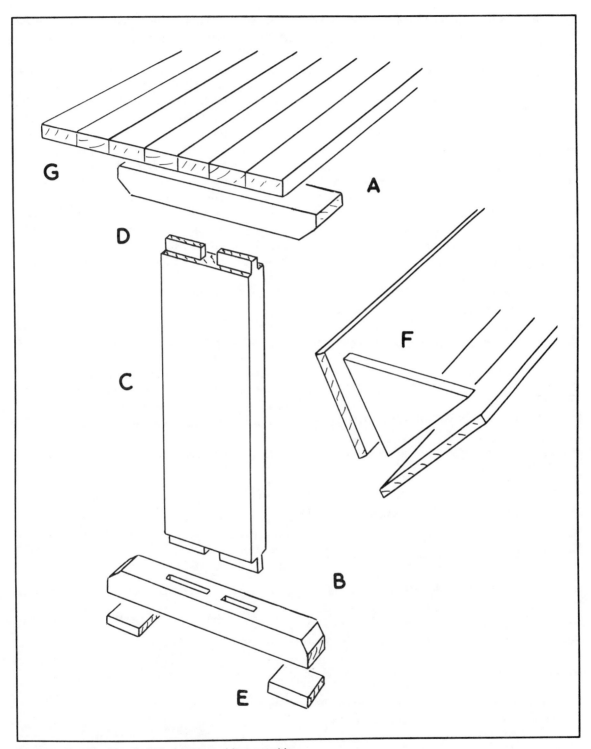

Fig. 6-12. Details of butcher block table and its assembly.

fit between them and form ends. Make up the trough to a length that will fit between the legs, to which it can be screwed from inside. Sight along the assembly to see that the legs are upright and parallel.

3. The top (Fig. 6-12G) extends 2 inches past the tops of the legs and is 2 inches wider than the top rails. Make it from a number of 1-inch thick strips. The drawing shows seven 2-inch pieces, but any width will do with random widths looking quite effective. If the bare top is to be used for working with food, choose a light, close-grained hardwood. Glue and clamp sufficient strips to allow a little waste for trimming to size and getting the ends square. Take sharpness off all edges and lightly round the corners.

4. Although one of the methods of attaching the top from below could be used, the butcher block top will look correct if screws are driven downwards in counterbored holes. The holes are then plugged with cross-grain pieces of the same wood as the top.

Materials List for Butcher Block Table

2 legs	1 × 6 × 24
2 rails	2 × 2 × 14
2 rails	2 × 2 × 12
2 trough sides	3/4 × 6 × 23
2 trough ends	3/4 × 4 × 9
1 top	1 × 14 × 28 (made up of glued strips)

TOWEL HOLDER

This holder allows four kitchen towels or other cloths to hang and dry (Fig. 6-13A). It screws to the wall and has four arms that fold against the wall when not in use, then rotate out as needed. As the arms have to be fairly slender for the best look, the wood should be a strong hardwood. A light color looks better than a dark one for kitchen use. The suggested sizes suit most towels (Fig. 6-13B).

1. Make the four arms first (Fig. 6-13C). Start with wood 1/2 inch thick and 1 1/2 inches wide. The arms taper from a 5/8-inch diameter at the pivot end to a 1/2-inch diameter at the tip (Fig. 6-14A). Cut to the outline, then plane the taper first to an octagonal section. Take off the angles of the octagon with a small plane, then round the wood by pulling a strip of abrasive paper around the arm (Fig. 6-15) before finishing by sanding lengthwise. Round the tips of the arms and try to make them all the same.

2. At the inner end, mark the center of each dowel pivot hole. Use that point as the center for a compass to draw the curve of the end (Fig. 6-14B). Cut the shape and drill the holes to fit the dowel.

3. Mark out the wood for the back. Put the four arms together to measure the thickness between the pivot blocks (Fig. 6-14C). The arms should fit tightly so they will stay in any position you set them and will not sag after long use.

4. Mark out the pivot blocks (Fig. 6-14D). They could be tenoned into the back or glued and screwed from behind. Drilling for the dowel pivot can be done more accurately before shaping. Drill through the blocks, then cut their curved outlines. Round the exposed parts. Using the arms as spacers, glue and screw the blocks to the back.

5. Drill holes at top and bottom for the fixing screws.

6. Before assembly, seal the wood pores to keep dirt out. A high gloss is not needed, only one coat of varnish or lacquer.

7. The dowel rod pivot could be left slightly too long during assembly, then its ends can be rounded (Fig. 6-14E). It should be a sufficiently tight fit without glue, then if you ever need to take the holder apart, the rod can be knocked out.

Materials List for Towel Holder

4 arms	1/2 × 1 1/2 × 18
1 back	1/2 × 2 × 9
2 blocks	1 × 2 × 3
1 pivot	8 × 1/2 diameter dowel rod

DRAWER TRAY

Many kitchen drawers can use fitted divisions, but

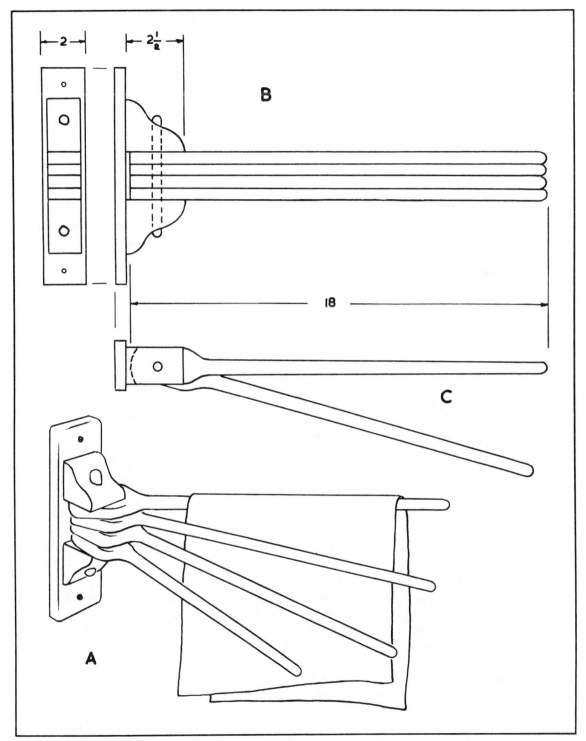

Fig. 6-13. A kitchen towel holder and dryer with four arms.

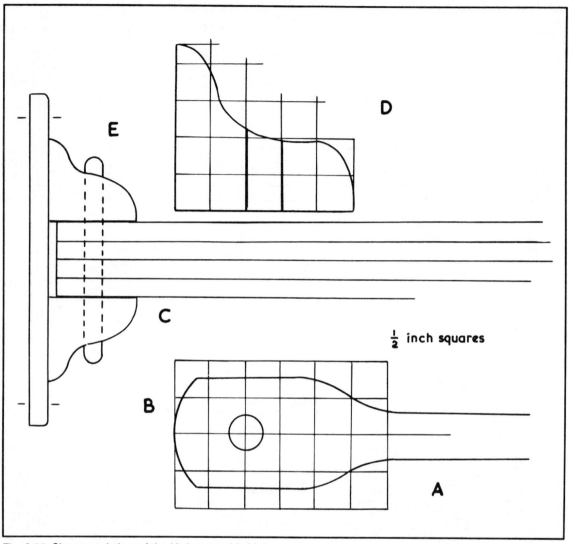

Fig. 6-14. Shapes and sizes of the kitchen towel holder.

a lift-out tray is even better. Contents can then be removed as a package for use elsewhere. A fitted tray may be as big as the drawer (Fig. 6-16) and lift out to expose other things underneath. It can also be on runners screwed to the sides of the drawer (Fig. 6-18A). It can still be lifted out, but it will also slide and give limited access below while in the drawer. In a very small drawer there might be no room for a tray, so any divisions have to be fitted directly to the drawer sides and front to get maximum capacity (Fig. 6-17).

To provide the greatest capacity in a tray and to look neat, the wood used should be thin. In most drawers the tray sides could be 3/8 inch thick or less and divisions should be not more than 3/16 inch thick. The bottom should be as thin as possible—1/8-inch plywood or hardboard could be used.

Tray sizes will depend on the drawer it is to fit and the cutlery or other contents. The depth of the tray can be about half that of the drawer, usually 2 inches or more.

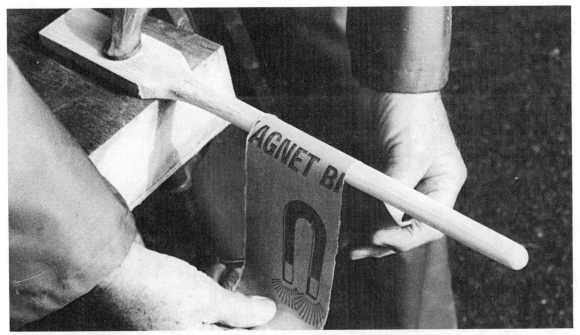

Fig. 6-15. The arm of a towel holder may be rounded using abrasive paper pulled around it.

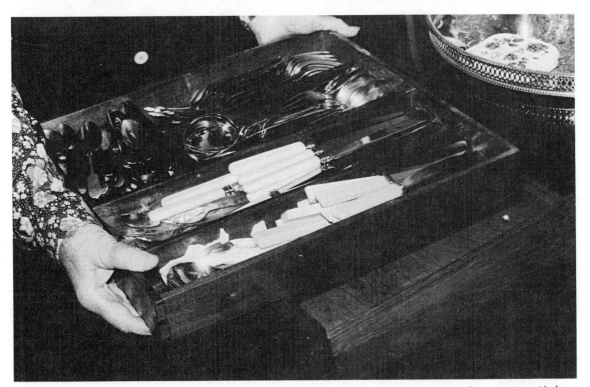

Fig. 6-16. A tray for cutlery may be full size or part of the size of a drawer. It lifts out to give access to the compartment below.

Fig. 6-17. A small drawer can be divided if there is no space for a tray.

1. Make the four tray sides. Box joints could be used at the corners, but dovetails are best (Fig. 6-18B).

2. Arrange the divisions to suit the contents. A common arrangement is shown in Fig. 6-18C. Keep the divisions below the tray edges.

3. With these thin sections ordinary dadoes are impractical. It is better to use triangular notches (Fig. 6-18D).

4. Where divisions join each other, very shallow triangular notches can be cut full depth.

5. The tops of some divisions can be hollowed (Fig. 6-18E) for ease in removing spoons etc. Round the top edges of all divisions.

6. If holes with 3/4-inch diameters are drilled in each side, you can get your fingers into them to lift the tray out of the drawer (Fig. 6-18F).

7. Assemble the four sides. Insert divisions from the bottom. You might prefer to delay cutting the ends of divisions to final lengths until just before fitting them, to get the closest joints.

8. Before fitting the bottom, glue cloth to its surface. Red or green will look good below cutlery. If you do this, apply any varnish or other finish to the wood before nailing or screwing on the cloth-covered bottom.

9. Fit the runners to the drawer sides so the tray top will be below the top of the drawer sides.

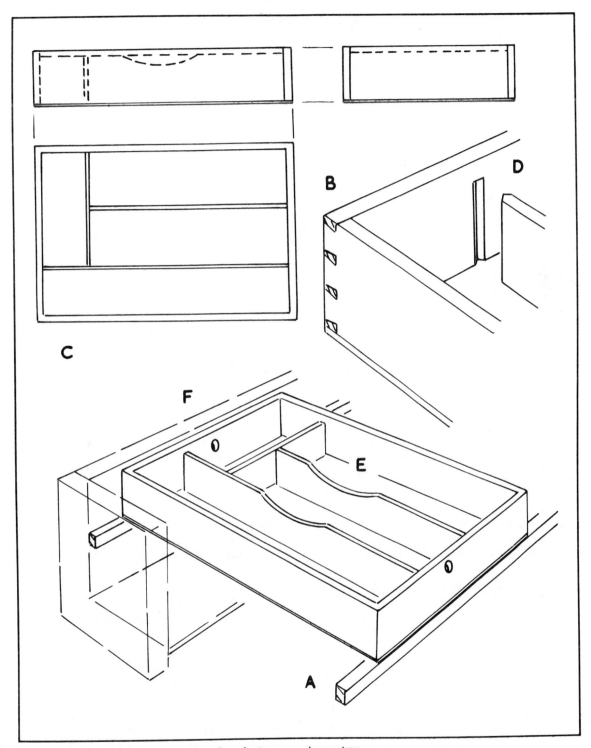

Fig. 6-18. Suggested layout and construction of a tray as a drawer tray.

Chapter 7

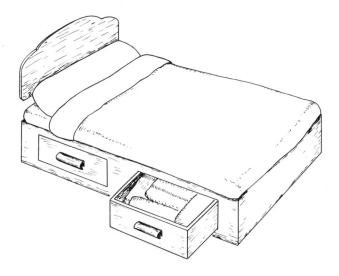

Bedroom

The bedroom offers as much scope for the amateur woodworker as any room in the home. You might be furnishing a new bedroom and want to make the bed as well as other furniture. Even if you have a bed, perhaps you want to make a headboard or arrange storage under it. You can also add the comfort and convenience of bedside tables, cabinets, and vanities.

A bedroom is not as active a place as other rooms. While you do not need wide open spaces, you do not want to overcrowd the room with furniture. Make sure anything new will have a real place and purpose. Storing clothing and bedding is often a problem. Projects that offer storage as well as another use are usually desirable.

This book is not concerned with built-in furniture. A bedroom often has plenty of built-in furniture and your projects should complement it. Too much built-in furniture can give a rather austere look to a bedroom. The freestanding furniture you make will soften and improve the general effect as well as personalize the room where you spend about

one-third of your life.

BED WITH DRAWERS

Space under a bed is often wasted, yet this is a useful area which may be put to good use in a small or overcrowded bedroom. Putting things loosely under a bed standing on legs is untidy, difficult to get to, and certainly not a place to put clothing or bedding, unless they are in bags or containers. It is better to make a bed that encloses the space with drawers.

This can be done in several ways. You have to relate the drawers to the space around the bed. It is no use fitting drawers if other furniture prevents them being pulled out. The size and shape of a bed will allow long drawers, but there has to be the space to use them. A drawer usually pulls across the bed, but a drawer at the foot of the bed may be more accessible. Under a narrow bed the drawers can be full width and pull from either side, as in Fig. 7-1. If the narrow bed is near a wall or something prevents movement one way, leave that

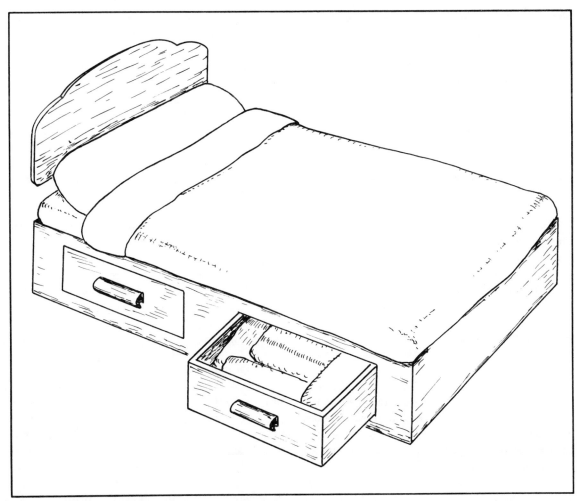

Fig. 7-1. A bed with headboard and two drawers underneath.

side blank. With a wide bed space to pull out a long crosswise drawer is unlikely, so there can be shorter drawers working against stops. Under a very wide bed there can be drawers on both sides.

One problem with an enclosed bed with drawers is its bulk compared with the usual bed on legs. This could be a nuisance when moving the bed. It helps if the bed is in two parts with a joint (Fig. 7-2A). The bed can then be taken apart at the center to form two boxes. With the headboard removed and the drawers pulled out, the individual parts are easy to manage and will pass through doorways or up stairs.

The bed drawn is made in the form of two in-

verted boxes, open towards the floor. It is intended to take a mattress 36 inches wide and 78 inches long, but could be modified to other sizes. If made much wider, some additional stiffening might be needed under the plywood top. They are two, almost identical boxes. The only differences are in the bolt holes for the headboard supports and for joining the boxes. As drawn, the drawers are arranged to pull out from either side. If that does not suit the surroundings, the drawers could be arranged to work one way. It would be quite simple to arrange the drawer in the box at the foot of the bed to pull out endwise.

The major parts of the bed are made of 1/2-inch

plywood framed around with 1-inch-by-2-inch strips, which could be softwood. All of these parts may be glued and held with finishing nails, either painted over or set below the surface and covered with filler, if a varnished finish is to be used. Although the plywood prevents the wood from warping, start with straight pieces, particularly for the drawers and their guides.

Joints could be cut between some parts of the framing, but it is satisfactory to use glue and nails for most parts and screws where endwise parts have to be secured.

1. Start by marking out the four sides (Fig. 7-2B). They are all the same if you are fitting drawers of the same size that operate both ways. Cut the drawer openings. Their depth is controlled by the framing strips. If these are not exactly 2 inches deep, it will not matter, but you should make the openings to match the actual wood.

2. The top framing strips go the full length of each side (Fig. 7-3A). Other short strips fill the gaps at the ends and beside the drawer openings (Fig. 7-3B).

3. Cut and fit the four ends (Fig. 7-3C). The plywood is attached to the sides, and the top and bottom edges are stiffened. See that the assemblies are square. You could cut the top pieces of plywood to size and use them for squaring, but do not attach them yet. Check that the two boxes match.

4. Where the drawers are to come, fit strips across at the top and bottom in line with the openings (Fig. 7-3D and E). Because they will form runners and kickers for the drawers, they should be absolutely straight and with their surfaces in line with the edges of the openings.

5. Attach strips outside these pieces, overlapping half their width, to rub against the sides of the drawers and act as guides (Fig. 7-3F and G). As you assemble these parts, check squareness across the bed.

6. Attach the top pieces of plywood. Trim edges if necessary. Put the boxes together and drill for two widely spaced bolts to hold them together—3/8 inch by 4 inches through the framing or 2 inches through the plywood only should be suitable. Put washers under the nut and bolt heads

to prevent pulling into the wood. If you expect to move the whole bed much, four bolts are preferable.

7. As the drawers have to pass through the bed both ways, the opposite fronts must be the same size as the drawer section (Fig. 7-2C). If you are making a drawer that will only work one way, the front could overlap the opening. In this case you do not have to be so careful about the fit of the drawer because the opening is hidden.

8. Cut the drawer fronts to fit the openings (Fig. 7-3H). Leave just enough clearance to permit easy movement.

9. Make the drawer sides the same depth (Fig. 7-3J).

10. The drawer framing can be wood 1-inch square or smaller—2-inch strips cut down the middle will do. Frame across the top and bottom of each drawer front. Make the drawer sides of plywood with strips to go between the front strips (Fig. 7-3K), but allow for the thickness of the bottom plywood. The side supports for the plywood bottom could be reduced to 1/2 inch thick.

11. Assemble the two sides and one drawer front and put the plywood bottom temporarily in position. You would not be able to put it in place with both fronts attached to the sides. Try the temporary assembly through a box to see if it runs smoothly. If there is any lack of symmetry, you might be able to correct it by planing the plywood. Complete the assembly of both drawers.

12. The drawer handles can be any type you wish. There will be less projection for bare legs to knock against if you choose bail handles that swing down.

13. Because the drawers are intended to be pulled out from either side, there cannot be any stop to hold them in the closed position. Spring ball catches can be used at the sides or bottom front edges. A ball set into the edge of the opening will then hit a catch plate on the edge of a drawer.

14. The headboard could be any design you wish, but a simple shaped piece of plywood on two supports is suggested (Fig. 7-4A). Make the plywood to match the width of the bed. If you shape the top, draw half the pattern full size on paper and

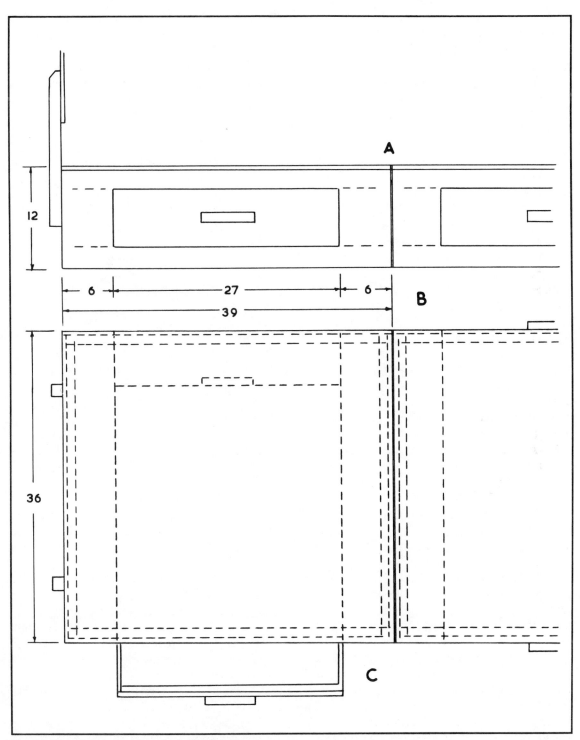

Fig. 7-2. Suggested sizes for a bed with drawers.

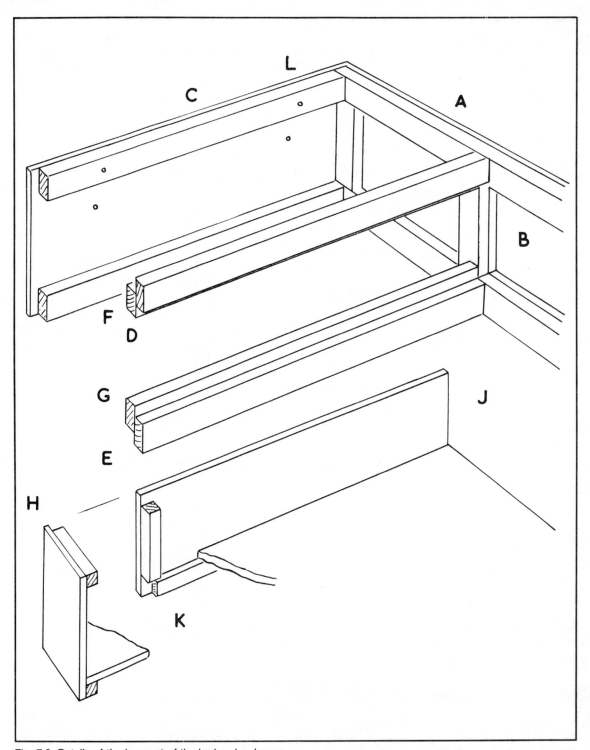

Fig. 7-3. Details of the box part of the bed and a drawer.

turn it over to make the outline symmetrical.

15. The headboard supports (Fig. 7-4B) are square strips glued and screwed to the headboard, then bolted to a box. Two holes in each support match two more in the box. For the strongest hold, secure the top bolts through the box framing (Fig. 7-3L). Coach bolts 3/8-inch diameter are suitable, with washers on each side. To adjust the headboard height, alternative sets of bolt holes could be drilled in the supports.

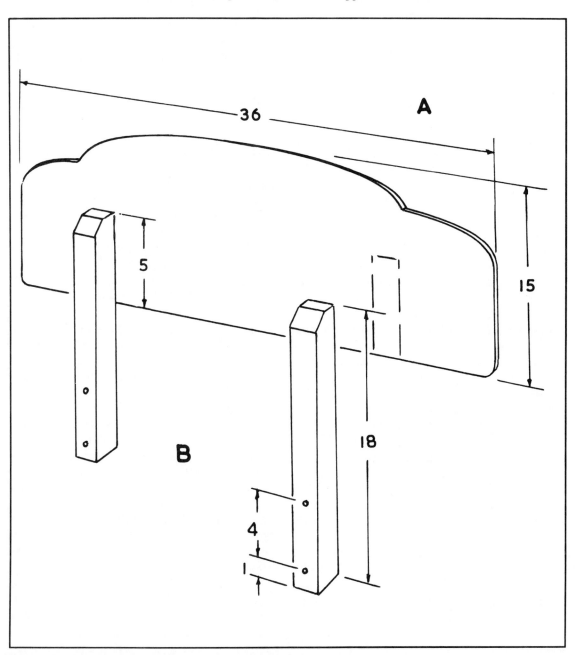

Fig. 7-4. Suggested design for a headboard on the bed with drawers.

Materials List for Bed with Drawers				
4 sides	12	× 39	× 1/2	plywood
4 ends	12	× 36	× 1/2	plywood
2 tops	36	× 39	× 1/2	plywood
8 side frames	1	× 2	× 39	
16 side frames	1	× 2	× 8	
8 end frames	1	× 2	× 34	
16 drawer strips	1	× 2	× 34	
4 drawer fronts	8	× 27	× 1/2	plywood
4 drawer sides	8	× 36	× 1/2	plywood
2 drawer bottoms	27	× 36	× 1/2	plywood
8 drawer front frames	1	× 1	× 27	
8 drawer front frames	1	× 1	× 7	
4 drawer bottom frames	1/2	× 1	× 36	
1 headboard	15	× 36	× 1/2	plywood
2 headboard supports	1 1/2	× 1 1/2	× 18	

OPEN-END BED

Modern mattresses with innersprings or thick pads of plastic or rubber foam provide ample support and comfort without the need for a box spring as well. A wooden bed can be made with a nonresilient base, which simplifies construction. A raised foot as well as a headboard keeps the mattress in place. Many types of bed ends can be devised, and some are quite elaborate. Basic ends could be plywood or made up of slats, as in Fig. 7-5.

The bed supports are boards laid across with narrow gaps, which provide ventilation. The head and footboards feature matching patterns of vertical slats between rails. The slats are 2 inches wide with gaps of about 3 inches. If the bed is redesigned for a different width, keep the gaps narrow enough so a child cannot get his head through.

The main bed parts should be a good hardwood, reasonably straight-grained for the sides and legs, to reduce any risk of warping. The baseboards could be softwood. There are several metal fittings available for bed assemblies, but are not used for this bed. It is usually impossible to move an assembled bed through normal doorways, so you must be able to remove the head and footboards from the sides to reduce bulk.

Sizes given (Fig. 7-6) suit a mattress 36 inches wide and 78 inches long. Adjust sizes to suit the mattress you intend to use. The sections of wood listed should be adequate for any bed up to 54 inches wide. Fit the legs with casters. Heights are shown from the floor; allowances must be made for the height of the casters.

The head and footboard assemblies should be made at the same time to match, then the other parts added. Mortise and tenon joints are shown, but dowels could be used in the slat and rail assemblies, if you wish.

1. Prepare the wood for the four legs, allowing for the caster depth at the bottom. Leave some extra length at the top until after the joints have been cut. Mark out the legs together (Fig. 7-7A) so positions that have to be the same are squared across in one action. Mark the depths of rails from the actual wood to allow for variations. The two sets of legs have to be paired.

2. Mark the wood for the rails so the lengths between shoulders are the same (Fig. 7-7B). Allow for tenons 1 inch long and at least 1/2 inch thick at the ends of the rails. Mark the mortises that take them on the legs.

3. Cut the wood for the slats (Fig. 7-7C). The lengths between shoulders should match the distance between mortises on the legs. Tenons can be 3/4 inch long and 5/16 or 3/8 inch thick. Check that all in each set of slats match.

4. You can experiment to get the same spacing all the way across a rail or measure each side of the centerline so spaces next to the legs will be narrower. Mark and cut all the mortise and tenon joints (Fig. 7-7D).

5. After the mortises for the rails have been cut in the legs, decorate the tops of the legs. They could be rounded or chamfered; here they are shown cut to a shallow square cone (Fig. 7-6A). Sloping 1/2 inch back from the end will be satisfactory.

6. The sides (Fig. 7-6B) should be checked for straightness. For their ends to be level with the outsides of the legs, they are given barefaced tenons (Fig. 7-7E). Cut the tenons half the thickness of the wood and to the full depth. This gives maximum

Fig. 7-5. An open-end bed with solid mattress supports.

rigidity to resist lengthwise loads applied when moving the bed.

7. Cut the mortises to a close fit on the tenons. These joints will have to be taken apart if the bed is disassembled. This may require driving out with a piece of wood as a punch.

8. Take the sharp edges off the legs, rails, and slats. Assemble both bed ends. Make up the slats and rails first, then join the rails to the legs. Check squareness and that head and footboard assemblies are the same width. Add the casters.

9. Have the wood for the base boards ready, but not yet cut to length. Use the thickness of this as a guide to the location of the supporting strips on the sides (Fig. 7-6C). Glue and screw these strips to the sides with their ends opposite the joint shoulders.

10. Drill through the mortises for two, 5/8-inch dowels (Fig. 7-7F). Mark similarly on the tenons, but slightly closer to the shoulders. How much

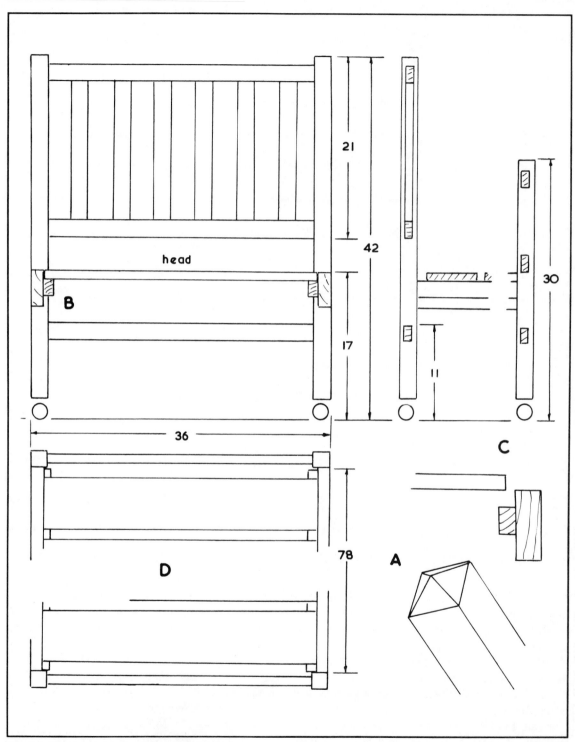

Fig. 7-6. Sizes and details of the open-end bed.

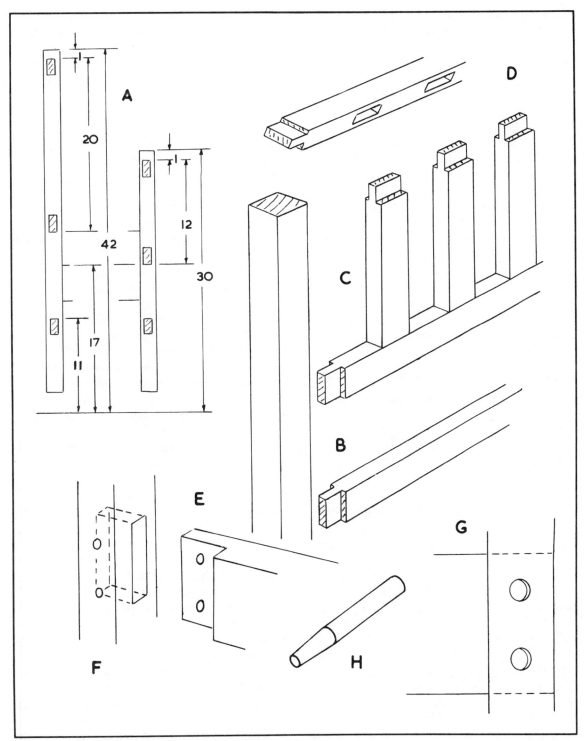

Fig. 7-7. Constructional details of the open-end bed.

closer depends on the wood, but 1/16 inch will be enough for close-grained hardwood, a little more for softwoods. In this way the joint will be pulled tight during assembly because of the offset holes (Fig. 7-7G).

11. Cut dowels with at least 2 inches parallel, then about 1 inch tapered (Fig. 7-7H). When you assemble the bed, drive the dowels from outside. The taper will then pull the tenon tighter and the parallel part will secure it. Drive until the end of the dowel is level outside. Leave the other end projecting inside so it can be driven back if you want to disassemble the bed. With all the dowels driven, the bed should be very steady and rigid.

12. Have the bed standing level. Measure diagonals to see that it is square. Cut the baseboards (Fig. 7-6D) to length. Fill the base, leaving gaps of about 1 inch. It might be satisfactory to merely put the boards in place before positioning the mattress, but they might move and the bed sides could bend. It will be better to drive one screw at each end of each board to locate and secure it.

Materials List for Open-end Bed			
2 legs	2	× 2 × 42	
2 legs	2	× 2 × 30	
6 rails	1	× 2 × 18	
6 rails	1	× 2 × 11	
2 sides	1 1/2	× 4 × 82	
2 side supports	1	× 2 × 78	
11 baseboards	1	× 6 × 34	
8 pegs	4	× 5/8 diameter dowel rods	

DIVAN BED WITH HEADBOARD

A modern hard-sided box mattress is almost a bed in itself. Put on the floor it is too low for comfortable use, but if it is raised, the construction of its supports can be quite simple. Without a headboard it could be put against a wall and used as a seat or sofa during the day, if it is covered in a way to disguise its night-time use as a bed. If its only use is as a bed, it is better with a headboard.

The arrangement is particularly suitable for a single bed or smaller child's bed. The bed should be designed to fit around the mattress. The bed shown in Fig. 7-8 is intended to suit a mattress 36 inches by 78 inches (Fig. 7-9). Do not make the woodwork too tight a fit around the mattress. Measure the actual size and allow at least 1/2 inch extra each way. Measure its depth and arrange for enough of it to come above the bed sides. Much depends on the construction of the mattress. If there is a rigid casing on the mattress, the wood can fit almost to that depth, but a softer foam-filled mattress may have the wood edge to half its depth. Making the wood too high will give a hard, uncomfortable edge when sitting on the bed.

The headboard is removable and could even be added later if you change the use of the bed. Taking it off makes the bed easier to pass through doorways when turned on edge. The headboard is given limited height adjustment. Anyone using high pillows may prefer the headboard higher, but otherwise it can be lowered a few inches.

If the bed covering hangs over the edges, not much of the woodwork will show in use. You could make almost all parts from softwood. The legs will show and they could be stained and varnished, although you might prefer to make them of a good hardwood. The headboard is a piece of plywood, preferably with an attractively veneered front surface, although it could be painted or upholstered.

1. Settle on the sizes to suit the mattress and lay out the bed parts to suit. Relate the sizes to those shown to get suitable proportions. The headboard should be arranged with its average lower edge height about 3 inches above the mattress top (Fig. 7-9A).

2. Decide on the corner joints. The sides might overlap the ends and be screwed. Arrange screws closer at the top where there is the most strain (Fig. 7-10A). Screws to attach the legs also strengthens the corners lower down. If the woodwork is expected to show later, counterbore and plug the screw heads.

3. A strong nailed joint can be made with a rabbet (Fig. 7-10B). Nails can then be driven both ways. If they are set below the surface and covered with filler, the result should be inconspicuous. The best corner, particularly if you want to show your

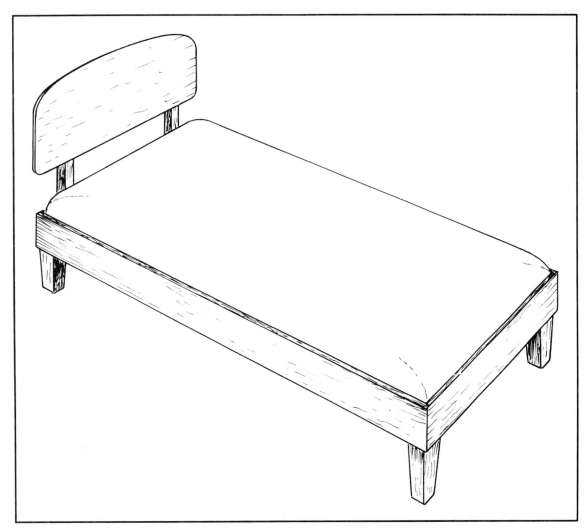

Fig. 7-8. A divan bed with headboard.

skill, is a dovetailed one (Fig. 7-10C).

4. The legs should come up to the same level as the supporting strips for the plywood under the mattress (Figs. 7-9B and 7-11A). The simplest legs are parallel and fitted inside the frame (Fig. 7-10D). This is satisfactory if you take the sharpness off the edges and bottom. Because the legs are not very obvious in the finished bed, you might find this arrangement suits your needs.

5. With the legs inside the frame, the loads are taken by just glue and screws. It is stronger to notch the tops of the legs to half the thickness of the frames (Fig. 7-10E) so that takes a share of the load. You could taper the outer two faces of each leg (Fig. 7-10F) or taper equally all around (Fig. 7-10G). In any case, take the sharpness off the bottom edges. An interesting shape looks like an angular cabriole leg (Fig. 7-10H). It is made with tapers on the two outer surfaces, but a foot is formed below them. If you have the use of a lathe, the lower part of each leg could be turned (Fig. 7-10J). When tapering the bottom, do not reduce the part in contact with the floor too much or it will mark the floor covering excessively.

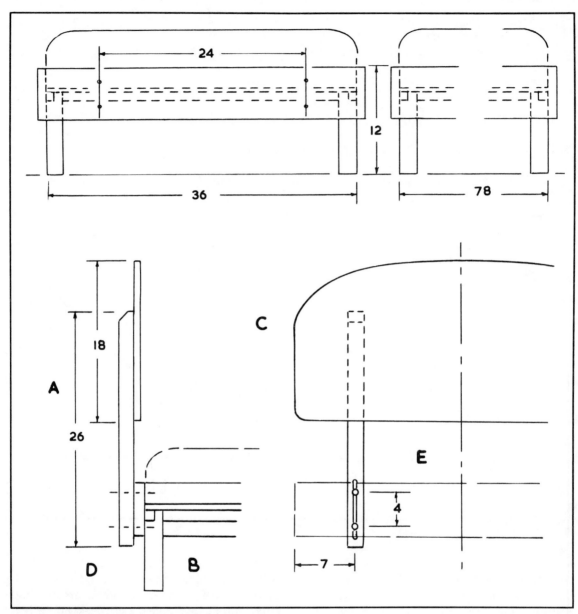

Fig. 7-9. Suggested sizes of a divan bed with headboard.

6. Assemble the frame parts with the legs. Check squareness by measuring diagonals, and see that the assembly is not twisted by sighting across it. Fit the bearer strips (Fig. 7-11B) level with and between the leg tops.

7. Cut the plywood (Fig. 7-11C) to rest on these strips. It does not have to be secured so it can

be lifted out when cleaning the bed. It should make a reasonable fit, however, to keep the bed in shape. Drill a few holes in it to provide ventilation for the mattress.

8. The headboard (Figs. 7-9C and 7-11D) is a piece of plywood that is veneered or upholstered on the front. It can be rectangular and have angled

corners or other straight-line outline, but curves are more restful than straight lines, and a sweeping curve is suggested. The supports are square strips glued and screwed to the back (Fig. 7-9D).

9. So there can be some height adjustment, the supports are slotted to fit over two bolts, each in the bed end (Fig. 7-11E). Coach bolts, 3/8-inch diameter, are suitable. Their square necks then slide in the slots and prevent turning when nuts are tightened inside the bed. Washers under the nuts prevent them from pulling into the wood. Position the holes in the bed end (Fig. 7-9E), then make the slots 6 inches or longer to allow for adjustment.

10. Fit casters or glides if desired. You might have to shorten legs during construction, if they lift the bed too high.

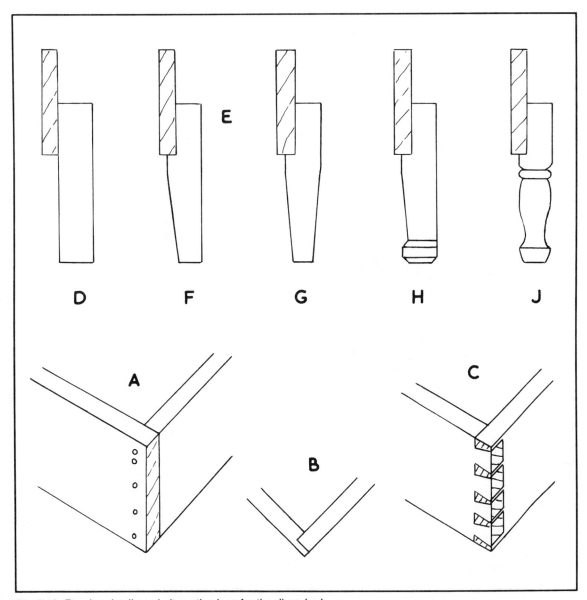

Fig. 7-10. Framing details and alternative legs for the divan bed.

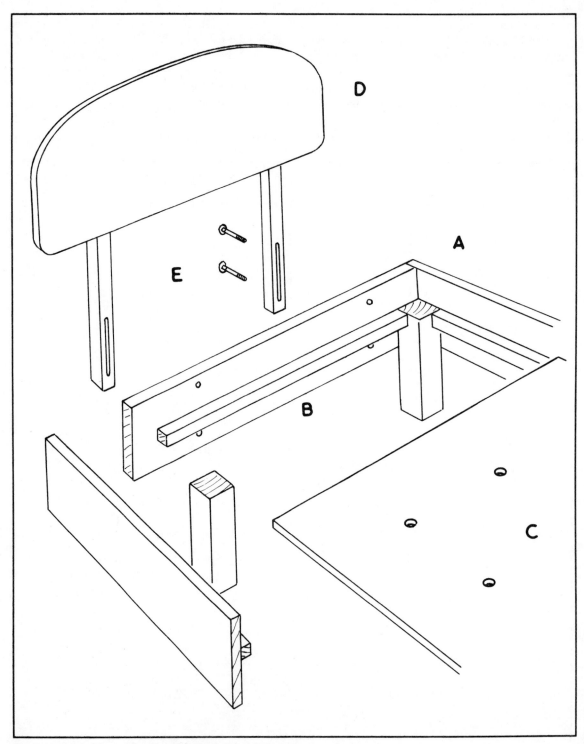

Fig. 7-11. Assembly and headboard details of the divan bed.

Materials List for Divan Bed with Headboard	
2 sides	1 × 6 × 82
2 ends	1 × 6 × 40
4 legs	2 × 2 × 9
2 bearers	1 × 1 × 76
2 bearers	1 × 1 × 34
1 base	36 × 78 × 1/2 plywood
1 headboard	18 × 40 × 1/2 plywood
2 headboard supports	1 1/2 × 1 1/2 × 26

BED ENDS

Innerspring and other mattresses may be supported on iron side pieces with fittings that attach to the bed ends. For many modern beds the foot does not extend above the mattress level. This design (Fig. 7-12) is intended to complete a bed where the mattress and its supports are ready to be attached to head and foot.

Size depends on the mattress; in this example it is 48 inches wide. The legs are 2 inches square, which is wide enough to take the metal end fittings.

They are usually mounted on casters. At the foot there is a simple board to link the legs at a level below the mattress top. The headboard can be made in an infinite number of ways, but is shown here to be fairly plain.

The legs should be made of a strong hardwood, as moving a bed may put considerable strain on them. The headboard could be solid wood, but it is more likely to be veneered plywood or particleboard.

1. Allow for the casters when deciding on height. They will probably be about 2 inches deep.

2. Prepare the wood for the legs (Fig. 7-13A and B). Square the bottoms and drill for casters. The tops are square against the boards, then bevelled. Take sharpness off all edges.

3. Make the footboard (Fig. 7-13C). Except for removing sharpness off edges, it needs no special treatment.

4. If the head is solid wood, glued strips make up the width.

5. Cut the head with its ends square to the bottom edge. Mark the center of the curve and its limits at the ends (Fig. 7-13D). Spring a batten

Fig. 7-12. A piece of veneered plywood makes a headboard with an elliptical edge.

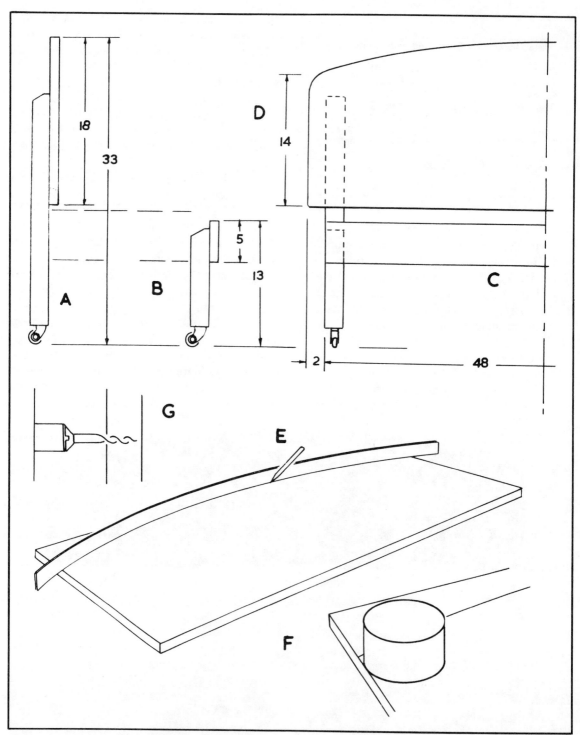

Fig. 7-13. Bed ends can be made to suit a box mattress.

through these points and draw the curve (Fig. 7-13E). Let the batten extend at the ends and bend it from its extremities. If you bend from the board edges only, the curve will be distorted. Draw the end curves around a paint can or something similar (Fig. 7-13F).

6. Cut the headboard to shape. Sand and round the edges of solid wood. The edge of veneered plywood or particleboard could be veneered. Alternatively, paint the edges an appropriate color.

7. Attach the legs to the boards with glue and counterbored screws (Fig. 7-13G). Plugs are not essential, but they improve appearance.

Materials List for Bed Ends

2 legs	2 × 2 × 27	
2 legs	2 × 2 × 12	
1 footboard	1 × 5 × 48	
1 headboard	1 × 18 × 52	

FITTED BEDHEAD

A bed can be more cozy if its head is enclosed both by a headboard and cabinets or side tables. For anyone who reads or handles business or household matters while sitting in bed, adequate surface and storage places hold papers and other things, such as a telephone, safely within reach. It is possible to have separate head and side tables with cabinets or cupboards, but it helps if all these things are joined in one unit.

This fitted bedhead (Fig. 7-14) has a large headboard that may hold a reading lamp. It extends over two side cabinets with doors to enclose shelf space. The bed is not attached. It is pushed between the cabinets so it can be pulled out for cleaning. The head assembly stands unaided by the bed.

Sizes must be adjusted to suit the bed. The width between the cabinets should be about 4 inches wider than the bed with its covering. Sizes in Fig. 7-15 suit a bed 48 inches wide and of average height. The main part of the head can be a plywood sheet 48 inches by 96 inches. For a wider bed

there must be a joint, probably at the center.

Many parts are fairly wide. Although the whole assembly looks very attractive in solid wood, the wide boards are expensive and hard to make up from narrower pieces. If you have suitable hardwood, it can be used to make the bedhead in the way described; it could also be made with veneered particleboard. The construction information is laid out to suit that material and has straight edges for veneering them to match the surface veneers.

You can also use plywood of sufficient thickness with its exposed edges lipped. This might be more suitable for a painted finish. If the large board at the back is plywood, either veneered or stained, the main assembly could then be veneered particleboard in a color to contrast with the plywood. Some edging and the handles could match the plywood.

Most of the construction can be with dowels. The large plywood assembly may have its framing and edges glued and held with pins sunk below the surface and covered with filler. Decide what you need and adjust sizes to suit. Check what standard widths of veneered particleboard are locally available. Slight variations in the size of your project to suit available materials may enable you to reduce the amount of veneering you have to do.

1. Lay out the plywood back. Mark the framing positions so screws or dowels holding the side cabinet parts will go through solid wood (Fig. 7-16A).

2. Frame the plywood. You could halve the strips together, but it should be strong enough to use the full-length pieces around the edges. Take the two intermediate rails across without breaks, then fit short vertical pieces between them (Fig. 7-16B). Use glue and sufficient pins or thin nails from the front to hold the parts close. Set the pins below the surface and fill to cover their heads. Plane the edges level and square.

3. Cover the top edges (Fig. 7-16C) using glue and pins. Round the front edges and fit the rear edges level. Miter the sloping sides and allow for their ends overlapping the cabinet sides (Fig. 7-16D).

4. Make the two cabinet sides (Figs. 7-15A and 7-17A). Mark on the overlap the positions of

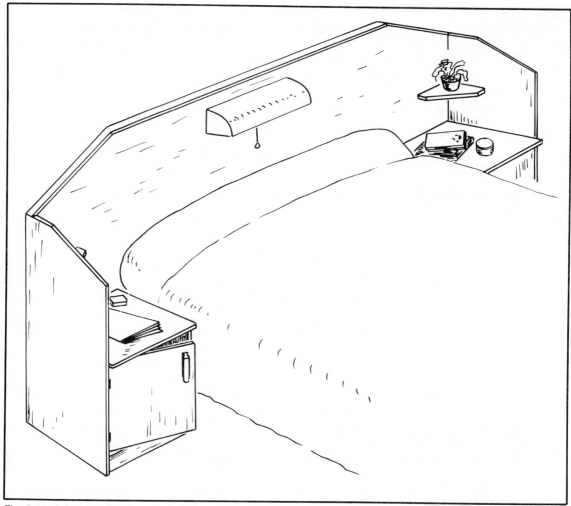

Fig. 7-14. A fitted bedhead can include many items in one unit.

the backboard and other parts. Keep those parts far enough forward to clear the overlap (Fig. 7-17B).

5. The cabinet bottoms (Figs. 7-15B and 7-17C) determine the sizes of the horizontal parts. Make the inside shelves (Fig. 7-17D) the same length, but the cabinet tops should extend forward and towards the bed by about 1 inch (Fig. 7-17E). A variation on the veneered edge for the cabinet top is to edge it with solid wood to match that around the back. An advantage of doing this is that you can round the corners and edges instead of leaving the hard edge of the particleboard (which is difficult to veneer on a curved edge), just where bare flesh comes against it.

6. The plinth (Fig. 7-17F) fits between the upright parts and is set back 1/2 inch under the bottom.

7. Make the inner sides (Fig. 7-17G) to match the sizes marked on the outer sides.

8. An upper shelf is optional (Fig. 7-17H) on one or both sides. The shelf size and shape are not critical and need not be added until you see how the whole bedhead will look when partly assembled.

9. Veneer any exposed edges that have been cut or are without the manufacturer's veneer.

10. Prepare the meeting surfaces for dowel

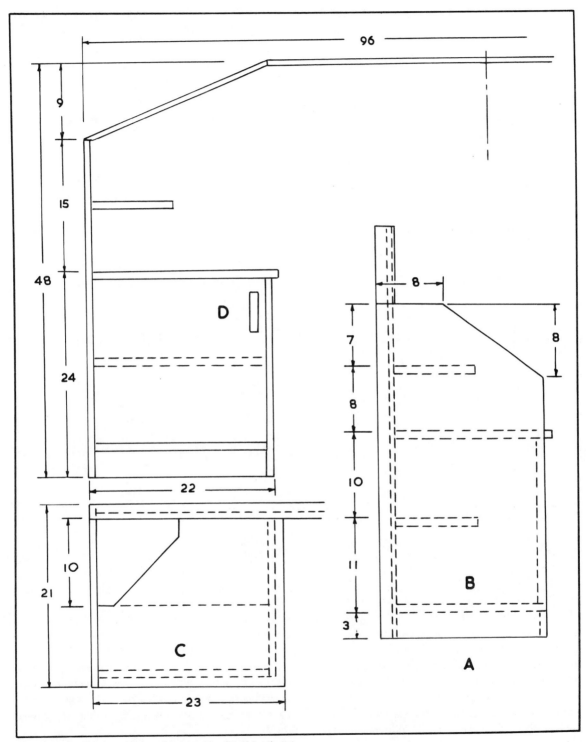

Fig. 7-15. Suggested sizes and layout of a fitted bedhead.

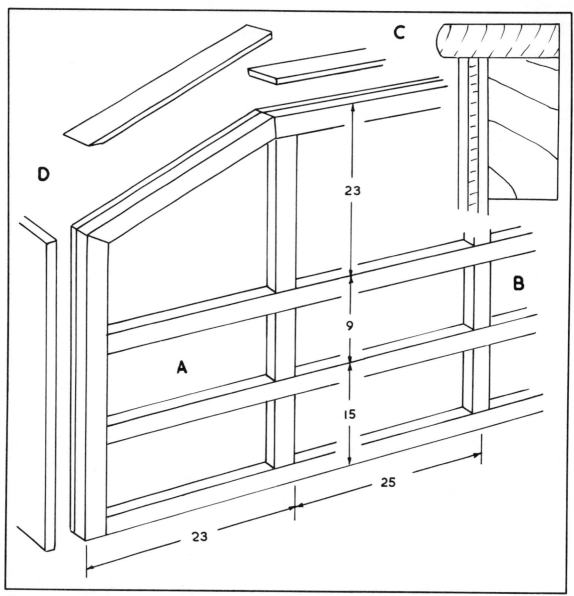

Fig. 7-16. Details of the back of the fitted bedhead.

joints, except that at the back you can screw through the framing on the plywood. Mark the positions on the front and drill through for screws. Where the cabinet sides overlap the back, use dowels. For these and all other joints it should be satisfactory to use 3/8-inch dowels spaced about 4 inches apart. Take them as deep as possible into the thickness of the particleboard and slightly deeper into edges.

11. Attach the plinths to the bottoms. Assemble the horizontal parts to the tall sides, then add the inner sides. Check squareness on the marked positions on the plywood. Dowel the sides to the back framing, then screw into the other parts from the back.

12. If the bedhead is to go against a wall, as

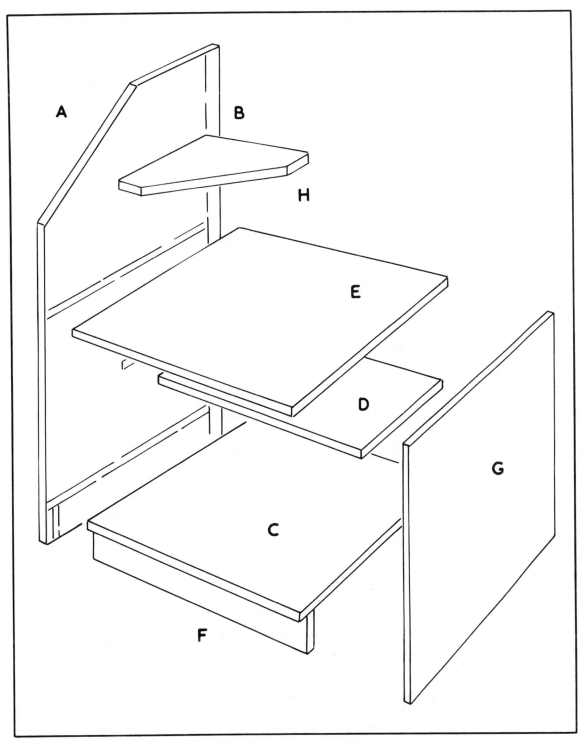

Fig. 7-17. How the parts at the side of the fitted bedhead go together.

is usual, there is no need to do anything to its rear surface. If it will be used away from a wall, secure another piece of plywood to the back with the edging wide enough to overlap it. If you are fitting any lighting to the head, do the wiring inside before adding the second piece of plywood.

13. The cabinets could be used without doors, or you could arrange a door at one side only. Make a door (Fig. 7-15C) to fit within its space easily. Veneer its edges. Fit hinges at the side away from the bed. At the other side fit a wood or metal handle fairly high (Fig. 7-15D) so it is easily reached from the bed. Put small pieces of wood at top and bottom to act as door stops. Use spring or magnetic catches—you do not want any fastener that needs an action other than a pull.

```
            Materials List for Fitted Bedhead

head
1 back                  48  × 96 × 3/8 plywood
3 back frames            1  × 2 × 96
1 back frame             1  × 2 × 50
2 back frames            1  × 2 × 30
2 back frames            1  × 2 × 40
3 back frames            1  × 2 × 22
3 back frames            1  × 2 × 6
3 back frames            1  × 2 × 12
1 back edging          1/2  × 2 × 50
2 back edgings         1/2  × 2 × 30


cabinets
2 sides                 3/4  × 21 × 40
2 sides                 3/4  × 19 1/2 × 24
2 bottoms               3/4  × 19 1/2 × 21
2 tops                  3/4  × 20 1/2 × 22
2 shelves               3/4  × 10 × 21
2 shelves               3/4  × 10 × 10
2 doors                 3/4  × 21 × 21
2 plinths               3/4  × 3 × 21
2 handles             1 1/8  × 1 1/8 × 6
```

UNDER-BED STORAGE BOX

If a bed stands on legs, there is space underneath that is often not used because it is not easily accessible without crawling on the floor. This box on casters (Fig. 7-18) can be pulled out easily to use the underbed space for storing spare bedding, chil-

dren's toys, and other things you want to keep, yet only need occasionally.

Sizes obviously depend on the bed and the clearance below the mattress. It may not be wise to make one box to fit the maximum space. You must consider space around the bed as well as under it. Two or more boxes fit the space better. In some rooms the box can pull out sideways. In others there may be more outside floor space to fit it in endwise. The drawing offers sizes to suggest proportions. The boards on top (Fig. 7-18A) help to stop the contents from rising and catching on the mattress or other obstructions. The casters could be small because they do not have to carry much load. If they are shallow, more height is available for storage.

Construction can be anything from nails to dovetails. As described, it is assumed that screws are being used. Staining and varnishing will make a box look better among other furniture. Obtain the casters first so you can allow for their height and the size blocks needed to fix them.

1. Make the four sides. There could be handles for pulling out, but slots about 1 1/2 inches by 6 inches are simpler and provide a good grip without projections (Fig. 7-18B). They could be cut in one side, opposite sides, or all four sides, depending on how you expect to move the box. Make them by drilling their ends and sawing between the holes. Round their edges.

2. Screw the sides together. Square the bottom so it will bring the assembly square as you screw it on.

3. Screw on the top strips over opposite sides.

4. Screw on the blocks under the corners and attach the casters.

```
            Materials List for Underbed Box

4 sides                 3/4  × 6 × 36
2 tops                  3/4  × 6 × 36
4 blocks                3/4  × 3 × 3
1 bottom                36  × 40 × 1/8 or 1/4
                        hardboard or plywood
```

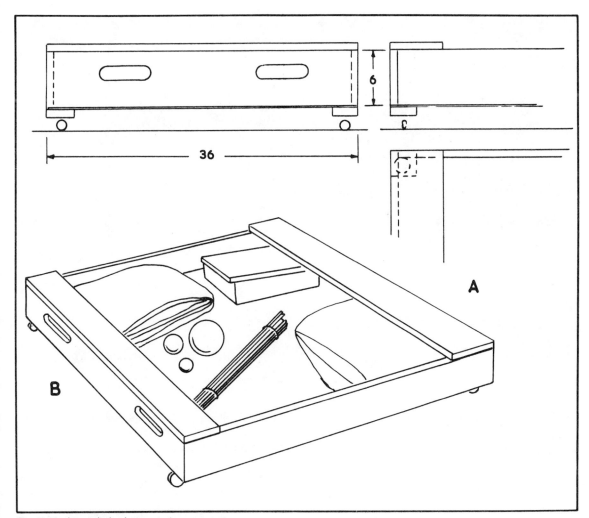

Fig. 7-18. An underbed storage box on casters.

HANGING SHELVES

Shelves or compartments can hang on the wall above a bedhead, over a desk or bench, or anywhere that books and other things should be kept together and off other furniture. This set of hanging shelves (Fig. 7-19) is used over twin beds to keep books and other things within reach.

The shelves shown are made of mahogany, but any hardwood can be used. Softwood might be suitable for a painted finish in a child's bedroom. Sizes may vary, but if the unit is made smaller, wood thickness should not be reduced because it will weaken joints. A much larger assembly should

be made with thicker wood.

Several different methods of construction are possible, depending on your wishes, skill, and available hand or power tools. The satisfactory use and appearance of the shelves is dependent on joints that will not fail.

1. Prepare the wood with all parts the same width and thickness.

2. Mark out the top board (Fig. 7-20A) with the positions of the other parts. Leave some excess length until you have decided on the methods of jointing.

3. Make the other lengthwise parts (Fig.

Fig. 7-19. This hanging shelf unit goes above twin beds and has a reading lamp at the center.

7-20B and C) using the top board as a guide.

4. Mark the four uprights (Fig. 7-20D) together, but leave some excess length so you can cut the chosen joints.

5. The drawing shows the corners without extensions (Fig. 7-20E). It is possible to let the shelves or the uprights extend (Fig. 7-20F and G) in some forms of construction. Some of these variations are dependent on the choice of joints, as detailed below.

6. The shelves photographed have through dovetails (Fig. 7-21A) cut by hand. The exposed joint details may be regarded as decorative. Note the tails are vertical, to take the hanging load. Machine-cut dovetails are equally suitable, but may not have the narrow pins that are a feature of handwork.

7. A simpler joint uses a rabbet (Fig. 7-21B) about two-thirds of the thickness of the top piece. This allows the upright piece to fit in and nails to be driven both ways to lock the joint. Use glue, but that is not very strong on end grain, so much of the load has to be taken by the fastenings. Screws are

too conspicuous, but finishing nails may be set below the surface and covered with filler. If you have the equipment to cut the joint, a rabbet and tongue (Fig. 7-21C) will join the wood without nails.

8. As with most furniture, it is possible to join the parts with dowels. Using these at corners without an overhang, however, does not leave much wood outside the dowel holes and the short grain may break out. It is better to extend the overlapping part (Figs. 7-20G and 7-21D). If you want the shelves to extend outwards, the dowelling will have to be downwards (Fig. 7-20F).

9. The raised shelf (Fig. 7-20C) may be fitted to the uprights with dowels, although a better joint is a stopped dado (Fig. 7-21E). Taking it through to the front would expose the end of the shelf unattractively.

10. Where the inner uprights join the top shelf there could be dowels. Tenons are an alternative, but they would have to go through for sufficient strength and their exposed ends might be regarded as ugly. A simple stopped dado, as at the ends of

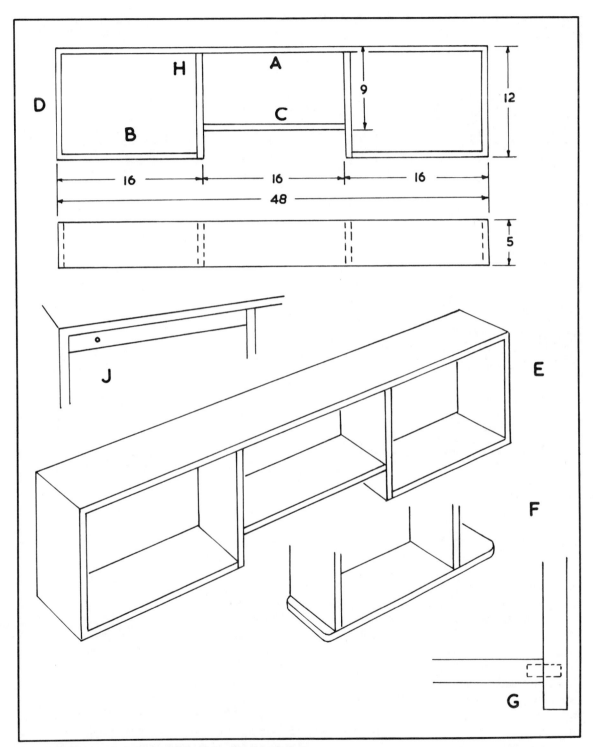

Fig. 7-20. Sizes and alternate details of the hanging shelves.

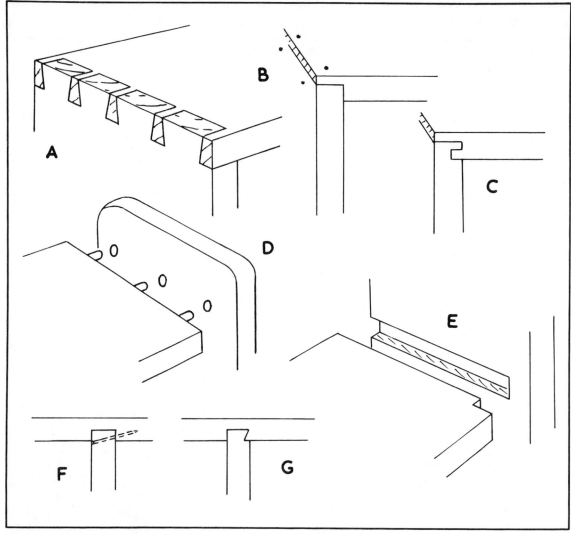

Fig. 7-21. Joints at the corners and divisions of the hanging shelves.

the middle shelf, might not be strong enough because of the weakness of end grain gluing, unless nails are driven diagonally (Fig. 7-21F). A dovetail stopped dado (Fig. 7-21G) will take downward loads without the help of nails.

11. The shelves could be attached to the wall with metal plates screwed to the backs of at least two uprights, with holes in extensions for the screws to the wall. Another way is to glue strips under the ends of the top shelf and screw through them (Fig. 7-20J).

Materials List for Hanging Shelves	
1 shelf	5/8 × 5 × 48
3 shelves	5/8 × 5 × 17
4 uprights	5/8 × 5 × 12
2 screw strips	5/8 × 1 × 15

SMALL CHEST OF DRAWERS

Particleboard in standard widths with veneer on surfaces and edges allows simple and effective construction. This chest (Fig. 7-22) is made mainly with 4-inch, 6-inch, and 15-inch widths. The dimensions can be modified to available stock sizes to avoid cutting to widths. The chest looks attractive if the main parts are covered with wood or wood-grained plastic and the drawer parts have a plain white plastic veneer. Strips of matching veneer will be needed for covering cut edges.

Dowels with a 3/8-inch diameter and spaced about 3 inches can be used for joints. Use a stop on the drill to get the maximum depth of holes in the thickness, but you can drill slightly deeper in the ends.

1. The drawer fronts are the controlling sizes (Fig. 7-23A). Cut them to size and veneer their ends.

2. Mark out the pair of ends (Fig. 7-23B) allowing 1/8 inch between drawer fronts and under the top. The difference in depth is made up at the bottom by the plinth. Mark across where the bottoms of the drawers will come.

3. Fit strips near the rear edges (Fig. 7-24A) to take the back.

4. Cut the drawer sides (Fig. 7-24B). Allow a little clearance inside the rear strips on the sides.

5. Use a router to groove the outside of each drawer 1/2 inch deep and 3/4 inch wide to within a 1/2 inch of the front (Figs. 7-23C and 7-24C).

6. Screw and glue runners to suit on the chest sides (Fig. 7-24D). Allow a little clearance at the chest front.

7. Groove the drawer sides for the drawer

Fig. 7-22. A small chest of drawers alongside a bedside cabinet.

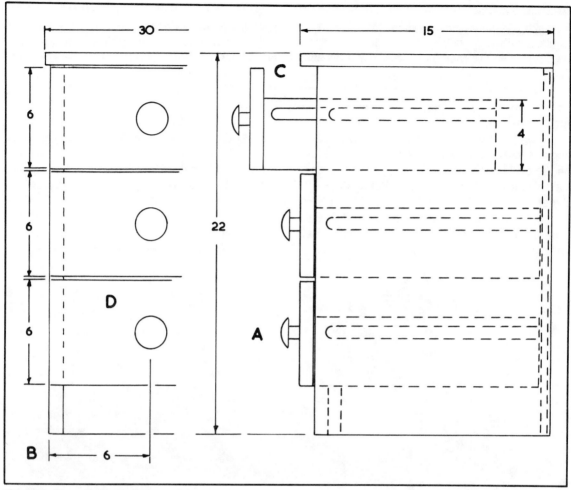

Fig. 7-23. Sizes of the small chest of drawers.

bottom (Fig. 7-24E). If you do not have a suitable cutter, use strips for the bottom to rest on (Fig. 7-24F).

8. A router can be used to groove the drawer fronts for the bottoms, but the grooves should stop within the thickness of each drawer side so its end does not show. Alternatively, put strips across for the bottom to rest on.

9. When the chest is assembled, the drawer fronts should come level with the outer surfaces of the sides. Mark the length of the top to allow for this and to overhang about 1/2 inch (Fig. 7-24G). Put a strip under the rear edge to take the back and match the strips on the sides.

10. Make the plinth (Fig. 7-24H) to fit between the sides. Mark its position on each end 3/4 inch back from the front.

11. Mark and drill all the dowel holes and prepare enough dowels.

12. Assemble the top and plinth to the sides. Have the back ready and glue and tack it to the strips to hold the assembly square. Check that the chest stands level.

13. Join the drawer sides to the fronts. Fit each drawer bottom loosely and check the drawer action on its slides. If satisfactory, add the drawer backs and fit the bottoms permanently. Make sure the drawer fronts close tightly against the chest sides.

The rear ends of the drawer sides should not hit the strips at the rear of the chest sides.

14. Knobs are shown (Fig. 7-23D), but there could be long handles on the drawers. Most types are fitted with screws from inside.

Materials List for Small Chest of Drawers

(all veneered particleboard unless marked)
3 drawer fronts	3/4 × 6 × 29	
6 drawer sides	3/4 × 4 × 14	
3 drawer backs	3/4 × 3 × 28	
3 drawer bottoms	14 × 29 × 1/8	hardboard
2 chest ends	3/4 × 14 × 22	
1 chest top	3/4 × 15 × 30	
1 chest plinth	3/4 × 3 × 29	
1 chest back	21 × 28 × 1/8	hardboard
6 drawer runners	3/8 × 3/4 × 14	hardwood
2 back fillets	3/8 × 3/8 × 22	hardwood
1 back fillet	3/8 × 3/8 × 29	hardwood

SMALL BEDSIDE CABINET

A cabinet that occupies a minimum space, yet has a reasonable capacity, may be all that can be put beside a bed in a small room. This one (Fig. 7-25) is made of veneered particleboard, either all one type of veneer or, if the cabinet is to match the small chest of drawers, wood-grained plastic veneer for most parts and white plastic veneer for the door. All main parts are joined with 3/8-inch dowels. The back is hardboard.

1. Mark out the pair of sides (Fig. 7-26A) with the top shelf 1/2 inch down and the other shelf positions marked.

2. Cut the three shelves to the same length and take 1/4 inch off the backs of the lower shelves to allow for the hardboard back (Fig. 7-27A).

3. Make and fit strips to go between the rear edges of the shelves (Fig. 7-27B).

4. Make the plinth (Figs. 7-26B and 7-27C).

5. Drill for and prepare sufficient dowels.

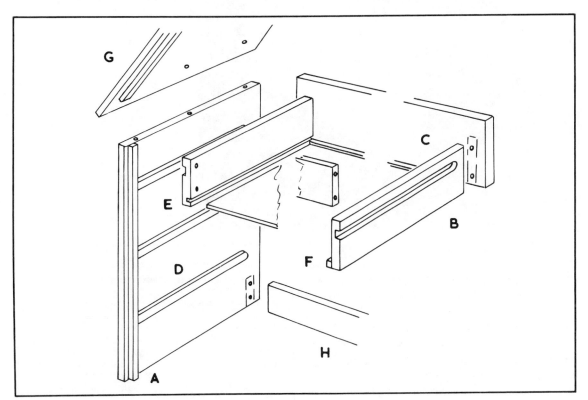

Fig. 7-24. How the parts of the small chest of drawers fit together.

Fig. 7-25. A small bedside cabinet made from veneered particleboard.

6. Join the parts together. Fit the back to hold the other parts square. Check that the assembly will stand level.

7. Make the door (Figs. 7-26C and 7-27D). It should be level at the sides and middle shelf, but may overhang at the bottom. Veneer any cut edges.

8. The door can swing on two thin hinges or throw-clear types might be fitted inside (Fig. 7-28). If spring hinges are used, there may be no need for a catch, otherwise fit a spring or magnetic fastener. Add a knob for opening.

Materials List for Small Bedside Cabinet

(all veneered particleboard unless marked)

2 sides	3/4 × 12 × 22
3 shelves	3/4 × 12 × 12
1 door	3/4 × 12 × 12
2 back fillets	3/8 × 3/8 × 11 hardwood
2 back fillets	3/8 × 3/8 × 7 hardwood
1 back	12 × 19 × 1/8 hardboard

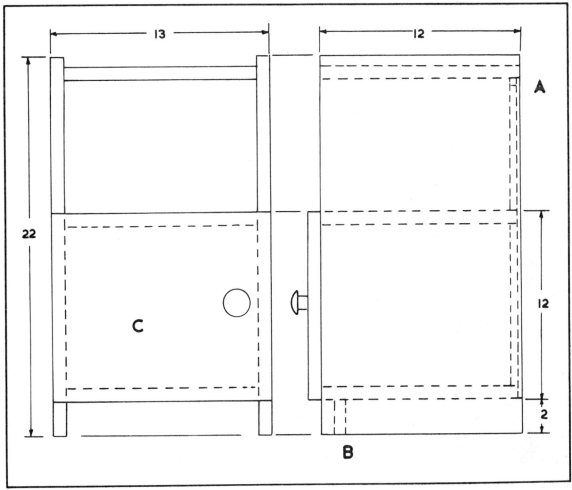

Fig. 7-26. Sizes of the small bedside cabinet.

DRESSER

A dressing table should provide one or more mirrors at a convenient height to use when standing or sitting. It should also have surface area suitable for many toilet articles. If it can also have drawers, it will store clothing and bedding. This dresser (Figs. 7-29 and 7-30) is a solid piece of furniture that does all that a good dresser should, and looks good as well.

The mirrors adjust so you can see yourself at several angles. The sunken top is shown with a glass cover. This and the two narrow drawers (Fig. 7-31) will hold a large accumulation of smaller items, while the full-width drawers have the capacity for anything up to folded blankets. The dresser proportions give an attractive appearance, but they could be modified to suit space or available materials.

The original dresser was designed to suit a quantity of mahogany already finished to a 3/4-inch thickness and 7-inch width. If wood is obtained in this section, it can be cut or made up to width so there is very little waste. The drawer interiors may be softwood. The handles shown are also mahogany, but this is a piece of furniture that might benefit in appearance from brass or other metal handles.

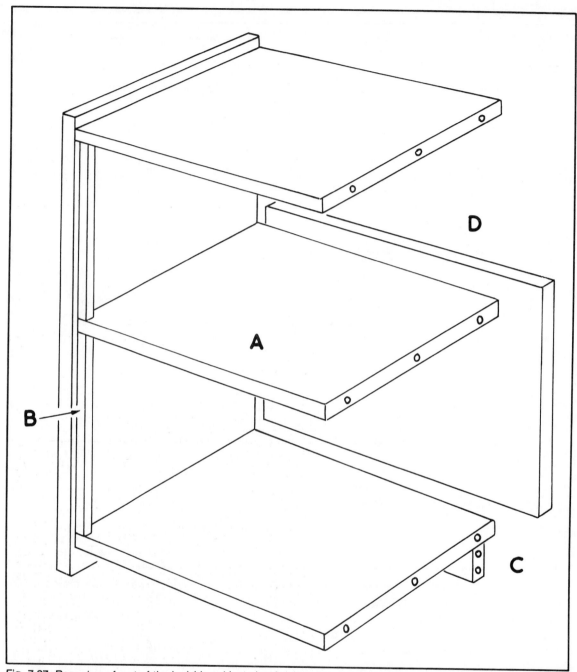

Fig. 7-27. Rear view of part of the bedside cabinet showing how the parts assemble.

It is possible to use the design for other materials, with a few adaptions. Veneered particleboard could be used for all the visible parts. It should have any cut ends veneered to match the surfaces and edges (Fig. 7-32A). Plywood could be used, but it should have an attractive veneer unless you intend to apply a painted finish. Edges should be lipped (Fig. 7-32B). You can get an attractive effect by having lips on the front edge in a color that contrasts with the surface veneer.

The choice of material will affect some details of construction. With solid wood you have the choice of a variety of joints, or you may substitute dowels in some parts. With particleboard or plywood, many cut joints are not practical and dowels must be used. Fortunately, dowels will give a satisfactory and sound construction, except the design may have to be altered slightly to accommodate them. The instructions assume the use of solid wood, with some guidance on what to do with other materials.

The top corners serve as examples of the variety of joints possible. The dresser in the photographs has secret dovetails, so the construction is hidden and only a miter shows on the surface. If dowels are used, in any material, the top may be level with the side. It is better with a slight overhang (Fig. 7-32C), however, particularly if you are using particleboard. The overhang prevents holes breaking out and hides any lack of tightness between parts.

In solid wood an alternative joint is a rabbet (Fig. 7-32D). In its simplest form glue could be supplemented by pins driven both ways, then set below the surface and covered with filler. As shown, thin dowels in the rabbet are hidden. If the overlap is rounded, the division between end and side grain will not be very apparent. This joint may be made with plywood, particularly if the plies are thick enough to make the overlap.

If you cannot make secret dovetails, but want to show your skill at dovetailing, you could use

Fig. 7-28. Throw-clear hinges allow the door to open, even if close to a wall or other piece of furniture.

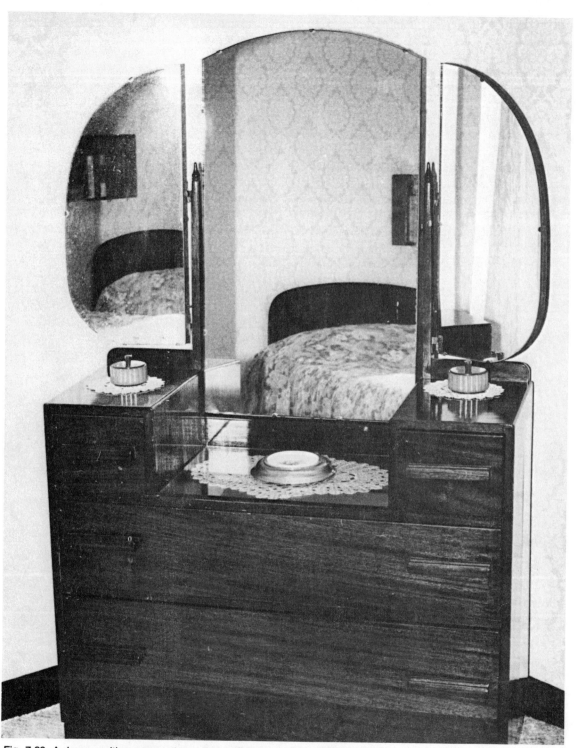

Fig. 7-29. A dresser with a recessed top, three mirrors, and four drawers.

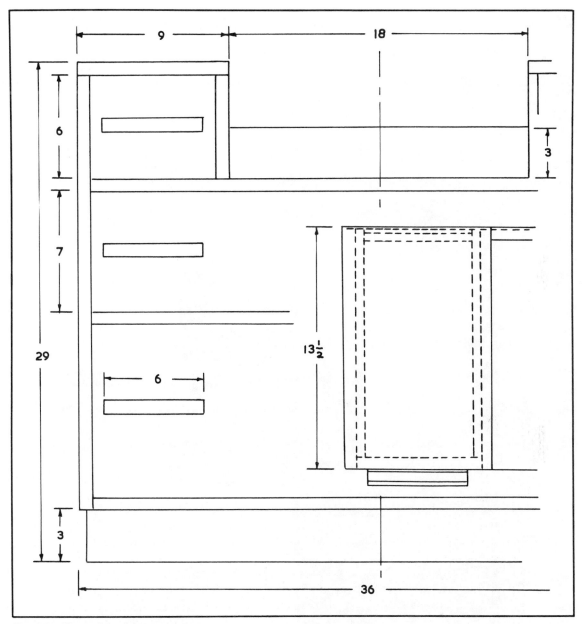

Fig. 7-30. Sizes of the dresser carcase.

stopped dovetails with the tails on the upright parts (Fig. 7-32E). The joints can be cut by hand or with the help of one of the power dovetail guides.

Where wide boards are required, it is probable they will have to be made by glueing narrow pieces—the 7-inch boards are convenient, but any pieces could be joined. So far as possible, match the grain. The pieces at the inside of the top drawer casing should have their grain vertical, although they are wider than they are deep. Prepare the pieces above the top drawers in the same way. The back may be hardboard or thin plywood.

173

Fig. 7-31. Each small drawer fits into a compartment at the side of the dresser.

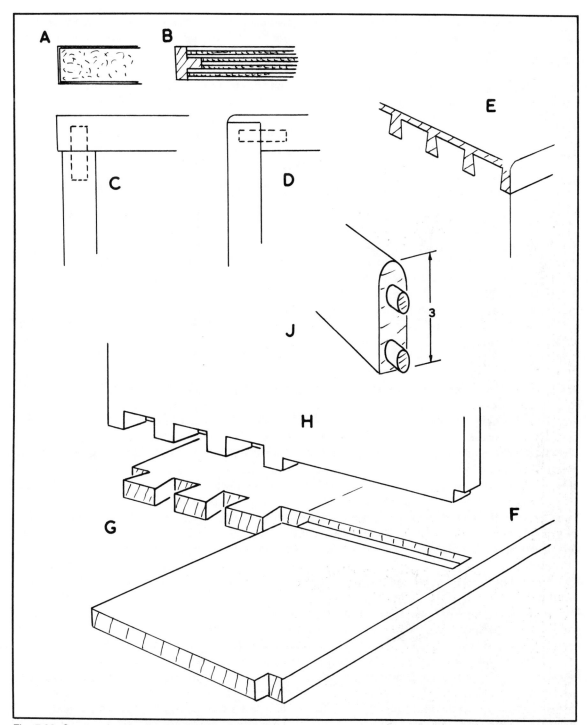

Fig. 7-32. Construction details of parts of the dresser.

1. Cut rabbets to suit the back on the rear edges of the sides, inner uprights, and the narrow tops. Mark out the pair of sides first as a guide to sizes when marking other parts (Fig. 7-33A). Allow for the actual thicknesses of wood and mark the depths of the drawers, but let the lower drawer come where it will, which will be about 10 inches. Some of the joint details can be marked later when the other parts are prepared, but at this stage you can determine their location. Leave a little excess wood at the ends.

2. Mark the inner uprights (Fig. 7-33B) to match the sizes on the sides.

3. The piece across that comes under the narrow drawers and forms the center recess could go all the way as a full-width board. If you have to glue to make up the width, only the front need go all the way (Fig. 7-33C). With this as a guide, mark the two narrow tops. The part across the recess does not have a rabbet at the back as it comes inside the plywood or hardboard, and there will be a cover strip in the recess over that edge.

4. Between the two long drawers there are strips across. At the front is a piece level with the edges of the sides. Cut it to fit into a stopped dado (Fig. 7-34A). There is a similar narrower piece at the back, but because its joint will be covered, there is no need for the dado to be stopped (Fig. 7-34B). After the two have been fitted, a drawer runner is screwed to each side (Fig. 7-34C).

5. At the bottom make two similar pieces to come between the bottom drawer and plinth, but at their ends dovetail into the sides. Fit drawer runners between these rails when the carcase (see Glossary) is assembled.

6. The top piece across can fit into wide stopped dado joints if it is taken full width across. If only half of it crosses, let it into narrower stopped dadoes (Fig. 7-34E) and screw on drawer runners behind it (Fig. 7-34F).

7. If the crosspiece is a full-width board, the inner uprights should be dowelled to it, whatever the material. An alternative for solid wood would be dadoes with tenons taken through as well, for maximum strength. If only part of the crosspiece goes all the way, the best joint for solid wood at the inner uprights combines a dado and dovetails. For the width of the extended part make a stopped dado (Fig. 7-32F). For the rest of the board width make dovetails (Fig. 7-32G). Note how the dado joint meets a pin of the dovetails (Fig. 7-32H).

8. The strip at the back of the sunk top (Fig. 7-32J) should have its top rounded and be prepared with short dowels at the ends. When it is fitted, it will be level with the edges of the inner uprights, so it overhangs the back of the part it rests on and will cover the edge of the carcase back. It will probably be sufficient to glue its long edge, but there could be screws upwards into it, if necessary.

9. Prepare the joints for the short top pieces above the drawers. Trim any excess length from the sides. See that ends are cut square.

10. Have all the joints prepared ready for assembly. This is not a project suitable for assembling in separate steps. Where dowels are to be used, make sure all holes are ready and dowels cut. Check parts in relation to each other. Crosswise parts should all be the same length between shoulders. Work should flow smoothly because there is little opportunity to make adjustments or alterations if preparations have been overlooked.

11. Assemble the long crosswise pieces to the sides. The dovetailed strips at the bottom will hold the sides in at that level. At the higher positions you might need clamps. You could also hold the joints tight with a few screws driven diagonally upwards through the dado joints, particularly if you need to release clamps for use elsewhere. Fit the recess back strip between the inner uprights and fit the uprights into the dadoes and dovetails of the main crosspiece. There can be screws through the dovetails, if needed to pull the joints tight, because they will be hidden in the finished dresser. Fit the short tops and check squareness of the whole assembly by measuring diagonals and correcting the shape before the glue sets.

12. Make the back from one piece of plywood or hardboard to fit into the rabbets, across under the strip in the recess, and low enough to cover the rear strip below the bottom drawer. Glue and screw the plywood in place.

13. The plinth lifts the dresser off the floor and

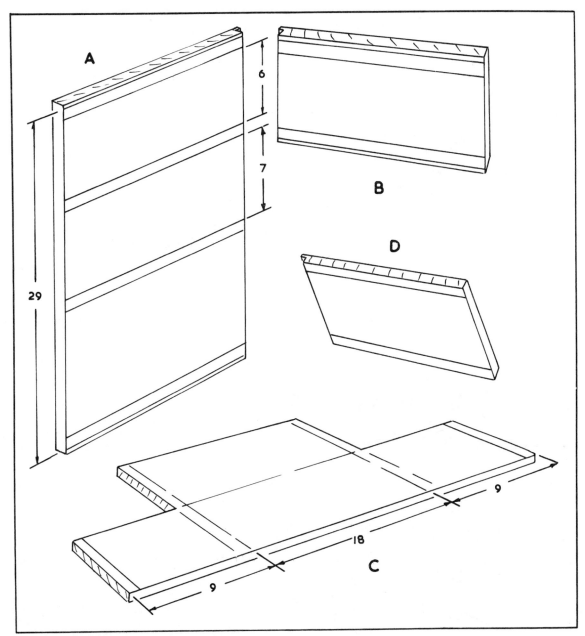

Fig. 7-33. Marking out the main parts of the dresser.

is set back at the sides and front by 1/2 inch for appearance and to make knocks from shoes less obvious. Unless the dresser is to stand in a position where it will be seen from all sides, there is no need for a back to the plinth. It is made of 3-inch wide strips mitered at the front, with the joints strengthened by blocks inside (Fig. 7-35). Fix it with screws driven downwards through the front strip and the bottom drawer runners. Make sure no screw heads stand above the wood surface.

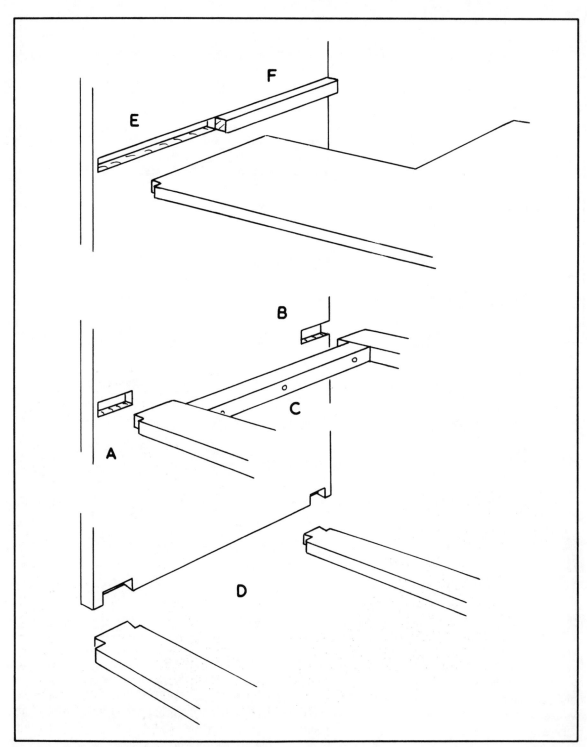

Fig. 7-34. Fitting the horizontal parts into an end of the dresser.

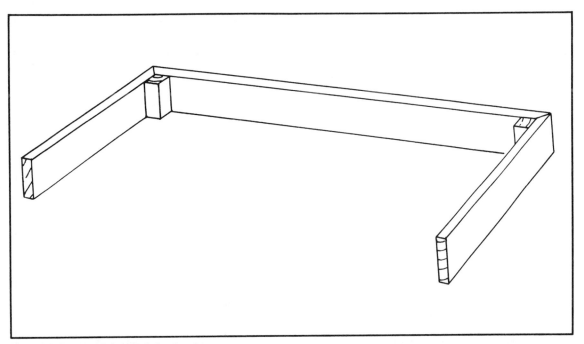

Fig. 7-35. Details of the plinth for the dresser.

Fig. 7-36. The drawers of the dresser are dovetailed and fitted with wooden handles.

14. It is suggested that the drawers (Fig. 7-36) are all made in the same manner in the traditional way, using dovetails. They could be made with simpler joints, but if this dresser is made in a good hardwood, it warrants the use of the best joints. The inner parts could be 1/2-inch softwood with thin plywood bottoms. Pieces will probably have to be joined to make up the width for the bottom drawer, but the others can be cut from 7-inch boards. The drawer fronts can stand forward about 1/8 inch from the framing and have rounded edges.

15. Prepare the material for a drawer. Groove

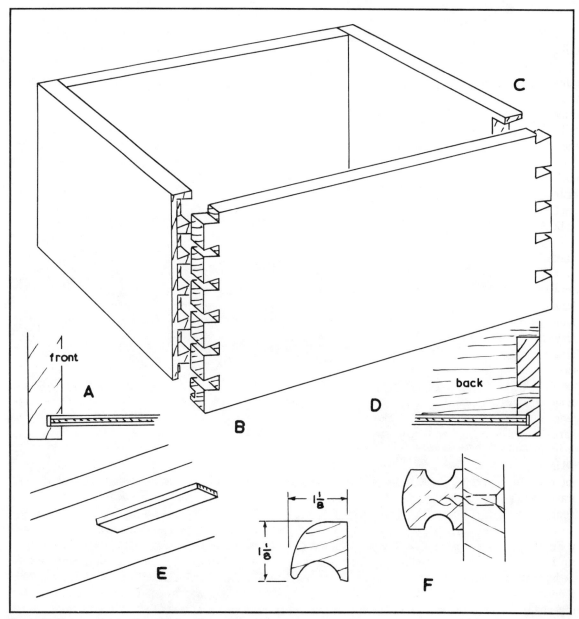

Fig. 7-37. Drawer construction and handle sections.

the front (Fig. 7-37A) and sides for the bottom. The drawer back will come above the bottom. Cut the front to be a close sliding fit into its opening. Cut the width of the drawer sides so they slide easily, although with minimum slackness in their openings. At this stage leave them too long. Make the back and bottom later.

16. Mark and cut the front joints. Cover the groove at the bottom of the front with a half dovetail at each side (Fig. 7-37B).

17. Make the sides short enough so they do not quite touch the carcase back when the front is in the right position. Mark and cut the joints for the drawer back (Fig. 7-37C) so the bottom half dovetail is high enough to take the bottom groove and the lower pin of the back (Fig. 7-37D).

18. Check the sizes of the drawer parts in the positions they have to fit. There can be some adjustment after they have been assembled, but the thickness of wood does not allow a great amount to be planed off.

19. Assemble a drawer with all the joints clamped tight. Make the bottom a little undersize so it will slide in easily from the rear under the drawer back. Leave it loose until the glue in the drawer joints has set. Clean off any excess glue and plane level any projecting parts of joints. Try the drawer in position and plane if necessary. When it is satisfactory, slide in the bottom and fix it by screwing upwards into the back.

20. Make all the drawers in the same way. Arrange stops under the rails at the front (Fig. 7-37E), centrally for the top drawers and a pair spread towards each side for the others. These should stop the drawer fronts when they are projecting about 1/8 inch from the carcase front. The drawers should not come against the back when pushed in. A drawer can be inserted or removed by tilting the front upwards so the back clears the stop.

21. Suggested sections for handles are shown in Fig. 7-37F. Make them in long lengths and cut off. Fix with glue and screws from inside. Center the handles across the top drawers and fit the others in line under them. To avoid the optical illusion of appearing too low, position each handle a little above the center of its front.

22. The supports for the mirrors have to be rigid because glass is heavy. The posts can be the same wood as used in general construction, but see that it is straight-grained. Cut the posts long enough to screw into the lower drawer dividers (Fig. 7-38A). Reduce that part to 1 inch thick. From 4 inches above the carcase top taper to a 3/4-inch square (Fig. 7-38B). For extra strength put a 1/4-inch dowel downwards into the top (Fig. 7-38C).

23. At the top of each post drill for the dowel from a finial (Fig. 7-38D), which you can turn or buy. Round the tapered edges of the posts, which must be fitted exactly vertical or the mirrors will exaggerate any discrepancies.

24. At the rear edges of the tops outside the posts fit short strips (Fig. 7-38E) with rounded edges and outer corners. Two dowels downwards will supplement glue.

25. Cut the plywood backboards for the mirrors and use them as templates when cutting or ordering the mirrors. The central mirror is a plain rectangle with a rounded top (Fig. 7-38F). Before deciding on its exact width, check the clearance needed for the pivots (see step 27). Set out the shapes of the side mirrors on a pattern of squares (Fig. 7-38G). If you modify the sizes, do not make the top angles of these mirrors too acute as they would be difficult to cut and liable to break in use.

26. Mount the mirrors to the backboards with metal clips over the edges. There will be a tendency for gravity to make the glass slide down, so have ample clips at the bottoms—four under the large mirror, then two at each side and top should be enough.

27. For the center mirror the pivots should screw to the posts and the curved pieces on the mirror backboard drop in. There should be a limited range of movement. These should provide enough friction to hold the mirror at any angle. If not, there can be a folding strut from the bottom of the backboard to the center of the rear rail below.

28. There could be ordinary hinges on the side mirrors. A neater one has a part with a pin on the mirror backboard dropping into a socket in a part on the post (Fig. 7-39). Fit two hinges on each side mirror.

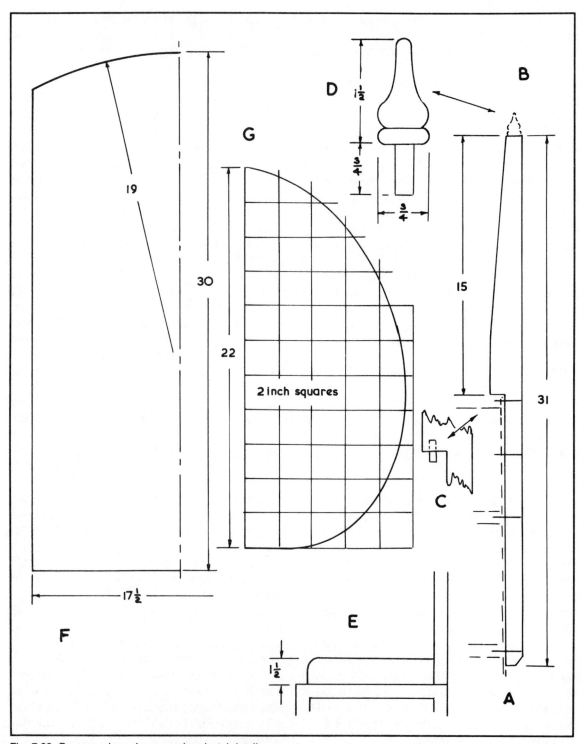

Fig. 7-38. Dresser mirror shapes and pedestal details.

Fig. 7-39. The central mirror has fittings that allow it to swing. The side mirrors are on vertical pivots. This side mirror has a friction arm to hold it in position.

Materials List for Dresser

carcase

2 sides	3/4 × 13 1/2 × 29
2 inner uprights	3/4 × 13 1/2 × 8 (grain short way)
2 tops	3/4 × 13 1/2 × 9 (grain short way)
1 top	3/4 × 13 1/2 × 36
2 drawer rails	3/4 × 3 × 36
2 drawer rails	3/4 × 2 × 36
1 back rail	3/4 × 3 × 18
2 back rails	3/4 × 1 1/2 × 9
6 drawer runners	3/4 × 1 × 8
1 plinth	3/4 × 3 × 35
2 plinths	3/4 × 3 × 13
1 back	26 × 36 × 1/8 or 1/4 hardboard or plywood

top drawers

2 fronts	3/4 × 6 × 8
4 sides	1/2 × 6 × 14
2 backs	1/2 × 6 × 8
2 bottoms	8 × 14 × 1/4 plywood

middle drawer

1 front	3/4 × 7 × 35
2 sides	1/2 × 7 × 14
1 back	1/2 × 7 × 35
1 bottom	14 × 35 × 1/4 plywood

bottom drawer

1 front	3/4 × 10 × 35
2 sides	1/2 × 10 × 14
1 back	1/2 × 10 × 35
1 bottom	14 × 35 × 1/4 plywood
6 drawer handles	1 1/8 × 1 1/8 × 6

mirrors

2 posts	3/4 × 2 × 31
2 finials	3/4 × 3/4 × 3
1 backboard	17 1/2 × 30 × 1/2 plywood
2 backboards	10 × 22 × 1/2 plywood

DRESSER STOOL

This is an upholstered stool (Fig. 7-40) intended for sitting in front of a dresser, but it could be a general-purpose seat for use in the bedroom or elsewhere. It could also be a piano stool.

The legs are splayed in the length, but parallel in the width. The top has a moderate overhang and its upholstery is adequate, although quite simple to make. Decoration is shown on the rails, but they could be left straight. The frame should be hardwood, probably matching other furniture in the room. The top covering could also match other fabrics nearby.

1. Set out half of the side view (Fig. 7-41A) to get the size and slope of each leg. The outside surfaces are straight. The slope starts 1 inch in from the edge of the top to directly under it at the floor. Both inner surfaces slope from 5 inches down to 1 inch square at the bottom (Fig. 7-41B).

2. Mark out the two pairs of legs. Cuts are square across the narrow way of the stool, but bevelled the other way. Leave some surplus wood at the top until after the joints have been cut.

3. Prepare the wood for the rails. Traditional joints to the legs are with tenons (Fig. 7-42A), made so the mortises meet and the ends of the tenons are mitered. You can also use 1/2-inch dowels. They can be staggered so the ends overlap in the legs (Fig. 7-42B), making a stronger joint than if they were on the same level and mitered.

4. Plow grooves on the inner surfaces (Fig. 7-42C) to take buttons to hold the top. Cut the mortise and tenon joints or drill for dowels.

5. If the lower edges of the rails are to be shaped, make templates of half or the whole shapes (Fig. 7-41C and D) working from the centers. Leave about 1 1/2 inches straight at each end. Mark the rails and cut the curves. Remove saw marks and take sharpness off edges.

6. Assemble the two long sides first, one over the other so they match, then add the short rails. If the top plywood has been cut to size, it can be used as a guide to flatness and squareness if the inverted framework is assembled over it.

7. Make buttons to hold the top (Fig. 7-42D). Two each side and one at the center of each end should be sufficient.

8. Plastic foam about 1 1/2 inch thick can be used for the top. Cut it slightly bigger than the plywood so it compresses at the edges when covered. Make the covering material large enough to go underneath to inside the rails when the stool is assem-

Fig. 7-40. A dresser stool with padded top.

bled (Fig. 7-42E) to keep a tidy appearance outside.

9. Tack the covering with enough tension to round the edges of the foam. Spacing tacks about 1 1/2 inches should suit most materials.

10. Fit the top to the framework with the buttons to test the fit, then remove the top while the woodwork is finished.

Materials List for Dresser Stool	
4 legs	1 1/2 × 1 1/2 × 16
2 rails	3/4 × 4 × 16
2 rails	3/4 × 4 × 13
1 top	14 × 17 × 1/2 plywood
6 buttons	1/2 × 1 1/2 × 1 1/2

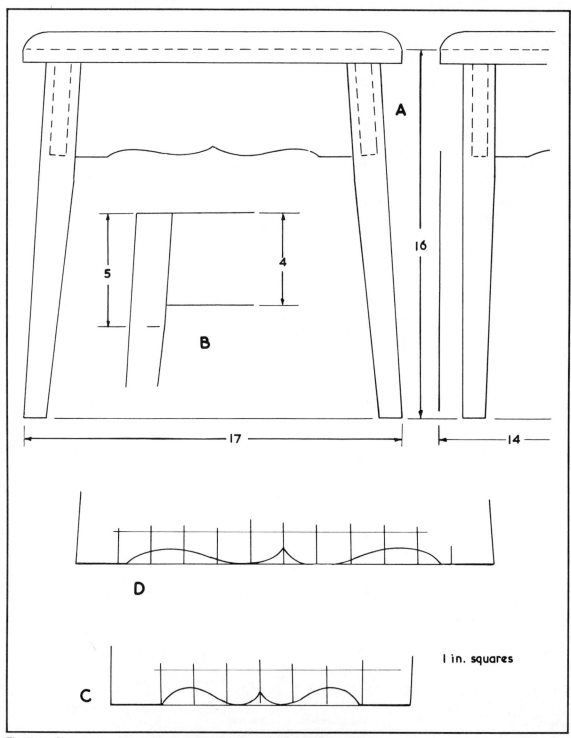

A

B

C

D

5

4

16

17

14

1 in. squares

Fig. 7-41. Sizes of the dresser stool and details of suggested edge decoration.

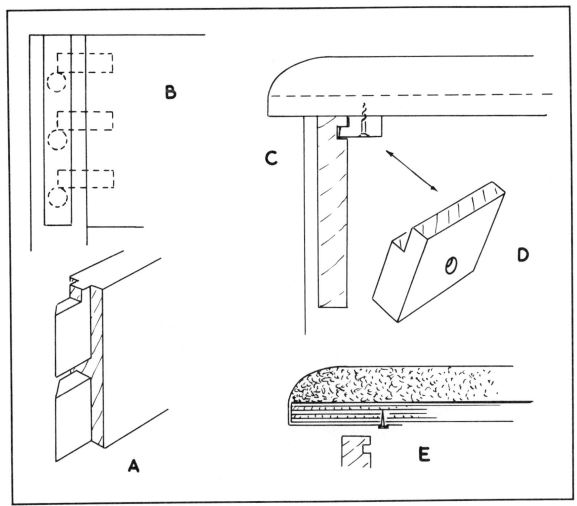

Fig. 7-42. Construction details of the dresser stool.

FULL-LENGTH MIRROR

A mirror that allows you to see yourself full length is welcome in a bedroom or dressing room. You can check to see if clothes fit correctly or to make sure everything is in place. Fortunately, to get a complete view of yourself does not necessitate having a life-size mirror. Because of the angle of sight in relation to the reflecting surface, you can see outside the actual dimensions of the mirror.

It is possible to arrange a comparatively small mirror that will reflect your full height, but that means careful angle and placing. It is usual to make the mirror bigger than the absolute minimum size to give ease of use and flexibility in positioning. The full-length mirror suggested (Fig. 7-43) gives a good view without the need for precise adjustment.

Glass is quite heavy, and a mirror of this size needs a strong frame and supports that are rigid and stable. It is unwise to use wood of very light sections. Heaviness in appearance is counteracted by rounding and tapering.

Sizes depend on the mirror. If it is possible, get a stock-size mirror within an inch or so of the drawn size (Fig. 7-44A). The mirror pivots should also be obtained before making the wood parts. Furniture hardware suppliers have several types of support

187

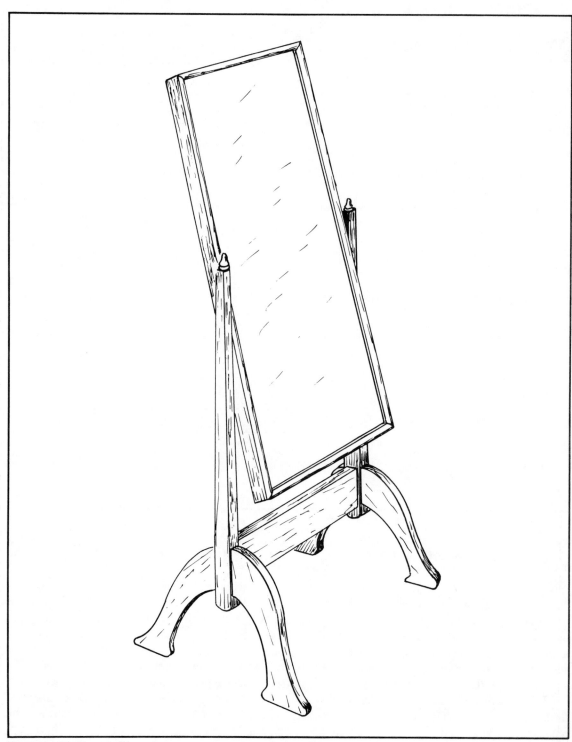

Fig. 7-43. A full-length tilting mirror.

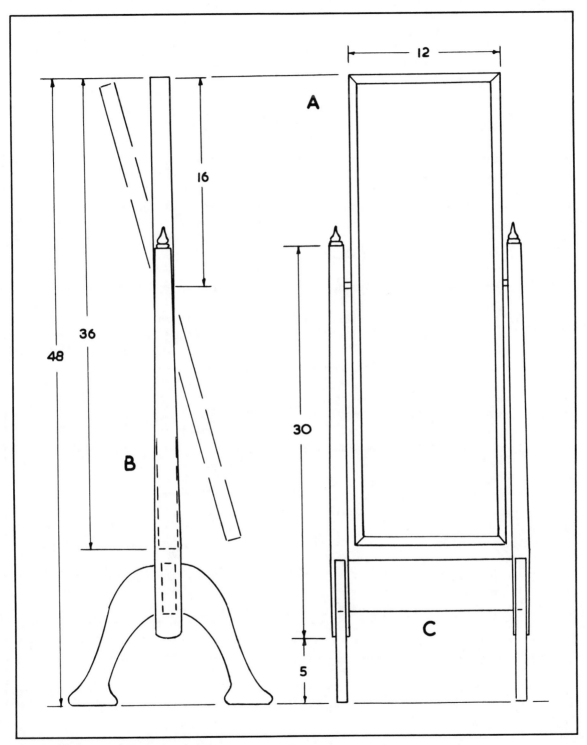

Fig. 7-44. Sizes of the full-length mirror.

for tilting mirrors. If possible, get a type that includes enough friction to hold the mirror at any angle. One suitable type has a tapered socket in a bracket to screw to the post and curved parts that drop into it and attach to the mirror side. The mirror is then held by its own weight, but can be lifted out. If the supports do not have enough friction, a folding metal strut between the center of the bottom of the mirror frame and the bottom rail will control the angle.

Choose a hardwood with reasonably straight grain, particularly for the posts. It is possible to mix woods effectively. The mirror frame could be a lighter color than its supports or the other way round.

The framed mirror with its supports governs other sizes, so make it first.

1. Prepare the wood for the mirror frame. Cut a rabbet to half the width and thickness (Fig. 7-45A). An elliptical rounding is shown on the front edge, but you could work any molding for which you have cutters.

2. Check the size of the mirror and make the frame so there is a small clearance all around. A tight fit might cause cracking. The edges of the mirror can be packed with strips of card to provide resilient packing and keep the glass central.

3. Miter the frame corners and reinforce the joints by drilling diagonally for 1/4-inch dowels (Fig. 7-45B). Glue the joints and the dowels, then plane the dowel ends level with the surfaces.

4. So the mirror does not reflect the grain in the rabbet, put black paint in the rabbet, whatever finish will be used outside.

5. There can be a trial assembly with the mirror, but delay its final fitting until all the wood is finished. Secure the mirror with strips of wood (Fig. 7-45C). These might be in short lengths, if it is not convenient to make them the full length of a side. Pin or screw them to the frame at fairly wide intervals. Close the back with a piece of thin plywood or hardboard. Keep it back from the frame edges and rounded so it is not very obvious from the front. If the glass is not to be installed in the frame until later, screw on the back temporarily to keep the

frame in shape while making the other parts for the support.

6. The posts are made from 1 1/2-inch by 2-inch wood, but the section is reduced for much of the length. Mark the post lengths and the positions of other parts (Figs. 7-44B and 7-45D). Taper from 8 inches above the lower end. In the wider direction taper equally from both sides to 1 1/4 inches at the top (Fig. 7-45E). In the other direction leave what will be the side towards the mirror straight, but taper the outside to 1 1/4 inches (Fig. 7-45F). Round the edges towards the top so the end finishes as a square with rounded corners. Drill centrally for the dowel of a finial. Suitable finials can be bought ready to fit, but a design is suggested if you want to turn your own (Fig. 7-45G). Round the bottoms of the posts, if you wish.

7. The rail has to provide the only transverse stiffness, and mortise and tenon joints (Fig. 7-46A) will give greater strength than dowelled joints. Arrange double tenons that go three-fourths of the way through the posts. Put the metal pivots against the sides of the mirror and measure the total width over them. This will be the length of the rail between its shoulders.

8. The feet must match each other and be mounted squarely because any errors will be very obvious. Draw the outline (Fig. 7-46B) and make a template, or complete one foot and use it to mark the others. Note that the grain should be in the long direction to reduce any risk of breakages at short grain. Leave on pieces for clamping (Fig. 7-46C) and cut them off after assembly. Round the exposed edges and give the feet a good sanding before assembling to the posts.

9. Assembly should be done in two stages. Glue and clamp the rail to the posts. Besides checking squareness, check that the width between the posts at the top is the same as at the bottom. Drill the legs and posts for 1/2-inch or 3/8-inch dowels. The dowels may enter the tenons to give both extra security.

10. The feet should stand without rocking. The bottom of one or more can be planed level so the posts stand upright.

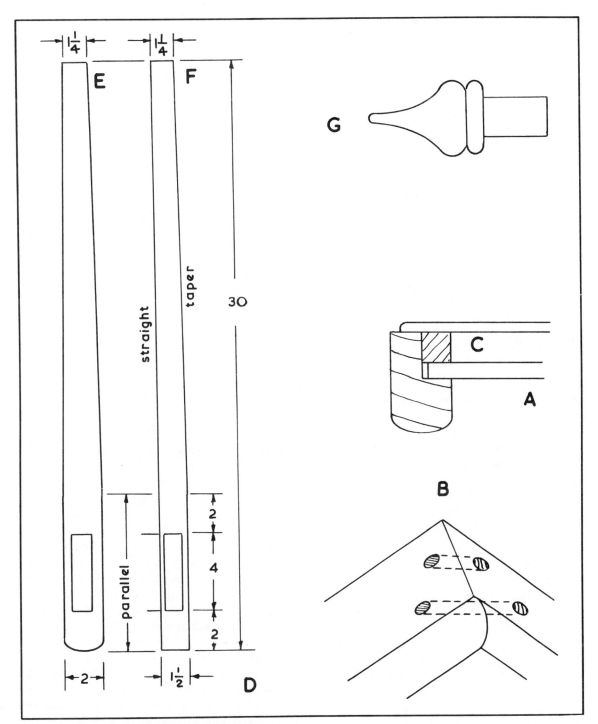

Fig. 7-45. Details of parts of the full-length mirror.

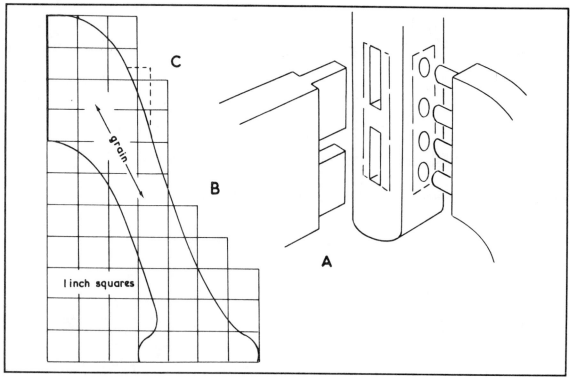

Fig. 7-46. Foot shape and assembly for the full-length mirror.

11. Sand, stain, and polish all the woodwork. Fit the mirror securely in its frame with its strips, which can be padded with paper to prevent damage to the mirror back. Screw the back on all round. Put the pivot fittings above the center of the mirror frame so it tends to swing to upright rather than turn over—how much depends on the friction in the pivots, but up to 2 inches above the center should be satisfactory.

Materials List for Full-length Mirror

2 mirror sides	3/4 × 1 1/2 × 36
2 mirror ends	3/4 × 1 1/2 × 12
2 mirror strips	3/8 × 3/8 × 35
2 mirror strips	3/8 × 3/8 × 11
1 mirror back	12 × 36 × 1/8 hardboard or plywood
2 posts	1 1/2 × 2 × 30
1 rail	1 × 4 × 16
4 feet	1 × 4 × 14
2 finials	1 1/4 × 1 1/4 × 3

CLOTHES RACK

A bedroom stand to hold your daytime clothes overnight will encourage tidiness and keep clothing in good shape. A stand has to be big enough to hold your clothing, yet not intrude too much into the available space.

This stand (Fig. 7-47) has a top that will take a shirt or blouse and jacket. Beneath it is a rail intended for slacks or pants or a skirt. At the bottom are rails for shoes or slippers. Other rails will take underclothing, stockings, ties, and similar things.

The legs, feet, and top rail should be made of hardwood to match nearby furniture. For a painted finish softwood might be chosen, but even under paint hardwood is stronger. The shaped top is 1/2 inch thick and would be most conveniently cut from plywood; it could also be made from solid wood. If the whole rack is to be stained, however, the plywood and dowel rails could be finished to match the main parts.

Check sizes in relation to your needs, but those

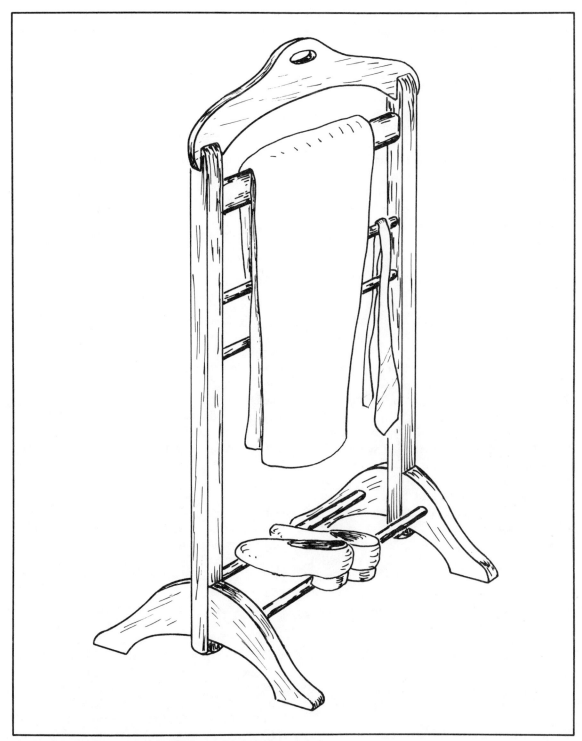

Fig. 7-47. A clothes rack holds daytime clothing overnight.

shown (Fig. 7-48) should be satisfactory. The feet occupy an 18-inch square on the floor. If you have to fit the rack into a confined space, the projection of the feet could be reduced by a few inches, with a slight loss of stability.

1. Make the two legs (Fig. 7-49A). Mark the slot at the top and the position of the rail. At the bottom the legs will extend 1 inch below the joint with the feet, and the end may be rounded. Leave the legs square, but later the top will be tapered and all edges rounded.

2. Mark out the shape of the top (Fig. 7-50A) symmetrically about a centerline. Except for where it will fit into the leg slots, round all edges thoroughly and sand them smooth. The hole is for lifting and should have its edges rounded.

3. Cut slots in the legs for the top (Fig. 7-49B). Taper and round the legs.

4. Make the rail (Figs. 7-48A and 7-49C) and cut the mortise and tenon joints. The rail is an important strength member, as well as somewhere to hang pants. Take stub tenons about halfway through the legs. Round the rail edges well.

5. Drill for the dowel rails (Fig. 7-48B). There could be two, as shown, or you could arrange others to suit your needs.

6. Mark out the feet (Fig. 7-50B). Use one to mark the others or make a template to mark them all. Make sure they match, are cleaned of saw marks on the edges, and have square surfaces where they will meet the legs. So the dowel joints can be clamped tightly, leave on small triangles (Fig. 7-50C) for the clamp, then cut these off and smooth the surfaces after the glue has set.

7. Drill the legs and feet for dowels (Fig. 7-50D). You can drill right through the legs, but it will be easier to get a tight assembly if the dowels are in two parts. Check that the two assemblies match and opposite feet are in line.

8. Make the shoe rails (Fig. 7-48C). They should penetrate the feet nearly 1 inch for strength, because they help maintain rigidity with the top rail.

9. Round the exposed edges of the legs and feet. Level any unevenness in the bottoms of the feet, if necessary.

10. Join the glued legs and feet with the top rail and round rods. Clamp the top rail tight. Adjust the width at the feet until the legs are the same distance apart at the bottom and top and the assembly is square.

11. Glue the shaped top into the leg slots. Glue alone might be sufficient, but you could put a dowel in each joint.

Materials List for Clothes Rack	
2 legs	1 1/4 × 1 1/4 × 34
4 feet	1 1/4 × 4 1/2 × 11
1 rail	1 × 2 × 18
1 top	1/2 × 8 × 20
2 rails	18 × 3/4 diameter
2 rails	18 × 1/2 diameter

WOVEN-TOP STOOL

A stool with interwoven cord forming a flat pattern on top can have a dual purpose. If made at the right height, it can serve as a seat in front of a dresser or when working on a table or as a bar stool. The slightly flexible top is more comfortable than a plain wood seat. With a close weave the stool can also serve as a table beside a bed or elsewhere.

Several materials can be used for the top. There are many attractive cords manufactured from man-made fibers, and the appearance of some natural cords also suit stools. Suitable cords are sold by craft shops especially for stool seating, or you can find other cords available in shops catering to boating needs. Seagrass is an attractive seating cord obtainable in hanks of natural color or already dyed. Most materials are available in several thicknesses. There is more work in weaving thin cord, and the result might not be as rigid when completed. Thick cord can be woven quickly, but if there are not many over-and-under tucks, the result is not so attractive. On this stool (Fig. 7-51), made 13 inches square, cord between 1/8-inch and 3/16-inch diameter should be satisfactory. Some cord is supplied in metric sizes; the near equivalents are 3 millimeters and 5 millimeters.

The frame is best made of strong hardwood. The joints should be mortise and tenon, because

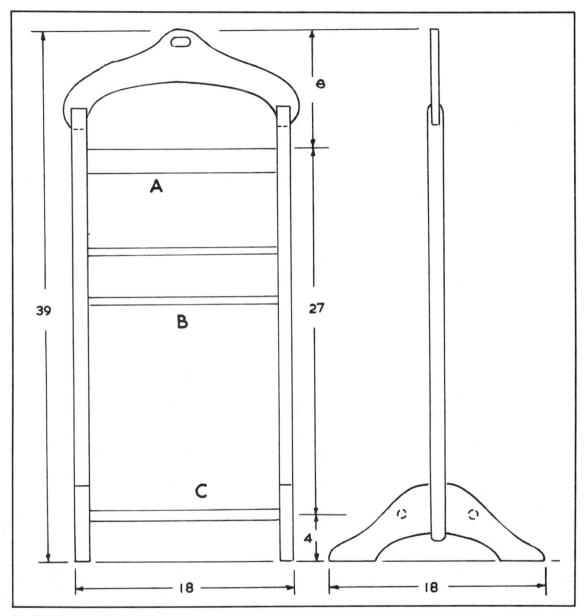

Fig. 7-48. Sizes of the clothes rack.

sections are not large enough for satisfactory dowel joints. If the stool is used as a seat, it must withstand the tendency of some users to rock on two legs. The combination of suitable wood, double lower rails, and good joints provide a good resistance to strain.

The frame can be stained and polished to match other furniture; the colors used in the top may match other fabrics. If there is no particular color needed, a natural cord one way and a colored one the other way suits most situations. Natural in both directions will give a traditional effect.

The framework has square rails at the top for the woven seat, and they must be at the same level.

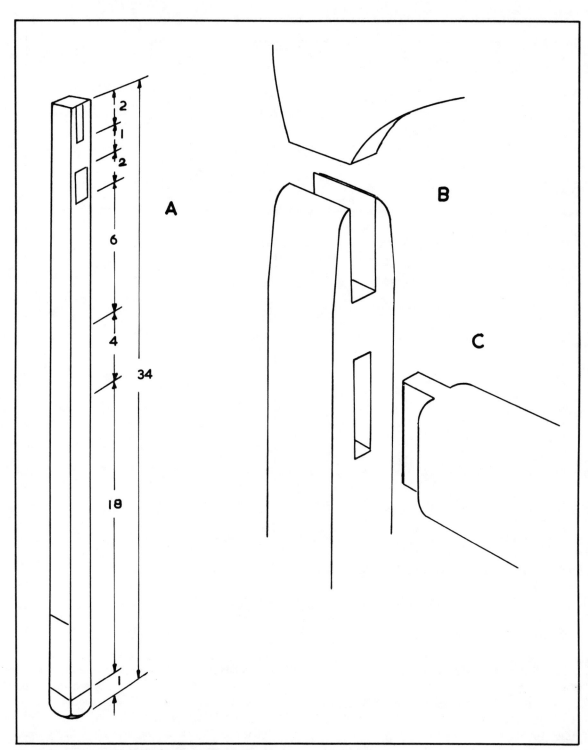

Fig. 7-49. Leg and rail details for the clothes rack.

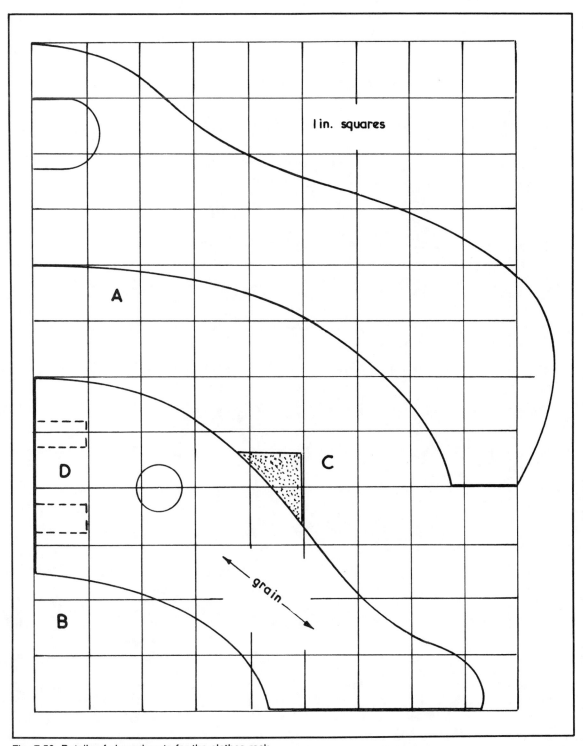

1 in. squares

A

C

D

B

grain

Fig. 7-50. Details of shaped parts for the clothes rack.

Fig. 7-51. A tall stool with a flat woven top can also be used as a bedside table.

The other rails can be higher one way than the other to allow tenons of greater length and strength. For maximum strength those rails have barefaced tenons, allowing thicker wood for maximum rigidity.

The sizes suggested make a stool that is a compromise between a seat and a bedside table. In a bedroom it can then have alternative uses.

1. Cut the wood for the legs overlong at first. Mark them together (Fig. 7-52A), so sizes match, but pair them in twos for the different heights of

the lower rails (Fig. 7-52B).

2. The stool does not have to be square, although that will suit most needs. It is shown 13 inches square over the legs, but it could be 12 inches by 15 inches or any size you wish. Mark the length between shoulders of all rails together if square, or all together each way if not square. It is the length between shoulders that is important—the actual tenons can be left long until the joints are cut.

3. Mark the top tenons long enough to almost

198

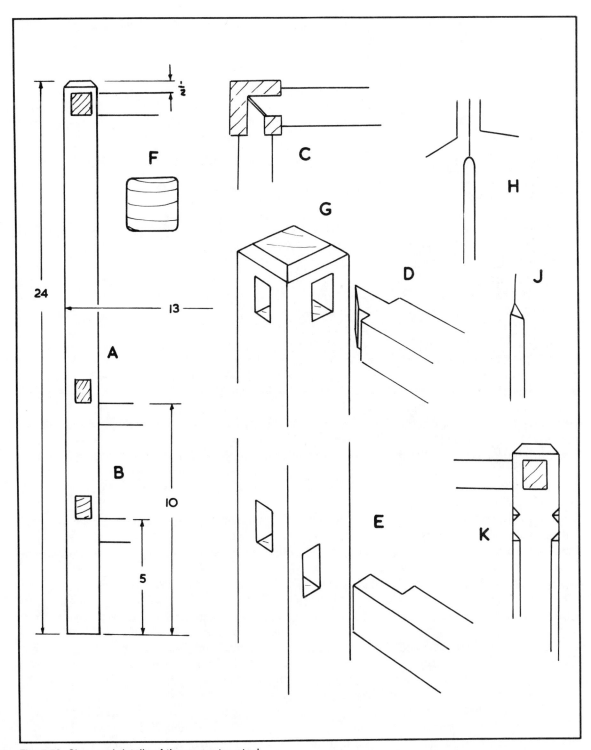

Fig. 7-52. Sizes and details of the woven-top stool.

meet (Fig. 7-52C). This will be about 1 inch, although the mitered ends reduce the effective length (Fig. 7-52D). Tenon thickness may be 1/2 inch. Mark and cut the tenons and their mortises at the same time.

4. For the lower rails cut away one side to leave tenons about 1 inch long (Fig. 7-52E). Mark mortises to suit.

5. Round the top rails slightly (Fig. 7-52F). Except for taking the sharpness off edges, leave the lower rails as they are.

6. Cut the legs to length. The tops could be rounded, shaped to a shallow cone, or bevelled all round, as shown (Fig. 7-52G). In the finished stool the tops of the legs are prominent; make sure shaping is even and surfaces are smooth.

7. The legs can be left square, but if some decoration is required, this can be done in the gaps between the bottom rails and the top. With a lathe you could do some turned decoration. Another way is to put a chamfer or bevel on the outer or all edges. A router would make a chamfer with rounded ends (Fig. 7-52H). The traditional *wagon bevelling* has triangular ends (Fig. 7-52J). The name comes from the decoration done on the edges of wood in oldtime wagons. A router bevel could be converted by handwork with a chisel. A further step is to make little nicks beyond the main bevels (Fig. 7-52K).

8. Any lack of squareness will be very obvious, so assemble carefully. Make up two opposite sides squarely and without twist. See that they match. Add the rails the other way, again checking squareness and measuring diagonals. It helps to assemble on a flat surface where you can stand back and look at the stool from several directions. If it looks right, you have a good stool. To get tight joints they should be clamped. If you do not have many clamps, pull the joints tight one way, then drive fine nails through the tenons from the inner surfaces of the legs. You can then move the clamps to the next joints.

9. For most stools it is advisable to stain and polish the wood before weaving the top. You might want to give a final coat of polish or varnish after the top has been worked because it is difficult to

avoid some abrasion of the wood as you move the stool around during weaving.

Weaving

10. The top is woven with groups of strands across and wraps around the rails between them, with the same arrangements both ways. Several combinations are possible, but four across and two wraps will make a pleasing top.

11. Make two or three shuttles from scrap wood (Fig. 7-53A). Exact sizes are not important. These are for winding cord used in putting on the pattern in the first direction.

12. Knot the end of the cord and tack it into a leg under a rail (Fig. 7-53B). Put on four turns across the stool with only a moderate tension; how tight depends on the stretch in the cord. Weaving the other way will tighten these turns. You have to judge the amount of tension needed to get a taut top.

13. Wrap around the rail opposite to where you started (Fig. 7-53C). Return underneath and wrap twice round the near rail (Fig. 7-53D). Take four more turns across and so on until you have covered the rails that way. Always wrap at the far side before the near side or you will get a diagonal crossing on top. Press the turns close together along the rails, but adjust the spacing so you get a full set of four across on completion. Finish by tacking to a leg underneath a rail in the same way as at the start.

14. If you have to join cords, make the knots underneath. Almost any joining knot will do, but the traditional one is a weaver's knot. Bend one end back and work the other around it (Fig. 7-53E, F, G).

15. In the other direction you cannot use the shuttles. Instead, you cut the cord into lengths as long as you want to handle. To weave them, make a wooden needle. Ash or hickory is best, but almost any wood will do if you are making one stool. Keep the needle thin—1/2 inch wide and 1/8 inch thick will do. The length should be more than the distance across the top. Put two holes in the end for the cord (Fig. 7-53H). With it you need a pointed rod, which could be a 1/2-inch dowel rod or a square

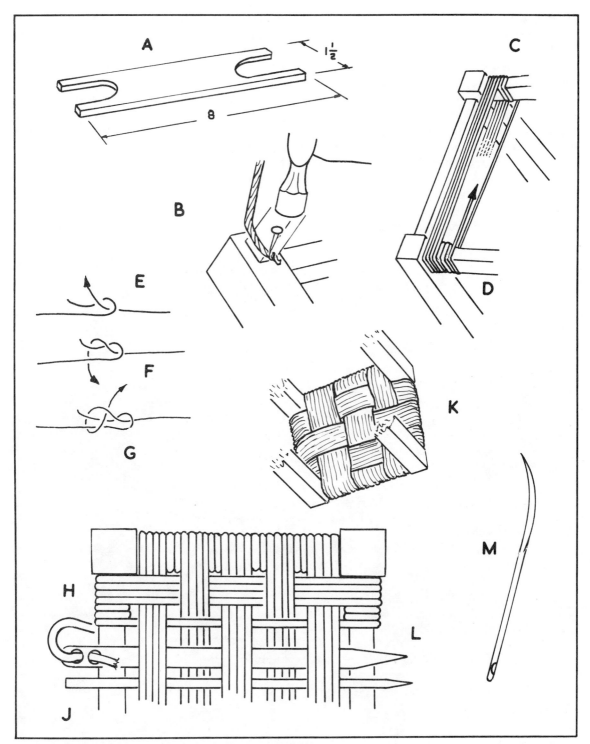

Fig. 7-53. Tools, knots, and method of weaving the top of the stool.

piece about the same section (Fig. 7-53J). Make the rod as long as the needle.

16. Tack the knotted end of the cord as you did in the first direction. Push the pointed rod through to separate the up and down groups. Pass the needle through, pulling the turns tight as you go. After four turns, push close together, wrap at the far side and return underneath to wrap on the near rail. There is no need to work the pattern underneath, but merely going across without tucking is unsatisfactory. A large interweave (Fig. 7-53K) will hold the cords together.

17. Pull out the rod and insert it in the opposite arrangement of cord groups, then pass the needle again (Fig. 7-53L). Continue in this way, pushing the turns close along rails and straight across the top. They will tend to curve. Use the point of the rod or needle to pull earlier groups of tucks back into straight lines.

18. As you get some way along with the tucking, tension will make it difficult to use the rod, so tuck with the needle as far as possible. Towards the end you cannot use the wood needle and might have to pass the cord end alone, but it is useful to have a steel needle (Fig. 7-53M) to pick your way across. It will help to pull earlier rows slightly hollow to make more space for the final tucking.

19. Check with a straightedge in both direc-

Fig. 7-54. Stool has its top worked in the traditional rush pattern.

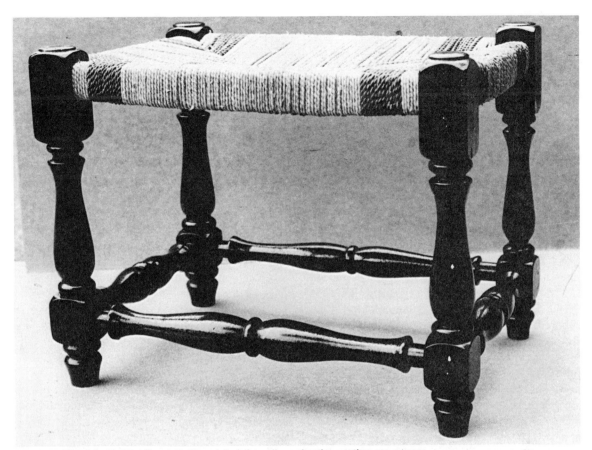

Fig. 7-55. Stool frame has its parts turned, but the rails under the seating are square.

tions and use the point of the rod to pull the rows straight. Finally tack underneath in the same way as at the start.

Materials List for Woven-Top Stool	
4 legs	1 1/2 × 1 1/2 × 24
4 top rails	1 × 1 × 13
8 lower rails	3/4 × 1 × 13

RUSH-PATTERN STOOL

A traditional method of seating stools and chairs used rushes twisted into a rope as work progressed. The resulting pattern was in a form tapering downwards from the corners to the center to provide an attractive and comfortable seat. The finished top design (Fig. 7-54) hides its method of construction, and the work of early craftsmen was probably regarded as a trade secret. In fact, the method of making such a seat top is surprisingly simple.

Twisting rushes may still be possible, but it is much easier and more convenient to use prepared cords. Very fine line is not advisable, but any natural or synthetic cord up to a 1/4-inch diameter can be used. The nearest in appearance to the traditional rushes is seagrass. It is in a form of rope sold by craft shops in its natural brown/green color or dyed in a few bright colors.

This stool could also be seated with a checker pattern, as described for the tall stool (Fig. 7-53). The rush pattern could be worked on that stool, but because it dips to the center to add to seating comfort, it would not be level enough for use as a table as well.

The stool frame shown (Fig. 7-55) has turned legs and lower rails. A design that does not need the use of a lathe is also suggested.

It would be unwise to use softwood because it might not provide sufficient strength in the joints. Any furniture hardwood can be used and finished as you wish. It is advisable to do any staining and at least the first coat of polish or varnish before working the top. Apply only a finishing coat later to reduce the risk of marking the seat with finishing materials.

The suggested size (Fig. 7-56) makes a comfortable occasional seat or footstool. It might be altered to a square or to a different size, but any variations will not affect the working of the top. Wood sections could be reduced slightly for a lighter stool, but a fairly substantial appearance of the framework goes with this type of top.

1. The wood for the legs should be carefully squared, although much of it will be turned away. Allow extra length at the tops for driving at the headstock. The tail center could go directly into the bottom of the leg. Center the wood by drawing diagonals so the square section runs true in the lathe.

2. It helps to mark the limits of the square parts before mounting the wood in the lathe. Use a narrow strip of wood to mark the positions of the parts of the turning. You can hold it alongside your work as a guide to where to cut. After turning one leg you can use it as a pattern as you turn others. You can use your own ideas for a leg pattern, but the suggested design (Fig. 7-57A) is a suitable match for the rails and seat.

3. Turn the parts between the squares, then the foot end. Round the corners of the squares. Get that part satisfactory before dealing with the top. At that end reduce the wood enough to turn a shallow button. Slightly dome the button and turn it down as far as possible before parting off. Because the buttons are prominent in the completed stool, do any hand sanding necessary to get a good shape and surface.

4. The shape of the long rails is shown (Fig. 7-57B). The short rails are similar, with the ends and central bead, but with the long curves shortened.

5. At the end of the rails turn the wood parallel or with a very slight taper to fit the holes that will be drilled in the legs. Use the drill (7/8 inch is suitable) to make a hole in a thin scrap piece of wood for testing the rail ends.

6. The top rails are 1 inch by 1 1/2 inches, with tenons 1/2 inch thick (Fig. 7-57C). Round the edges that will come under the seating cord. Mark and cut the mortises in the legs deep enough to meet, then miter the ends of the tenons (Fig. 7-57D).

7. The holes for the lower rails need not go quite as deep (Fig. 7-57E). The rail ends should be partially mitered (Fig. 7-57F).

8. Assemble the two long sides first. Clamp the top rail joints tight. Their shoulders will set the size, but you can move the bottom rail joints in or out to get the assembly square. The joints can be locked while the glue is still soft with pins or fine nails driven through them from inside the legs. See that opposite sides match. Add the rails the other way and leave the framework on a flat surface while the glue sets.

9. Do any preliminary finishing that seems advisable before working the top. The top rails will be completely hidden; there is no need for stain or polish on them.

10. To make a stool without a lathe, the square legs can be bevelled top and bottom (Fig. 7-56A). The bottom rails can be square and may be a little higher than in a turned stool frame (Fig. 7-56B). The legs could be left plain, although wagon bevelling will improve appearance (Fig. 7-56C).

Seating

11. Make a few scrap wood shuttles for winding the cord, rope, or seagrass (Fig. 7-53A). A wooden needle and a pointed rod, also on that drawing, are not essential. They can be used towards the end of the pattern, if you have them.

12. Load several shuttles with cord. The amount on each does not matter. Nearly all joins will be hidden inside the pattern.

13. Knot one end of cord and tack it to the inside of a rail (Fig. 7-58A). From there take the cord over the next rail close to the leg, underneath and

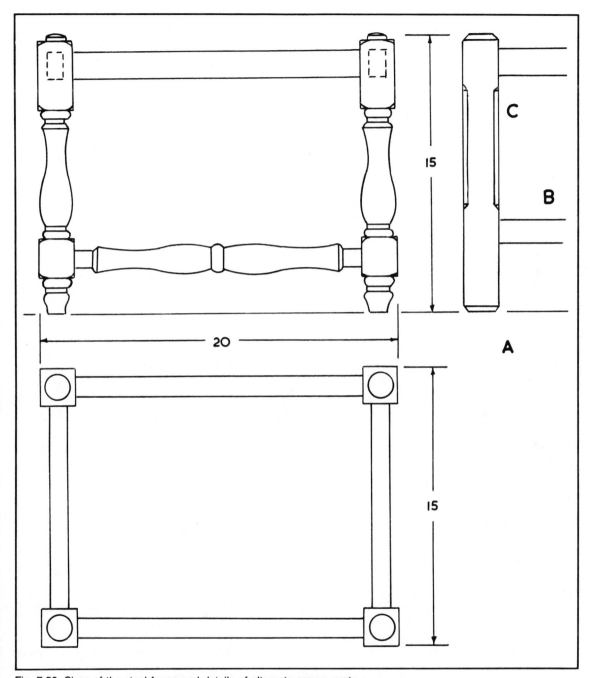

Fig. 7-56. Sizes of the stool frame and details of alternate square parts.

back over and under the first rail (Fig. 7-58B). That is the entire action that has to be mastered. Most further work is just repetition.

14. From the first corner go to the rails at the next leg and do the same. Pull as tight as possible with every action you take. When you come around

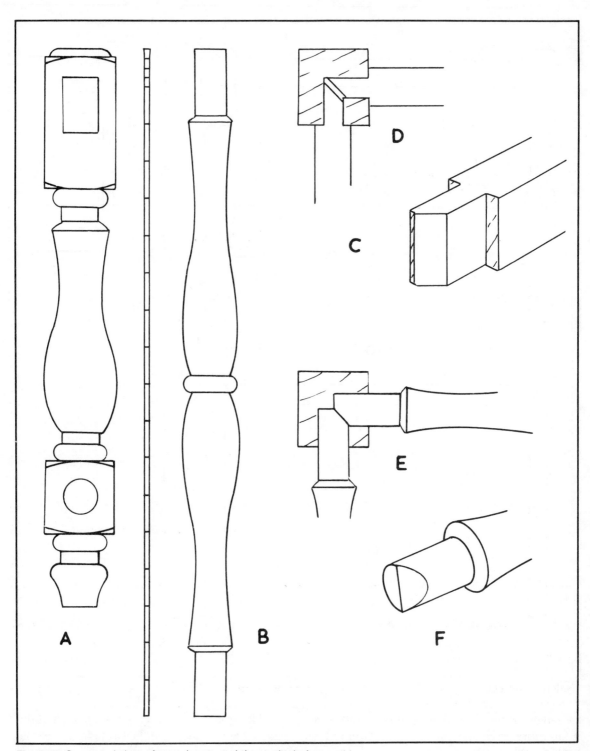

Fig. 7-57. Suggested sizes of turned parts and the method of assembly.

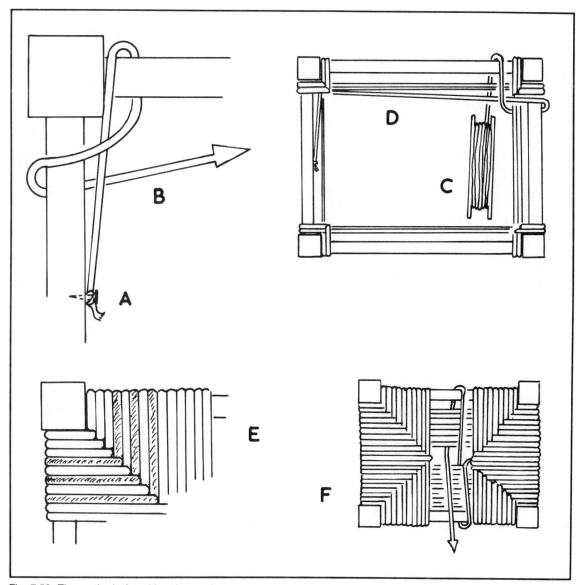

Fig. 7-58. The method of working the stool seat.

to the corner where you started, make the next wraps close alongside the first, and so on (Fig. 7-58C).

15. This will build up a pattern of turns developing from each corner, with the same design above and below. Check tension and squareness. Keep the turns pushed tight towards the legs so the rails do not show between turns. Check frequently that the lines of cord are square at each corner, and the lines of the pattern on top point squarely towards the opposite sides.

16. The cords going from corner to corner will be hidden when the seat has been completed. Any joins should be made along them (Fig. 7-58D) with weaver's knots (Fig. 7-53E, F, G).

17. There is little scope for variations in the pattern, but you can include other colors. They could be worked in anywhere and look best near

Fig. 7-59. Nearing the end of working the stool seat, with figure-eight turns being taken. The lengthwise parts that will be hidden may be seen in the space.

the corners (Fig. 7-58E). Arrange the colored cords as you wish. Make sure you have the same full arrangement showing on top at each corner, with knots where you change color in the lines between corners.

18. Continue until the short rails are filled. Press the turns tight along the rails so you get in as many as possible on the short rails. Insufficient turns here will lead to gaps near the center of the seat.

19. Change to going over and under in a figure-eight manner on the long rails (Fig. 7-58F). As with the previous wrapping, pull every turn tight as it is made and press the turns tight together on the rails. Use a pointed stick to push them close at the crossing. If you have to make any joins in this part, have the knots underneath. Leave the ends a few inches long so they can be turned in and buried.

20. Get in as many figure-eight turns as possi-

ble (Fig. 7-59). You will not be able to use a shuttle, but the loose cord must be passed through. A wood needle (Fig. 7-53H) is useful. Finally, gaps to pass the end will have to be forced open with a pointed stick to allow the maximum number of turns to be passed.

21. Take the last turn under and tack through it into the rail. Cut off with a few inches to bury inside.

Materials List for Rush-pattern Stool

4 legs	2 × 2 × 17
2 bottom rails	1 1/2 × 1 1/2 × 20
2 bottom rails	1 1/2 × 1 1/2 × 15
2 top rails	1 × 1 1/2 × 20
2 top rails	1 × 1 1/2 × 15

Chapter 8

Child's Room

A child's room is often more than just a bedroom. It might serve a child from babyhood right up to the teenage years, so its contents must change. It might also be the place for playing and studying. Some of the requirements are similar to those for an adult, although sometimes scaled down, but there are many specialized needs.

Some of the furniture described for other rooms also has a place in a room for children, and there are things described in this chapter that could have uses elsewhere. Furniture in a child's room has to suit his or her size and be functional and attractive, in that order. A child is more concerned with the use of a thing than with its appearance. Furniture needs to stand up to misuse and be safe. If a child can damage himself or the furniture, there is a good chance that he will find a way of doing that.

Safety should be kept in mind at all times during construction. Joints must be strong, corners should be rounded, edges should be smooth and unlikely to splinter. There should be no projecting nail or screw heads and nothing that small hands could pry away. Paint or other finishes should be nontoxic if a youngster bites or sucks them.

FOLDING CRIB

A crib is an important item for a year or two of a child's life, then it may not be needed again for some time. It is helpful if it can be taken down or folded for storage. Being able to fold it is also useful if you want to take it with you on an overnight visit.

A crib, whether it folds or not, must be stable. A boisterous child must not be able to rock it over. He should not be able to get out. There should be no risk of him getting hurt. There must be no gaps he can get his head through. Any access arrangements have to be secure against investigating hands from inside.

Although the crib may not have long-term use, it should look good and blend with other furniture. To keep it light and of good appearance it should be made of hardwood and given a good finish.

Sizes depend on the mattress. A common size is 24 inches by 48 inches. The mattress should be obtained first so variations of size can be allowed for. This crib (Fig. 8-1) is designed around a mattress of that size. One or both sides of the crib can be swung down for easy access. The mattress frame holds the crib in shape. When it is lifted out the two ends fold inwards to bring the sides towards each other. Although height and length remain the same, the closed thickness is no more than 6 inches. There is no fear of inadvertent folding when the crib is in use.

Most parts are made from square strips, with the upright spindles made from dowel rods. To en-

Fig. 8-1. A folding crib may have one or both sides lowered. When the mattress frame is removed, the ends hinge so the sides fold flat.

sure satisfactory construction, make sure all the wood sections are the same before you start.

Check that sizes suit your mattress (Fig. 8-2A). It is the inside measurement between the legs (Fig. 8-2B) that is important. The mattress frame (Fig. 8-2C) fits between the sides and its ends extend through the ends of the crib.

1. Mark out the four legs. If only one side is to swing open, the front legs (Fig. 8-3A) will not have top mortises. They will be joined with rails lower down. If the other side is to open, it is made the same, otherwise rails will come at top and bottom (Fig. 8-3B).

2. At the same time, mark out the ends of the opening frame (Fig. 8-3C).

3. The lengthwise rails (Fig. 8-2D) are all the same. At the ends arrange stub tenons into the legs (Fig. 8-3D). Mark all the rails together for the spindle holes, which can be at 4-inch centers. If making the crib to other sizes, do not exceed this spacing between spindles because of the risk of a child getting his head through. Use a stop on the drill press to get all holes the same depth—5/8 inch deep is suitable.

4. Cut mortises in the legs and round the leg tops (Fig. 8-3E). Join the rails to the legs with spindles between them. Check that the opposite sides match, are square, and without twist.

5. Make the opening frame an easy fit between its legs. Use simple tenons at the top (Fig. 8-3D), but haunch them at the bottom (Fig. 8-3F). Space the spindles to match those in the fixed part.

6. The two end frames are in two parts so they will fold (Fig. 8-2E), but they should be made the full width and cut apart after the spindles have been glued in. Mark the rails for six spindles equally spaced (Fig. 8-2F). To keep the rails the same distance apart as those in the unopening side, use two pieces of scrap wood as spacers while glueing in the spindles (Fig. 8-2G). Cut the rails at their centers and mark the meeting ends to avoid confusion during assembly.

7. Fit hinges inside and out on the ends (Fig. 8-2E) and test the folding action. At the back, hinge to the long rail. At the front, hinge to the leg.

8. Make the mattress frame (Fig. 8-2C) with its sides long enough to pass through the crib ends. Make the ends of the mattress frame to hold the sides far enough apart to slip inside the legs at the corners. Join the frame parts with stub tenons (Fig. 8-3G). Round the projecting ends.

9. Cover the mattress frame with a wire mesh or thin plywood or hardboard. If the base is made in this way, drill ventilating holes in it (Fig. 8-3H)—1-inch holes spaced 6 inches apart should be satisfactory. Nail or screw the base to the frame.

10. Hinge the opening frame to the rail below it. If necessary, notch to clear the hinges on the folding ends. At its ends the opening frame can be held up with bolts on the outside (Fig. 8-3J).

11. Sand all parts. Take off all sharp edges and corners. The screws to the hinges should fit level and not be roughened by a slipping screwdriver. Pay particular attention to the hinges joining the ends to the inside of the legs because they will be within reach of prying hands. If necessary, file off the edges and corners of these hinges.

Materials List for Folding Crib

4 legs	1 1/4 × 1 1/4 × 36
4 rails	1 1/4 × 1 1/4 × 50
4 rails	1 1/4 × 1 1/4 × 24
2 opening frames	1 1/4 × 1 1/4 × 14
2 opening frames	1 1/4 × 1 1/4 × 48
2 mattress frames	1 × 2 × 51
2 mattress frames	1 × 2 × 24
1 mattress base	24 × 48 × 1/8 or 1/4 hardboard or plywood
34 spindles	24 × 1/2 dowel rods

LOW STACKING BEDS

With two children sleeping in a room, there may be little space around the beds and other furniture for play space. Even if there is normally only one adult or child sleeping in the room, you might need an extra bed occasionally for a guest. One solution to these problems is to arrange two beds that will stack. If the beds are made low, it is possible to have the combination little more than the height of

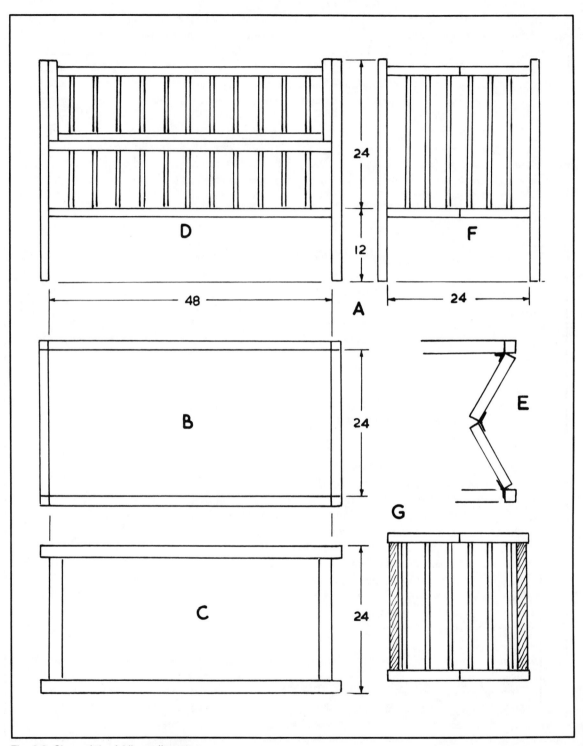

Fig. 8-2. Sizes of the folding crib parts.

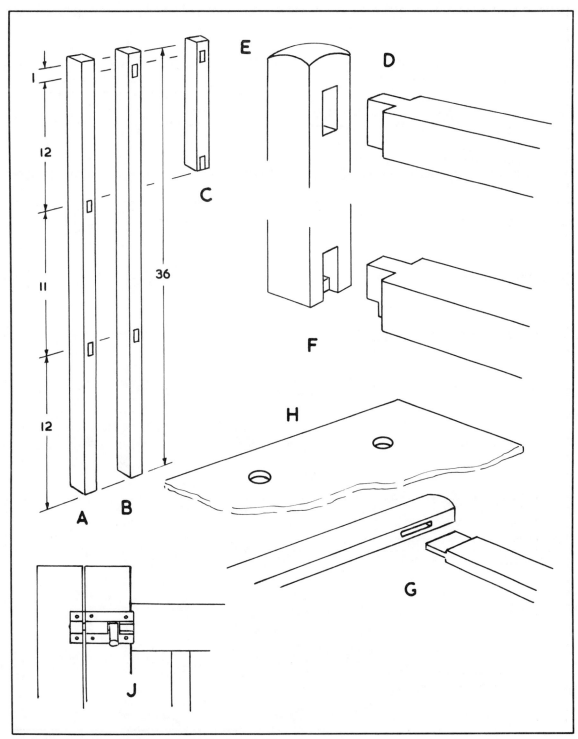

Fig. 8-3. Leg sizes and construction details of the folding crib.

a single bed. While the separated beds may be low, they are not so close to the floor as to be inconvenient to use.

If a room is to have day use, it is possible to cover the stacked beds so they appear as a single settee. Pillows could then become daytime cushions, possibly with covers to match the bed covering. In this pair of beds (Fig. 8-4), removable headboards are suggested (Fig. 8-5A). They could be stored under the bottom bed. It is possible to leave bedding on the mattresses, but whether it will

be possible to leave the pillows on the lower one depends on the thickness of its mattress.

The beds are drawn to fit mattresses 30 inches wide by 78 inches long and up to 6 inches thick. It is advisable to get the mattresses before making the wood parts, in case there are differences in size. With the beds stacked, the upper surface of a 6-inch mattress is about 20 inches from the floor. Individual beds are then about 10 inches high.

For a painted finish, softwood could be used for all parts. Hardwood would look better for a polished

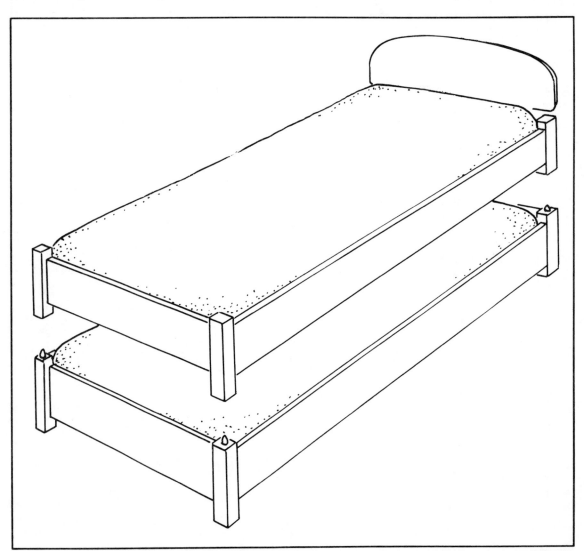

Fig. 8-4. These low stacking beds fit together to make one unit.

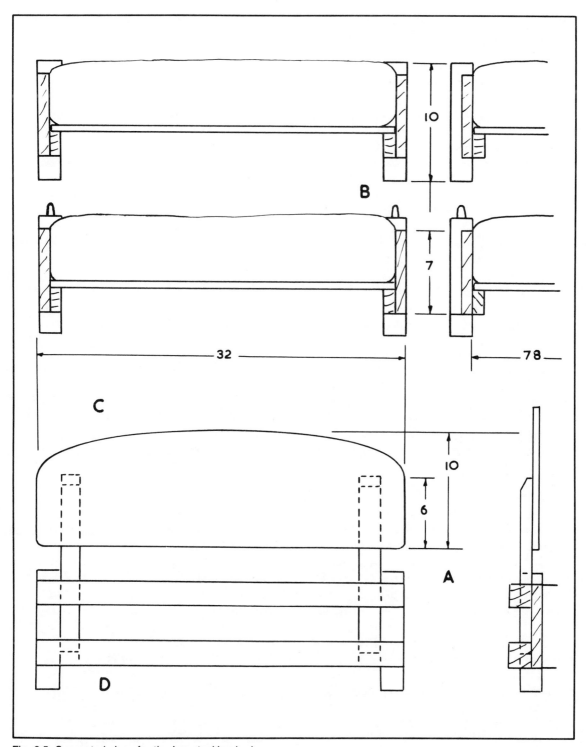

Fig. 8-5. Suggested sizes for the low stacking beds.

finish, although the mattress supports could be softwood in any case. The mattresses rest on plywood. The headboard is plywood, preferably faced with veneer if the bed is to have a polished finish. The two beds are identical except for the arrangement of locating dowels.

1. Mark out the legs (Fig. 8-6A). The side rails are level with the outsides of the legs (Fig. 8-6B), and the end rails are level with the inside surfaces (Fig. 8-6C).

2. Make the side rails and end rails. Use double tenons into the legs and take the tenons on the end rails deep enough to meet those on the side rails.

3. Glue and screw on the mattress support strips (Fig. 8-6D), inside the rails level with their bottom edges.

4. Drill the tops of the bottom bed legs and the bottoms of the top bed legs for the locating dowels. These can be 3/4-inch diameter glued into the bottom legs and projecting about 1 inch to fit into the holes in the top legs. Round and taper the dowel tops for an easy fit (Fig. 8-5B).

5. Assemble the frames. Check squareness and try the top bed on the lower one so they match.

6. Cut the mattress plywood bases to fit in. They do not have to be fixed down, although a few screws into the support strips help keep the beds in shape. Drill ventilating holes in the plywood. Ten, 1-inch holes should be adequate.

7. The headboards are optional. You might settle for one only, if the second bed will only have occasional use. Cut the plywood to any shape you wish; an elliptical top edge is shown (Fig. 8-5C).

8. Mount the headboard on its supports spaced so they will slide between the bed legs (Fig. 8-5D). Screws can be driven in counterbored holes in the backs of the supports and plugs put over their heads.

9. To hold the headboard in place, put two guides (Fig. 8-6E) across the top and bottom of the bed end. They are cut away to make slots for the supports as they overlap the bed legs. Both are made the same, but include blocks in the bottom one (Fig. 8-6F) to prevent the supports from dropping too far.

Materials List for Low Stacking Beds	
8 legs	2 × 2 × 10
4 sides	1 × 7 × 80
4 ends	1 × 7 × 30
4 mattress supports	1 × 2 × 78
4 mattress supports	1 × 2 × 32
2 bottoms	30 × 78 × 1/2 plywood
2 headboards	12 × 32 × 1/2 plywood
4 headboard supports	1 × 2 × 15
4 headboard guides	2 × 2 × 32

BUNK BED

A two-tier bed is the obvious space saver for two children sleeping in the same room. It appeals to them and can be just as safe and comfortable as separate beds. If made long enough, it can also be used by adults. In any case, children grow rapidly, and it is worthwhile providing ample length when building the bed.

This bunk bed (Fig. 8-7) is designed around 36-inch-by-78-inch mattresses, which could be any thickness. Other sizes are possible with the same construction, but a much greater width is not recommended.

The overall height gives sufficient headroom for the user of the bottom bed, while not making the top bed too high for reaching to arrange coverings. The bed is intended to have enough clearance below for a trundle bed (see next project).

There could be guards on both sides of the top bed (Fig. 8-8A). If it is going against a wall, you might decide that a single one will be enough. The ladder is shown attached to the bed sides (Fig. 8-8B), but it could be made as a loose one that hooks over the top bed side. There are panels between the legs at the head and foot at each level. They could be the same height at each end or made about 3 inches lower at the foot end (Fig. 8-8C).

The bunk bed could be made from softwood and painted, but it would be stronger and look better if made of hardwood. Choose straight-grained

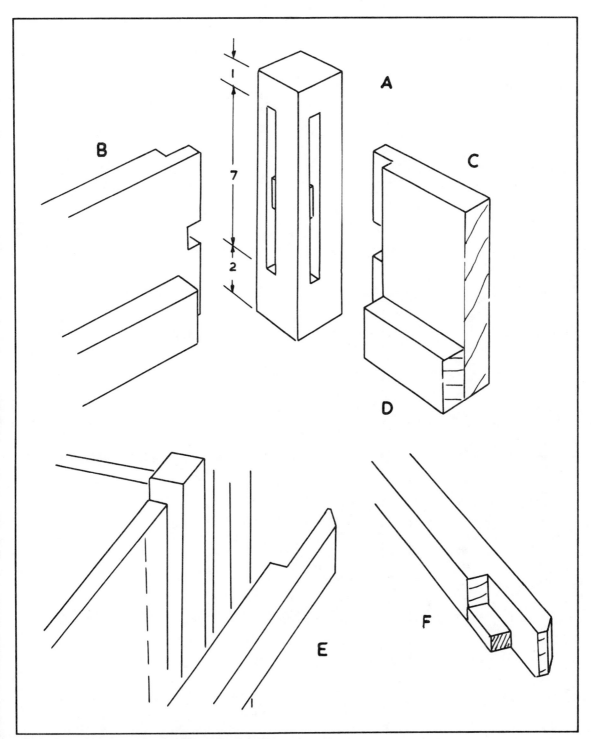

Fig. 8-6. Construction details of the low stacking beds.

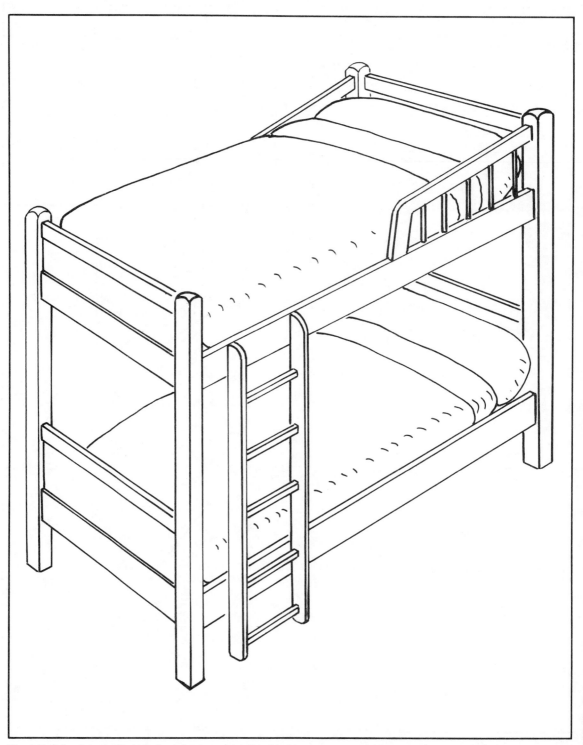

Fig. 8-7. A bunk bed with guards at the top and a fixed ladder.

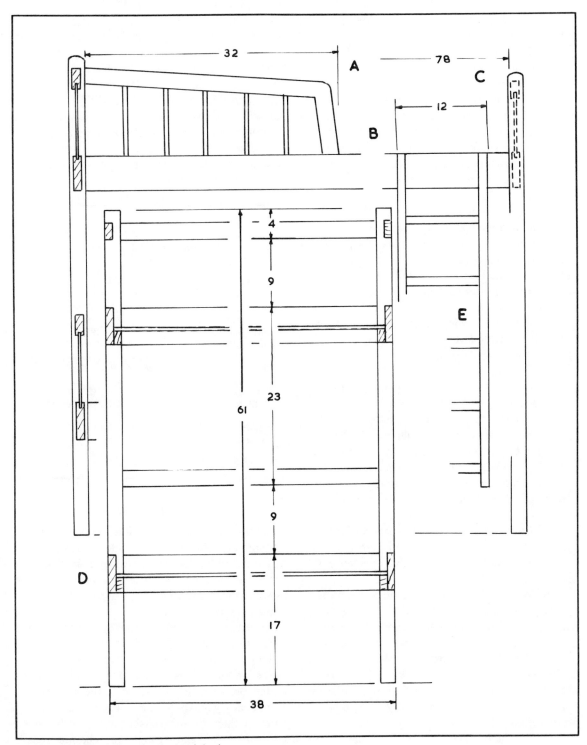

Fig. 8-8. Suggested sizes for the bunk bed.

wood for the legs to reduce the risk of warping in either case.

1. Prepare the wood for the legs and mark out the positions of the other parts (Fig. 8-8D). Leave extra wood at the top until after the joints have been cut, then round the wood (Fig. 8-9A).

2. Cut the pieces for the sides and ends at the bed levels. The joints can be similar to those at the corners of the stacked beds (Fig. 8-6A, B, C). Attach the mattress support rails level with the lower edges and cut off level with the shoulders of the tenons.

3. At the same time mark out the rails that will come at the tops of the panels (Fig. 8-9B). Groove them and the wide rails to take the plywood panels. Use plain tenons at the ends of the narrow rails. With a suitable router bit and a guide it is possible to groove the legs for the panels between mortises. Without this equipment you can avoid grooves in the legs by letting the plywood into the rails only and pin quarter-round molding each side of the plywood on the legs (Fig. 8-9C).

4. Prepare the parts for the guards (Figs. 8-8A and 8-9D). They are shown sloping, but could be made square. If sloping, set out the shape full size and make the parts to this drawing. Allow for tenons into the legs and bed rails (Fig. 8-9E). Cut the end of the tenon into the rail upright for ease of fitting. The best joint at the corner of the guard is an open mortise and tenon, or bridle, joint that is rounded. Use 1/2-inch or thicker dowel rods, at about 4-inch spacing.

5. Have the plywood end panels ready, then assemble the bed ends first. The panels should keep the assembly square, but check that opposite ends match, particularly at bed level.

6. With the parts on a flat surface, join the end with the lengthwise parts, including the guards, which will hold the other parts square. Remember to check squareness as viewed from above as well.

7. The plywood bases for the mattresses could be single sheets, but they would be easier to handle if made in two parts. Drill some ventilating holes. Either fit the sheets loosely or hold them down with a few screws.

8. The ladder could reach the floor or stop about 2 inches below the bottom rung. To make rung spacing even, divide the height of the top bed edge from the floor by six to give gaps just over 8 inches. This should suit most children. Make the ladder sides (Fig. 8-8E). Round all edges of the rungs and the exposed edges of the ladder sides. Allow for a curved top and mark the positions of the rungs (Fig. 8-9F). Make the tenons 3/4 inch thick and secure each with a wedge as well as glue. Attach the ladder with screws driven outwards through the bed sides.

Materials List for Bunk Beds

4 legs	2 × 2 × 62
4 sides	1 × 5 × 80
4 ends	1 × 5 × 38
4 mattress supports	1 × 2 × 78
4 mattress supports	1 × 2 × 36
4 end rails	1 × 2 × 38
2 end panels	11 × 35 × 1/4 plywood
2 end panels	8 × 35 × 1/4 plywood
2 bed bases	36 × 79 × 1/2 plywood
2 guards	1 × 2 × 37
2 guards	1 × 2 × 12
10 guards	12 × 1/2 diameter dowel rods
2 ladder side	1 × 2 × 45
5 ladder rungs	1 × 1 × 12

TRUNDLE BED

The original trundle, or truckle, bed was a simple resting place that was kept under a lady's bed to be pulled out for her servant to sleep on. The modern version is a low bed on casters that can be kept out of the way under another bed to pull out for an extra person.

Because the trundle is really just a box to hold a mattress, it can be any size to suit your needs, as long as it goes under the chosen bed. The trundle bed in Fig. 8-10 is intended for a child and stows under the bunk bed described as the last project. With bedding and pillows it will be about 10 inches from the floor. It can be pushed under the bunk bed either from one side or one end. The mattress is

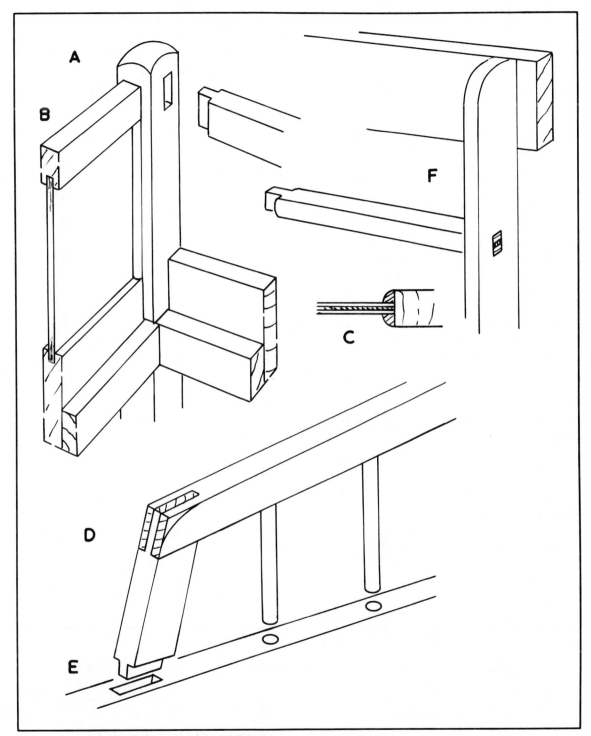

Fig. 8-9. Assembly details for parts of the bunk bed.

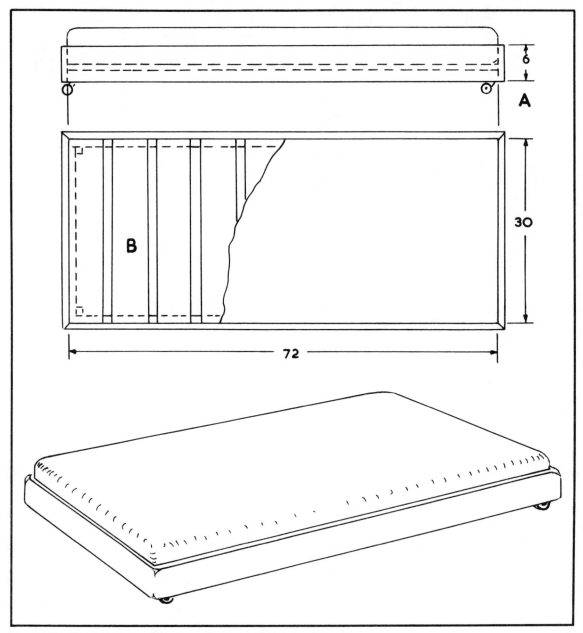

Fig. 8-10. A trundle bed on casters to go under another bed.

supported on boards, but the base could be ply-wood. Similarly, the bunk bed and others shown with plywood bases could have boards.

For the sake of appearance the outside parts could be hardwood to match other furniture. Be-cause none of the other wood in the bed shows, it

could be softwood. Obtain the mattress first and use it to determine actual sizes of the woodwork.

1. Make the box sides and ends (Figs. 8-10A and 8-11A). Round the outer edges. There could be molding worked on the faces if you wish. Miter the corners (Fig. 8-11B) to a size that will fit easily

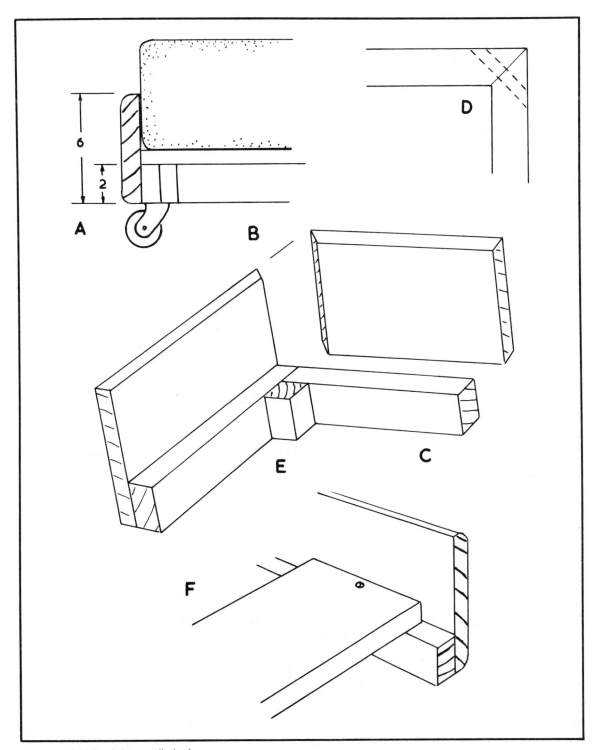

Fig. 8-11. Details of the trundle bed.

around the mattress.

2. Inside these pieces screw and glue bearers (Fig. 8-11C). They do not have to be mitered and can overlap at the corners.

3. Assemble these parts. The bearers will strengthen the miters, but above them use 1/4-inch dowels across (Fig. 8-11D). Glue long dowels in and plane them level. Round the corners of the box.

4. The corners will need extra area to take the casters. This is most easily done with blocks glued in (Fig. 8-11E).

5. The exact widths of the boards across to support the mattress are not critical. Here 6-inch boards are shown (Fig. 8-10B). Gaps should not be more than 1 1/2 inches with the end boards close to the box framing. A single screw at its end (Fig. 8-11F) secures each board, but does not restrict expansion and contraction.

6. Fit the casters. Try the action and stow the trundle bed under the other bed. If satisfactory, apply a finish.

Materials List for Trundle Bed	
2 sides	3/4 × 6 × 74
2 ends	3/4 × 6 × 32
2 bearers	1 × 2 × 73
2 bearers	1 × 2 × 2
10 mattress boards	3/4 × 6 × 30

PLAYPEN

To keep a crawling child safe and happy without constant attention might only be a problem for a short time. Any restraint need not be more elaborate than necessary, unless it will be used for several children. This simply-constructed playpen (Fig. 8-12) is large enough to allow a baby room to play with toys, yet it folds flat when not in use. A floor that fits in and reduces to half size keeps the open playpen in shape with no fear of accidental folding. It also protects the room floor.

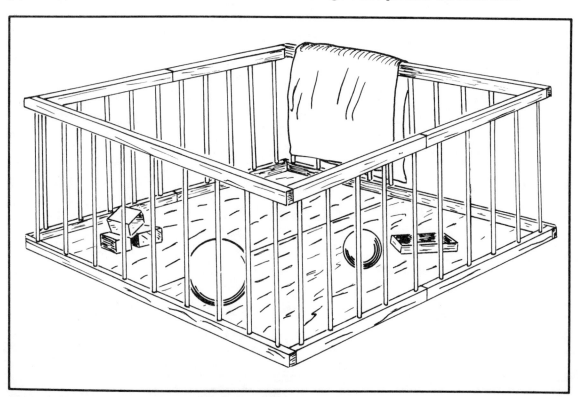

Fig. 8-12. This playpen has a removable floor and folds flat.

The pen folds to about 25 inches by 44 inches and 5 inches thick. It opens almost square. The bottom is in two parts, which may be hinged, so the folded floor is about 21 inches by 40 inches and 1 inch thick. If sizes are altered, keep the spindles close enough so a child cannot stick his head between them at any point. The spindles are hardwood dowel rods. The frame parts are preferably made of hardwood.

1. Prepare the wood for the rails. For the long sides (Fig. 8-13A) the top and bottom are the same. For the short sides (Fig. 8-13B) there are hinged joints at the middle.

2. Mark the hole positions in the top and bottom rails together for a perfect match. Drill evenly and fairly deeply (Fig. 8-14A) because the rung joints are all that provide rigidity to the frames. The holes are all 4 inches apart. The only different measurements are at the corners (Fig. 8-13C). The hinged joints in the short pieces come midway between dowel holes. Round all edges.

3. Use temporary strips to hold the top and bottom rails at the correct distance apart while assembling. All sections will then finish at the same height.

4. To prevent the playpen from being accidentally lifted in use, extend four metal plates under the plywood floor. Make them from 2-inch square pieces of 16 gauge aluminum or brass and place them under the long sides (Fig. 8-14B and C).

5. The corner hinges come inside and might be touched by the baby. File off all sharp edges. Drive the screws carefully so the screwdriver does not slip and roughen the slots.

6. Join the two pairs of folding sections with their hinges outside while the rail ends are pushed tightly together. At the corners have the rails level outside while fitting the hinges inside (Figs. 8-13D and 8-14E).

7. Test the opening and closing action.

8. Make the two pieces of plywood floor to be an easy fit with their joints towards the long sides of the pen (Fig. 8-13E). If they are to be joined, arrange the hinges to be underneath when the pen is in use.

9. To keep the wood clean and hygienic, paint or varnish it. The floor section can be covered with something waterproof, but not slippery.

Materials List for Playpen	
4 rails	1 × 2 × 44
8 rails	1 × 2 × 22
2 floors	21 × 40 × 1/2 plywood
42 spindles	24 × 1/2 or 5/8 dowel rods

CHILD'S PLAY CHAIR

Children's furniture has to be strong and safe, particularly if a child uses it while unattended. This means strong and simple construction. A chair will almost certainly be stood on as well as used for a seat. To make the risk of tipping minimal, the seat must not extend over the legs more than a small amount. A chair might be preferable to a stool for an adventurous child who wants to use it to reach higher, because it gives him something to hold. A child is unlikely to be concerned with comfort. He will not sit for long and will treat the chair more as a plaything.

This chair (Fig. 8-15) is simple in appearance and construction. It stands steady, can be climbed on, and may be put on its back or side when the child exercises his ingenuity and imagination to improvise cars and other make-believe things.

The wood can be hard or soft, but any type liable to splinter should be avoided. Finish can be paint or varnish, mainly to seal the wood as well as to improve appearance. The sizes shown (Fig. 8-16) could be altered to suit your child, but children grow rapidly and the chair may only have a use for a year or two. Dowels are suggested, but the rails could be tenoned to the legs if you wish. Three, 1/2-inch dowels at each place should be sufficient.

1. Mark out and cut the rear legs (Figs. 8-16A and 8-17A). Notch at the top so the back will have its surface 1/8 inch forward of the leg (Fig. 8-17B). Allow for rail joints both ways (Fig. 8-17C).

2. Mark the front legs from the rear legs and mark on them the positions of the rail dowels in the same way.

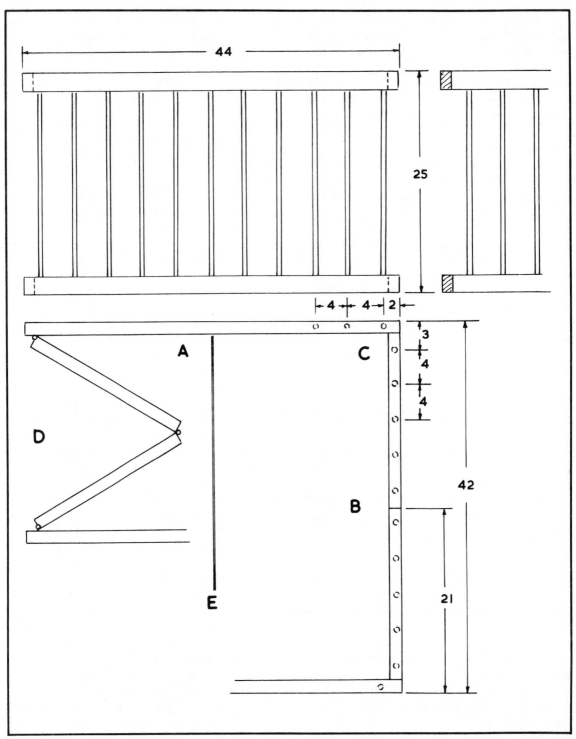

Fig. 8-13. Sizes of the playpen.

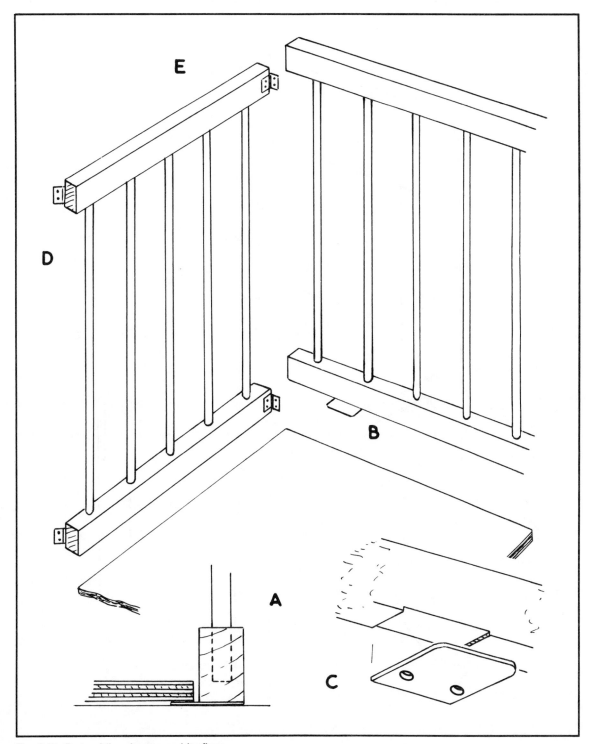

Fig. 8-14. Parts of the playpen and its floor.

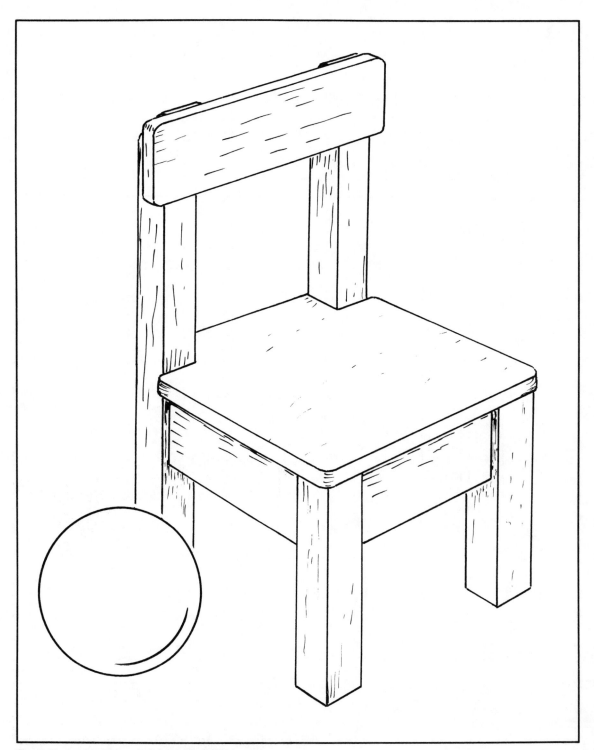

Fig. 8-15. A robust play chair for a small child.

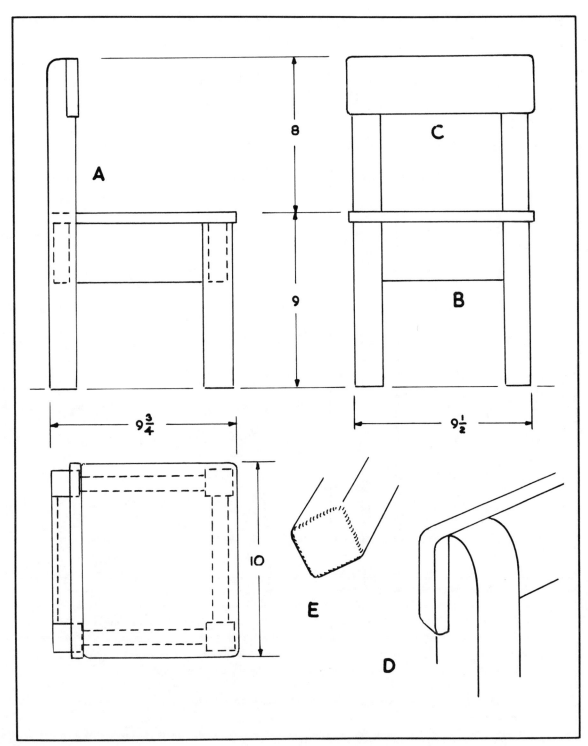

Fig. 8-16. Sizes of the play chair.

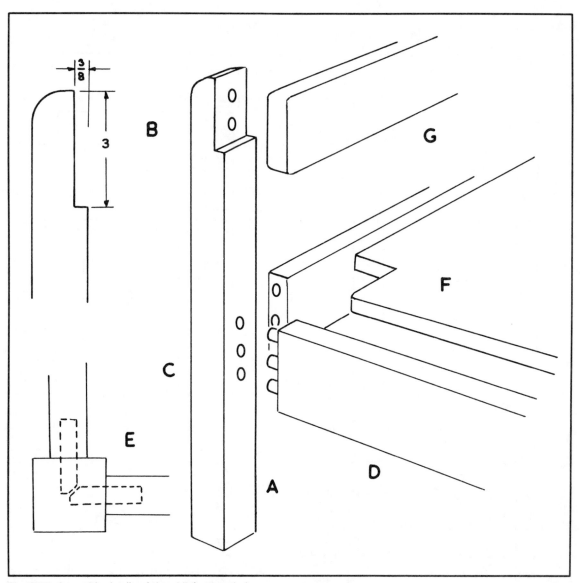

Fig. 8-17. Assembly details of the child's play chair.

3. Make the rails (Figs. 8-16B and 8-17D), which are the same both ways. Cut their lengths so the chair size will be 9 1/2 inches over the legs. To give them sufficient length, miter the dowel ends in the legs (Fig. 8-17E).

4. Join the rails to the legs. Be sure the assembly is square in all directions.

5. Cut the seat to size so it notches around the rear legs (Fig. 8-17F) and is level with their rear edges. On the other edges it should be 1/4 inch outside the tops of the legs. Round its corners and edges. Sand the edges of all other parts so no sharp angles are exposed.

6. Fix the seat with glue and a few fine screws. Sink them below the surface and cover with filler.

7. Make the back (Figs. 8-16C and 8-17G). Extend it 1/4 inch outside the legs and round the

corners and edges (Fig. 8-16D). Glue and screw it or make the joints with dowels.

8. Check that the chair stands level. If necessary, trim the bottoms of one or more legs, then round their ends (Fig. 8-16E) to reduce the risk of splitting.

9. The back could be decorated with a decal picture or a name.

```
Materials List for a Child's Play Chair

2 legs        1 1/2 × 1 1/2 × 17
2 legs        1 1/2 × 1 1/2 × 9
4 rails       3/4 × 3 × 7
1 seat        1/2 × 10 × 10
1 back        1/2 × 3 × 10
```

DISPLAY SHELVES

Small display shelves are often made straight, but curves may be more attractive than straight lines. This little block of two shelves (Fig. 8-18) has all curved edges, except for the parts against the wall. Hardwood 1/2 inch thick is suitable, although slightly thicker softwood could be used. The suggested sizes should suit a young person's collection of small treasures and souvenirs, but sizes can be modified or the numbers and spacings of shelves altered without affecting the general design.

1. Mark out the two ends (Fig. 8-19A). A pattern of 1-inch squares indicate the curved outline (Fig. 8-20A).

2. Mark out the shelf shapes in a similar way (Fig. 8-20B). Mark the tenons on the shelves and mortises in the ends together to match. Cut these joints (Fig. 8-19B) before shaping the outlines. Make sure all saw marks are removed from the shaped edges and take off any sharpness.

3. The scalloped shelf supports are cut from one piece of wood and glued in place. Make them the same length as the shelves between shoulders (Fig. 8-19C). Mark and drill 1-inch holes along the center of the strip of wood (Fig. 8-20C). After drilling, cut away a 1/4-inch wide space through the holes (Fig. 8-20D). Round the projecting pieces between the remains of the holes (Fig. 8-20E) and take

any sharpness off the edges of the holes.

4. Glue the supports to the shelves and let it set. Assemble the shelves to the ends. Check squareness by measuring diagonals and see that there is no twist.

5. The block of shelves can be hung with screw plates projecting from the top shelf or inside the sides near their tops.

```
Materials List for Display Shelves

2 sides       1/2 × 6 × 18
2 shelves     1/2 × 7 × 26
1 support     1/2 × 3 1/4 × 23
```

UTILITY STAND

Some furniture to take apart is often unsteady when assembled. This stand (Fig. 8-21) is made as four units that can be joined permanently or taken apart for convenience in transport or to store flat. Because of the use of made-up parts between the legs, the assembled stand should be quite steady in use.

A boxed unit forms the top and a shelf below serves as a book rack. Because neither of these break down into smaller parts, they keep their shape and strength without being bulky. The supports are two pairs of legs with rails between. The box and book rack screw or bolt between to make the complete stand.

The stand has many uses. A student might use it as a dresser or desk, with papers and books stored below. In a younger child's room the top might display models or collected items, while magazines, books, and boxes of toys could go below. In a family room or den the stand could go near a wall for storage or as a table for food and drink. When taken apart the four units can travel inside a car or be stored in a closet.

The leg assemblies should be solid wood. The box and book rack could be veneered particleboard dowelled together. The instructions are for 1/2-inch plywood without any attempt to disguise its use. The joints suggested, if carefully made, can then be regarded as design features in this piece of fur-

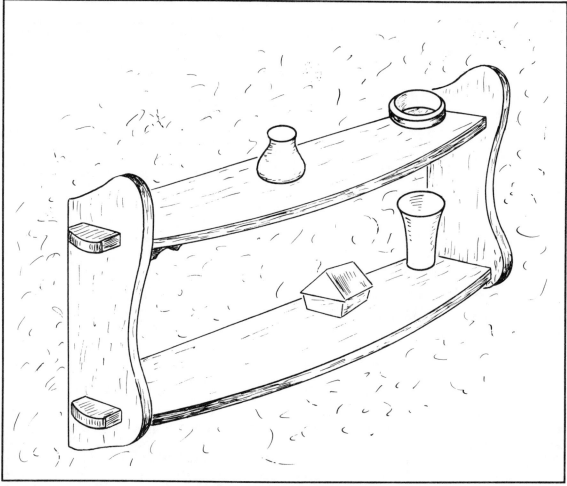

Fig. 8-18. These display shelves are decorated by curved edges and tusk tenons.

niture. It should get some of its attraction from the fact that it is functional and looks it.

1. The box is intended to open through, but the back might be closed if required. Cut the plywood for the four parts (Figs. 8-22A and 8-23A). Square all the panels to the full size of the box. Finger joints are suggested (Fig. 8-22B). Each finger may be 1 inch wide, which conveniently gives eight one way and seven the other. Let the fingers extend through very slightly to allow for planing off after the glue has set. A few pins can be driven and set below the surface to hold the parts while the glue sets, if there is any difficulty in arranging sufficient clamps.

2. Cut the plywood for the book rack ends (Fig. 8-23B) and the pieces for the lengthwise parts (Fig. 8-22C). Similar finger joints can be used. Arrange it so the bottom of the back fits into a socket at each end (Fig. 8-22D). The fingers of the bottom are also arranged for the rear edge to enter a socket (Fig. 8-22E). Be careful to make the box and the book rack square and exactly the same length.

3. The legs are splayed symmetrically. Set out the main lines of an end (Fig. 8-22F). The legs should go 1 inch above the top of the box. The legs spread at the bottom to 3 inches wider than the box, for stability. If you alter sizes, make sure an adequate spread is allowed.

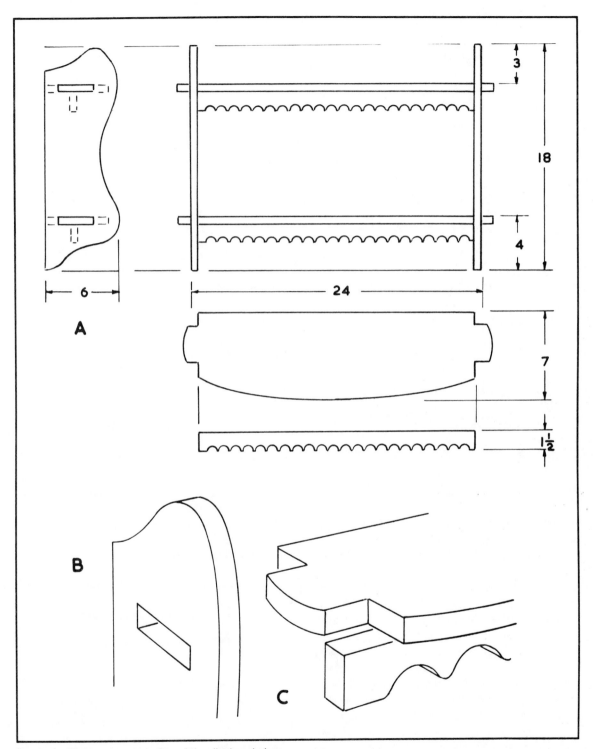

Fig. 8-19. Sizes and construction of the display shelves.

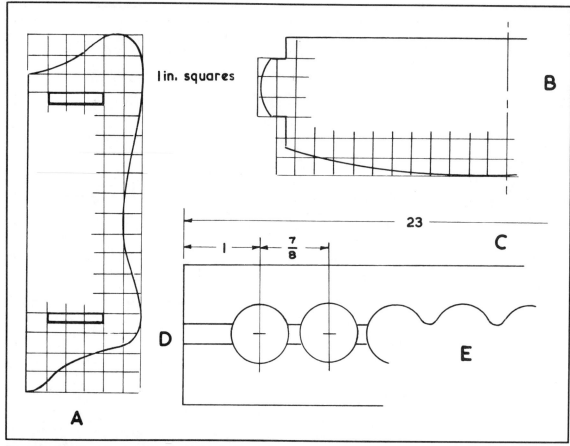

Fig. 8-20. Details of the curved parts of the display shelves.

4. The rails may be cut against the legs and dowelled (Fig. 8-23C). They might also be given extra length to be tenoned. This would be stronger, particularly if the stand is taken apart and transported frequently. Round the top rails and legs (Fig. 8-23D).

5. Mark the positions of the legs on the box and the box on the legs. If the stand is expected to be put together and probably never taken apart again, you could use screws, which might also be driven from inside the box into the legs, for neatness. If you want to take it apart and assemble it many times, it is better to use bolts. Plated or brass 1/4-inch coach bolts, with their heads outside (Fig. 8-22G), could be used and would look smart.

6. Decide on the angle you want for the book rack. In the end view shown, it is 70 degrees to vertical (Fig. 8-22H). Mount it with screws or bolts to the rails in a similar way to the box. Mark the meeting surfaces of the parts which bolt together because it is unlikely that the holes at opposite sides will be exactly the same spacing.

Materials List for Utility Stand	
2 box panels	1/2 × 15 × 20
2 box panels	1/2 × 7 × 15
2 book rack ends	1/2 × 7 × 9
1 book rack back	1/2 × 7 × 20
1 book rack bottom	1/2 × 5 × 20
2 legs	1 × 1 1/2 × 35
2 rails	1 × 3 × 9
2 rails	1 × 3 × 17

Fig. 8-21. This utility stand is designed to take down for transport or storage.

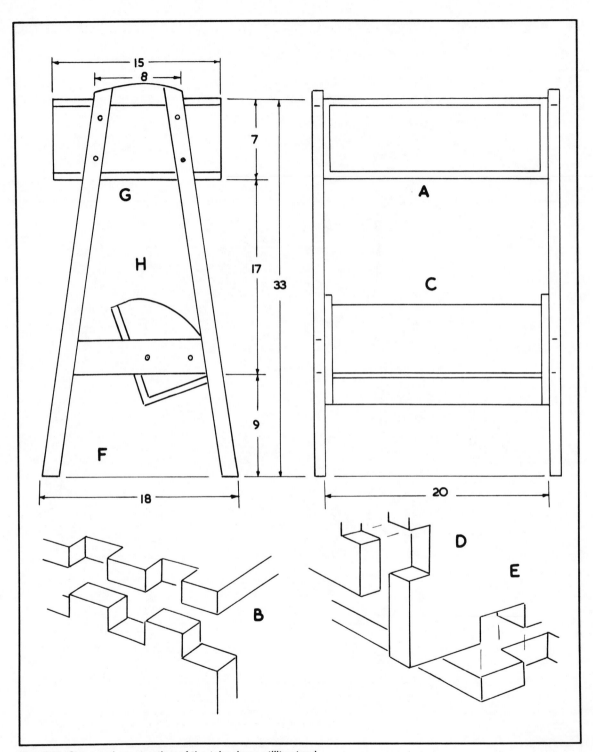

Fig. 8-22. Sizes and construction of the take-down utility stand.

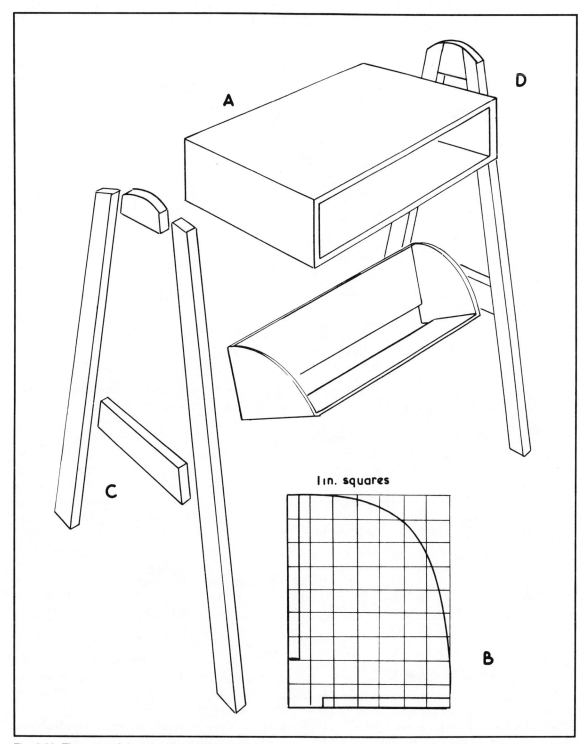

Fig. 8-23. The parts of the take-down utility stand.

Chapter 9

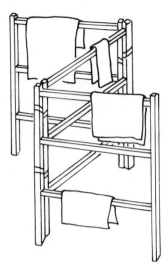

Laundry

A separate laundry room is usually full—housing a washing machine, dryer, and other essential equipment. As the room is often not very big, there cannot be much additional furniture. It is a help if at least some new items can be taken apart or fold so they occupy little space when not needed.

A few items of furniture described elsewhere in the book might be used in the laundry. Anyone using the laundry room will be glad of a seat and storage facilities. To avoid cluttering the laundry room with too many things, some items may be brought in only as required. The projects in this chapter are primarily for the laundry, but some might find a second place in a bathroom or bedroom.

LAUNDRY HAMPER

Somewhere to put soiled linen is necessary in a laundry room, but it could also be used in a bathroom or bedroom. The container could be carried with its contents to the laundry, especially if it is

light and portable. In many homes there are never enough laundry containers, particularly if there are several children in the family. Such a hamper does not have to be an elaborate piece of furniture of difficult construction. This hamper (Fig. 9-1) is simple and inexpensive to make. It uses panels of hardboard, preferably of the oil-tempered type, although ordinary well-painted hardboard should have a long life. The panels fit into slotted legs, and the plywood top may be used as a seat. Use softwood or hardwood for the other parts. Glue all parts together. Where solid wood goes against hardboard, panel pins are inconspicuous and can be used as well.

Sizes are not critical, but those shown (Fig. 9-2) give a useful capacity in a hamper that does not take up much space and is easy to carry.

1. Prepare the wood for the legs (Figs. 9-2A and 9-3A). This is 7/8-inch square and the grooves to take the hardboard are plowed 1/4 inch deep and 1/4 inch from the outer surfaces. Round the outer corners. Make sure the grooves are all the same depth and the hardwood fits closely.

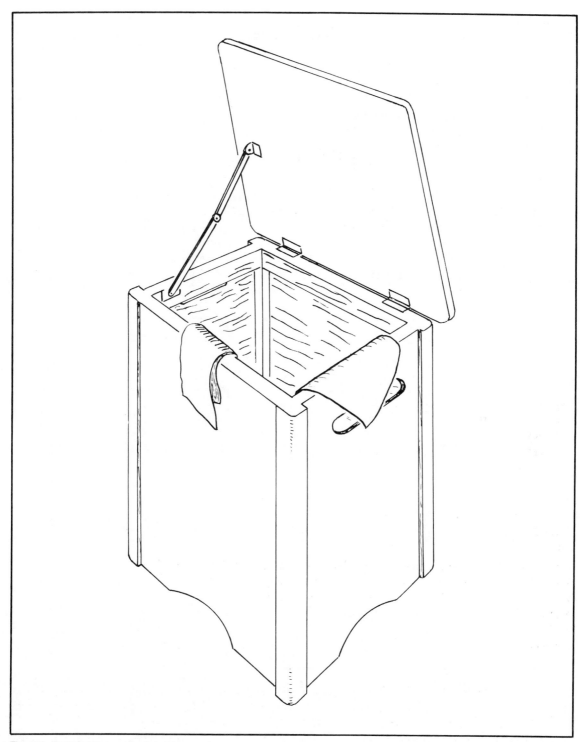

Fig. 9-1. A portable laundry hamper.

2. Cut the hardwood panels to size. Check that corners are square. So the hamper will stand without wobbling on slightly uneven surfaces, cut away the bottom edges. A curve starting 3 inches in from the corners and going about 3/4 inch deep is satisfactory (Fig. 9-2B and C).

3. Make hand holes at the sides, 1 inch deep and 5 inches wide, below where the top stiffening strip comes. Make the holes by drilling the ends and sawing away the waste between. Round the edges of the holes.

4. Fit strips across the insides of the panels. Cut back to allow the panels into the grooves (Fig. 9-3B). Lightly round the exposed inner edges of the strips. The thickness of each strip should fill the gap between the panel and the leg edge (Fig. 9-3C). Shape the bottom strips to the curves already cut in the hardboard.

5. Assemble the back and front of the hamper first. At the top of the back put a strip across the outside to come level with the leg surfaces (Fig. 9-3D) to take hinges.

6. Prepare the bottom hardboard to rest on the bottom strips (Fig. 9-3E). Notch it to fit around the legs at the corners. Have it ready to go in as you fit the side panels because it cannot be put in after the hamper has been made up with four panels. The bottom will hold the hamper square. Check squareness at the top while the bottom is standing on a flat surface to make sure there is no twist.

7. Cut the plywood lid (Fig. 9-2E) to overlap 1/2 inch on three sides, but to be level at the back (Fig. 9-3F) so hinges can be fitted. An overhanging edge would hit the back of the box if opened too far and strain the hinges and their screws.

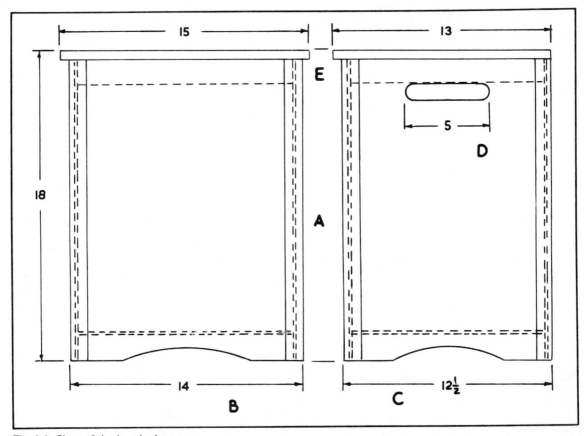

Fig. 9-2. Sizes of the laundry hamper.

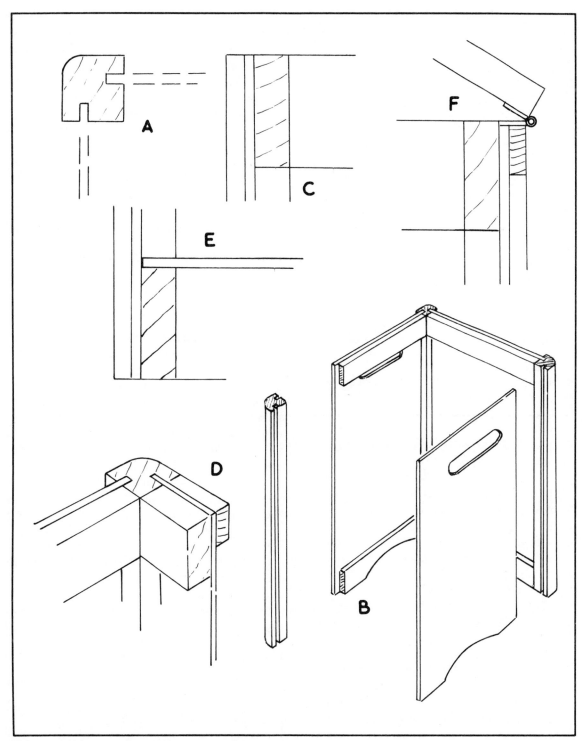

Fig. 9-3. Assembly details of the laundry hamper.

Round the corners of the lid and take sharpness off edges all round. Two, 2-inch hinges can be used. Let them into the top edge of the hamper. They could also go on the surface of the plywood. Let the hinge knuckles project from the wood surfaces so the lid will swing freely.

8. There could be a folding stay for the lid, as shown in Fig. 9-1, if you wish. A simpler alternative would be a cord between screw eyes or a length of tape, screwed or nailed on.

9. Paint the hamper thoroughly inside and out, including below the bottom, to prevent moisture entering the wood and hardboard.

Materials List for Laundry Hamper

4 legs	7/8 × 7/8 × 18
4 strips	1/2 × 1 1/2 × 13
4 strips	1/2 × 1 1/2 × 12
1 strip	1/4 × 1 × 13
2 panels	13 × 18 × 1/8 hardboard
2 panels	12 × 18 × 1/8 hardboard
1 bottom	12 × 13 × 1/8 hardboard
1 lid	13 × 15 × 1/2 plywood

FOLDING LAUNDRY TABLE

Although space is often restricted in the laundry room, there are occasions when a table is needed for folding clothing, bedding, and other articles just washed. A permanent table might occupy too much space when it is not needed, so a take-down or folding table has to be the choice. Most folding tables keep the top full size and that may be bigger than you want to stow. A folding table could be made with a top that folds in half.

The table (Fig. 9-4A) is intended for this purpose. It is light with the construction just strong enough for folding sheets and similar things. It is not intended for general use, cannot be sat on, or used for any hobby that involves hammering or other heavy work. Outside of the laundry it would serve for cutting and pasting wallpaper, but otherwise it should be kept for the work it is designed for.

The top is 1/2-inch plywood and folds to 20 inches by 24 inches and about 1 inch thick. The leg frames are about the same size with three loose strips. All of the framing could be softwood, but hardwood will have a longer life. Stresses have to be taken by the notched joints, which might wear and slacken earlier in softwood than in hardwood, but either should give a useful life.

1. Make the top lengthwise strips (Fig. 9-5A) and the bottom strip (Fig. 9-5B). Mark the notches on all three strips together. Use the actual wood that will be across the legs to mark the widths of the notches. Cut them 1 1/8 inches deep (Fig. 9-5C).

2. Make the leg assemblies (Fig. 9-5D). The legs and rails may overlap and be glued and screwed or nailed. Cut notches in the rails to fit those in the lengthwise rails (Fig. 9-5E). At the top they come against the legs (Fig. 9-4B). At the bottom they are centered. Try the parts together. The joints should press into place and fully close with hand pressure, but avoid slackness. Two, 1 1/8-inch notches together leave the tops of the long supports 3/4 inch above the legs. Check that this is the same at all corners.

3. Make the two parts of the top (Fig. 9-4C). Round the edges and outer corners. Join the parts with three, 2-inch hinges underneath—one in the center and the others near the edges (Fig. 9-4D).

4. Drill for 1/2-inch dowels, 2 inches from the ends of the top rails (Fig. 9-4E). Drill matching holes in the top. They can go right through; then you can see from above where all dowels are located during assembly. Cut the dowels to come level with the top surface. Glue them in the rails and sand them so they fit easily into the holes in the top.

5. Ideally the parts will be so accurate that they will fit in several ways. It does not matter if they do not, providing you mark the joints that make the best fits.

Materials List for Folding Laundry Table

2 rails	1 × 3 × 44
1 rail	1 × 3 × 40
4 legs	1 × 3 × 26
4 rails	1 × 3 × 18
2 tops	20 × 24 × 1/2 plywood

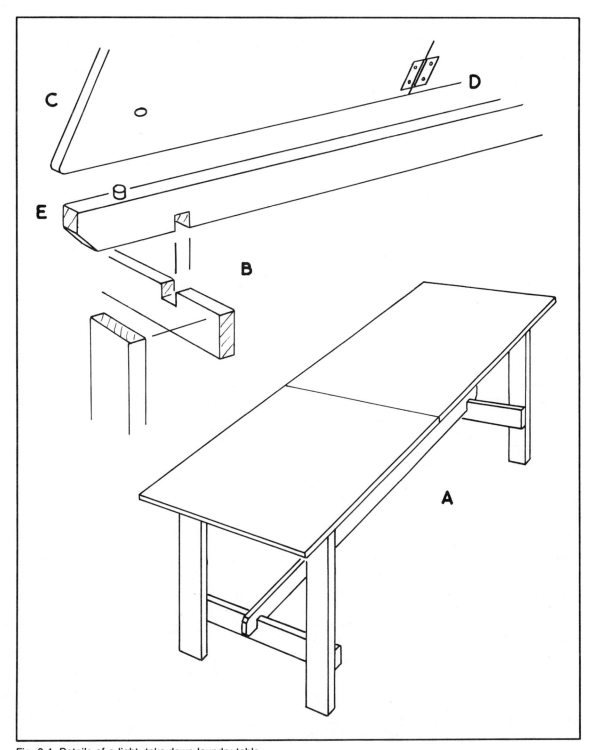

Fig. 9-4. Details of a light, take-down laundry table.

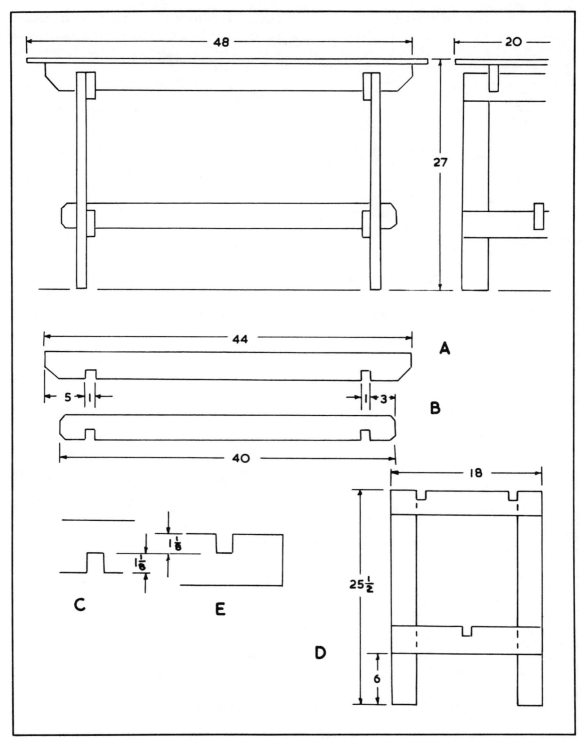

Fig. 9-5. Sizes of the take-down laundry table.

CLOTHES RAIL

If a large number of clothes have to be hung up, either for storage or for drying or airing, a long rail provides compact accommodation. A short version could be used in a bedroom for overnight clothes storage. If you receive many guests the rail makes a place for their outdoor clothes. If the amount of clothes is too great for a clothes closet, some can be hung on a rail.

The suggested clothes rail (Fig. 9-6) also has

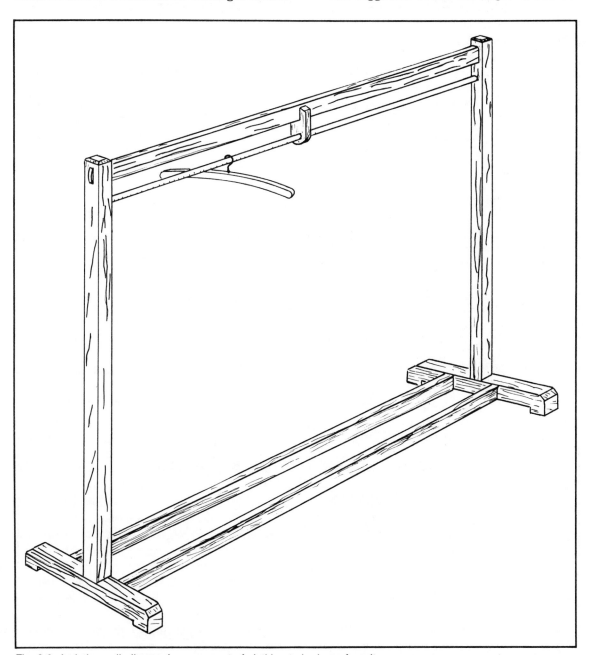

Fig. 9-6. A clothes rail allows a large amount of clothing to be hung from it.

two bottom rails that provide strength and are suitable for spacing shoes to air-dry if necessary. The assembly can be stationary or move on casters.

Different heights and lengths are suggested. If long dresses or coats are to be hung, the taller arrangement will be needed. The chosen length will depend on the quantity of clothing as well as available space. The hanging rail suggested is 1/2-inch dowel rod. A short rack should be stiff enough with only support at the ends. For a long rail with a full load, a center support is advisable. If dowel rods are not available in sufficient length, there could be a joint in a hole in the center support.

Although it would be possible to join the parts with dowels, the assembly will be stronger with mortise and tenon joints. These are advised (Fig. 9-8) because there could be considerable strains on the rail if it is knocked hard in use.

Hard or softwood can be used. For laundry purposes painted softwood is satisfactory. If a varnished or polished finish on a rack to be used elsewhere is desired, a good hardwood would look better.

1. Decide on the sizes (Fig. 9-7).

2. Mark out the posts (Fig. 9-7A) and leave a little excess length until after the joints have been cut.

3. Mark out and cut the bases (Fig. 9-7B) and feet (Fig. 9-7C).

4. The mortises on the posts and bases go right through. Mark them on both sides for accuracy and cut from both sides to prevent the grain from breaking out.

5. The three rails are the same length between shoulders. The tenons on the top rails are full depth (Fig. 9-8A), while those on the shoe rails are shorter and arranged double across (Fig. 9-8B) to allow for the different grain direction in the bases.

6. Complete the marking and cutting of the mortise and tenon joints. The top rail tenons should extend through the posts and their ends are rounded (Fig. 9-8C).

7. Make and glue and nail or screw the feet to the bases.

8. Assemble the posts to the bases. Careful

squaring is important. The tenons could have one or more saw cuts across so wedges can be driven in to give maximum strength in each joint. Trim the tenon ends and bevel underneath.

9. If there is to be a center support, fit it over the top rail (Fig. 9-8D) to which it can be held with glue and a dowel through. Make sure the hole for the dowel hanging rail is the same distance down from the top rail as the holes in the posts.

10. Join the support to the top rail, then join all the lengthwise parts to the end assemblies. Check squareness in the length by measuring diagonals. If there is a tendency to pull out of square, a diagonal strip can be clamped temporarily across the rack until the glue has set.

11. If casters are to be fitted, drill for them or screw them to the feet.

Materials List for Clothes Rail	
2 posts	2 × 2 × 48 or 72
2 bases	2 × 2 × 18
4 feet	1 × 2 × 2
2 shoe rails	1 × 2 × 30 or 50
1 top rail	1 × 2 × 30 or 50
1 clothes rail	30 or 50 × 1/2 diameter
1 clothes rail support, if needed	1 × 2 × 6

TAKE-DOWN DRYING RACK

When only a few small things have to be hung to air or dry, it is useful to have some rods to hang them on. You might not have space to store such an arrangement, however.

This drying rack (Fig. 9-9) supports three, 36-inch dowel rods on light legs. The rods can be removed easily, and all the parts store out of the way until needed again. Any dowel rods can be used and the legs and feet may be softwood to keep all parts lightweight.

1. Obtain the dowel rods and check their diameters in holes drilled in scrap wood. They should make an easy push fit. Round their ends. In use they should go right through the legs and project a short distance.

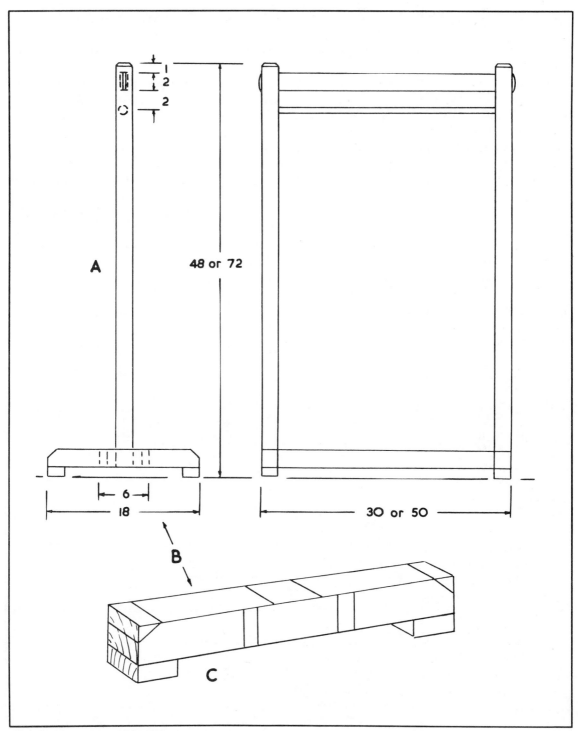

Fig. 9-7. Sizes of the clothes rail.

2. Make the legs (Fig. 9-9A), drilling squarely through them.

3. Make the feet with mortise and tenon joints to the legs (Fig. 9-9B). Taper the ends and cut underneath so the feet will stand level.

4. Assemble the ends to match and stand squarely. Round or bevel the tops of the legs.

5. It will probably be best to leave the wood untreated and wash it occasionally.

Materials List for Take-Down Drying Rack	
2 legs	1 × 1 × 36
2 feet	1 × 2 × 12
3 rails	36 × 1/2 diameter dowel rods

FOLDING DRYING RACK

For drying or airing clothes indoors, you need plenty of rails or lines spaced to give a good clearance from each other. When not in use, the rack should store out of the way. This airer (Figs. 9-10 and 9-11) has a large number of rails 24 inches long on a frame that opens to 42 or 60 inches high, yet it closes to about 6 inches thick and 24 inches square. It stands on the floor or could go inside a bath. It can hang on a wall or suspend from a cord. As shown, it adjusts to two heights, but extra notches at the bottom would allow other adjustments. If you have a height problem, the drying rack can be made a different size or some parts omitted, with the bottom notches as needed.

The important parts are the dowel rod rails,

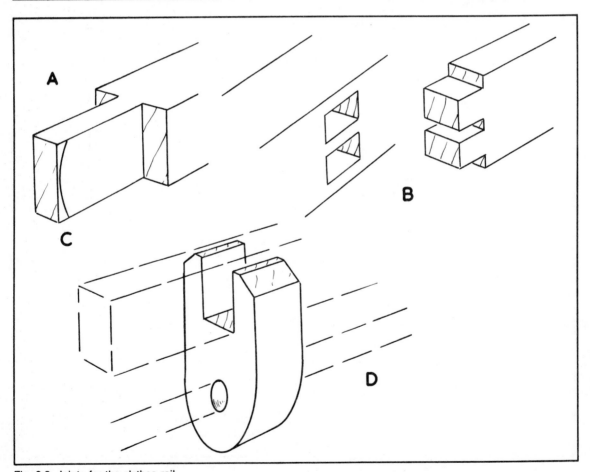

Fig. 9-8. Joints for the clothes rail.

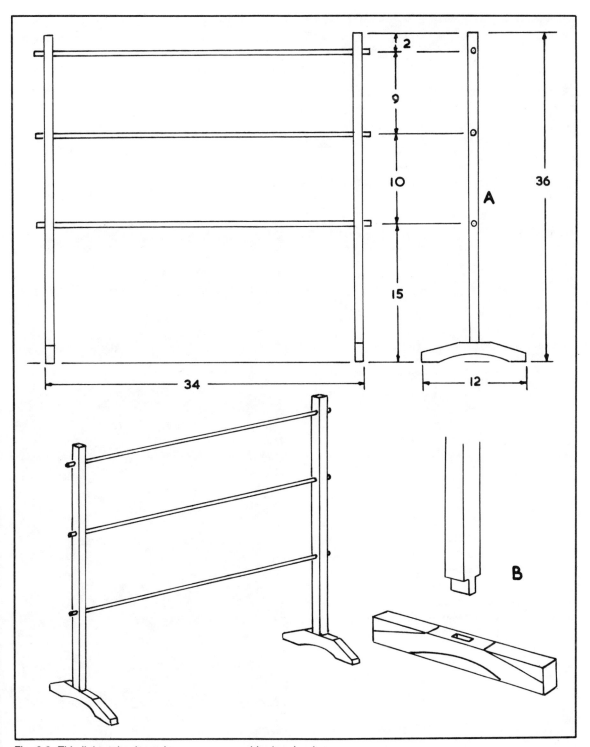

Fig. 9-9. This light, take-down dryer uses removable dowel rods.

Fig. 9-10. This folding clothes dryer compresses until all the parts fit against each other.

dowel rod economically if you alter the rail lengths slightly, although do not shorten them too much.

The completed dryer could be left as bare wood or finished with one or two coats of varnish to seal the grain. Boat varnish is best for damp conditions.

The assembly does not include any metal. Waterproof glue in the joints can be reinforced by pins or thin nails, preferably brass or other metal that will not corrode. Similarly, the screws and washers that hold the turnbuttons are better if not steel.

The assembly is made up with similar outer

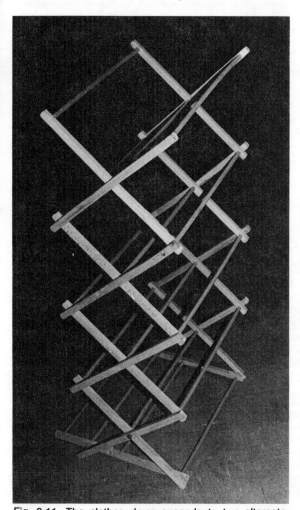

Fig. 9-11. The clothes dryer expands to two alternate heights.

which should be straight hardwood and true to size. The framework should be straight hardwood, preferably the same as the dowels. If the drying rack is to open and close without difficulty, it is important that holes are drilled square to the surface and all at the same spacings. The use of a drill press or a drill in a stand is advisable as is a jig or template to drill through. Alternatively, parts could be marked out in batches, using one strip as the master.

The sizes shown (Fig. 9-12) will make a rack to suit most needs. If you want to stand it in the bath, sizes may have to be altered so the base fits in. You may also be able to cut stock lengths of

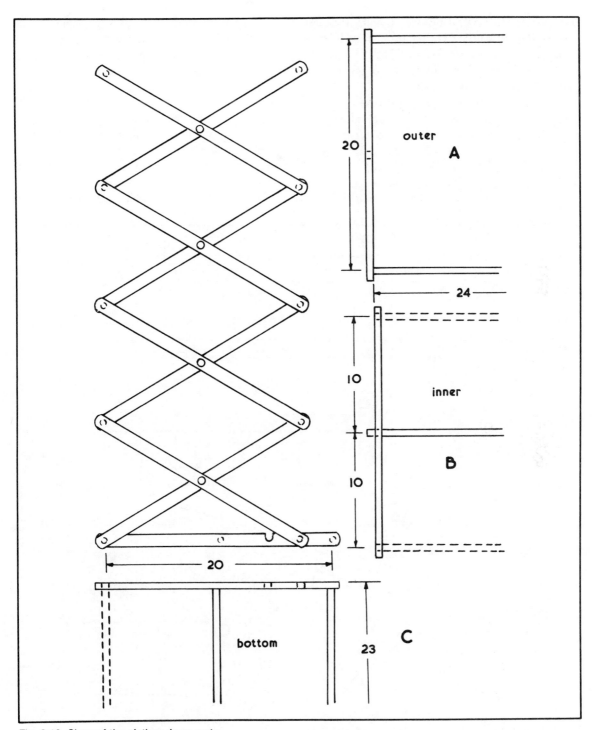

Fig. 9-12. Sizes of the clothes dryer parts.

frames (Fig. 9-12A) fitting over matching inner frames (Fig. 9-12B). The bottom frame (Fig. 9-12C) then fits into the inner frame. Widths therefore have to be made to fit with clearance for movement and allowance for wood thickness.

1. Make sixteen strips (Fig. 9-13A). Round the ends. Drill the center hole through all strips. For the eight strips that will make outer frames, drill the end holes as deep as possible without breaking through the far side. Drill right through at the end positions on the strips that will make inner frames. The two pairs that will make the top

and lower inner frames can have their upper holes only drilled part way for neatness. If you wish to avoid confusion, drill all end holes only part way, and continue them through as you need open holes.

2. The two bottom strips (Fig. 9-13B) have the same main sizes as the other strips, but only the hole to the left of the drawing goes right through. The others are stopped. Make the notches by drilling holes and sawing into them (Fig. 9-13C). Use a round file or abrasive paper on a dowel rod to enlarge the slots so a rail will drop in easily. To ensure enough wood underneath the slot for

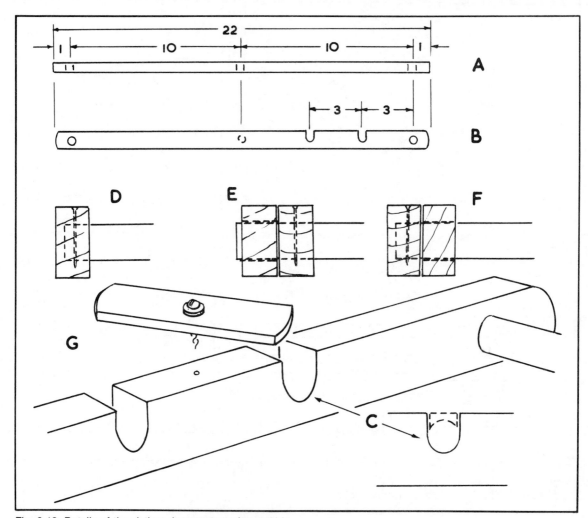

Fig. 9-13. Details of the clothes dryer parts and assembly.

strength, drill the holes only a short distance below the top edge.

3. Assemble the bottom first. Its overall width controls the inside width of the inner frames (Fig. 9-12C). Fit dowels into the stopped holes. Pin through each glued joint (Fig. 9-13D). Check that the sides are parallel and the frame square.

4. Work from this bottom upwards assembling the other parts. Slide the holes of the bottom frame on the rail of the next frame before that frame is assembled further. As you progress, the dowel rod at the center should project far enough to go through the strip of an outer frame (Fig. 9-13E). The hole in the outer frame may have to be eased by filing or sanding so it pivots easily. At the ends of the outer frames the dowel rods are fixed in them (Fig. 9-13F) and the holes in the inner frame must pivot. In this way the frames are locked so folding and opening is possible, but the assembly cannot fall apart.

5. Try the action of the rack, both closed and open, using both pairs of notches in the bottom. Make a turnbutton for each side of the bottom (Fig. 9-13G) long enough to go over the notches to prevent the rack from being accidentally folded when in use.

Materials List for Folding Drying Rack

18 strips	1/2 × 3/4 × 22
2 turnbuttons	1/4 × 3/4 × 5
16 rails	24 × 1/2 diameter dowel rods

FOLD-FLAT DRYING RACK

A simple fold-flat drying rack has attractions where space is limited. This rack (Fig. 9-14) has more rail space than the previous racks and is in three similar parts, although it could be made with only two. It provides about 20 feet of rail space on frames 27 inches by 36 inches, which fold flat to about 3 inches thick.

All the parts are 1-inch square and could be

softwood, although strength depends on the joints and hardwood joints would be better able to stand up to heavy use. It is possible to use dowel rods instead of square rails, but the rack would not be as rigid. With the specified wood sizes, satisfactory joints between rails and legs could not be made with dowels.

The parts are hinged with webbing or tape about 1 inch wide. By taking it in a figure-eight manner around the legs, the frames can be folded flat on each other either way or stood at any intermediate angle.

1. Mark out the legs all together to match rail positions (Fig. 9-14A).

2. Mark out the rails together (Fig. 9-14B). Mark out and cut mortise and tenon joints to the legs (Fig. 9-14C). Saw cut the tenons so wedges can be used for maximum strength when the parts are glued.

3. Round the edges of the rails. Round or bevel the tops of the legs and take the sharpness off their edges and bottoms.

4. Assemble the frames. Get the first flat and square and use it as a pattern for the others, so they will match when folded. Plane off the wedges and ends of tenons when the glue has set.

5. Make the webbing hinges. Use tacks with large heads, preferably copper or other metal that will not corrode when damp. Start on one leg, tacking below a rail, then go around the other leg so the webbing parts cross. Finally tack on the same surface as the starting end. On the other leg tack on the same surface as the rails (Fig. 9-14D). It may be advisable to try a temporary hinge assembly with a single tack in each place to discover the best arrangement and tension to suit the particular webbing. Have it fairly tight to allow for stretch. Two hinges on each pair of legs should be sufficient.

Materials List for Fold-Flat Drying Rack

6 legs	1 × 1 × 36
9 rails	1 × 1 × 28

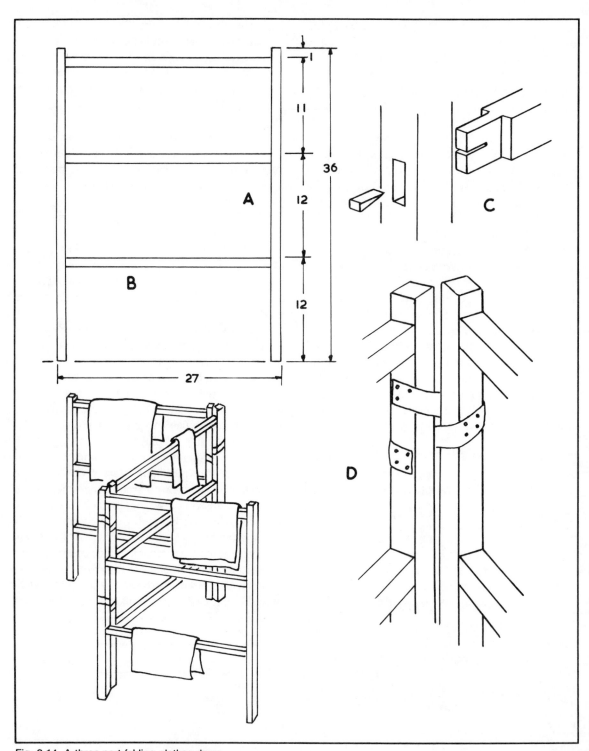

Fig. 9-14. A three-part folding clothes dryer.

Chapter 10

Bathroom

The bathrooms in many homes are no bigger than necessary to accommodate the essential built-in things. There is usually little room for added furniture, though extra facilities may be needed. Some smaller items can stand on existing shelves or ledges. Others can be attached to the walls. It is helpful if an item has a dual purpose—you may sit on it as well as store things in it; a mirror may have storage behind it.

What you make for a bathroom depends on its size and what is already there. Several small items might improve facilities without obstruction. Furniture used elsewhere can be brought into a bathroom, but projects specially suitable for the bathroom are described in this chapter.

UTILITY SHELF UNIT

A simple storage unit for small items, with shelf and drawer, could be appropriate for a bathroom. It can hold the many washing and beauty aids that accumulate there. It can stand on a table, shelf, or desk, or hang on a wall. It might go on a ledge behind a bed for books, drinks, and ornaments.

The design shown in Fig. 10-1 has a Victorian appearance that may appeal to scroll saw enthusiasts. For a modern effect the curves could be eased to a more angular outline, or the back could be cut straight across and the ends given simple bevels.

As shown, the unit is made with solid wood not more than 5/8 inch thick. With a suitable hardwood, it might only be 1/2 inch thick. Pieces might have to be joined to make up widths. If a painted finish is used to disguise edges, the whole unit can be made of plywood. Veneered particleboard can be used for most parts, but that is unsuitable for nearly all curved decoration. Any outlines have to be straight lines, although there could be long sweeping curves at the back to allow for covering with strip veneer.

Sizes can be modified. As shown in Fig. 10-2, the shelf is set back from the width of the bottom, and there is a central drawer with ample capacity for small items. The upper parts of the back and

Fig. 10-1. A utility shelf unit adds decoration to a bathroom.

ends stand high enough to retain a row of books standing on edge. They also prevent other things from falling off and form a good background for displayed ornaments. The back is high enough to take screws for hanging on a wall.

1. Decide on the method of construction. The lengthwise parts can be joined to the ends with dowels (Fig. 10-2A) taken as deep as possible into the ends. Dowels taken right through (Fig. 10-2B), are stronger, and their exposed ends might be regarded as decoration in some circumstances. Exposed screw heads are unacceptable, except possibly in a storeroom or workshop, but screws could be counterbored and plugged. A cross-grain plug of the same wood as the end would be inconspicuous (Fig. 10-2C). Shelf ends could go into dado slots (Fig. 10-2D) and the ends of the bottoms into rabbets. Screws could then be driven upwards to supplement glue. Drive shelf screws upwards before fitting the bottom or there will not be space for a screwdriver. Whatever joints are used at the ends, the pieces at the sides of the drawer and the back to other parts are best dowelled.

2. Set out the shapes of the ends and back (Fig. 10-3A and B). One end can be used to mark the other so they match. Make a paper or card template of half the back and turn it over on the centerline. Mark on these pieces where the other parts come.

3. Make the shelf (Fig. 10-3C) and bottom (Fig. 10-3D) as well as the pieces at the sides of the drawer (Fig. 10-3E). If you are using solid wood, the grain of these last pieces should be upright.

4. Cut or drill, as far as possible, for all joints, then do the shaping on the ends and back. Make sure saw marks are removed and the edges finished square across and smooth. Be careful to keep the shapes symmetrical.

5. The feet shown are square blocks screwed and glued on (Fig. 10-3F). If you have access to a lathe, they could be turned buttons with dowels to fit into holes in the bottom. Round feet are particularly appropriate to the Victorian appearance of the suggested shaped outline.

6. Assemble all parts. There should be little difficulty with squareness as the parts will hold each other square during the fitting of joints. Be particularly careful, however, that the pieces of the sides

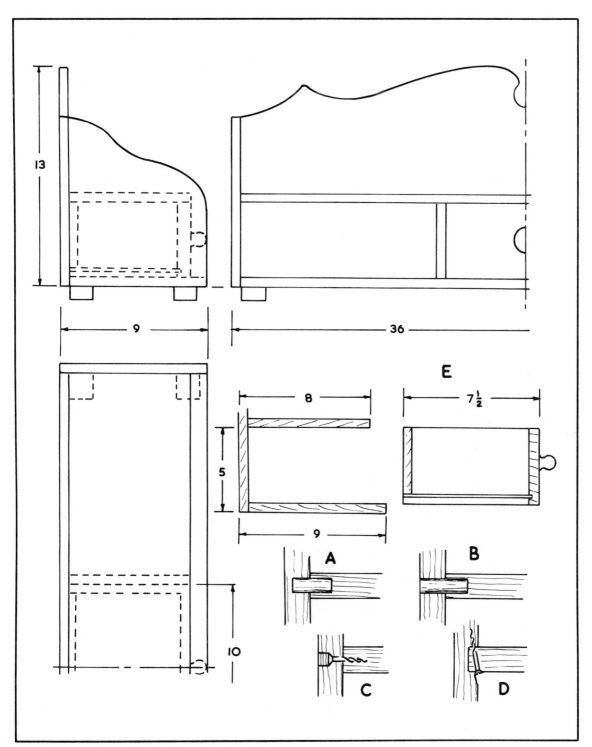

Fig. 10-2. Sizes and construction of the utility shelf unit.

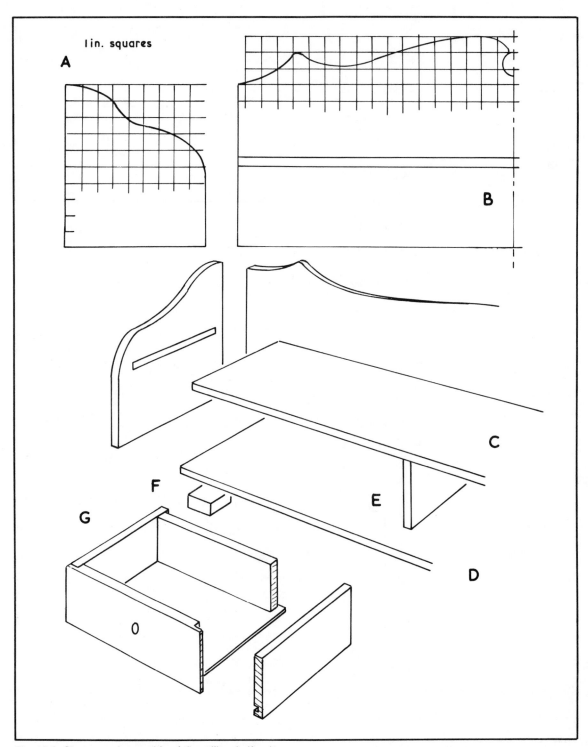

1 in. squares

A

B

C

D

E

F

G

0

Fig. 10-3. Shapes and assembly of the utility shelf unit.

of the drawer opening are square across or you might have difficulty with the fit and movement of the drawer.

7. The drawer (Figs. 10-2E and 10-3G) might have the sides dovetailed to the front or another drawer joint used. It is shown with the sides fitting into rabbets in the front with screws and glue to hold the parts together.

8. Make the drawer front to be an easy fit into the opening. Cut the width of the wood for the sides to slide easily in the space. Plow grooves in these parts to take the bottom.

9. Join the drawer sides to the front and slide in the bottom temporarily. Trim the sides so the drawer stops with the front level with the shelf. When you are satisfied with the fit of the drawer, make its back and assemble the parts with glue and screws.

10. A turned wood knob fitted with a dowel suits the curved decoration, but any type of drawer pull or knob could be fitted.

Materials List for Utility Shelf Unit

2 ends	5/8 × 9 × 10
1 back	5/8 × 13 × 36
1 bottom	5/8 × 8 1/2 × 36
1 shelf	5/8 × 7 1/2 × 36
2 drawer pieces	5/8 × 4 1/2 × 7 1/2
4 feet	1 × 1 1/2 × 1 1/2
1 drawer front	5/8 × 4 1/2 × 10
2 drawer sides	1/2 × 4 1/2 × 7 1/2
1 drawer back	1/2 × 4 × 10
1 drawer bottom	1/8 × 7 1/2 × 10 hard-board or plywood

TOWEL RAIL

In a bathroom there are often more towels than existing rails or hooks. This towel rail (Fig. 10-4) allows two or more towels to be spread on rails and two more to be hung at the ends. The rails might also have a use in a kitchen or bedroom.

The assembly can be screwed to the wall or the back of a door. It may also be more convenient to hang it from an existing rail, over the edge of a radiator, or on the rim of a bath. For screwing to the wall, the bracket backs are wood and extend to take screw holes. For hanging, the backs could be strips of aluminum or other noncorrosive metal screwed on.

The rails are hardwood dowel rods, but the other parts could be any wood if a painted finish is to be used.

1. Decide on the length. A short assembly for folded towels could have 1/2-inch dowel rods, but for longer rails, a 5/8-inch diameter would be better.

2. Mark the hole centers in the brackets (Fig. 10-5A) and use these as centers for a compass to draw the outlines. Drill the top holes right through, but stop the others about halfway. Cut the shapes and round the edges. For greatest strength, cut the wood so the grain is diagonal in the direction indicated.

3. Make the backs (Fig. 10-5B). Drill for screws into the other parts and into the wall. Round the exposed edges.

4. If metal hangers are to be used (Fig. 10-5C), bend the tops to suit what they have to fit and the bottoms to hold off the wood to bring the brackets upright. Drill for screws into the brackets.

5. Round the ends of the dowel rod that will go through. Make curved notches in it (Fig. 10-5D) to retain anything hung there.

6. Assemble with glue and screws, then finish with paint.

Materials List for Towel Rail

2 brackets	5/8 × 4 × 6
2 bracket backs	5/8 × 2 × 6
2 rails	1/2 or 5/8 diameter, length as required
2 metal hangers, if required,	1/8 × 5/8 aluminum

BATHROOM STOOL

A seat that also provides storage is valuable in the often restricted space of a bathroom. This stool (Fig. 10-6) is at a comfortable height and has a drawer with a cupboard below it. It gives maximum

Fig. 10-4. A double towel rail with space for extra towels at the ends.

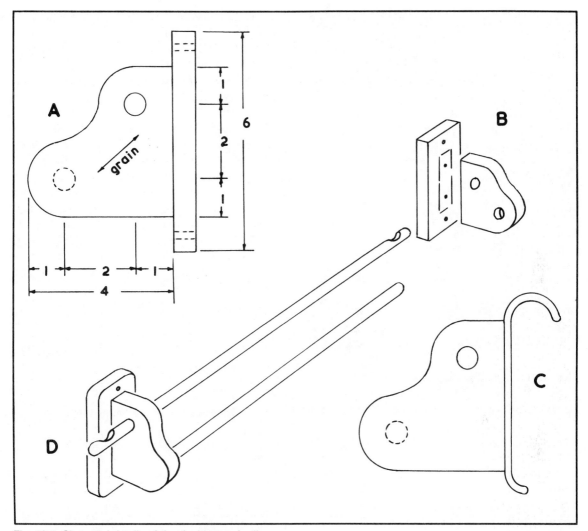

Fig. 10-5. Sizes and details of the double towel rail.

room for many of the small items that are kept in a bathroom.

If you want to have a painted finish, the stool can be made of softwood with hardboard or thin plywood panels. Decide on the choice of panel material first because these control several sizes.

1. Make the four legs slightly overlong at first, until joints have been cut. Plow grooves for the panels on two surfaces of each rear leg (Fig. 10-7A) and on one surface of each front leg. Make the grooves reasonably deep—5/16 inch should be possible in wood of the specified section.

2. Mark the positions of the rails on the legs. Make sure the front legs (Fig. 10-7B) are marked as a pair.

3. Mark all the rails the same length with tenons to fit in the grooves to keep outside edges level with the leg surfaces. Groove those that will take panels. The two top side rails are extra wide (Fig. 10-7C) to act as drawer kickers. The front bottom rail (Fig. 10-7D) is set back by the thickness of the door (Fig. 10-7E).

4. Cut mortises for the front rails in the legs.
5. Cut the panels for the sides slightly under-

Fig. 10-6. A bathroom stool with a drawer and a cupboard.

size so they will not press on the bottoms of the grooves and prevent the rail joints pulling tight.

6. Assemble the pair of sides with glue. Check squareness, flatness, and that they match each other.

7. At the drawer rail level on each side, put a packing to come level with the inner surface of the legs (Fig. 10-7F) to be a drawer guide. On this put a strip (Fig. 10-7G) with its top level with the front rail to act as a drawer runner.

8. Make up the back panel with its rails (Fig. 10-7H).

9. Prepare the bottom (Fig. 10-8A), which will have to be fitted in as the stool frame is assembled. It rests on the rails, is notched around the legs, and has its front edge level with the bottom rail.

10. Join the sides with the back panel and crosswise rails. The bottom should hold the assembly square, but check squareness at the top and see that the legs stand level.

11. Remove any surplus glue, particularly where the drawer will slide.

12. Make the drawer front (Fig. 10-8B) an easy fit in its opening. Cut the drawer sides (Fig. 10-8C) to slide freely. Groove these parts for the bottom. Rabbet the ends of the front and join the sides to it with glue and screws.

13. Fit the drawer bottom loosely and slide the drawer in place. When it is satisfactory, fit its back (Fig. 10-8D) over the bottom between the sides.

14. Make the top; set back 1/8 inch all around. The stool in the photograph has cork over the wood. The top could also be upholstered before fitting. Glue and screw down the top and glue on the cork.

15. The door is a piece of plywood (Fig. 10-7J) between the legs, under the drawer rail, and overlapping the bottom rail. Fit it with two hinges and a spring or other catch.

16. The stool pictured has wooden handles, which could be made, but metal ones may be used on the door and drawer. Those shown at the side are not essential, but they are useful if the stool has to be lifted often.

Materials List for Bathroom Stool	
4 legs	1 1/4 × 1 1/4 × 20
6 rails	1 1/4 × 1 1/4 × 12
1 rail	3/4 × 1 1/4 × 12
2 rails	1 1/4 × 1 3/4 × 12
3 panels	11 × 18 × 1/8 or 1/4 hardboard or plywood
2 drawer guides	1/2 × 2 × 1
2 drawer runners	1/2 × 1 1/4 × 10
1 top	1/2 × 12 × 12
1 bottom	1/2 × 12 × 12
1 door	1/2 × 10 × 12
1 drawer front	5/8 × 4 × 10
2 drawer sides	1/2 × 4 × 11
1 drawer back	1/2 × 3 1/2 × 10
1 drawer bottom	10 × 10 × 1/8 or 1/4 hardboard or plywood

BATH HOLDALL

A rack or trough to rest across the sides of the tub provides a place for soap, sponges, brushes, and the many things you want within reach (Fig. 10-9). Because it is not fixed, it can be moved to where you need it or lifted out. It could even serve as a book

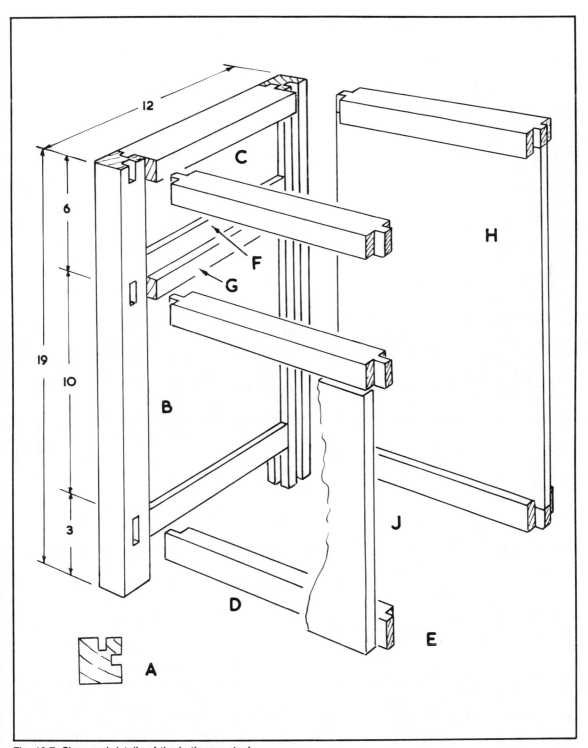

Fig. 10-7. Sizes and details of the bathroom stool.

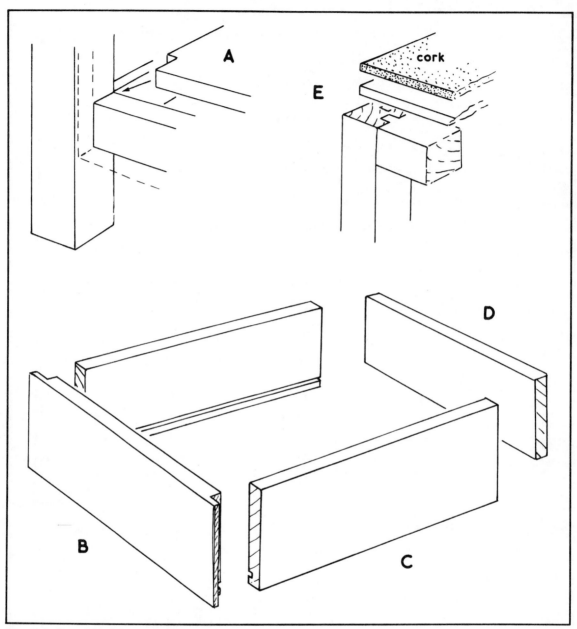

Fig. 10-8. Assembly of the stool and its drawer.

rest if you enjoy reading in the tub.

The material may be hard or softwood. The joints should be made with a waterproof glue, however, and the finish should be water-resistant. The joints are made with dowels and the bottom consists of dowel rods.

Sizes will have to be adjusted to suit your tub. The holdall does not have to be a tight fit. Give it plenty of clearance, but make sure that when it slides fully one way the ends cannot drop inside. The sizes shown are a guide to proportions (Fig. 10-10).

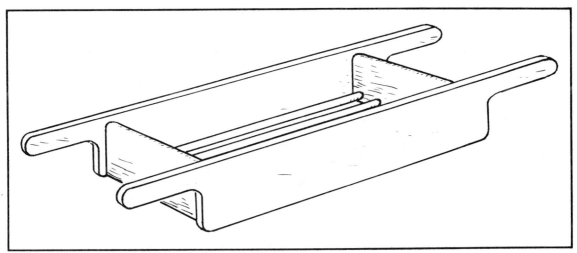

Fig. 10-9. This holdall is intended to rest across a tub bath.

1. Mark out the two sides (Fig. 10-10A) together with the positions of the ends and the shapes of the arms drawn.

2. Cut the end pieces (Fig. 10-10B) and mark the positions of the bottom dowel rods. These could be 1/2-inch diameter and the joints made with 1/4-inch dowels. Drill for all dowels. Go as deep as possible into the thickness of the wood without the drill point breaking through.

3. Cut the arms on the sides (Fig. 10-10C). Round the ends and the top edges of all parts. Take the sharpness off other edges.

4. Glue the dowel rods into the ends and the ends to the sides, tightly and squarely.

```
            Materials List for Bath Holdall

2 sides                 1/2  × 4 × 30
2 ends                  1/2  × 3 1/2 × 6
5 dowel rods            18   × 1/2 diameter
```

BATHROOM CABINET

A wall-mounted cabinet in a bathroom can accommodate the small things that accumulate there. It also keeps such things as medicines and pills out of reach of small prying hands. A mirror on the door is an extra bonus.

This cabinet can be fitted under a shelf (Fig. 10-11) or screwed through the back into a wall. There are two ways of mounting a mirror. If you want to fit a lock, frame the front. If you want a spring or magnetic catch, use either door construction. The simplest way to make the cabinet is with nails or screws. At the other extreme are dovetailed corners. Between these methods are rabbets and other corner joints.

A painted finish will hide the method of construction. Softwood can be used. Any plywood should be a waterproof type.

The available mirror will determine the size of the cabinet. You can also get a mirror cut to specification.

1. Prepare the wood for the sides, top, and bottom. The back might be nailed directly on. If you want to hide its edges, cut rabbets in the rear of the main parts to suit it.

2. Cut the top and bottom wide until you have made the door because they should overlap the door by a small amount. They would not look right if finished too narrow.

3. Of the two types of door suggested, the simplest is a piece of plywood the same size as the mirror with metal clips screwed around the edges (Fig. 10-12A). The plywood edges may be lipped, but a painted finish directly on the plywood should hide its details.

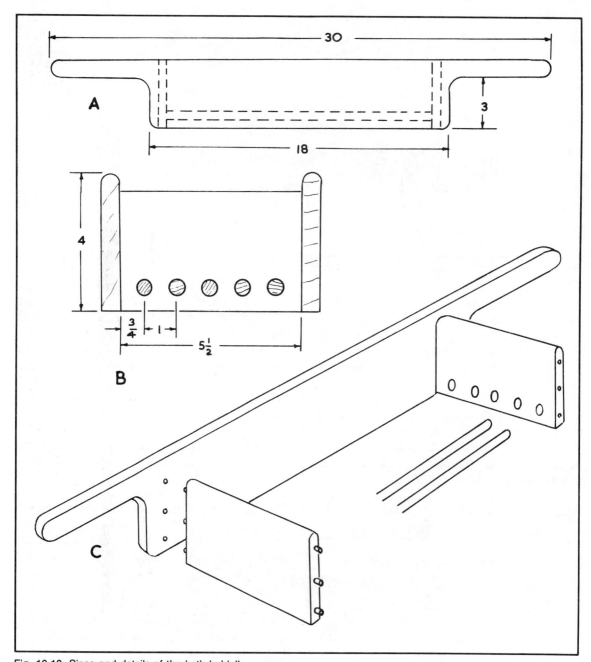

Fig. 10-10. Sizes and details of the bath holdall.

4. The other type of door is built up with a frame. At the back is a sheet of plywood (Fig. 10-12B), which could be lipped. Inside this are strips of wood the same thickness as the mirror (Fig. 10-12C), then wide pieces frame the front (Fig. 10-12D).

5. Miter the visible door corners. Assemble by screwing from the back. Use glue as well, if you

Fig. 10-11. A bathroom cabinet with a mirror front.

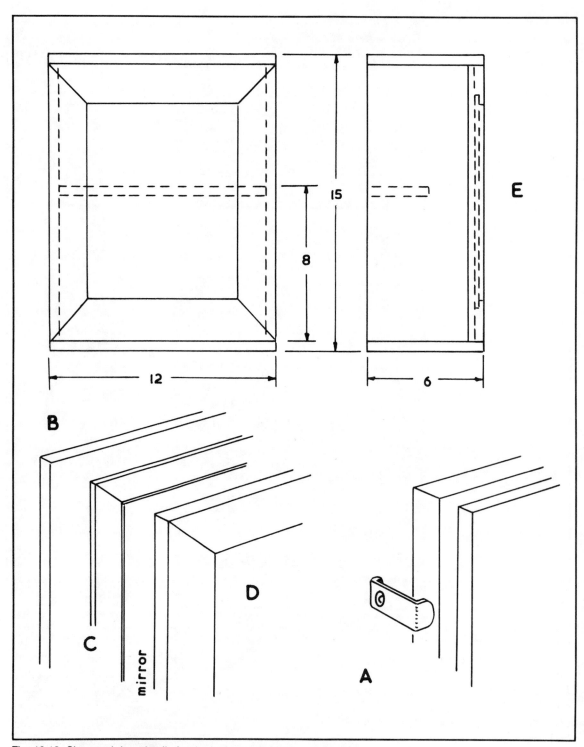

Fig. 10-12. Sizes and door details for the bathroom cabinet.

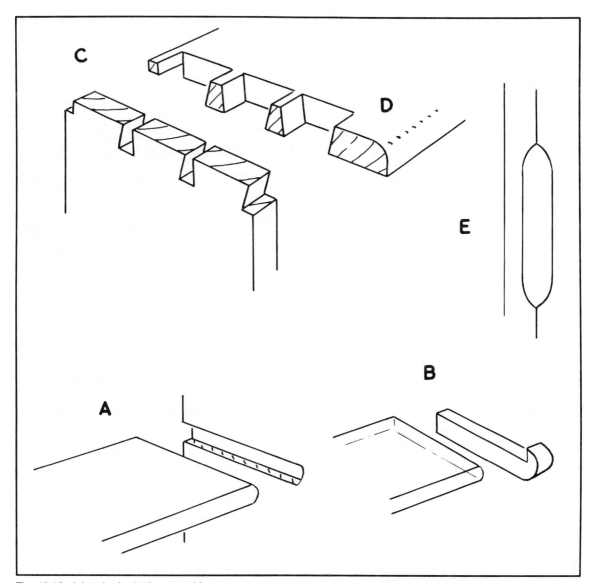

Fig. 10-13. Joints in the bathroom cabinet.

wish, but if you plan to take the glass out later, omit the glue from at least one layer.

6. Inside there should be a shelf just above the center (Fig. 10-12E). It can be wood or glass. Round the front of a wood shelf and fit it into dadoes (Fig. 10-13A). A glass shelf could go into dadoes, but is better supported on brackets so it can be lifted out (Fig. 10-13B).

7. The cabinet corner joints have to allow for the rabbets at the back. If dovetails are used (Fig. 10-13C), cut the rear edge of the last tail upright against the rabbet and notch the overlapping parts.

8. Round the top and bottom front edges (Fig. 10-13D) and the sides of the door.

9. Hinge the door at the more convenient side and fit a catch or lock at the other side. There could be a knob or handle for opening, or simply notch the cabinet side (Fig. 10-13E) so you can put fingers

behind the door to pull it. If that is not enough space, cut a matching notch in the door as well.

WASTEBASKET

A wooden waste bin can be attractive as well as sturdy. This wastebasket (Fig. 10-14) can be painted to match other furniture in a bathroom or stained and polished to stand beside a desk or sewing table. It is substantial enough to take the waste from a hobby in your den or shop.

Plywood 1/4 inch thick and framed with strips 3/4 inch square is suggested. Hardboard 1/8 inch thick could be substituted or thicker plywood used for tough conditions. If the contents are liable to be damp, marine or exterior grade plywood and waterproof glue will make a watertight wooden bucket.

The slight taper shown (Fig. 10-15) allows the contents to be tipped out easily, but is not enough to make the fitting of corner angles difficult. If the sizes are altered, do not give the sides too much flare.

1. Make two opposite sides, symmetrical about centerlines, with strips pinned and glued at the edges (Fig. 10-15A). Round the tops of these strips (Fig. 10-16A).

2. Make the other two sides 1/2 inch wider (Figs. 10-15B and 10-16B).

3. Join the four sides with pins and glue.

4. Prepare the wood that will make the strips around the base by planing to the same angle as the sides (Fig. 10-15C).

Fig. 10-14. A wastebasket particularly suitable for a bathroom.

5. Fit the strips around the bottom edge (Fig. 10-16C). They are shown mitered (Fig. 10-15D). For a painted finish that will hide constructional details, they could be overlapped.

6. Add the bottom (Fig. 10-16D) and four square feet at the corners (Fig. 10-16E).

7. Put strips around the top (Fig. 10-16F).

8. Round all exposed edges and finish with several coats of paint.

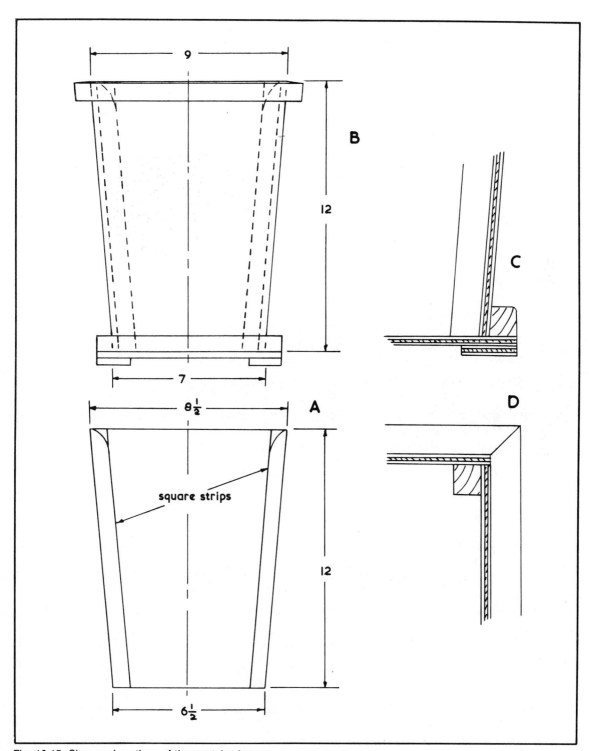

Fig. 10-15. Sizes and sections of the wastebasket.

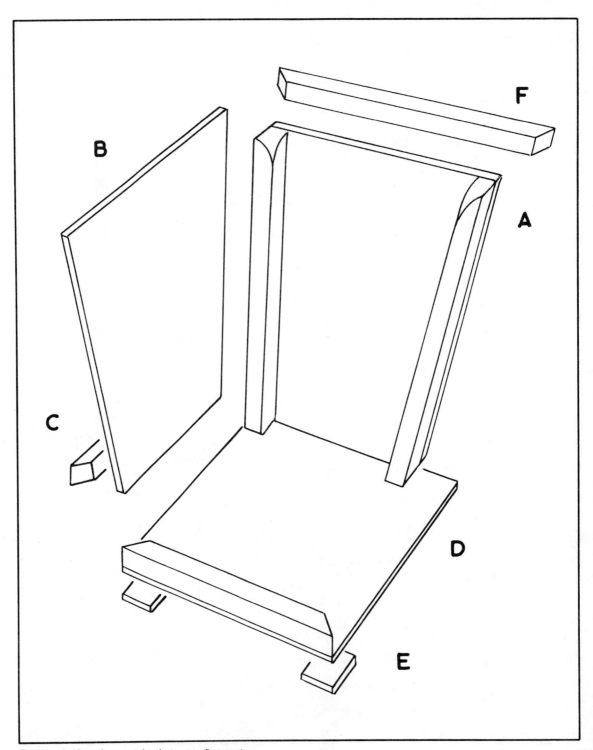

Fig. 10-16. How the wastebasket parts fit together.

Chapter 11

Den

The den can be a playroom, particularly if there are many young members of the family. It can be a hobby room, where a variety of things are tackled, such as sewing or modelmaking; or a music room, if that is your inclination. It can be just a place to relax without the need to wipe your shoes or watch out for the furniture.

Whatever the need, and that might change with a growing family, the furniture is usually a more casual type. This does not mean it need not be soundly constructed, although sometimes the finish, or lack of it, may reflect the surroundings.

DEN TABLE

In a den, playroom, or shop any table needs to be robust and adaptable to a variety of uses. It might not need the finish given to furniture for other rooms in the house. In fact, if it looks functional, it might be a better match for its surroundings than a more delicately finished piece.

This table (Fig. 11-1) is a size intended to be used beside or amongst chairs. It is strong enough

in itself to be used as a seat, and it might support wood being sawn or otherwise processed. The edges will take clamps. It matches the den chair (Fig. 11-4) and can be used with one or more of them.

The parts may be standard softwood stock and the top fir plywood. All of the rails are notched 1/4 inch deep into the legs. They can be held there with glue and screws, but dowels 1/2 inch or larger (Fig. 11-2A) will allow the framework to be built without metal fasteners. Alternatively, screws could be counterbored in the rails so dowel plugs may be glued in over them. In both cases, the dowels planed level with the surface will add to the functional appearance of the table.

The sizes suggested (Fig. 11-2B) can be altered without affecting construction. The table would probably not be made much smaller, but it could be enlarged up to workbench size for hobby use.

1. Prepare the two pairs of legs (Fig. 11-3A). Across the 2-inch width the notches are on the outside (Fig. 11-2C); in the other direction they are on

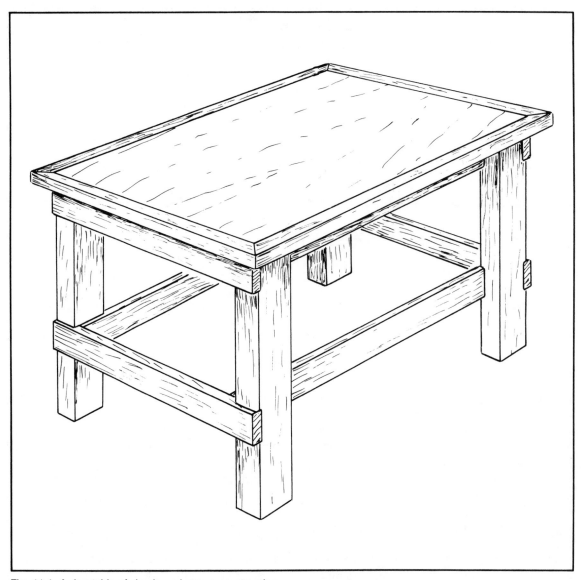

Fig. 11-1. A den table of simple and strong construction.

the insides of the legs (Fig. 11-2D). Use the actual wood for the rails to set the widths of the notches.

2. Make the four lengthwise rails (Fig. 11-3B) and join them to the legs. Check squareness and that opposite sides match.

3. Do the same with the short rails (Fig. 11-3C). Measure diagonals to check that the assembly is square.

4. Cut the top plywood level with the outer rails and the leg surfaces the other way (Fig. 11-3D). Fit it to the framework. Drive screws downwards into the rails and the leg tops. It would be neater to use nails, set below the surface and covered with filler. In any case, glue to the rails as well.

5. Plane the plywood edges level. Fit the lips (Fig. 11-3E) against the edges and nail to the plywood, the rails, and the legs. Mitered corners look

274

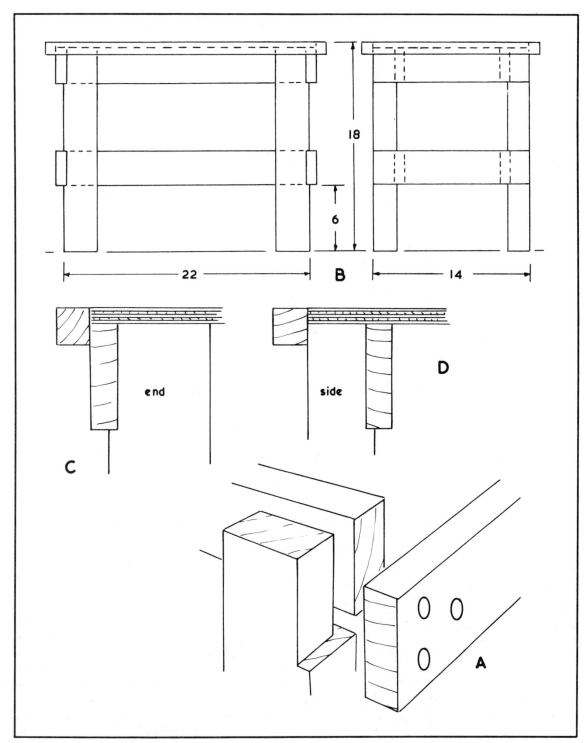

Fig. 11-2. Sizes and details of the den table.

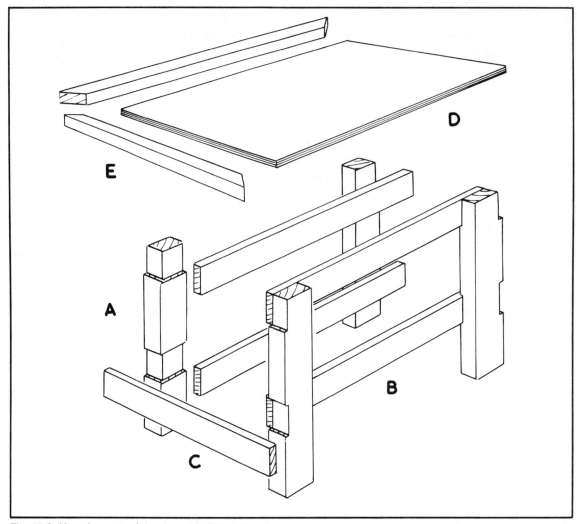

Fig. 11-3. How the parts of the den table fit together.

best, but the lip edges could overlap. In either case, round the corners and take the sharpness off exposed edges.

Materials List for Den Table

4 legs	2 × 3 × 18
4 rails	3/4 × 3 × 22
4 rails	3/4 × 3 × 14
1 top	16 × 24 × 1/2 plywood
2 lips	1 × 1 × 26
2 lips	1 × 1 × 18

DEN CHAIR

Like the den table (Fig. 11-1), this chair (Fig. 11-4) is functional and robust. Despite its workmanlike appearance, it is comfortable. Construction is very similar to the table, with rails let 1/4 inch into the legs. Stock sizes of softwood are used, and the joints may be screwed or dowelled.

There are two cushions, not attached to the chair, that may be made or bought. If they are bought, they should be obtained first so sizes of the woodwork can be modified to suit. They could be made by covering 4-inch thick slabs of plastic foam.

They are simple rectangular shapes. The cloth covering is sewn on three sides inside-out, and after turning the right way, the foam is inserted and the fourth side sewn. If these sides are brought together in use, the outside seams will not show.

The seat cushion is supported on rubber webbing arranged front to back of the chair. The strips are about 2 inches wide with gaps of less than 1 inch between strips. Clips squeeze and grip the ends, then press into grooves in the wood. The front groove is in a strip inside the front rail (Fig. 11-5A). At the back the webbing goes over the edge of a rail and into a groove at its rear (Fig. 11-5B). The webbing has to be tensioned to give the right amount of support. Get the webbing and clips before making the woodwork so grooves can be made to suit the end clips.

1. Make the two pairs of legs. They are the

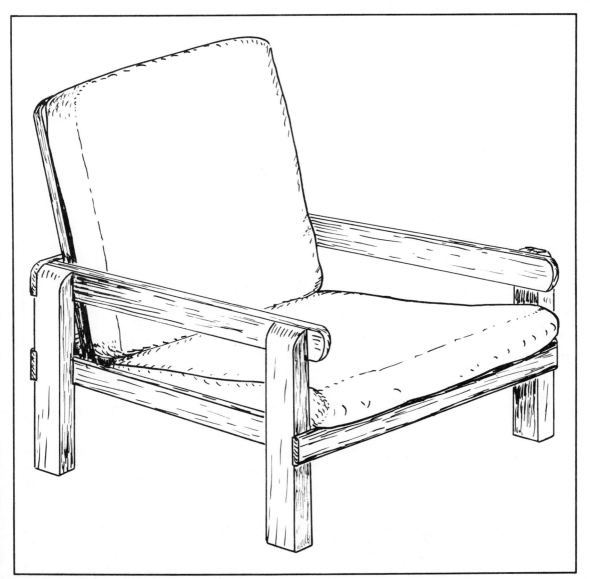

Fig. 11-4. A den chair to match the den table.

same except the front legs (Fig. 11-6A) are not notched for the top rail, which comes at the back (Fig. 11-6B).

2. Make the rails at seat level (Fig. 11-6C) and those that form the arms (Fig. 11-6D). Round the fronts of the arms and the tops of the legs. Prepare the seat rails to take the tenons on the rear web-

bing rail (Fig. 11-5C).

3. Join the parts to make the pair of opposite sides.

4. Prepare the three crosswise rails. They are the same except the outside edges of the front one should be well rounded (Fig. 11-5D).

5. Make the rear webbing rail. Plow the

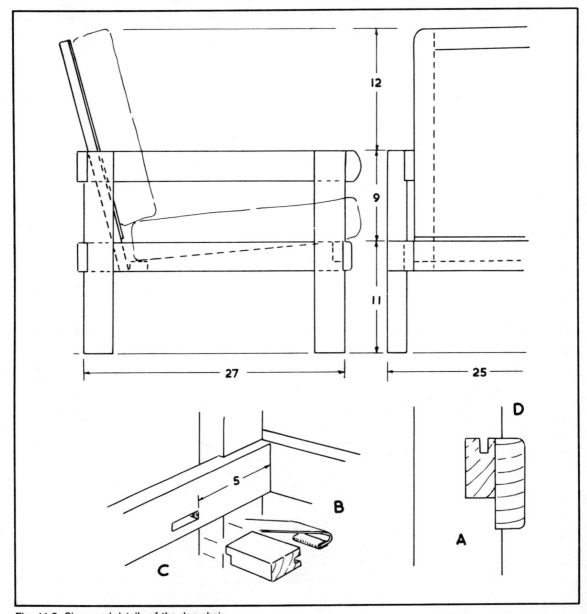

Fig. 11-5. Sizes and details of the den chair.

278

groove below center. That allows the load to be on a thicker part and keeps the groove away from the tenons.

6. Join the side frames with the three main rails and the rear webbing rail. Check squareness in all directions.

7. Make the front webbing rail (Figs. 11-5A and 11-6E) to fit between the front legs. Glue and screw it to the front rail.

8. The frame for the back cushion fits between the chair sides. It rests against the top rear rail and is screwed to the two rails at each side. Cut the back plywood to size (Fig. 11-6F). Glue and screw the framing strips to it (Fig. 11-6G) with some surplus left at the bottom of the side pieces.

9. Experiment with the angle of the back, testing it for comfort preferably with the webbing fitted and the cushions in place. Mark the best position. Round the top corners and edges. Cut off any unwanted wood and screw to the back through the side rails.

Materials List for Den Chair	
4 legs	2 × 3 × 20
2 rails	1 × 3 × 27
2 rails	1 × 3 × 30
3 rails	1 × 3 × 25
2 webbing rails	1 × 2 × 25
1 back	21 × 22 × 1/2 plywood

ROUND PLYWOOD TABLE

This is a little table suitable for drinks and snacks (Fig. 11-7). It is of light construction and is easily carried. The main parts are 1/2-inch plywood, with the legs formed by two pieces notched together. The parts (Fig. 11-8) could be prefabricated for several tables at one time. This is a table for almost any room, but is particularly suitable as a side drinks table in a den.

If a hardwood plywood is chosen, the table could be varnished. The top might have an attractive veneer left clear, while the edge is darkened. The table in the photograph has a Formica top and the edge is painted black. If fir plywood is used,

a painted finish would be better.

For stability it is inadvisable for the top to overhang very much. It is shown 1 inch bigger than the legs (Fig. 11-9).

1. Set out the shapes of the leg parts (Fig. 11-9A). If several tables are made, a hardboard half-template would ensure uniformity.

2. Cut the curves, but do not cut the tenons until the rails are made. Cut the matching slots to be a tight push fit. The legs should assemble square and level (Fig. 11-10A).

3. Make the two top rails (Fig 11-10B). Their length is the same as the width of the legs. Cut a halving joint at the center so the surfaces finish level (Fig. 11-10C). Mark the mortises to fit the tenons on the legs. Cut these joints (Fig. 11-9B).

4. Remove all saw marks and round all edges, except where joints come.

5. Glue the rails together, checking that they are square. Glue the legs together and to the rails. Check that the assembly stands level.

6. The top is shown with square edges (Fig. 11-10D). It could be rounded or molded, but plywood will not take fine detail on its edge. There could be plastic or veneer glued round as a lip. Cut the shape of the top as accurately as possible because discrepancies will be obvious. The outline could be octagonal if you wish.

Materials List for Round Plywood Table	
2 legs	14 × 18 × 1/2 plywood
1 top	15 × 15 × 1/2 plywood
2 rails	3/4 × 1 1/2 × 14

PIANO STOOL

For sitting at a piano or organ a seat should be higher than a normal chair. Some piano stools are very ornate, but nearly all are arranged with a box seat so sheet music and other things can be stored inside. This piano stool (Fig.11-11) is simple, both in appearance and construction. Besides its use as a piano stool, it could be a seat when working at a hobby or craft at a table. Its extra height will al-

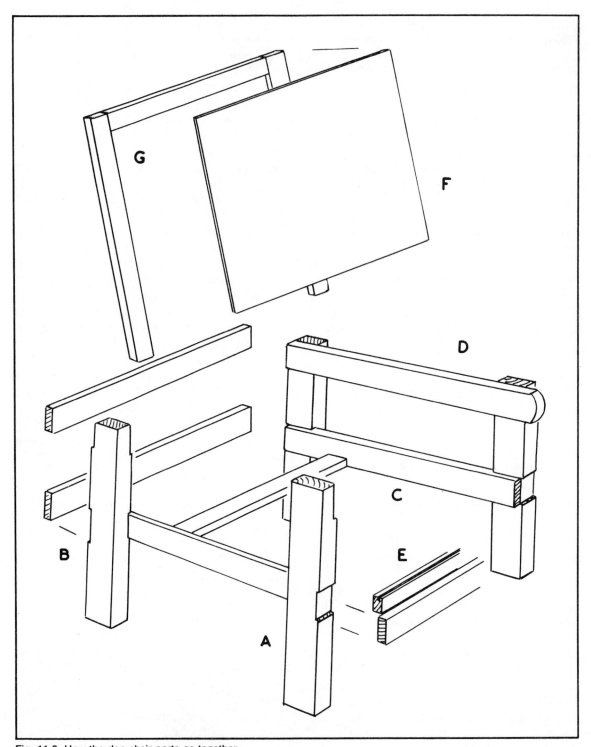

Fig. 11-6. How the den chair parts go together.

Fig. 11-7. A plywood table with a round top.

low a better reach over a larger area.

Construction is similar to many small tables with rails between legs. In addition, a bottom fits inside the rails and a top hinges open and is lightly upholstered. Very deep soft seating is not advisable when playing a piano. The basic outline is without ornamentation because the proportions are all that are required to give a pleasing appearance. Some decoration of the lower edges of the rails is possible, however. The overhang of the top hides the upper parts.

The wood should be close-grained hardwood.

Straight-grained pieces should be chosen for the legs to reduce the risk of warping. Dowelled construction is shown, but the rails could be tenoned if extra length is required.

1. The sizes shown (Fig. 11-12) makes a stool of suitable size for a piano of normal size in most surroundings. For use with some organs it can be made longer.

2. Start with the legs (Fig. 11-12A). Keep the tops square to 2 inches below the rail positions, then taper to 1 inch square on the inner surfaces only so the outer corners remain upright.

3. Cut the wood for the long and short rails (Fig. 11-12B and C), carefully squaring the ends. Mark out for three, 1/2-inch dowels in each end (Fig. 11-12D). Cut the dowels so they will go as far as possible into each leg (Fig. 11-12E).

4. Mark and drill the legs (Fig. 11-12F) to keep the outside surfaces of the legs and rails level.

5. Groove the lower edges of the rails to take the plywood bottom (Fig. 11-12G). Where these grooves meet the legs, mark and cut across the corners (Fig. 11-12H). Do not go so deeply that these diagonal cuts reach the bottoms of the grooves in the rails as this might weaken the legs. It will be sufficient to go only far enough to meet the inner surfaces of the rails, then the plywood corners will be trimmed to suit (Fig. 11-12J).

6. If the rails are to be decorated, do this before assembly. There could be a bead worked along the bottom edge (Fig. 11-13A) or a molding made

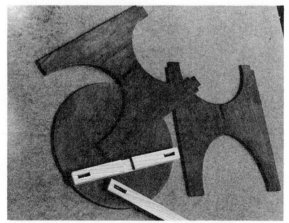

Fig. 11-8. The parts of the round plywood table.

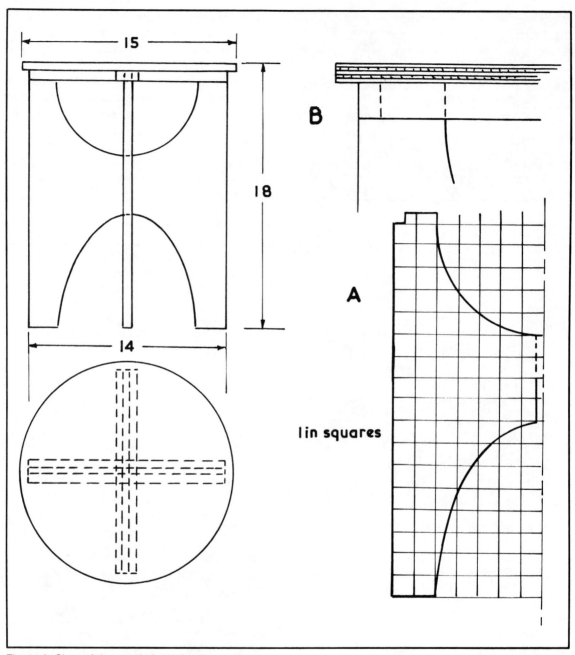

Fig. 11-9. Sizes of the round plywood table.

there. The edge could be shaped slightly (Fig. 11-13B). Do not cut into the groove for the bottom or raise it excessively because the box will be too shallow.

7. Assemble in two stages. Join the long rails to their legs. Square one set and check that it is free from twist, then assemble the opposite long side to make a matching pair to it. Let the glue in these

joints set. Cut the plywood bottom to size. It should not be such a close fit as to press on the bottoms of the grooves because it might prevent the dowelled joints from pressing together tightly. Assemble the short rails and the bottom to the other assemblies. The bottom will hold all parts square, but see that the legs stand level on a flat surface.

Stand back and look at the stool from several directions to see that it appears upright.

8. The top is a piece of 1/2-inch plywood (Fig. 11-13C) with foam padding and a fabric cover. Cut the plywood to overhang the main assembly by 1 1/2 inches all around. Cut a moderate curve on what will be the bottom edges (Fig. 11-13D).

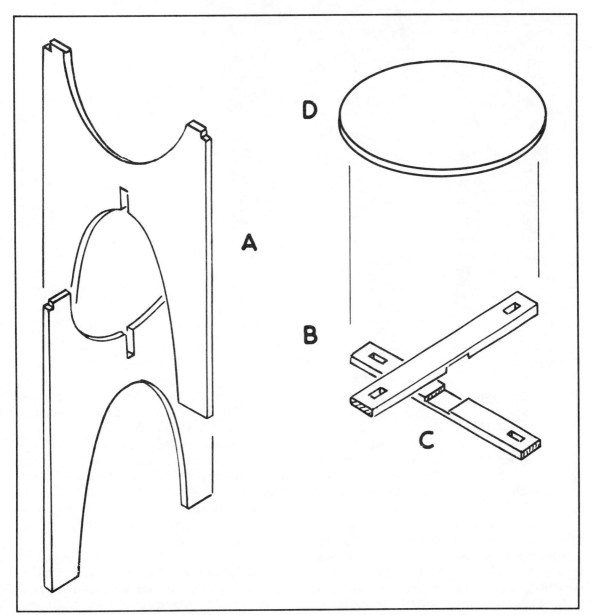

Fig. 11-10. Assembly of the round plywood table.

Fig. 11-11. A piano stool with storage space under its padded top.

9. Cut a piece of 1/4-inch plywood or 1/8-inch hardboard 3/4 inch smaller than the top all round (Fig. 11-13E). The upholstery will be buttoned. Besides improving appearance, this stops the padding from moving under the fabric. Four buttons are suggested (Fig. 11-13F). They could be arranged squarely, as shown, or as a diamond pattern. There might be more, arranged in other ways, if you wish. To allow for buttoning, drill both pieces of plywood with 1/4-inch holes below where the buttons will come.

10. Cut a piece of plastic or rubber foam about 1 inch thick and 1/2 inch bigger each way than the plywood top. Bevel its lower edges. This allows it to take a smooth curve and compress slightly to avoid the plywood showing a hard edge. Cover with fabric, stretching enough to shape the upper surface, by pulling into 3/8-inch tacks about 1 inch

from the plywood edge. The number of tacks will depend on the cloth and how it shapes, but 1 1/2-inch spacing is appropriate.

11. After upholstering the top, position the plywood or hardboard covering piece so the holes match. Screw it in place to hide and retain the tacks.

12. Buttons may be bought covered with fabric to match or plain buttons of matching or contrasting color could be used. Have a needle with stout thread. Underneath there could be flat buttons with two holes. Short pegs or dowels can be used (Fig. 11-13G). Drill across so the needle can be pushed through.

13. Use the needle to take the thread up through the wood and covering from below. Put the button on the thread and take the needle down close to where the thread comes up. Underneath, knot the thread through the peg or flat button, adjust-

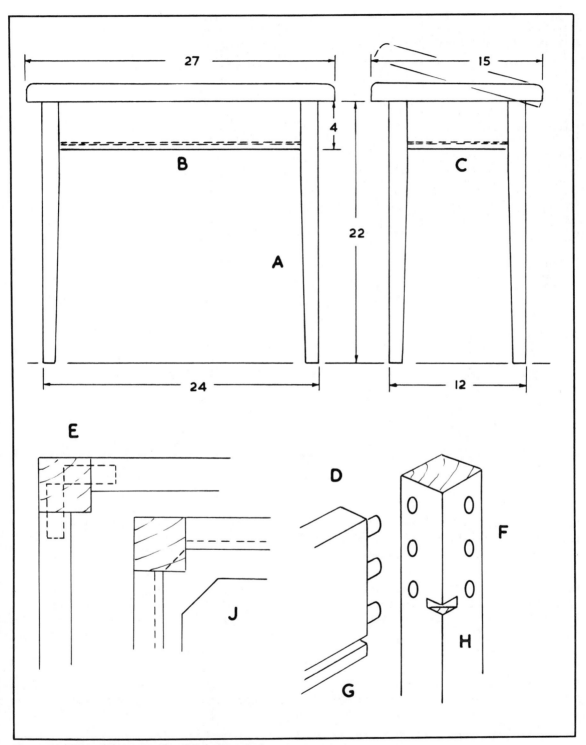

Fig. 11-12. Sizes and construction of the piano stool.

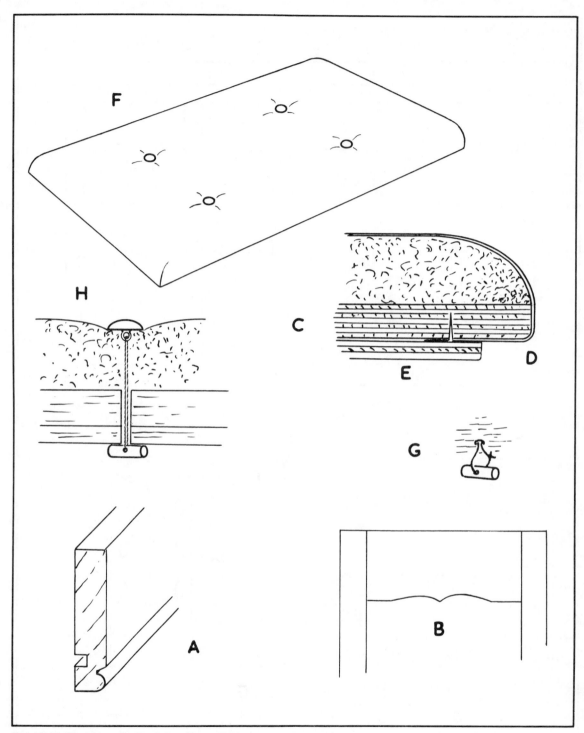

Fig. 11-13. The top and rails of the piano stool.

ing tension so the button on top is pulled level or below the surface (Fig. 12-13H). Get the same tension on all buttons. More information on buttoning is given in Chapter 1.

14. Hinge the top to a long rail. Two, 3-inch hinges should be adequate. Let them into the rail edge so the lid closes flat, but not so deeply that the hinged edge meets before the others and the lid has to be forced down. This will strain the hinge screws. Arrange the hinge knuckles clear of the rail edge. When the lid is opened, it will stop at an angle slightly further than upright. There should be no need for any other support, but you could fit a folding metal stay or fit a cord between two screw eyes.

15. Before finishing the wood, remove the top after a trial assembly. This will protect the fabric from being marked by stain or varnish or other finish.

Materials List for Piano Stool	
4 legs	1 1/2 × 1 1/2 × 22
2 rails	7/8 × 4 × 21
2 rails	7/8 × 4 × 9
1 bottom	10 × 22 × 1/4 plywood
1 top	15 × 27 × 1/2 plywood
1 top	14 × 26 × 1/4 plywood
	or 1/8 inch hardboard

SEWING BOX

This box (Fig. 11-14) is intended to hold sewing equipment and it might also suit a knitting or crochet enthusiast. There is a large container and a drawer below for small things. A tray might be fitted in the box and the drawer could have divisions. The legs support the box at a convenient height for the user to reach it while sitting in a chair.

The main parts should be solid wood with the grain the long way of each piece. The deckle edges are then all cut in end grain, except for the drawer front. If you prefer the box without this decoration, the corners could all be cut square and edges straight. Box parts are dowelled together. If the wood is 5/8 inch thick, dowels could be 5/16 inch

or 3/8 inch at about 2-inch intervals. The legs may be dowelled, or alternatively, screwed from inside the box.

1. Mark out the wood for the two sides (Figs. 11-15A and 11-16A). If you lay out the shapes and positions of other parts on one side, that will serve as a guide when making and fitting them.

2. Make a template (Fig.11-17A) of the shaped ends wide enough to suit the drawer front and lid edges. Mark its centerline and use it over the centerlines of the narrower sides to draw their end shapes.

3. Make the lid (Fig. 11-16B) the same length as the sides. Make the back (Figs. 11-15B and 11-16C) to match the lid, but cut down in depth to allow for the lid coming between the sides. Make the front in the same way, but narrow enough to allow for the drawer (Figs. 11-15C and 11-16D).

4. Do the end shaping, checking that the patterns look alike and the edges are smooth.

5. Join the four box parts with dowels. Use the lid to check squareness.

6. The bottom of the box is a piece of plywood or hardboard supported in strips glued and nailed or screwed inside the box (Fig. 11-16E).

7. The drawer fills the space under the box bottom (Fig. 11-16F). Cut its sides and back to a width to suit. Plow grooves for the bottom and for the runners (Fig. 11-15D). Because the drawer front goes below the sides to provide a grip for pulling out, a separate handle is not needed. Use the template to mark the lower edge (Figs. 11-15E and 11-16G). Notch the front to take the sides (Fig. 11-15F). Cut the sides to length so when the drawer is shut, its back will come against the box back and its front will be level with the box front. Fit drawer runners to the box sides. Assemble the drawer with glue and dowels and screws.

8. The lid pivots on two screws and is positioned so it rests on the box back and front when it is closed. When it is opened, it swings to vertical or slightly past it (Fig. 11-15G). Round-head screws, 10 gauge by 2 inches long, are suitable. For greatest strength, screw threads should go right through the sides and be entirely buried in the lid. Dowels could be used as pivots, but they would be difficult to

Fig. 11-14. A sewing box with a top compartment and a drawer below.

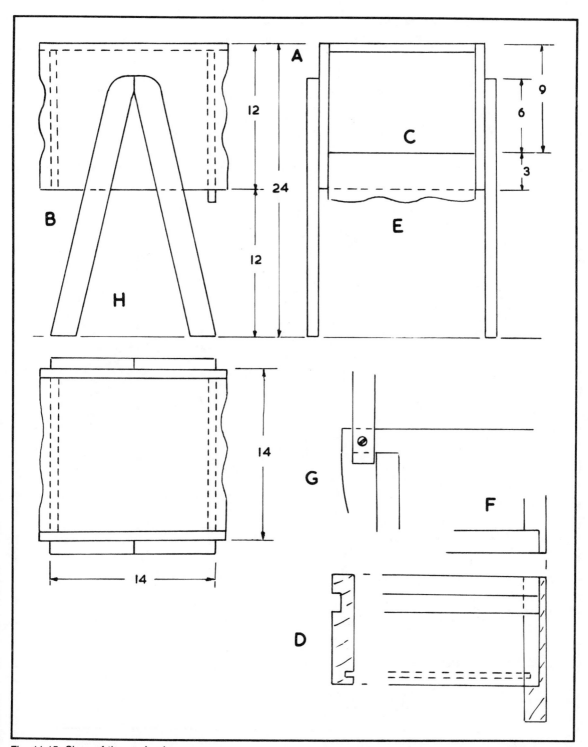

Fig. 11-15. Sizes of the sewing box.

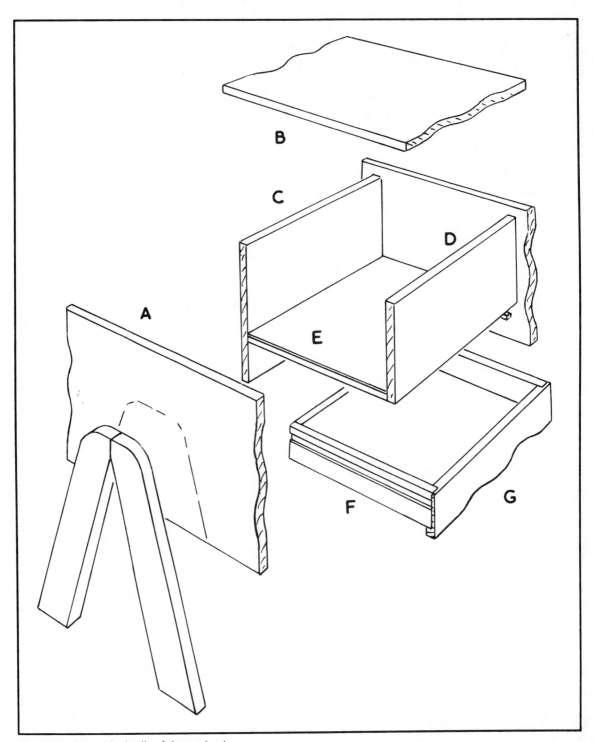

Fig. 11-16. Assembly details of the sewing box.

remove if that ever became necessary.

9. Set out the main lines of an end view full size (Fig.11-15H) to get the shape and sizes of the legs. Their bottoms spread to the width of the box. Make the legs and attach them to the box. Spread screws or dowels widely for greatest strength. Sight across when assembling to check that leg angles match.

10. If a tray is needed in the box, it can be made to slide on two bearers (Fig. 11-17B). If it is made half the width of the box, it will allow reasonable access to the contents below and can be lifted out when required.

11. Divisions in the drawer separate small items. They can be fitted to suit your needs during construction. To allow for changes in requirements, they might be made movable. One way of doing this is to put V-shaped grooves in the drawer, possibly at 1-inch intervals, then make divisions to fit into them (Fig. 11-17C). Because they drop in without glue, they can be lifted out and rearranged.

Materials List for Sewing Box	
2 sides	5/8 × 12 × 16
1 back	5/8 × 12 × 13
1 front	5/8 × 9 × 13
1 bottom	13 × 13 × 1/8 or 1/4 hardboard or plywood
4 bottom bearers	1/2 × 1/2 × 13
2 drawer sides	1/2 × 3 × 14
1 drawer back	1/2 × 3 × 14
1 drawer front	5/8 × 4 × 14
1 drawer bottom	14 × 14 × 1/8 or 1/4 hardboard or plywood
2 drawer runners	3/8 × 1/2 × 14
4 legs	1 × 2 × 24

SPRING-ACTION FOLDING TABLE

There are many ways of making tables which fold flat, and most of them require specific actions to lock them with the legs in position or stowed. One way of providing a nearly automatic lock up and down is to use a spring action provided by flexible wooden laths. The laths engage with notches to hold the legs firmly in the upright position, and they press against their rails to keep them closely folded

under the top. When opening, the legs spring into place automatically; but for closing, the laths have to be lifted out of their notches.

There could be a single lath under a small coffee table (Fig. 11-18), but for a larger table (Fig. 11-19), it is better to have two. Sizes and proportions are controlled by the need to fold the legs to fit within each other and within the table length (Fig. 11-20A).

Ash and hickory are the woods most suitable for the spring laths. Any wood could be chosen for the other parts. The top might be made up from solid wood boards glued together or from veneered particleboard. For a lighter table it might be plywood with the edges improved by lips.

It is helpful to use the underside of the top to lay out the other parts. The opposing legs are best arranged to fit into each other without excessive clearance. The inside legs at one end should not be positioned towards each other any further than necessary. The laths and their notches come only a short distance inside them.

1. Mark out the top. Fit the end rails to its underside (Fig. 11-20B) with 1/2-inch clearance at their ends.

2. Make the two leg rails (Figs. 11-20C and 11-21A). Mark on them the positions of the legs. On one they are at the ends of the rails (Fig. 11-21B). On the other they are set in 2 inches (Fig. 11-21C).

3. Make the legs. The top 6 inches remain parallel. Notch to half the thickness of the rails (Fig. 11-21D). Leave the notched side of each leg straight, but taper the opposite side to 1 3/8-inches square at the bottom. For the legs that are outside when folded, taper the inner surfaces in the same way (Fig. 11-20D). For the legs that will be inside when folded, taper the outer surfaces to match (Fig. 11-20E).

4. Cut the wood for the laths (Fig. 11-21E), but leave it long. Also have the central blocks (Fig. 11-21F) and covers (Fig. 11-21G) ready.

5. Mark the notches on the leg rails 1/2 inch inside the positions of the two closer legs (Fig. 11-21H). Cut them with notches to let the laths go in their full depth, but to be a loose fit in the width.

6. Join the legs to their rails with glue and

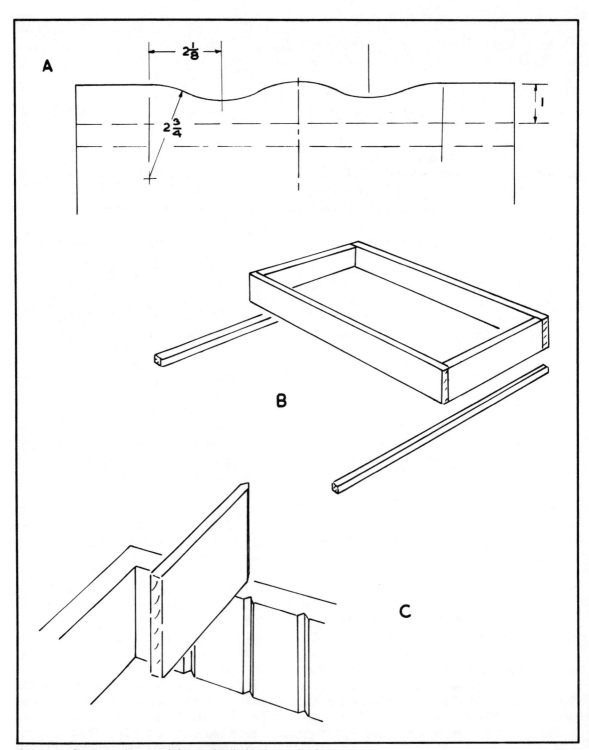

Fig. 11-17. Shapes and tray and drawer details for the sewing box.

Fig. 11-18. A folding table where the legs are held open and closed with a flexible lath.

screws. Check squareness and the folded fit by laying the assemblies on the inverted top.

7. Position the lath blocks and glue and screw them to the top. Temporarily screw the laths and covers to the blocks. Two thin screws will probably be enough. Many thick screws would weaken the wood, reducing springiness, and possibly causing breakage.

8. Stand the leg assemblies in position against the top rails on the inverted top, letting the spring laths extend over the rails. Mark where the ends of the laths have to fit into the notches. Dismantle and trim the lath ends, preferably cutting slightly too long at first to make a close fit during the final assembly.

9. Much of the load on the table when it is in use comes on the hinges. They should be strong—as long as the width of a leg and with holes for enough stout screws. Attach the hinges to the tops of the legs so their knuckles are level with the tops. In this way the legs as well as the hinges will take the load.

10. Position each leg assembly tight against its top rail, which will help the hinges keep the legs upright.

11. Screw the laths and their covers in position and try the opening and closing action. There should be no need for glue on the lath attachments.

12. The legs, rails, and laths should have their edges rounded. Leave the edge of the top square,

or you can round or mold it. The finish will depend on the intended use.

Materials List for Spring-Action Folding Table	
1 top	5/8 × 24 × 44
2 top rails	1 1/2 × 1 1/2 × 23
2 leg rails	1 × 4 × 23
4 legs	2 × 2 × 28
2 laths	3/8 × 2 × 38
2 blocks	2 × 2 × 3
2 covers	1/2 × 2 × 7

SMOKER'S STAND

An ashtray on a stand at a convenient height for use beside a chair will be welcomed by a smoker as well as the home lover concerned with ash dropping on a carpet. This stand has a shelf as well as an ashtray (Fig. 11-22). It becomes a smoker's companion with places for packets, pouches, matches, and other needs. Details of the top are dependent on the size of an available ashtray. The drawings assume a metal one with a rim that fits into a hole—in this case 4 inches across. Obtain the ashtray first and make the top to suit.

The stand in the photograph was made completely of oak. Most hardwoods are suitable, but they must be properly seasoned to reduce the risk of shelves warping. It does not matter if the square wood is slightly undersize after planing, but the shelves should not finish much under 1/2 inch thick.

It would not be difficult to alter the design to have round shelves. They are shown octagonal (Fig. 11-23). Hexagons would be inappropriate as the six sides would not relate to the square section posts and other parts.

1. Make the three shelves first. Mark out the

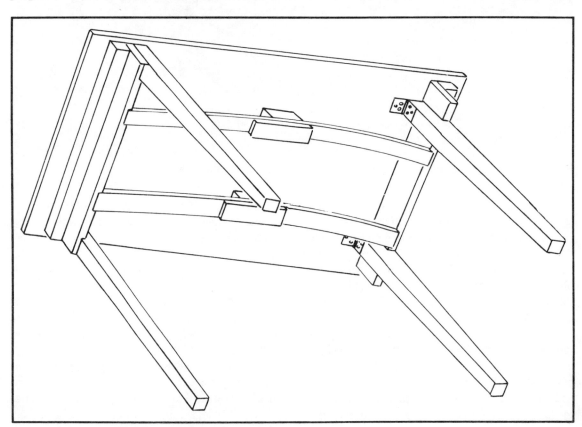

Fig. 11-19. The underside of a spring-action folding table.

294

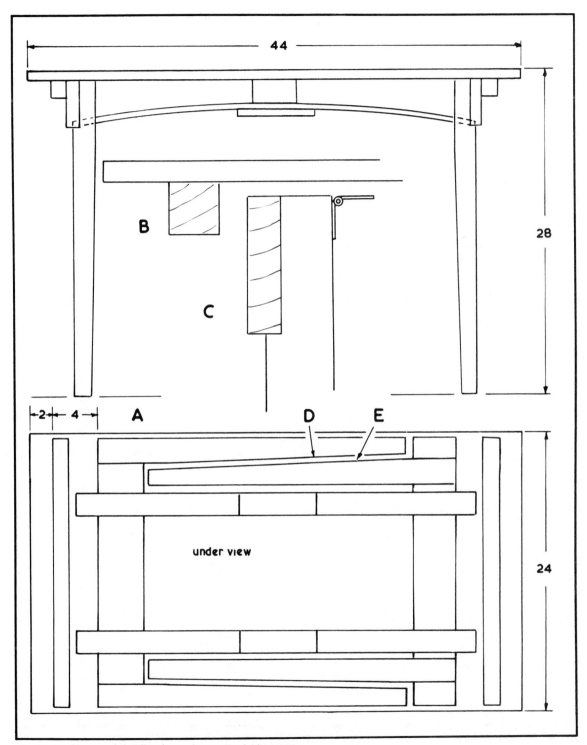

Fig. 11-20. Sizes and details of a spring-action folding table.

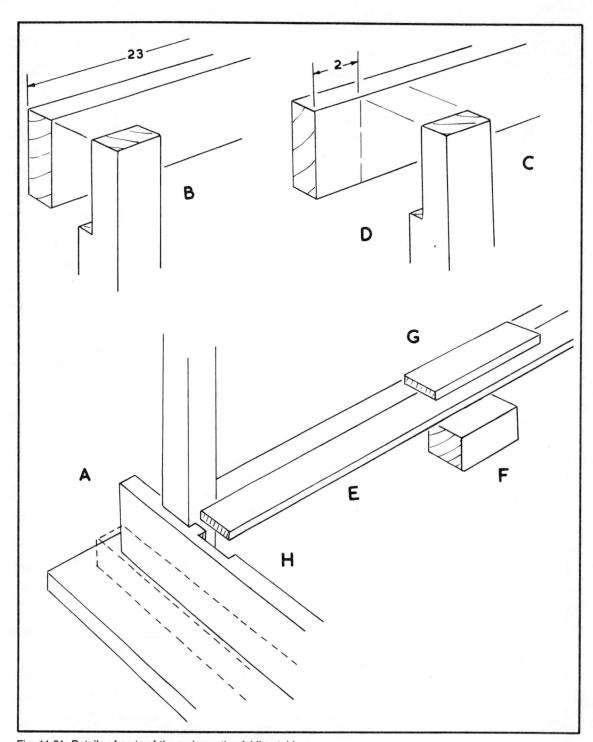

Fig. 11-21. Details of parts of the spring-action folding table.

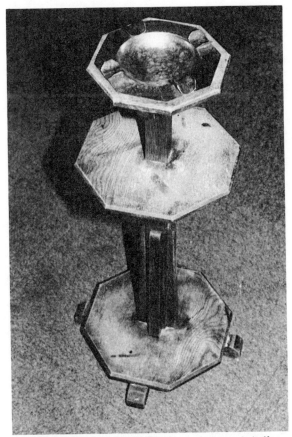

Fig. 11-22. A smoker's stand with an ashtray and shelf on a steady base.

wood to squares of the sizes shown (Fig. 11-23). To convert the squares to octagons, draw diagonals (Fig. 11-24A). Find the length of half a diagonal. Measure half diagonal lengths both ways from each corner along the sides of the square (Fig.11-24B) or use a compass to swing to these positions from each corner. Join these points. If you check the lengths of these marked lines, they should be the same as the distances along the edges of the square between them. Cut each shelf to these lines.

2. The edges could be molded in any way you wish. They could be rounded. If they are to be left square, take the sharpness off the edges or give them slight bevels or roundings.

3. The top shelf needs a hole to match the ashtray (Fig. 11-23A). A 4-inch circle is shown. Leave the holes for joints at the centers of the other

shelves until the parts that fit them are made.

4. Make the pillar with a joint at the center shelf. The long piece from below has two tenons and the short piece from above has one tenon to fit between them (Fig. 11-24C). Mark out and cut these tenons before cutting the wood to length. Make a mortise in the middle shelf to suit (Fig. 11-23B). Take care to get a good fit in this joint, so it will have adequate strength when glued.

5. Make two crossing pieces under the top shelf (Fig. 11-23C). They are reduced to half thickness and a halving joint is made between them (Fig. 11-24D and E). Sizes might have to be adjusted if the ashtray requires a different size hole. Arrange the ends to be a width that will fit under the wood around the ashtray hole. Taper the ends.

6. Make a tenon on the short part of the pillar to fit through the center halving joint (Fig. 11-24F).

7. Make the feet (Fig. 11-23D). Cut away 1/2 inch beneath (Fig. 11-24G) and bevel the ends. Make a halving joint at the center so the legs fit level under the bottom shelf.

8. The pillar will have a tenon to fit into the bottom shelf, similar to the top of the short part. It may go through the shelf and into the top part only of the halving joint in the feet underneath.

9. Make the four decorative pieces to fit around the pillar (Fig. 11-23E). They are parallel in width, but taper to rounded tops (Fig. 11-24H).

10. Assemble the crossing pieces to the top shelf. Glue only should be sufficient.

11. Assemble the feet to the bottom shelf with glue as well as screws driven upwards.

12. When the glue in these assemblies has set, glue the sections of the pillar into them. Be careful that they are square when you check both ways.

13. Make the joint of the pillar tenons into the mortise in the middle shelf. Clamp this tight or put weights on top. See that the pillar parts are in line and the shelf is parallel with the floor.

14. Add the four pieces around the bottom of the pillar. They can be held with glue only. Fine pins can also be driven to prevent the pieces from moving while the glue sets.

15. Scrape off surplus glue and finish the stand

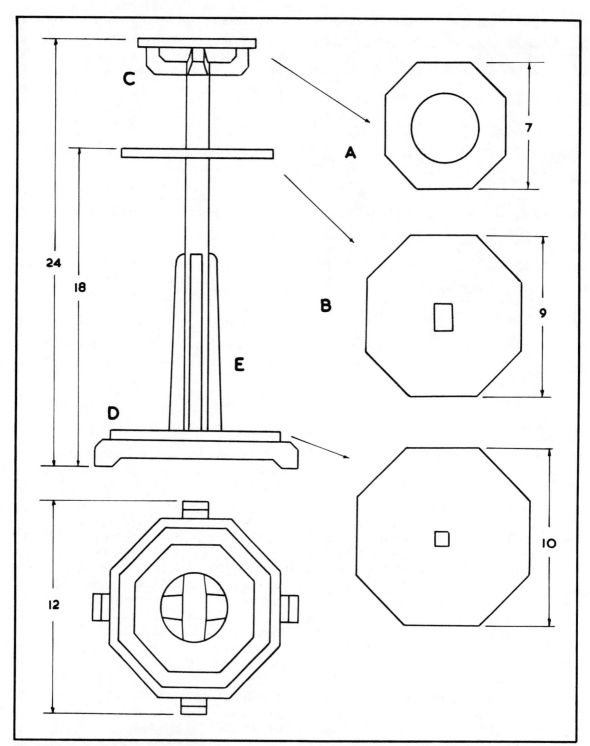

Fig. 11-23. Sizes of the smoker's stand.

298

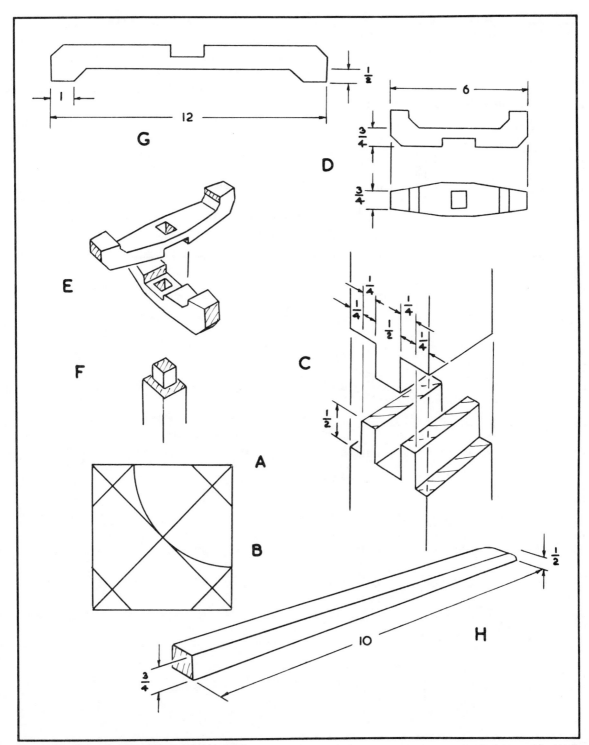

Fig. 11-24. Sizes of parts of the smoker's stand.

with stain and varnish or polish. Glides could be put under the feet or cloth can be glued on to prevent the stand from slipping or marking the floor.

Materials List for Smoker's Stand

1 shelf	1/2 × 10 × 10
1 shelf	1/2 × 9 × 9
1 shelf	1/2 × 7 × 7
2 feet	1 1/2 × 1 1/2 × 12
2 top supports	1 1/2 × 1 1/2 × 6
1 pillar	1 1/2 × 1 1/2 × 18
1 pillar	1 1/2 × 1 1/2 × 6
4 pieces	3/4 × 3/4 × 10

COTTAGE STOOL

Before the days of chairs for everyone, many people sat on stools or benches. They also served as steps or a surface to work on. This type of substantial stool has uses in a den and elsewhere for extra seating.

The stool shown in Fig. 11-25 is at a comfortable height for sitting, but is strong enough to stand rough treatment. The corners of the legs extend outside the area of the top to give stability. The slot in the top allows your fingers through for lifting.

The stool looks good if made of hardwood and given a clear finish. It can be lighter if made of softwood and painted.

Fig. 11-25. A strong cottage stool.

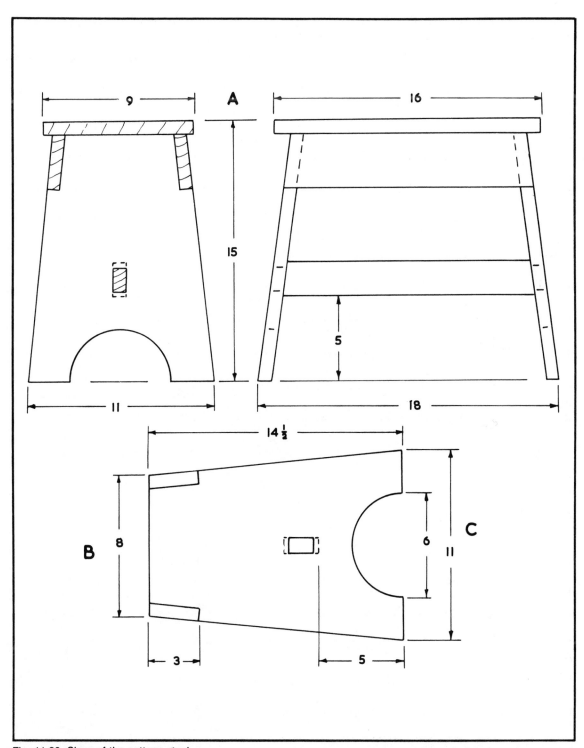

Fig. 11-26. Sizes of the cottage stool.

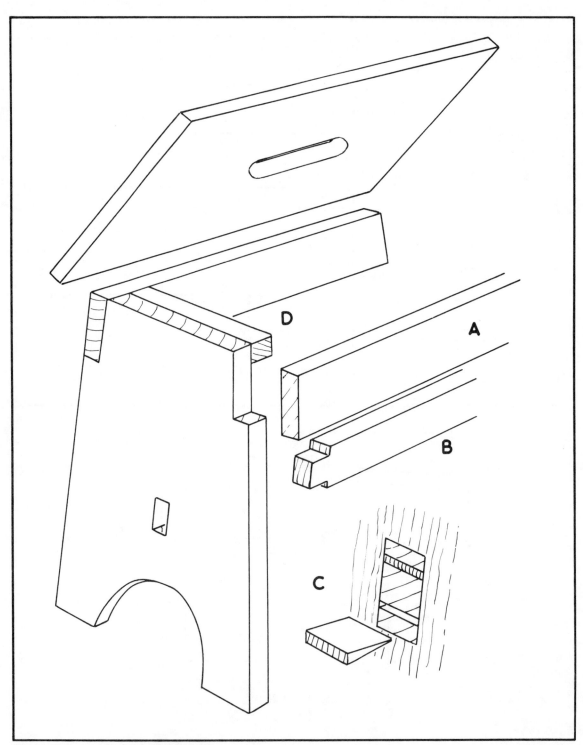

Fig. 11-27. Assembly of the cottage stool.

1. Draw the end view and at least half of the side view (Fig. 11-26A), preferably full size. This is necessary to get the angles for the joints and some of the edges.

2. Mark out the two ends (Fig. 11-26B). Cut top and bottom to the angles given by your drawing. Make semicircular cuts to leave feet (Fig. 11-26C).

3. Notch for the top rails (Fig. 11-27A). They are square on their bottom edges and bevelled to fit under the stool top. Mark the lengths and bevels of the top rails, but do not cut to the final length until after fitting.

4. Make the center rail (Fig. 11-27B) to the length and angle specified on your drawing. Cut the mortise and tenon joints, making the tenons slightly overlength.

5. Saw slots across the tenons. Assemble this rail to the ends and secure it with wedges (Fig. 11-27C) as well as glue.

6. Check that the feet stand level and the assembly is not twisted. Check the spacing at the top with the top rails. When the shape is satisfactory, glue and screw on the top rails. Let the glue set, then trim off wood ends.

7. Put strips across for screwing on the top (Fig. 11-27D).

8. Cut the board for the top so it overhangs the other parts 1/2 inch to 3/4 inch all around.

9. Make a slot at the center of the top about 1 inch by 5 inches and round its edges. Round the corners and outer edges of the top.

10. Screw upwards through the end strips into the top. If more screws are required and you do not wish to screw downwards into the rails, put more strips inside the top rails for screwing upwards.

Materials List for Cottage Stool	
2 ends	3/4 × 11 × 15
2 top rails	3/4 × 3 × 16
1 center rail	3/4 × 2 × 18
2 end strips	3/4 × 3/4 × 7
1 top	3/4 × 9 × 16

Chapter 12

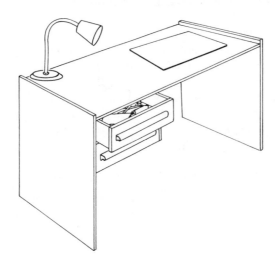

Study

I n every home there are accounts to keep, letters to write, plans to be made, and school work to be done. Sometimes such officelike activity is increased by adults and children needing space for research, somewhere to study, and a place to read undisturbed. A hobby, such as stamp collecting, may call for space to store books and specimens away from the general activity of the house.

These needs are best met by a special study or quiet den. We might not all be able to allocate a room for this exclusive use, but it is something to aim for. Perhaps a desk in a corner of a living room or a bedroom will have to do. This can be equipped to serve study needs in a compact way.

The paperwork involved in running a home, as well as that associated with hobbies, or association or club activities, should be handled in a businesslike way. There are several pieces of furniture that can help you towards that end.

DROP-FRONT DESK

A drop-front desk or bureau has several attractions.

It can be a pleasing piece of furniture in almost any room because its prime function is concealed. It keeps all the accumulation of correspondence, brochures, bills, and other papers tidily together and out of sight. It provides you with a good working area with most of your needs already in front of you when you open the flap. The lower part provides plenty of storage capacity, which does not have to be reduced and arranged at one side as happens with some table desks.

The desk in Fig. 12-1 is of a reasonable size, although it could be altered to suit your needs or available space. As drawn (Fig. 12-2), there is one full-width, narrow drawer; a half-width, slightly deeper drawer, and a file drawer. Opposite the drawers is a roomy cupboard. It would be easy to alter the layout so there are all full-width drawers or more narrow drawers in place of the cupboard. The cupboard and narrow drawers could be changed to suit your needs. When the flap is lowered, it is supported level on slides at each side. They work like small vertical drawers and push back out of the way when the desk is closed.

Fig. 12-1. A drop-front desk with storage inside and in drawers.

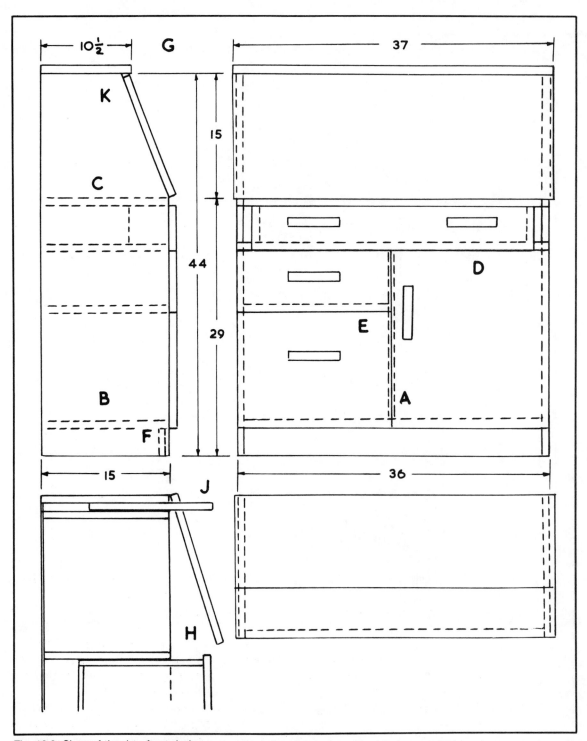

Fig. 12-2. Sizes of the drop-front desk.

The desk would look very attractive made out of solid wood. The widest parts are the ends, and they would have to be made by glueing two or more boards. If the flap is made of solid wood it, like the cupboard door, would look best panelled.

If solid wood is unavailable or too costly, the desk can be made with nearly all the main parts veneered particleboard. With either material it is possible, and quite satisfactory, to make most of the joints with dowels, although there are places where tenons or dadoes are more appropriate for solid wood. The instructions that follow are for dowelled construction, but an enthusiastic woodworker will see where other types of joints can be used. Whatever the material used for the main construction, internal framing and drawer parts are better made of solid wood. The pigeon holes inside the top also look better in thin solid wood. The desk back and drawer bottoms may be hardboard or thin plywood.

Select all the materials, including hinges and handles, before starting work. You can then relate sizes where applicable and match parts as you progress.

1. Mark out the left-hand side (Fig. 12-3A) first and use this as your pattern for sizes and locations of several other parts. The opposite side will match it, except it does not need the intermediate drawer runner (Fig. 12-3B). The partition (Fig. 12-2A) should match the first side as high as the long drawer rail. At the rear, the two ends are best rabbeted to take the back panel (Fig. 12-3C). If you do not have facilities for cutting rabbets in particleboard, the panel could be screwed to the edges, but that would expose its own edges. It would be better fitted inside with wood fillets (Fig. 12-3D) arranged between the other parts attached to the sides. Make the partition narrower, so it comes inside the back.

2. Cut the slopes on the ends. Veneer the cut edges if veneered particleboard is used.

3. Make the bottom (Figs. 12-2B and 12-3E) and shelf (Fig. 12-2C) the same and use them to control the lengths of other horizontal parts. Mark on them the position of the partition. It will probably be centered, but it does not have to be if a wider or narrower drawer arrangement suits your needs better.

4. Make the long drawer rail (Figs. 12-2D and 12-3F) the same length and 4 inches wide. On this and the underside of the shelf, mark the positions of the dividers where the slides will be (Fig. 12-3G). The slide can be particleboard, but even if the rest of the construction is particleboard, solid wood slides would be stronger and have a longer life. The fronts might be veneered to match the surrounding parts, if you wish. The fronts of the slides could have narrow drop handles or be notched for fingertips on the outer surfaces. Another way to provide a grip is with a finger notch at the bottom (Fig. 12-3H).

5. The dividers extend 5 inches back over the drawer rail and the 2-inch wide drawer runner (Fig. 12-3J). There is a strip behind the guide. The slide is given a stop to hit the guide when the slide is out to its limit (Fig. 12-3K). Prepare these parts, but do not assemble them until you are ready to put the whole carcass together.

6. Make the drawer rail between the two narrow drawers (Fig. 12-2E). At its ends are runners for the drawer (Fig. 12-3L). The deep drawer uses the carcass bottom as its runner.

7. Prepare all joints for dowels. For the main construction 3/8-inch dowels about 3 inches apart should be satisfactory. Dowel the drawer runners to their rails to keep them level in use. Make sure the dividers allow the slides to pass easily, but with not so much clearance that they wobble about. The slides can be planed in depth to fit vertically after the other parts have been assembled.

8. Make the plinth (Fig. 12-2F) the same length as the bottom and glue and dowel it. Set it back 1/2 inch from the front.

9. Make the top (Fig. 12-2G) to extend 1/2 inch over each side. It is level at the back, but extends 1 1/2 inches at the front to overhang the flap. Veneer its ends if it has a veneered surface. Prepare the rear edges to take the back. Prepare the top and sides for dowel joints.

10. Cut the back panel close to size and ready to be planed to fit exactly when the carcass is assembled. Make sure all dowel holes are drilled and

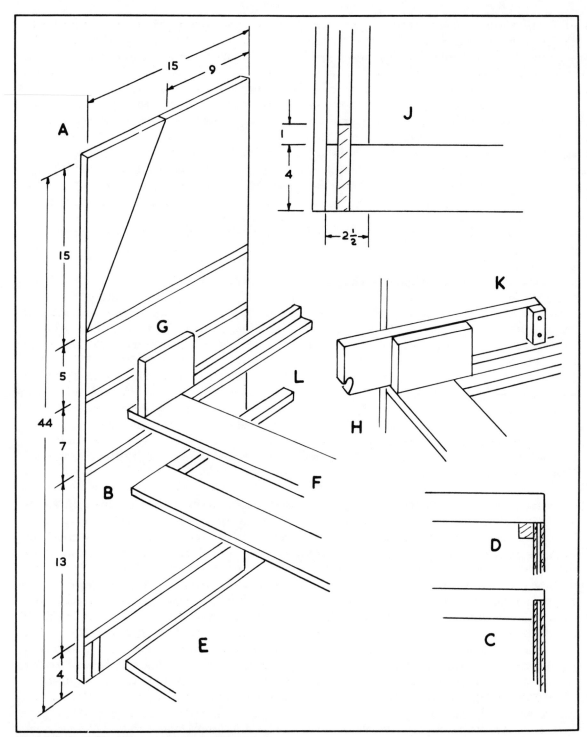

Fig. 12-3. Assembly at one end of the drop-front desk.

sufficient dowels are cut and ready.

11. The drawer runners and slide guides may be attached to their rails now or built in as you assemble the main parts. Take care during assembly that all front edges of the carcass finish level.

12. Start the main assembly by fitting the partition in place between the long drawer rail and the bottom, then join the drawer rails, the shelf, and the bottom to the sides. Clamp all joints tightly. Fit in the back panel with glue and screws to hold the assembly square. Also check squareness at the front by measuring diagonals there. When you are satisfied with the assembly up to this stage, add the top. Leave the desk flat on its back or standing on a level surface until the glue has set.

13. The drop front overlaps the edges of the desk front. The top of the long narrow shelf is level with the underside of the main shelf to leave space for the lowered flap. Its ends overlap the slide guides, and its lower edge overlaps the rail below. The full-width, drawer front comes under the overlapping top drawer. It overlaps the desk side and goes halfway over the front of the partition (Fig. 12-2H). The deep file drawer front is similar, with its lower edge overlapping the carcass bottom.

14. Make all the drawer fronts. If using veneered particleboard, veneer the ends and any cut edges.

15. Make the drawer sides to fit smoothly into place. Leave them too long at this stage. If possible, groove them for the bottoms (Fig. 12-4A). Otherwise, allow for narrow fillets (Fig. 12-4B). If you have a suitable router cutter to make stopped grooves in the drawer fronts, prepare them to match the grooves in the sides. Grooves plowed right through would show unattractively on the ends. If the fronts cannot be grooved, you can use fillets across the side grooves or fillets to support the front edges of the bottoms.

16. If the deep file drawer is to be used for general storage, it may be best to have the sides and back as deep as the front. If it is to be filled with papers in files or books standing on edge, the sides and back might be lower. In this case, make the sides about half the height of the front and screw kickers to the side and partition (Fig. 12-4C),

otherwise the drawer will tilt as it is pulled out.

17. Make the drawer backs to fit above the drawer bottoms. Have all the parts of a drawer ready. Cut the sides square at the front and prepare them for dowels to the drawer front (Fig. 12-4D). Arrange the dowels fairly close together (Fig. 12-5) for maximum strength in these positions where they have to withstand loads. Cut the sides short enough to not hit the carcass back when closed. The drawer should be stopped by the front against the framework edges when it is pushed in.

18. Assemble the drawer sides to the front and slide in the bottom from the back. Fit the back between the sides, using dowels or screws. Screw the bottom upwards into the back. Make and fit all the drawers in this way.

19. The slides can be made and fitted. Their front edges come level with the drawer fronts or level with the carcass edges. Make their length so they stop at the right distance when they touch the back of the carcass. Screw on to them small stops to limit the amount a slide can be pulled out (Fig. 12-3K). If you use screws without glue, a slide can be removed if you ever need to service it.

20. If particleboard is used, make the door with similar overlaps to the drawers, going over the carcass edge (Fig. 12-2J), and halfway over the partition with some clearance between it and the drawers.

21. If the flap is made of particleboard, make it in the same way as the door. Its lower edge comes on the level of the top of the shelf, where it will be hinged. Its top should clear the overhang of the desk top (Fig. 12-2K), but do not make the space there any greater than necessary. The edges of the flap should be level with the ends of the top.

22. If solid wood is used, the flap and door will look better if they are framed and panelled. Using solid wood without framing risks warping. The panel of the door could be veneered plywood let into grooves in the frame (Fig. 12-6A). Because the flap must have a flat working surface, plywood should be thicker if this construction is used (Fig. 12-6B). Its outside will look the same as the door.

23. The best flap and door will have solid wood for the panels, nearly as thick as the framing. At

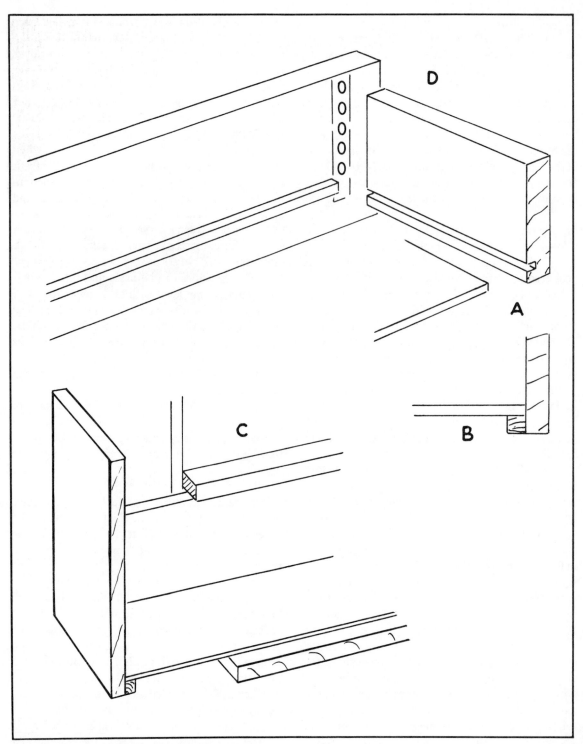

Fig. 12-4. Drawer construction for the drop-front desk.

Fig. 12-5. Dowels into deep holes in the front secure the parts at a drawer corner.

the front it is fielded by cutting its edge back (Fig. 12-6C). A simpler alternative to this is to make plywood panels and glue on centered pieces (Fig. 12-6D).

24. For door and flap the vertical parts of the frame should reach the top and bottom edges, then the horizontal parts are tenoned into them (Fig. 12-6E). Mitered corners are inappropriate and too weak. Use stub tenons at least as thick as the width of the grooves.

25. It is possible to build in the partitions and shelves in the top with dowels and dadoes into the surrounding parts, but it is easier and looks better to make a unit to fit in. It might be in wood of contrasting color and could be held in place with a few screws.

26. You can arrange the compartments to suit your needs. Some of these desks have been made with secret drawers and ingenious ways of closing and operating drawers and doors. The example (Fig. 12-7A) shows typical methods of construction, which can be adapted. It is unwise to use very thick wood, which looks ugly, or have too many divisions,

shelves, and other compartments because too much space will be taken up with wood. There is no need for the unit to reach the full height of the available space. Its top can form a shelf for the many things that do not have their own divisions.

27. Make the unit as a box to slide into place. Corners could be nailed or screwed, dovetailed, or joined by any box corner joint. Details at the corners will not show after the unit is in place. It could be used without its own back, but a piece of hardboard may be used if you wish (Fig. 12-7B).

28. Within the box are vertical divisions. These and the horizontal parts could be dowelled or nailed, but a better way is to use stopped dadoes (Fig. 12-7C).

29. A small drawer is always useful. This can be made with any of the usual drawer constructions. It will open easier if it is not as wide as its depth back to front.

30. Vertical dividers can be used in a compartment to allow such things as envelopes and postcards to stand on edge (Fig. 12-7D). The dividers are better made of thinner wood, which might be

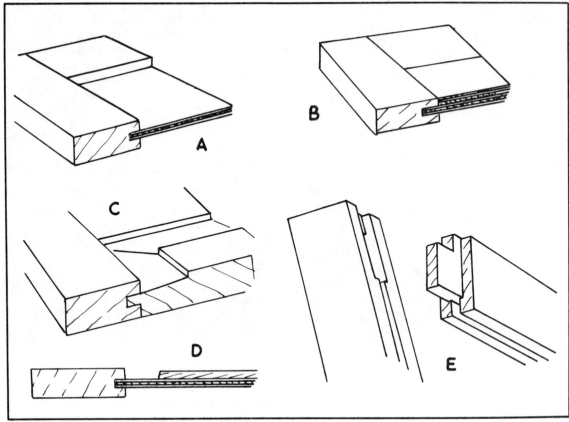

Fig. 12-6. Alternate constructions for the door and flap of the drop-front desk.

fitted into triangular grooves (Fig. 12-7E) instead of ordinary dadoes. If the front edges of these and other vertical parts are hollowed (Fig. 12-7F), it is easier to get a finger grip on the contents.

31. For most purposes there should be one fairly large compartment kept for books (Fig. 12-7G). Round all the forward edges of the unit because you will be reaching into the front frequently and do not want to bring your hand against sharp or rough edges.

32. The flap can be attached with several separate hinges. A long piano hinge on its edge and the edge of the shelf, however, screwed on so its knuckle comes level with the upper surface when the flap is down, is best.

33. When you finish the desk, put strips of cloth on the top edges of the slides, either all over the exposed surfaces or 3 inches along the end, to prevent the flap from being marked.

34. There is no need to put a handle on the flap because you can put your fingers around its overlapping edges to open it. It does not need a fastener because gravity will keep it closed, but you might wish to fit a lock.

35. The door and drawers should have matching handles. On solid wood they might be ornate brass ones. In some situations it is better to let flush handles into hollows or to fit hanging rails so projections are small. Wood handles could be made, similar to those suggested for several other projects. Put handles slightly higher than the centers of the drawers. Space the handles on the long drawer to match those in the middle of the narrow drawers. Fit the door handle fairly high so a user does not have to bend much to reach it. Fit a fastener to hold the door close against the partition.

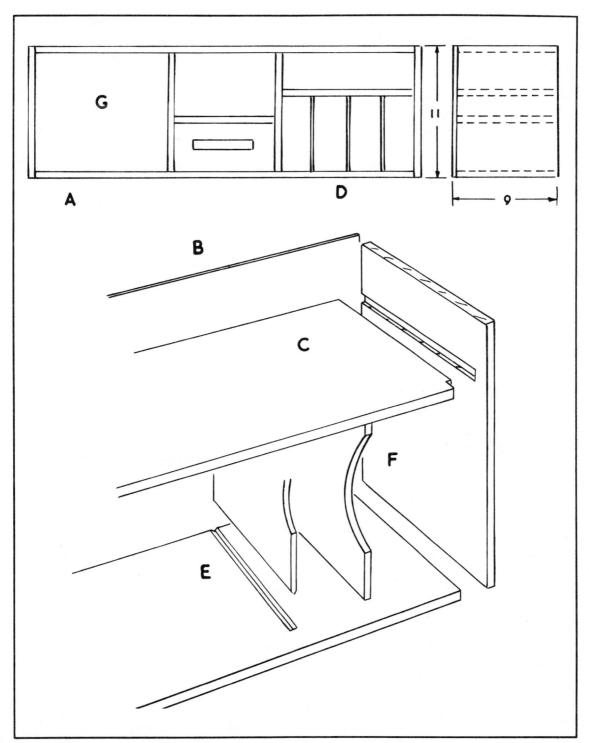

Fig. 12-7. Details of the racks inside the drop-front desk.

Materials List for Drop-Front Desk
veneered particleboard or solid wood

2 sides	3/4 × 15 × 44
1 partition	3/4 × 15 × 25
1 bottom	3/4 × 15 × 35
1 shelf	3/4 × 15 × 35
1 top	3/4 × 10 1/2 × 37
1 drawer rail	3/4 × 4 × 35
1 drawer rail	3/4 × 4 × 18
2 slide guides	3/4 × 5 × 5
1 plinth	3/4 × 4 × 35
1 drawer front	3/4 × 5 × 35
1 drawer front	3/4 × 7 × 18
1 drawer front	3/4 × 13 × 18
1 door	3/4 × 18 × 20 (or see below)
1 flap	3/4 × 17 × 37 (or see below)

solid wood

2 drawer runners	3/4 × 2 1/2 × 11
2 drawer runners	3/4 × 1 × 11
2 drawer guides	3/4 × 1 × 10
2 drawer kickers	3/4 × 1 × 15
2 slides	3/4 × 5 × 16
2 drawer sides	5/8 × 5 × 15
1 drawer back	5/8 × 4 × 35
4 drawer sides	5/8 × 7 × 15
2 drawer backs	5/8 × 6 × 18
1 unit top	1/2 × 9 × 35
1 unit bottom	1/2 × 9 × 35
2 unit ends	1/2 × 9 × 11
2 unit divisions	1/2 × 9 × 11
1 unit shelf	1/2 × 9 × 12
1 unit shelf	1/2 × 9 × 9
3 dividers	1/4 × 8 × 8
drawer front	1/2 × 4 × 36

alternative for solid-panelled door

2 pieces	3/4 × 3 × 20
2 pieces	3/4 × 3 × 18
1 panel	1/2 × 14 × 16

alternative for solid-panelled flap

2 pieces	3/4 × 3 × 17
2 pieces	3/4 × 3 × 37
1 panel	3/4 × 13 × 34

hardboard or plywood 1/8 or 1/4 thick

1 back	37 × 42
1 drawer bottom	15 × 35
2 drawer bottoms	15 × 18
1 unit back	11 × 35

DESK OR WORKTABLE

A table with a good working area and some drawers will serve as a compact office for your domestic accounts, needlework, or a hobby. When not in use it could serve as a side table or might be pressed into use for a meal. In a bedroom the same table could become a dresser if a mirror is stood on it.

This desk (Fig. 12-8) takes advantage of the availability of wide pieces of particleboard already veneered with wood or plastic on the surfaces and edges. The finished desk has a modern, clean look. It might seem austere, but it has a workmanlike and functional appearance that fits in with modern decor.

Nearly all the parts are 3/4-inch particleboard. You may choose veneer to give the appearance you want. Joints are made with dowels, although there is some wood reinforcement that can be screwed. The insides of the drawers can be particleboard, but solid wood makes drawers that fit a slide better. Long wood handles are shown on the drawers. They have the advantage of providing a grip anywhere, even if you reach for one without looking. The drawers are shown on the left, which will be convenient if you work mainly on top with your right hand, but they can be reversed.

Sizes here will suit most needs, but can be altered if the desk has to fit into a particular position or the stock widths of particleboard are different from those specified. This desk is intended to be a partner to the next project, so you might wish to arrange the combined sizes to fit in a particular place.

1. Mark out the end where the drawers are to come (Figs. 12-9A and 12-10A). Use this as a guide to sizes and positions of other parts. At the front allow for the thickness of the drawer fronts and for the back at the other edge. The depth of the two-drawer compartment below the top should be the same as the depth of the board forming the back. Make the opposite end to match (Fig. 12-9B).

2. Make the vertical part of the drawer compartment (Figs. 12-9C and 12-10B) to come under the top, against the back, and outside the drawer ends. Mark on it the location of the drawer runner to match the other end.

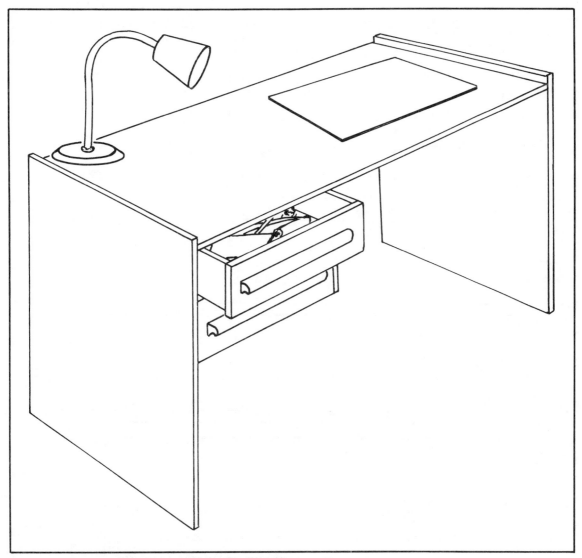

Fig. 12-8. A desk or worktable made from veneered particleboard.

3. Make the drawer compartment bottom (Figs. 12-9D and 12-10C) to fit inside the back, below the drawers, and set back from the other parts at the front.

4. Make the back to fit between the ends (Fig. 12-10D). Make the front rail (Figs. 12-9E and 12-10E) so its length plus the drawer compartment is the same as the length of the back. Make the top (Fig. 12-10F) to the same total length. In this type of furniture where finished shapes have nothing to

disguise them, careful cutting of exactly square ends is very important.

5. If the particleboard is bought with the edges as well as the surfaces veneered, the only cut ends of the parts made so far that will have to be veneered are the tops of the table ends.

6. Mark out the dowelled joints—3/8-inch dowels at 3-inch intervals should be satisfactory. Drill for dowels as deeply as the thickness permits. Check parts in position and have all dowels ready

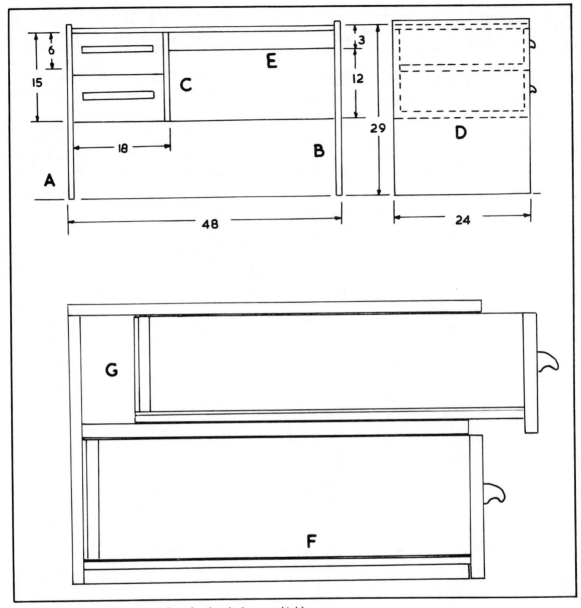

Fig. 12-9. Sizes and drawer sections for the desk or worktable.

so these parts can be joined in one glueing session.

7. Most of the loads come across dowel joints, and there is little parting strain on them. The exception is where the top of the vertical part of the drawer compartment meets the table top. Cut a strengthening strip of wood (Fig. 12-9G) to screw both ways into that joint.

8. Screw and glue the drawer runners (Fig. 12-10H) in the marked positions. Their forward ends are kept back to clear the thickness of the drawer fronts.

9. Make the top drawer front to overlap the ends of the drawer runners. Make the lower drawer front to fit below it and overlap the bottom of the

drawer compartment. Veneer the cut ends and edges so the finished fronts fit easily into place without excessive clearance.

10. If the drawer sides are to be particleboard, it would be difficult to groove them for the bottoms. Instead you can attach pieces of wood about 1/4-inch square inside the lower edges and attach the drawer bottom to them. Put a matching strip across the inside of each drawer front.

11. If wood is used for the sides and back of the drawers, groove the sides for the bottom (Fig. 12-9F). Dowel the sides to the front and put a strip across the front below the groove edges to support the bottom there. Fit the back between the sides above the bottom (Fig. 12-9G).

12. When the drawers are fully in, the fronts should be level all around. This could be arranged by letting the drawer fronts hit the runners or case

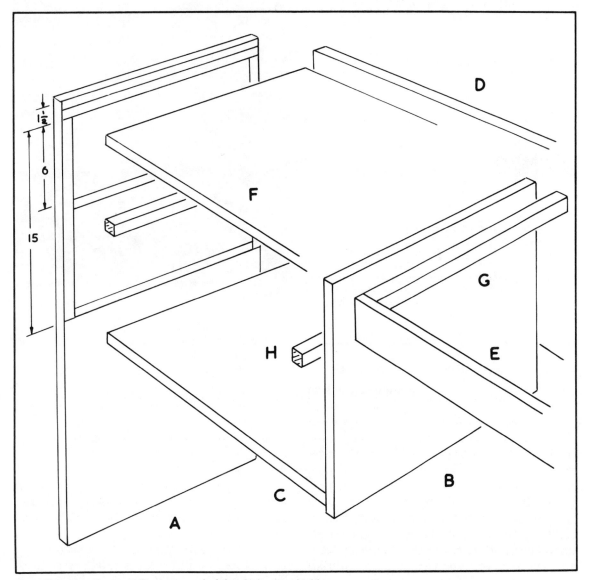

Fig. 12-10. How the parts fit at one end of the desk or worktable.

bottom. It is better to avoid strain on the fronts by leaving a little clearance there and planing off the backs of the drawers so they are stopped by hitting the table back.

13. Long wood handles shaped from square strips are suggested, but you could use metal or plastic ones, bolted through or screwed from inside.

Materials List for Desk or Worktable veneered particleboard 3/4 thick	
2 ends	24 × 30
1 top	24 × 47
1 back	15 × 47
1 drawer compartment	15 × 24
1 drawer compartment	18 × 24
1 front rail	3 × 20
1 drawer front	7 × 18
1 drawer front	8 × 18
wood	
1 top strengthener	1 × 1 × 24
2 drawer runners	3/4 × 3/4 × 24
2 drawer sides	1/2 × 6 × 24
2 drawer sides	1/2 × 7 × 24
1 drawer back	1/2 × 5 × 18
1 drawer back	1/2 × 6 × 18
2 drawer bottoms	18 × 24 × 1/8 or 1/4 hardboard or plywood
2 drawer handles	1 1/4 × 1 1/4 × 15

COMPANION CHEST OF DRAWERS

The desk described in Fig. 12-8 is unlikely to hold all the papers for domestic, gardening, or hobby interests. Some sort of filing cabinet is necessary as well, but an ordinary office filing cabinet looks out of place in a home. Usually one large filing drawer as well as shallow drawers for smaller items, loose papers, etc., is sufficient.

A suitable chest of drawers with one filing drawer could be made of solid wood throughout by traditional methods (Fig. 12-11). The project described in Fig. 12-12 has a similar capacity and is designed to be a companion to the desk in Fig. 12-8. Its appearance is similar and it is equally simple to

Fig. 12-11. A chest of drawers with a filing drawer suitable as a companion to a desk.

construct. The height is comparable to the desk, and this unit could stand alongside for use as an extension of the working surface. The two might be arranged alongside or square to each other in the corner of a room reserved as a study.

As with the desk, the main parts are veneered particleboard, but solid wood is best for the internal parts of the drawers. The two top drawers overhang their runners. The bottom drawer is within the bottom and has reduced depth at its sides. It could be made the same depth all around, but if files are stowed crosswise, the low sides are adequate and may make access to files, large catalogs, and similar bulky items easier.

Much of the work is similar to making the previous project, and it will be helpful to read those instructions. Check on the suitability of sizes (Fig.

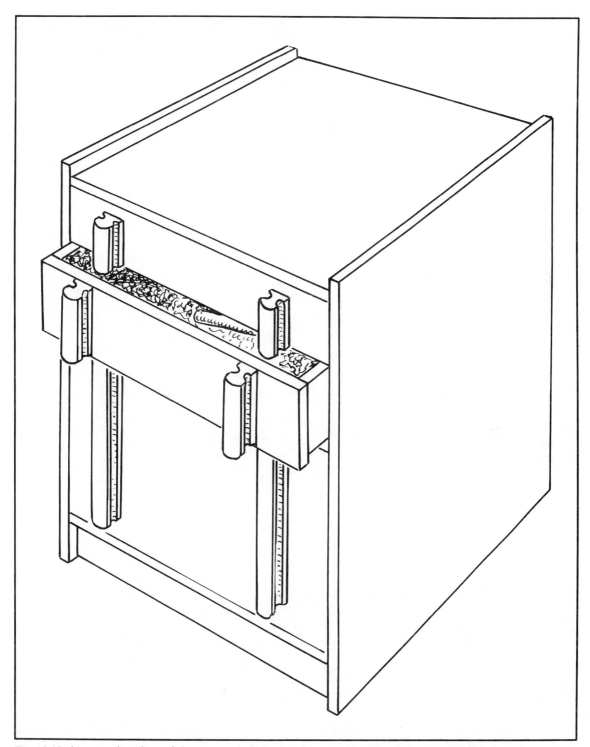

Fig. 12-12. A companion chest of drawers made from particleboard and suitable for use with the last project.

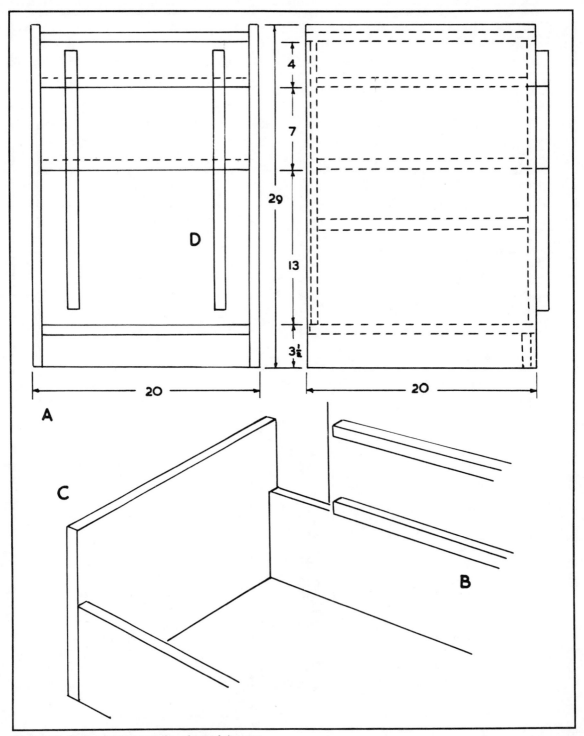

Fig. 12-13. Sizes of the companion chest of drawers.

12-13A) in relation to your needs and the availability of particleboard panels.

1. Mark out the pair of sides (Fig. 12-14A) showing the positions of other parts. The top will be the full width, and the bottom is set back a little at the rear. The plinth comes 1/2 inch in from the front. At the rear there has to be an allowance for the back behind the drawer runners (see #3).

2. Allow for the two drawers to overlap their runners. For the low sides of the bottom drawer there has to be a pair of kickers (Figs. 12-13B and 12-14C), which are necessary to prevent the drawer from tilting as it is pulled out.

3. There is no need to use particleboard for the back. Instead there can be a piece of hardboard or thin plywood. It comes between the sides and under the top, but the bottom can be cut back enough for it to overlap because its edge will not show. The back need not reach the floor. To support the back, put strips of 1/2-inch square wood at the sides and under the top (Fig. 12-14D) far enough in for the back to come slightly below the surrounding surfaces.

4. Make the top (Fig. 12-14E) the full width to fit between the sides. Make the bottom a similar size (Fig. 12-14F), but cut away the back enough to take the rear plywood or hardboard.

5. Veneer the tops of the sides and any other cut edges that are visible.

6. Attach the strips that hold the back. Take the drawer runners and kickers up to them. Glue and a few screws will hold these parts.

7. Prepare the particleboard parts for the dowel joints—3/8-inch dowels at about 3-inch spacing should be satisfactory.

8. Join the plinth to the bottom, and the top and bottom to the sides. Have the back ready and fit it in to hold the assembly square.

9. Make the drawers with particleboard sides and back or use solid wood, as described for the last project. With wood, the sides can be grooved for the bottom, then a strip put across as a front support (Fig. 12-14G). Make the drawers so they close against the strips holding the back of the chest, then they act as stops when the fronts are level. The bottom drawer front extends above its sides (Fig. 12-13C).

10. There could be horizontal handles on the drawers, either wood similar to those described for the desk, or purchased metal or plastic ones. Alternative vertical handles are shown (Figs. 12-12 and 12-13D). The handles can be made in long pieces and cut to suit the drawers. The sections should give a good finger grip on both sides (Fig. 12-14H). Attach with screws driven from inside the drawers.

Materials List for Companion Chest of Drawers

veneered particleboard 3/4 thick

2 sides	20 × 29
1 top	20 × 20
1 bottom	20 × 20
1 drawer front	4 × 20
1 drawer front	7 × 20
1 drawer front	13 × 20

wood

6 drawer runners	3/4 × 3/4 × 19
2 drawer sides	1/2 × 3 1/4 × 19
1 drawer back	1/2 × 3 × 19
2 drawer sides	1/2 × 6 1/4 × 19
1 drawer back	1/2 × 6 × 19
2 drawer sides	1/2 × 8 × 19
1 drawer back	1/2 × 7 1/2 × 19
3 drawer bottoms	19 × 19 × 1/8 or 1/4 hardboard or plywood
2 back frames	1/2 × 1/2 × 25
1 back frame	1/2 × 1/2 × 19
1 back	20 × 25 × 1/8 or 1/4 hardboard or plywood
handles from	1 1/4 × 1 1/4 × 46

BOOKCASE TABLE

A block of shelves at table height has many uses in a study or elsewhere. It can stand against a wall and serve as a sideboard as well as somewhere to store small items and books. It could make a stand for a television or radio set. Away from the wall it could be used as a low room divider with access from both sides.

This bookcase table (Fig. 12-15) has space for two rooms of books, including large volumes. There

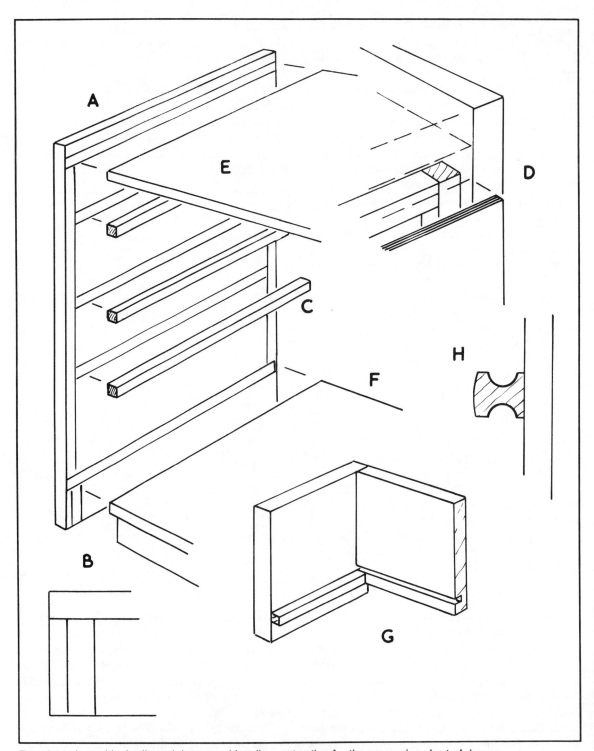

Fig. 12-14. Assembly details and drawer and handle construction for the companion chest of drawers.

Fig. 12-15. A bookcase at table height.

are extensions for ornaments and a top large enough for various uses. The back is open, except for the central strut, which contributes rigidity to the assembly as well as providing support for the shelves.

Solid wood could be used, but the design is also suitable for veneered particleboard. Joints are dowelled, except that the back is notched into the middle shelf.

1. Make three shelves the same size (Fig. 12-16A). Veneer the ends to match the sides and surfaces.

2. Cut the two pairs of uprights (Fig. 12-16B and C). Mark out their positions on the shelves and

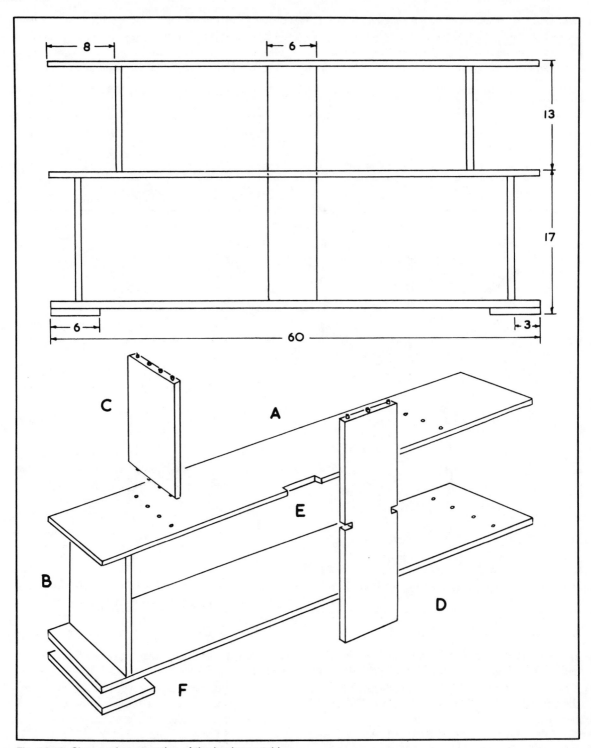

Fig. 12-16. Sizes and construction of the bookcase table.

positions of dowels on all parts—four, 3/8-inch dowels at each joint should be sufficient.

3. The back (Fig. 12-16D) is in one piece. Use dowelled joints at top and bottom of it. At the middle shelf, notch each side of the back, then cut away the shelf to fit (Fig. 12-16E). It may be sufficient to glue the parts together here, or you can include dowels.

4. Make the two feet (Fig. 12-16F). Glue and screw them under the ends of the bottom shelf.

5. Start assembly from the bottom up. Fit the back notch into the middle shelf before dowelling it, then the two uprights into the two lower shelves. Add the other uprights and the top. During assembly the back should pull the other parts square, but check that the shelf ends finish vertically above each other and that the whole assembly is square.

Materials List for Bookcase Table

3 shelves	3/4 × 10 × 60
2 uprights	3/4 × 10 × 13
2 uprights	3/4 × 10 × 16
1 back	3/4 × 6 × 30

STEPPED BOOKCASE

The plainness of a block of shelves to hold books can be eased by arranging them in steps. This bookcase (Fig. 12-17) has one straight upright end. The other end is stepped so there are short ledges for vases or ornaments. Although intended to hold books, the shelves are equally suitable for other things. Because the back is not fully closed, there are strips to prevent books pushing through and to keep other articles in place. They also provide stiffness and prevent the bookcase being pushed out of shape or the shelf joints strained. The stepped ends are arranged to extend slightly above the ledges to prevent anything from slipping off.

Sizes could be varied or the bookcase made the other way around to suit your room arrangements. If made much larger, the shelf thickness should be increased to resist bending—a load of books can be quite heavy.

The bookcase could be made of solid wood, although this method of construction is particularly suitable for veneered particleboard. It would be possible to use dado joints in solid wood, but for particleboard and solid wood, dowels are more suitable. For most joints, 3/8-inch dowels spaced 3 inches apart are appropriate.

1. Mark out the tall side (Fig. 12-18A) with the positions and thicknesses of all parts shown. Use this as a guide when marking all other upright pieces.

2. Mark out the three stepped sides (Fig. 12-18B, C, D) from the tall side. Make sure all tops and sides stand the same amount above the shelves. If using solid wood, square and smooth the tops of the sides. Their corners could be rounded. If using veneered particleboard, veneer the tops to match the edges and surfaces.

3. Cut the shelving to length (Fig. 12-18E, F, G, H) and make the plinth (Fig. 12-18J) and back strips to the same lengths.

4. Mark where the upper two sides will stand on their shelves, using the shorter shelves as a guide to distances.

5. Locate where the parts will come in assembly (Fig. 12-19) and mark and drill for dowels. Drill as deeply as possible in the side surfaces.

6. Assembly can be done in one glueing session. It helps to drive and glue all the dowels into the ends of boards first. Work from the bottom of the bookcase upwards, fitting the shelves and other crosswise parts between sides.

7. Check squareness and sight across the back to see that there is no twist. Leave the assembly on its back or standing on a flat surface until the glue sets. Clean off surplus glue and apply a finish.

Materials List for Stepped Bookcase

2 shelves	3/4 × 8 × 30
1 shelf	3/4 × 8 × 25
1 shelf	3/4 × 8 × 20
1 side	3/4 × 8 × 35
1 side	3/4 × 8 × 16
1 side	3/4 × 8 × 12
1 side	3/4 × 8 × 10
1 plinth	3/4 × 3 × 30
1 back	3/4 × 3 × 30
1 back	3/4 × 3 × 25
1 back	3/4 × 3 × 20

Fig. 12-17. A bookcase arranged in steps.

TELEPHONE SEAT

If you have the spare space for a telephone on a desk or table with a convenient seat, that may be all you need. In many homes, however, a piece of furniture that provides a seat and a support for the telephone, as well as storage for directories, books, or magazines, is welcomed. The seat in Fig. 12-20 allows the sitter to be at the right, but it could be made the other way around if that is more convenient.

As shown, construction is with dowels, using veneered particleboard or thick plywood. Solid wood could be used, but suitable wood can be difficult to get, and boards would have to be glued to make up widths.

The seat takes a 15-inch square cushion. Un-

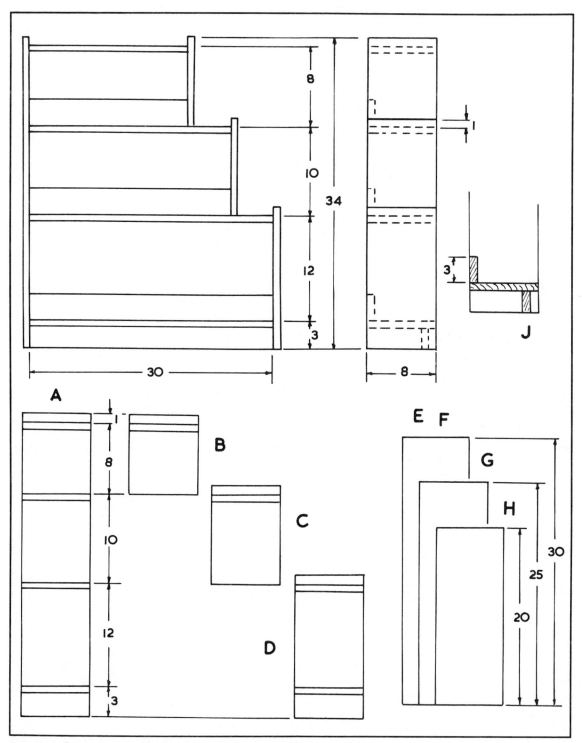

Fig. 12-18. Sizes of the bookcase with details of the stepped parts.

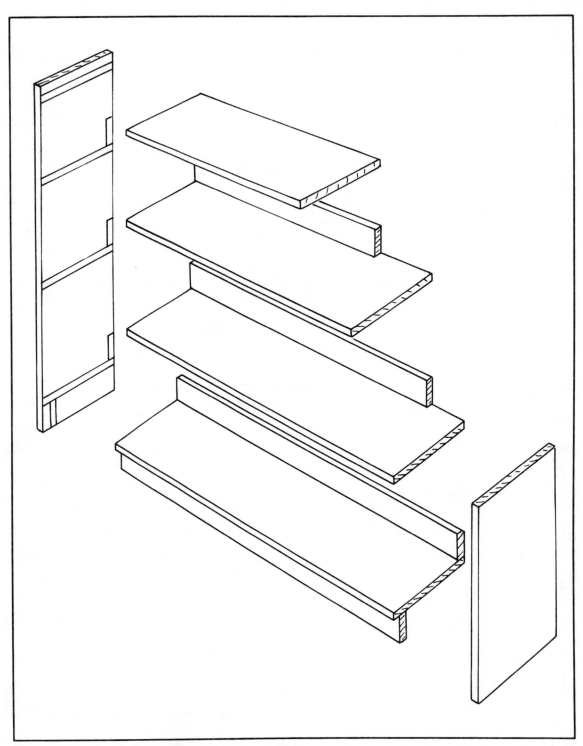

Fig. 12-19. How the stepped bookcase parts are assembled.

Fig. 12-20. A telephone seat with storage for directories and other books.

less you plan to make this yourself, a suitable cushion should be obtained first and the wood sizes adapted to suit it, if necessary.

If particleboard is used, exposed cut edges should be veneered to match the surfaces (Fig. 12-21A). For plywood there could be solid wood glued and pinned on (Fig. 12-21B) or strips could be made to fit into plowed groves (Fig. 12-21C). If the material is 5/8 inch or 3/4 inch thick, the dowels in the joints could be a 5/16-inch or 3/8-inch diameter, spaced about 4 inches apart. Mark out carefully to match parts because uneven edges or lack of squareness in this type of furniture is very obvious.

1. Make the two seat sides (Fig. 12-22A) and the division (Fig. 12-22B) and bottom (Fig. 12-22C) to fit between them. Make the plinth the same length as the bottom (Fig. 12-22D). Mark and drill the dowel holes in these parts.

2. It is advisable to make the top (Fig. 12-22E) to overlap the other parts by about 1/8 inch all around. This allows for slight errors in joints and sizes that would show if you tried to work to the exact size. Make the stiffener under the top (Fig. 12-22F).

3. The seat can now be assembled as a unit, or it can be left until the shelf section is made.

4. The shelves (Fig. 12-22G) are narrower than the end (Fig. 12-22H) by the thickness of the back.

5. The top rail (Fig. 12-22J) goes over the back and the top shelf (Fig. 12-21D).

6. A division is suggested (Fig. 12-22K), but this is not essential. It prevents books falling over and separates different items. Cut a plinth the same length as the shelves (Fig. 12-22L).

7. Check that the shelf positions at their ends suit the spacing for the division, then drill for all dowels.

8. When the parts are joined, include strips inside the back (Fig. 12-21E) to support its ends.

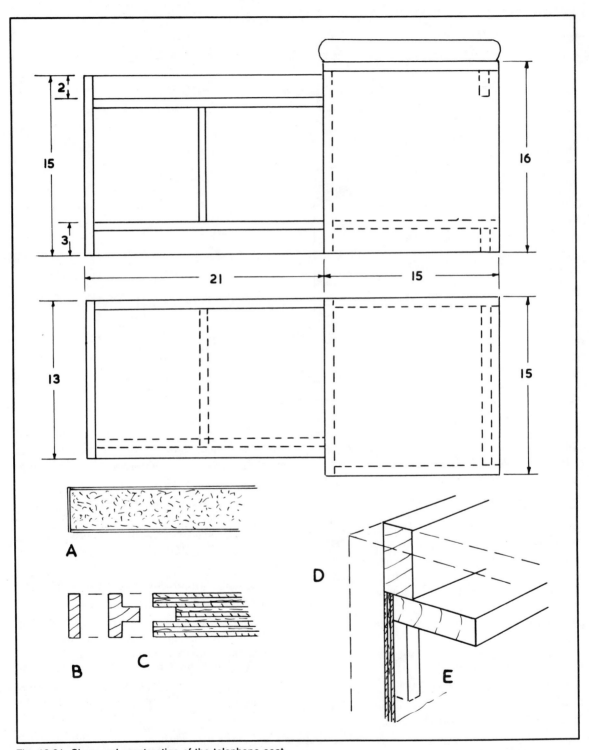

Fig. 12-21. Sizes and construction of the telephone seat.

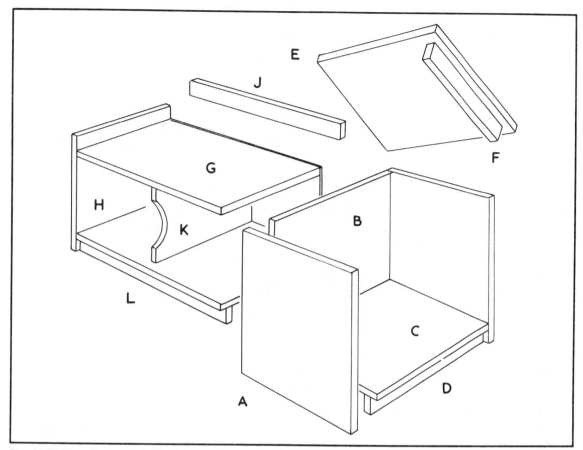

Fig. 12-22. How the parts of the telephone seat fit together.

Materials List for Telephone Seat

(all solid wood, particleboard, or plywood, 5/8 inch or 3/4 inch thick, except for back parts)

2 seat sides	15 × 16
1 seat bottom	15 × 15
1 seat division	15 × 16
1 seat top	15 1/4 × 15 1/4
1 seat plinth	2 1/2 × 15
1 seat stiffener	2 1/2 × 15
2 shelves	13 × 21
1 shelf division	10 × 12
1 end	13 × 15
1 rail	2 × 21
1 plinth	2 1/4 × 21
1 back	13 × 21 × 1/8 or 1/4 hardboard or plywood
2 back supports	3/8 × 3/8 × 11

CLOSED MAGAZINE RACK

A collection of magazines, even if they are in an open rack, can look untidy. The rack in Fig. 12-23 has space for a large number of magazines in a bin which is normally enclosed in a case, but can be tilted to give easy access to all of them. The unit then serves as a chairside or small coffee table. The bin stays closed under its own weight and the weight of its contents. There is no need for any fastener.

The sizes given (Fig. 12-24) should suit most magazines. The rack might have to be altered if you want to include folded newspapers. It is advisable to work from the inside outwards, making the bin to suit the magazines and the case to suit the bin. The bin could be made of 1/2-inch plywood with a veneered outer surface. Assembly might be with

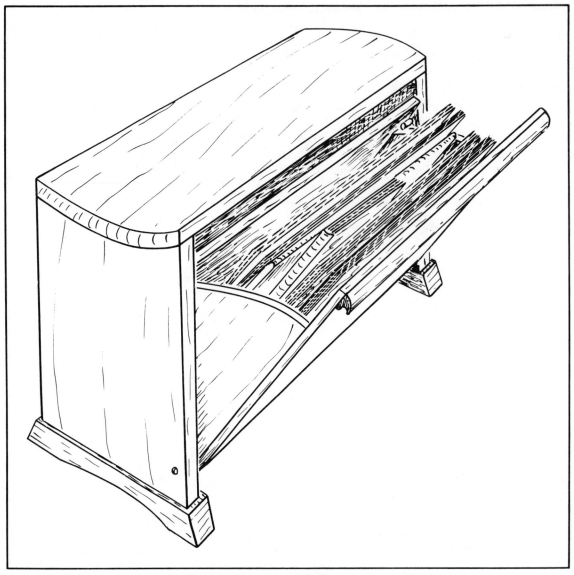

Fig. 12-23. A closed magazine rack with a hinged container that fits under the small tabletop.

glue and thin screws, although nails set below the surface and covered with filler are less conspicuous. The case is better made with solid wood and the parts dowelled.

The bin pivots on two round-head screws. Its movement is limited by pegs in the case ends near the top. They hold the bin vertical when the assembly is closed and prevent the bin from swinging too far forward when opened. Careful location of the

pivot points and stop pegs is important, but easy to arrange.

1. Cut the parts for the bin (Figs. 12-24A and 12-25A). The ends attach to the bottom, then the back and front go over their edges. The pivot point (Fig. 12-24B) is 3/4 inch in from the bottom and front surfaces. Use that as the center to draw the curves of the tops of the ends (Fig. 12-24C).

2. Assemble the bin. Drill small holes at the

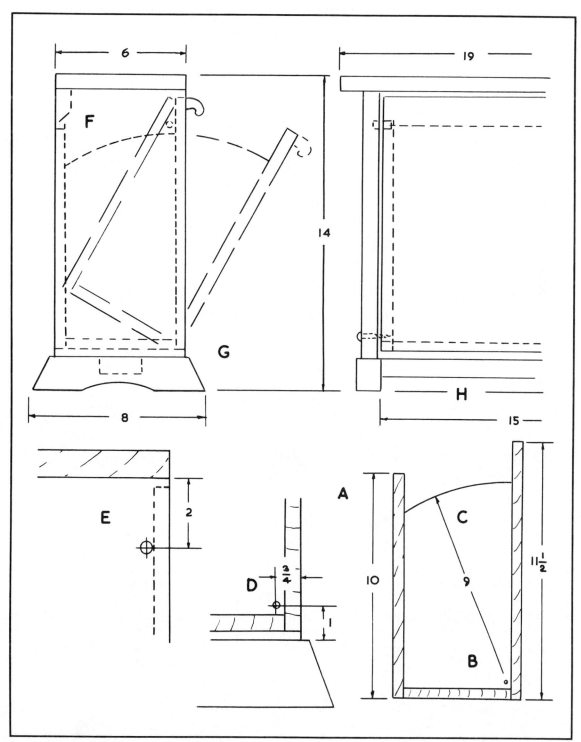

Fig. 12-24. Sizes of the closed magazine rack.

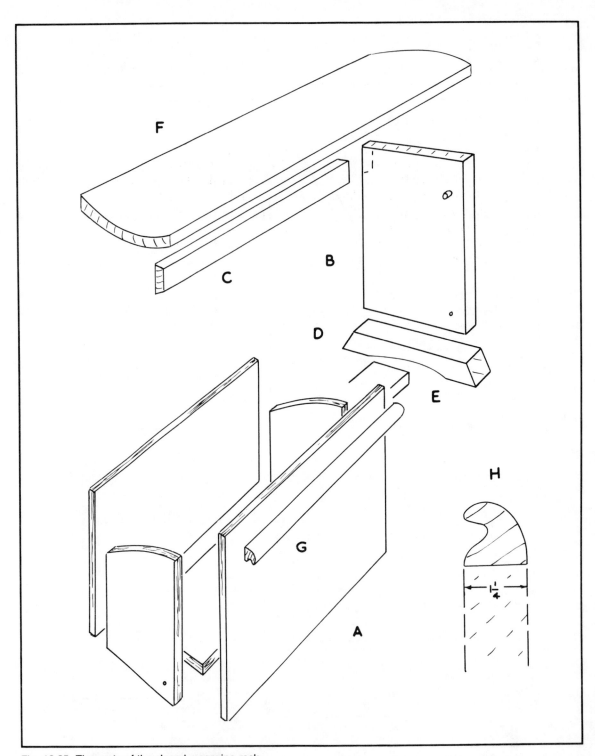

Fig. 12-25. The parts of the closed magazine rack.

pivot positions to locate the screw points.

3. The key parts of the case are the ends (Fig. 12-25B). The height should be 1/4 inch above and below the front of the bin. Use the actual bin as your guide to size. Mark the pivot positions (Fig. 12-24D) on each end and drill for the screws (10 gauge by 1 1/4 inches would be suitable). The stop pegs are short pieces of 3/8-inch dowel rod (Fig. 12-24E). Drill the holes in positions that allow the outside of the dowel to stop the bin front level with the edge of the case. It will then stop the back of the bin at the correct position when it is tilted.

4. The back rail (Figs. 12-24F and 12-25C) contributes stiffness to the case. Mark the outline of the back rail on an end. Put a temporary screw through the pivot hole and a piece of dowel in the stop hole. Try the action of the bin against the end. Besides the front finishing level with the edge, the back of the bin should close level with the other edge.

5. Add feet to the ends (Figs. 12-24G and 12-25D). Hollow the bottom edges to help the rack stand level.

6. Make the back rail. Bevel its lower edge so it does not interfere with the action of the bin back when it is moved. The length of the rail should be sufficient to allow the bin to swing between the ends easily. Allow for washers on the pivot screws.

7. Use the back rail as a guide for the length of the bottom rail (Figs. 12-24H and 12-25E). Allow for the thickness of the feet.

8. Make the top (Fig. 12-25F) the same width as the ends but with curved overlapping extensions.

9. Assemble the case with dowels—3/8-inch dowels at 2-inch intervals should be satisfactory. Check the fit of the bin during the case assembly, particularly the clearance at the ends which should fit squarely.

10. Any type of handle can be used on the bin. The grip must allow for a pull outwards. A metal or plastic handle at the center would do, but a full-length wood one is shown (Fig. 12-25G). If you make it, the shaping is best done on the edge of a wider board, which is cut off after shaping is completed (Fig. 12-25H).

11. Glue in the dowel stops. Put in the bin and fit the pivot screws and washers. If the action is satisfactory, remove the screws to release the bin so all the wood can be reached for finishing before final assembly.

Materials List for Closed Magazine Rack	
1 bin front	1/2 × 11 1/2 × 15
1 bin back	1/2 × 10 × 15
1 bin bottom	1/2 × 5 × 15
2 bin ends	1/2 × 5 × 10
2 case ends	3/4 × 6 × 12
1 case top	3/4 × 6 × 19
2 case feet	1 × 1 1/2 × 8
1 case back rail	1 × 2 × 17
1 case bottom rail	1 × 2 × 16

Chapter 13

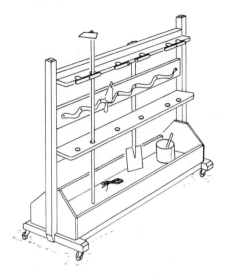

Storeroom

N ot every home has a room exclusively for storage. One is certainly useful, but many of us have to make do with part of the garage or a playroom. Whether we have a separate room or not, we all have a storage problem. Things in storage take up less space if they are on shelves or racks or in containers. They are tidier and can be stored systematically to make it easier to find what you want. You can make a few pieces of furniture to store your books and magazines, hobby materials, tools for occasional use and gardening equipment.

Strength is usually important. The quality of finish need not be very high unless you want to store things in a living room. The rack, boxes, or shelving could then be made of good wood and given a finish to match other furniture.

The projects that follow may suit you as described, or they can be altered and developed to match particular needs. For the beginning wood-worker who does not yet feel capable of making high-quality furniture, storage items that are more utilitarian will serve as an introduction and provide an opportunity to develop skills.

SHELF UNIT

Shelves for storage, which are intended to be functional rather than decorative, may be needed in a storeroom, garage, or anywhere utility is the main requirement. They should be strong and rigid. It is an advantage if they can be disassembled when they are no longer needed or if you decide to rearrange storage.

This shelf unit (Fig. 13-1) could be assembled permanently or rely on screws without glue, so it can be taken apart. Sizes can be varied to suit your needs, to fit a space, or to use available materials. The lower spaces between shelves are usually wider than higher ones because heavier and bulkier items are stored on lower shelves to maintain stability (Fig. 13-2).

Any wood can be used. The shelves can be solid wood, thick plywood, particleboard, or hardboard framed with solid wood. The only joints to cut are shallow dadoes to locate the shelves. Choose wood free from large knots and with reasonably straight grain. The finish applied depends on use. If the

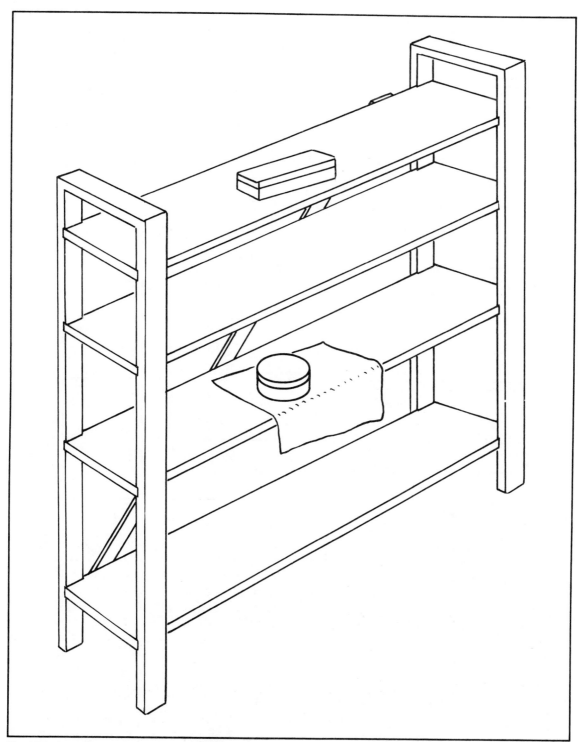

Fig. 13-1. A simple shelf unit for general storage.

337

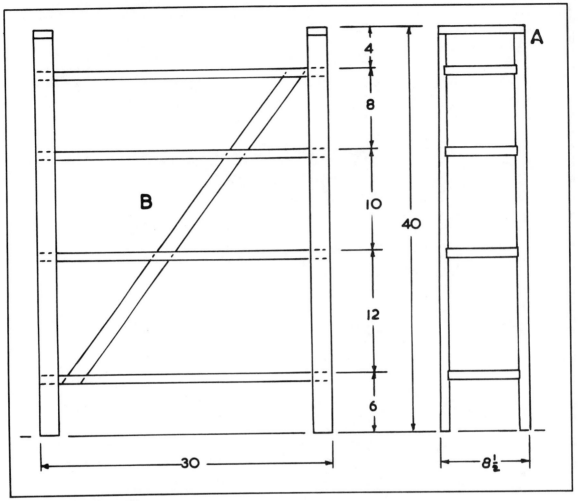

Fig. 13-2. Sizes of the shelf unit.

wood is left untreated, it will absorb dirt. It is better to give it at least one coat of paint or varnish to seal the grain, even if the shelf unit is located in an unimportant position.

1. Decide on the construction of the shelves. If solid wood, thick plywood, or particleboard, mark and cut them to size (Fig. 13-3A). If you think they might not be stiff enough for the intended load, add centered lengthwise stiffeners (Fig. 13-3B).

2. If you use hardboard or thin plywood, pin and glue strips underneath (Fig. 13-3C). Include centered crosspieces (Fig. 13-3D), more than pictured here if you think them necessary.

3. Mark out the uprights (Fig. 13-3E) together. The dadoes should match the shelf thicknesses and need be no more than 1/4 inch deep. Keeping them shallow locates each shelf without weakening the wood. Drill for one screw at each joint (Fig. 13-3F).

4. Assemble the shelves and uprights. Caps at the ends (Figs. 13-2A and 13-3G) are not essential, but they secure the uprights and help to prevent items falling off. Cut rabbets and screw downwards.

5. The assembly may be sufficiently rigid as it is, particularly if it fits into a room corner or

338

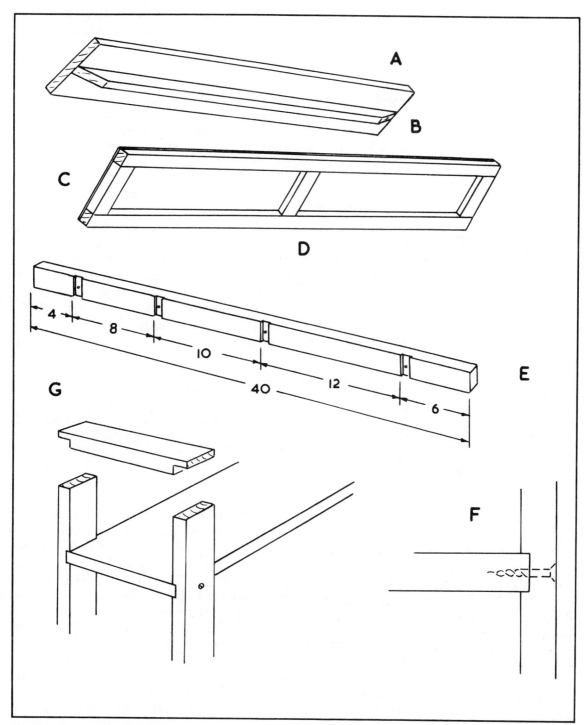

Fig. 13-3. Parts of the shelf unit.

against something else. Otherwise a diagonal strut at the back (Fig. 13-2B) can be screwed to the shelves after checking general squareness.

```
         Materials List for Shelf Unit

  4 uprights            1  × 2 × 40
  2 caps                1  × 2 × 9
  4 shelves             1  × 7 × 30
  1 diagonal strut      3/4 × 1 1/2 × 42
```

CORNER SHELVES

The corner of a room is often the least used part due to the difficulty of putting accessible furniture there. Something square, placed diagonally, wastes a large triangle behind it. There are special corner cabinets and various pieces of furniture for use in more important rooms. For simple shelf space in a storeroom, garage, or shop, however, a simple block of shelves arranged across a corner provides storage with direct access. Single shelves on battens may be suitable, but a complete unit is probably better.

The shelves could fill the space from floor to ceiling, from floor to table height, or hang from the wall. A simple triangular shelf does not offer much storage space, yet it is unwise to make it too large by extending it along the walls. Shelf area is better increased by extending it a short distance along the wall, then squaring off a small part on each side before cutting across at an angle.

The example in Fig. 13-4 has the shelves 24 inches along each wall. The useful increase in shelf area obtained by first cutting square from each wall can be seen in the plan view (Fig. 13-5A). The unit, as drawn, provides plenty of storage. The instructions apply to this size, but the same method can be used for shelves of very different sizes.

The shelves are drawn the same size both ways, so the front is at 45 degrees to a square corner. If it would suit your situation better, the shelves could extend more one way than the other. Making one way much less than the other reduces useful area, however. If there is no pressing reason for an unequal shape, it is better to have 45-degree shelves.

For most situations the main parts can be softwood and the shelves particleboard or thick plywood. Assembly can be accomplished with glue and screws or nails, then all parts finished with paint.

In this design two frames fit against the wall. Their parts are assembled with halving joints. In making accurate joints, it helps if all the wood is machined to exactly the same size. Mark the widths and depths of all the joints, then when you cut them with hand or power tools, they will fit uniformly.

1. Mark out the four uprights (Figs. 13-5B and 13-6A) together so they match.

2. Because one frame overlaps the other in the corner (Fig. 13-5C), make one frame narrower than the other by the thickness of the wood. Cut the four crosspieces for each frame (Fig. 13-5D). In all the frame parts leave a little excess on the lengths, which will be planed off after assembly.

3. Cut the halving joints. Join the frame parts with glue. If necessary, drive screws or nails from the frame sides that will be towards the wall.

4. Examine the place where the shelves are to go. The corner will probably not be sharp. For a close fit, round or bevel the edge of the frame that goes into the corner.

5. Do not assume that the corner is square, or you may make the shelves square and find that there are gaps at the back or front. Obtain the actual angle by measuring a distance along each wall from the corner to marked points, then measure the distance between these points (Fig. 13-6D). In this case, 24 inches each way from the corner will do. Set out the triangle from a straight edge on a piece of hardboard and cut it. Use that instead of a square when making the shelves, if the corner is not 90 degrees.

6. Mark out and cut the shelves (Figs. 13-5A and 13-6B). Notch around the uprights. Do not plane the front edges until the other edges fit to keep them level with the frames.

7. Round the projecting shelf edges. If veneered particleboard is used, the edges could be veneered to match the surfaces. If the shelves are

Fig. 13-4. A block of corner shelves.

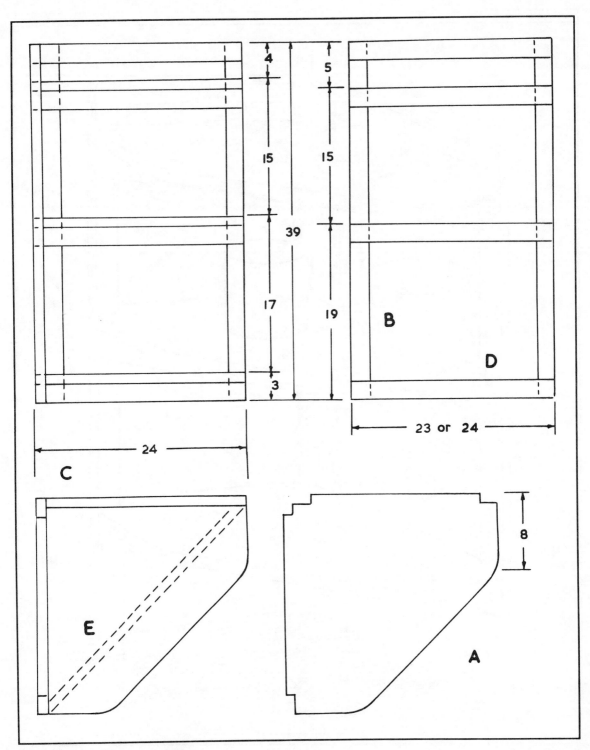

Fig. 13-5. Sizes of the corner shelves.

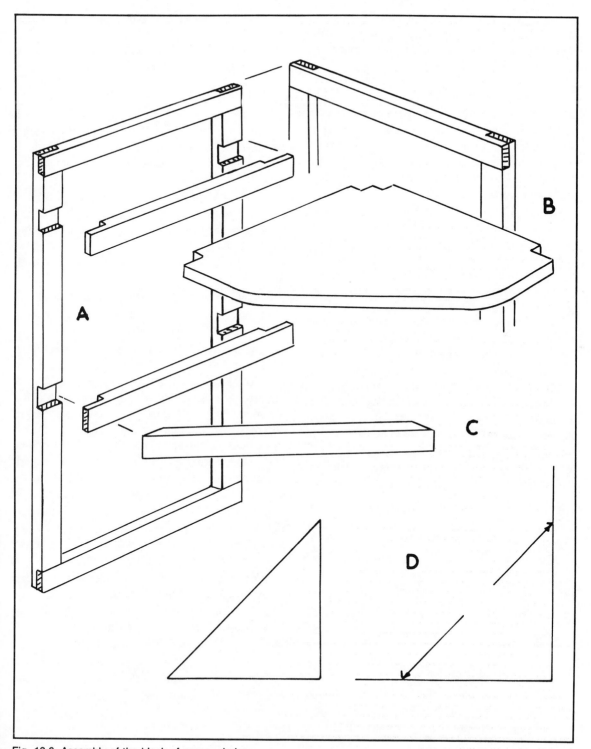

Fig. 13-6. Assembly of the block of corner shelves.

plywood, solid wood lips can be added to improve the appearance of the edges. In a storeroom or shop it may be sufficient to leave the edges untreated except for sanding. Round the exposed edges and corner of the frames.

8. If the assembly is to stand on the floor, a screw each way at the top to prevent tilting may be all the attachment to the wall that is needed. If the shelves are to hang, the number of screws needed into the wall will be governed by the expected load. Those towards the outside will be more effective than those near the corner.

9. It is possible to join the frames together and fix the shelves to them before fitting to the wall, but a good fit is easier to obtain if the frames are mounted on the walls before finally fixing the shelves to them. Join the frames together with a few screws to keep them in the correct relative position, then screw the frames to the walls.

10. Get the top shelf to be as accurate a fit as possible, because it cannot be removed once the frames are attached to the walls. The other shelves can be tilted and removed if you have to do any adjusting. Screw the shelves to their supports.

11. The shelves are probably stiff enough, but if you think the material used is too flexible or the shelves will be heavily loaded, there can be diagonal supports below (Fig. 13-6C). Cut the pieces to fit between the edges of the frames (Fig. 13-5E), then glue and screw them to the frames and shelves.

Materials List for Corner Shelves

4 uprights	1 × 2 × 39
4 crosspieces	1 × 2 × 24
4 crosspieces	1 × 2× 23
3 shelves	3/4 or 1 × 16 × 34
3 supports	1 × 2 × 34

SHOE STAND

If shoes are not kept together in a rack, they look untidy and can be difficult to find. There can be a built-in rack in a closet; if not, a freestanding rack may be put in a convenient place or moved as needed.

This shoe stand (Fig. 13-7) holds a large number of shoes. It has a compartment at the bottom for cleaning materials and small things that will not go on the rack.

The main parts are solid wood and the shoe supports are dowel rods. The back is plywood or hardboard. A painted finish is probably most suitable, but a good hardwood could be polished or varnished.

1. Mark out the pair of sides (Figs. 13-8A and 13-9A). The slopes are 60 degrees to the back. A suitable spacing for the dowel rods is 2 inches from front and back edges.

2. Rabbet the rear edges to take the back (Fig. 13-9B).

3. Cut the wood for the three shelves all the same length. Use them as guides to groove widths when cutting the dado joints (Fig. 13-9C).

4. The dowels could go right through the sides, but the shoe stand will look better if they do not. Stopping them reduces the glue area. To get the strongest joints in these blind holes, use fox wedging (Fig. 13-9D). Drill as deeply as possible, without the drill point breaking through. Make a saw cut across the end of the dowel and cut a short wedge to go into it. When the assembly is clamped, the wedge will spread the glued dowel end into its hole for maximum strength.

5. Have the back ready so it can be fitted during assembly to keep the parts square while the glue sets. Fit the shelves and dowels to the sides, drawing as tightly as possible with clamps.

6. Provide extra strength with blocks screwed and glued below the bottom shelf joints (Fig. 13-9E). Similar pieces can go under the top shelf. Keep them back from the front edges and bevel them so they are inconspicuous.

7. At the bottom, the door (Fig. 13-8B) is hinged at its lower edge (Fig. 13-9F) so the contents are easily seen and removed. Fit a centered handle near the top. Spring or magnetic catches at the sides will hold the door shut.

Fig. 13-7. A shoe stand with storage at the bottom.

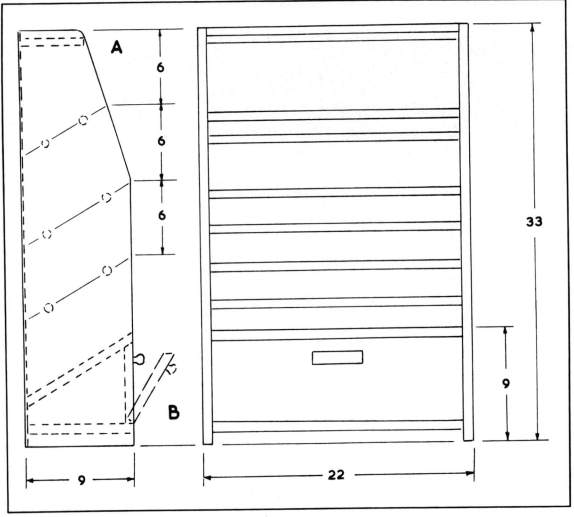

Fig. 13-8. Sizes of the shoe stand.

Materials List for Shoe Stand

2 sides	3/4 × 9 × 33
1 shelf	3/4 × 11 × 22
1 shelf	3/4 × 9 × 22
1 shelf	3/4 × 5 × 22
6 rails	22 × 3/4 diameter dowel rods
1 door	3/4 × 7 × 22
1 back	22 × 33 × 1/8 hardboard

WINE STORAGE RACK

Bottles of wine are best stored on their sides, preferably with a downward slope towards the cork. The bottles must not roll about the rack. Its size and capacity depends on how much wine you want to store at any time. The rack can also serve other purposes.

The rack in Fig. 13-10 holds and separates twelve bottles. There is a shelf for glasses and other things and a top at working height where you can open bottles or display ornaments. In its plain, un-

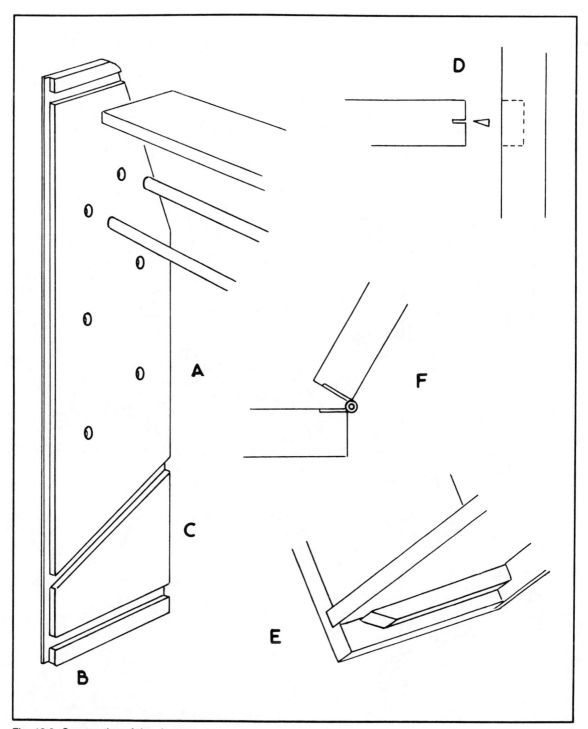

Fig. 13-9. Construction of the shoe stand.

Fig. 13-10. A wine storage rack with a working top.

treated form the rack can go in a storeroom, cellar, or any cool place. With a better finish and a table cloth in position, it could be used in a living room.

Construction may be entirely of softwood, with most parts 1-inch-by-2-inch sections. Dowelled assembly is suggested, with two, 3/8-inch dowels in each joint, but the framing can be joined with mortise and tenon joints if you wish.

The bottle rails are the same back and front. This means that bottles can be put in either way and the neck will come lower than the body both ways. Bottle sizes vary, but the cutout shapes in the rails, as shown, should suit most wine bottles. The designed size is for bottles up to a 4-inch diameter and 12 inches tall.

1. Mark out the bottle rails first (Fig. 13-11A). Make a template of one-and-a-half hollows (Fig. 13-12A). Locate the centers of the hollows along a rail and use the template overlapping curves to draw shapes. Cut one rail and use it to mark the others. Round the edges in the curves and underneath the upper rails where your hands might touch when removing bottles from below.

2. Set out the four legs (Fig. 13-11B) with the positions of other parts marked on them.

3. Make the two feet (Figs. 13-11C and 13-12B). Bevel the ends and cut away underneath so the rack is more likely to stand level if the floor is slightly uneven. Use the marked locations of the legs on the feet as a guide to the length of other parts between the legs (Fig. 13-12C).

4. Drill for dowels and assemble the end frames. Check that they are square and match as a pair.

5. Make the shelf with its ends to fit between the legs and the same length between shoulders as the bottle rails (Figs. 13-11D and 13-12D).

6. Drill for dowels and join the end frames with the bottle rails and shelf. Check squareness with the rack standing on a level surface.

7. Make the top (Fig. 13-11E) to overhang the other parts by 1 inch. The edge can be left square, rounded, or molded. If there is any shaping of the top edges, the long edge of the shelf is treated in the same way.

8. Even if the rack is to be used in a storeroom and its finish is unimportant, the wood should be given one or two coats of varnish or lacquer. This seals the grain and prevents it from absorbing spilled liquid and attracting dirt.

Materials List for Wine Storage Rack	
4 bottle rails	1 × 2 × 32
4 legs	1 × 2 × 30
2 feet	1 × 2 × 14
4 spacers	1 × 2 × 7
1 shelf	1 × 8 × 33
1 top	1 × 12 × 35

STACKING BOXES

If you want to store quantities of smaller things, whether they are nuts and bolts, potatoes, or children's building bricks, boxes are preferable to chests of drawers or other substantial furniture. If the boxes are made to stack, you can store many things while only occupying the floor space of one box.

The sizes depend on your needs, but they must be identical if they are to stack. If your needs vary, the overall sizes could suit the largest capacity required, and some boxes could have divisions for things needing less space.

The suggested boxes (Fig. 13-13) are a size and proportion to stand safely three or four high. Keeping the measurements different each way stops anyone trying to fit the boxes together in the wrong way, as might happen if they were near square.

The boxes could be made of solid wood or plywood. The corners could be simply nailed, or you could show your skill with dovetails or other joints.

1. Prepare all the wood needed for the same sections, then vital parts will match.

2. Mark out the openings in the fronts (Fig. 13-13A). Leave enough straight at the top for the runner ends to be covered when another box is put in. Cut about 4 inches deep so a hand could be put in without removing the box above. Round the edges.

3. The sides could have lifting handles, but

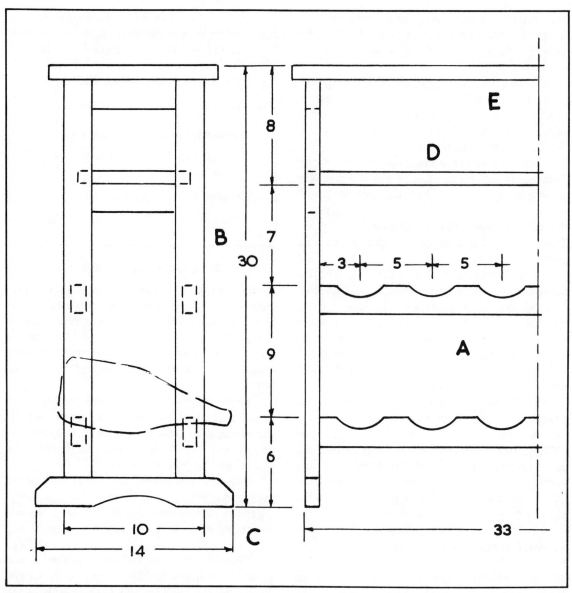

Fig. 13-11. Sizes of the wine storage rack.

hand slots serve the same purpose without projecting. Make the slots (Fig. 13-13B) 6 inches long and 1 1/2 inches wide by drilling at the ends and sawing away the waste. Round the edges.

4. If the corners are to be nailed, drive the nails in dovetail fashion. Put the top ones close together to resist any spreading loads there (Fig. 13-13C).

5. Comb joints can be used so nails can be driven both ways. This joint is particularly suitable for plywood (Fig. 13-13D).

6. Attach the bottom with screws or dovetail nailing.

7. To act as feet and locate one box on top of another, fit strips underneath (Fig. 13-13E). Cut these runners so they drop in easily without slack.

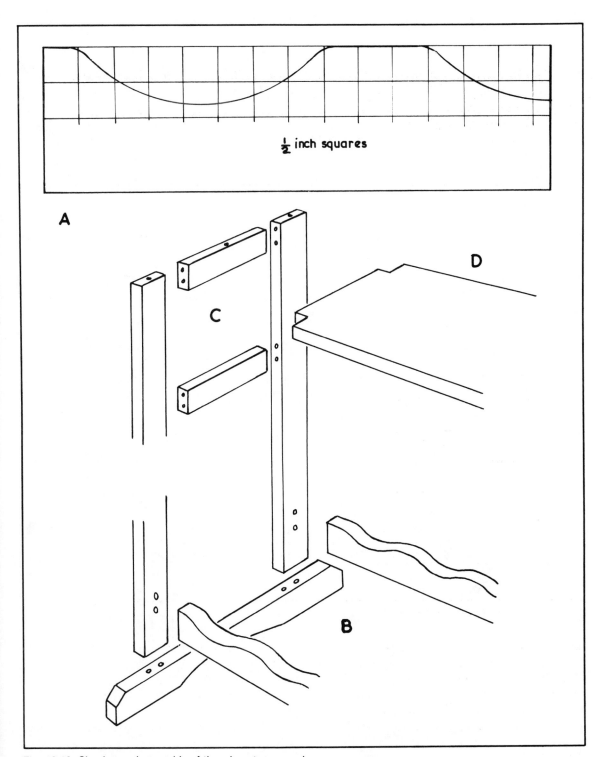

½ inch squares

A

C

D

B

Fig. 13-12. Shaping and assembly of the wine storage rack.

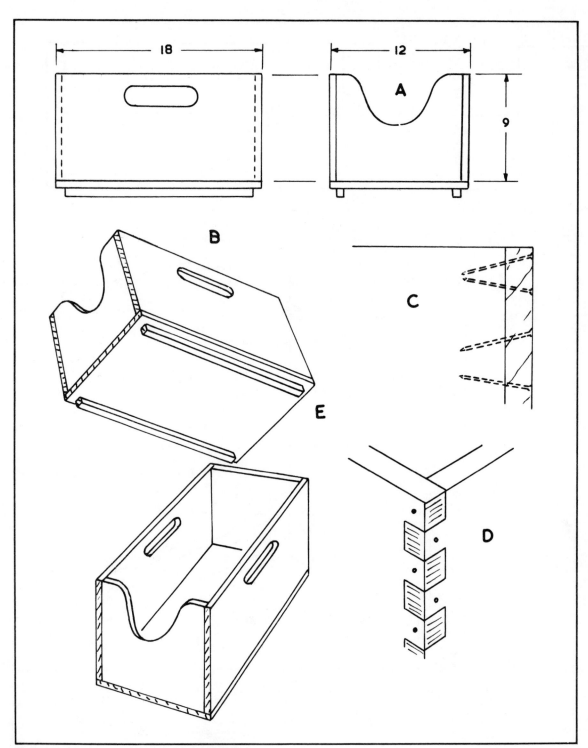

Fig. 13-13. Stacking box sizes and construction.

They should not have to be forced in.

GARDEN TOOL RACK

Many of us keep garden tools in a corner of the garage or spread them in several places. The tools can suffer or get in the way and we do not always know where to find them. It helps to store the tools on racks, but there might not be enough wall space for all of them. A freestanding rack can hold the hand tools and small equipment all together and protected. If it is on wheels, it can be pushed out of the way when not in use and pulled out to an accessible position when needed.

This rack (Fig. 13-14) is about 48 inches high and wide, with places for long and short tools of various sorts. At the bottom is a roomy container to hold the ends of the long tools and accommodate all the small things that a gardener accumulates. The feet are spread wide enough to provide stability, and they can be fitted with industrial-type, rubber-tired casters for mobility. The suggested sizes (Fig. 13-15) should suit most needs. Do not make the rack too small. Start with a few extra spaces for the tools that will, almost inevitably, be acquired.

Construction can be with softwood, except for the hardwood turnbuttons. The box will probably get wet, so any plywood should be exterior or marine grade.

1. Mark out the posts (Fig. 13-15A) with the positions of the other parts. Test the longest hoe or similar tool that will fit into holes. In use you will have to lift it clear of the lower shelf. Is there enough headroom to allow this in your storeroom or garage?

2. Make the two feet (Fig. 13-15B). Cut the joints between the posts and the feet (Fig. 13-16A). The notches are shallow, as the top surfaces of the feet have to extend under the box.

3. Make the box, (Fig. 13-15C) because it controls the sizes of some other parts. Its base is 14 inches wide and the ends extend 12 inches up the posts to serve as stiffening brackets. Nail or screw the base and ends to the solid wood sides. An overall box length of 44 inches should be satisfactory.

4. Make the two bottom rails (Fig. 13-15D). Their ends could be dowelled to the feet or joined with stub tenons (Fig. 13-16B). Let the outside edges of the rails come under the outside edges of the box.

5. Make the two, 2-inch square rails and the one flat one (Fig. 13-15E) using the box as a guide to length. Joints to the posts could be dowels or stub tenons (Fig. 13-16C).

6. The top rail (Fig. 13-15F) can have pegs for hanging tools. For spades and similar things with loop handles, there may be single pegs or two spaced close together. For T shaped handles fit pairs of pegs. Make them 1/2-inch or 3/4-inch dowels, tilted upwards (Fig. 13-16D), so tools will not fall off when the rack is moved.

7. Under the top rail and projection the other way, make a shelf pierced with slots (Fig. 13-15G). The slots are to take tools with long parallel handles. Slots made by drilling 1 1/2-inch holes and sawing into them should give ample clearance. Make the holes quite close to the shelf edge. Spacing should suit your tools. Where the working ends will not interfere with each other, they can be quite close, but if the tool has a broad top, you must arrange wider spacing.

8. The lower shelf is on top of its rail and is wider than the top one (Fig. 13-15H). Drill 1 1/2-inch holes in positions to match those in the top shelf (Fig. 13-16E).

9. Shape the tops of the posts. Take off any sharp edges on all parts. Round the outer corners of the shelves.

10. Glue and nail or screw the shelves to their rails. Join all the lengthwise parts to the posts. Screw in the box at the same time as fitting the bottom rails.

11. To retain the tools in the slotted shelf, make turnbuttons. Where the slots are close, one

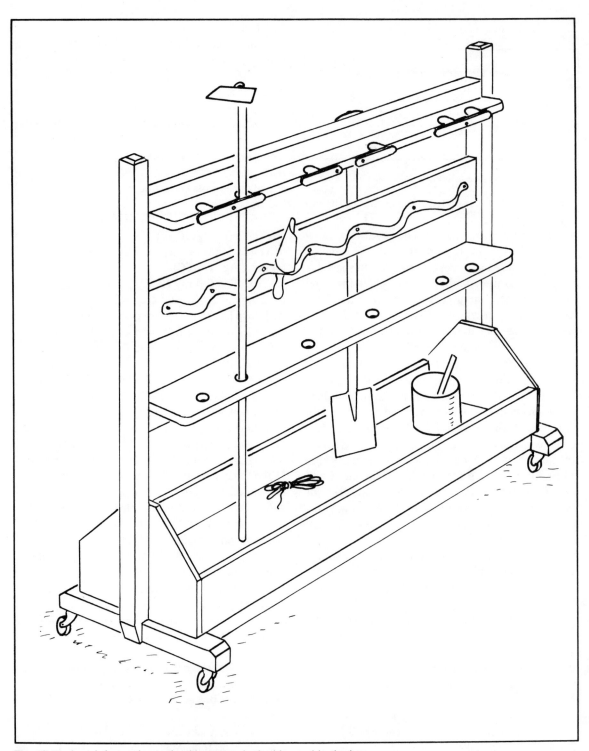

Fig. 13-14. A rack for garden tools with storage both sides and in the box.

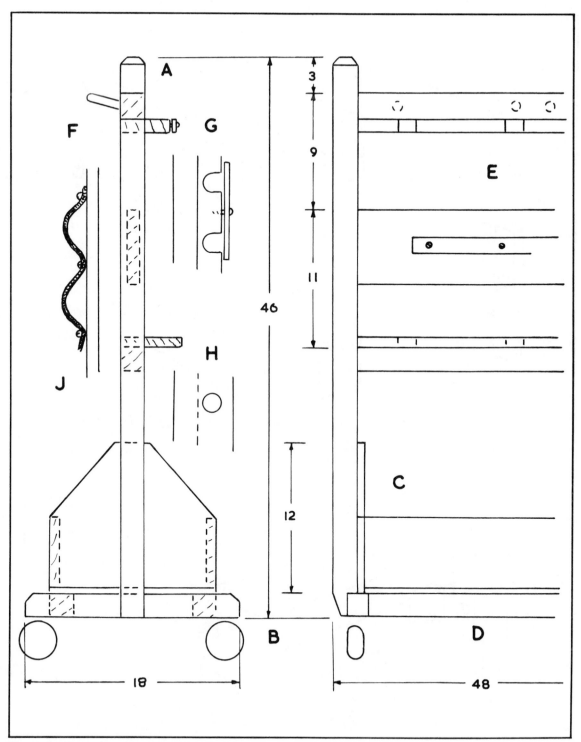

Fig. 13-15. Sizes of the garden tool rack.

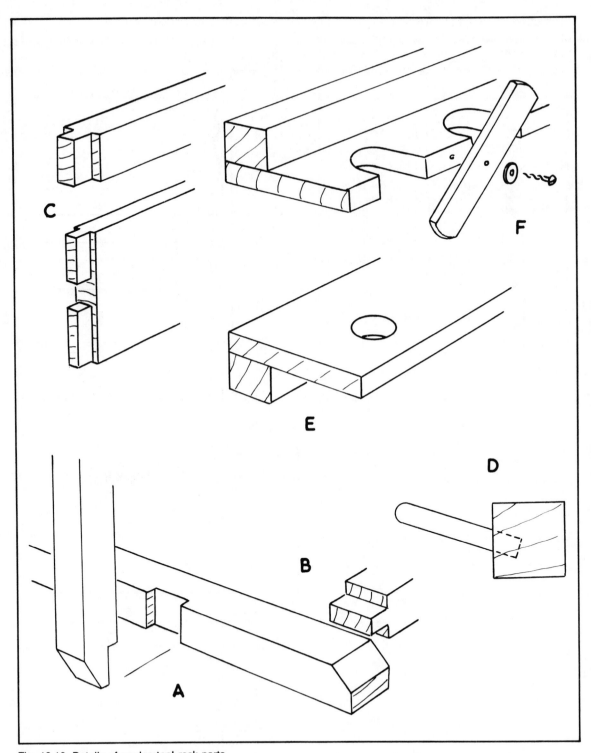

Fig. 13-16. Details of garden tool rack parts.

turnbutton can go over two slots (Fig. 13-15G). If the slots are more widely spaced, make a turnbutton for each slot. A fiber washer between a turnbutton and the shelf edge can provide friction if the turnbutton tends to drop out of position.

12. For small tools there can be loops along both sides of the wide board (Fig. 13-15J). Webbing 1 inch wide is suitable. Fasten the loops with screws through large washers. Arrange loops of different sizes to accommodate various tools.

13. A few drainage holes in the bottom of the box will reduce the risk of water being trapped. Although the rack could be used without treatment, it will look better if painted.

14. Screw on casters if the rack is to be mobile.

Materials List for Garden Tool Rack	
2 posts	2 × 2 × 46
2 feet	2 × 2 × 18
4 rails	2 × 2 × 48
1 rail	1 × 6 × 48
2 box sides	3/4 × 6 × 48
1 box bottom	14 × 44 × 1/2 plywood
2 box ends	12 × 14 × 1/2 plywood

Glossary

Glossary

The making of furniture forms only part of the craft of woodworking. The selection of words that follows are some that are particularly appropriate to the subjects of this book. This glossary may be helpful to readers unfamiliar with the language of craftwork.

annular rings—The concentric rings in the cross section of a tree that form the grain pattern; one ring is added each year.

apron—A piece of wood below a drawer that may be straight or have its lower edge decorated by molding, shaping, or carving.

arris—The line or sharp edge between two flat surfaces.

autumn growth—Part of an annual ring in a tree. It is formed as the sap descends.

backboard—The piece of wood closing the back of a cabinet or other piece of furniture.

backflap hinge—A hinge designed to swing back further than a normal hinge, often used for drop leaf tables.

bail—A swinging loop handle.

barefaced tenon—A tenon shoulder on one face only.

base—The foundation of anything. The main bottom portion of an assembly.

batten—Any narrow strip of wood. Any board fitted across other boards to join them (also called a *cleat*), to cover a gap between them, or to prevent warping.

bias—Cloth cut diagonal to the weave.

blind—Not all the way through; a mortise for a short tenon or a stopped hole for a dowel, for example.

bracket—An angular piece used to strengthen a corner in an assembly or to hold a shelf or flap.

bureau—A writing desk with a front that closes and has storage places inside.

burl—An outgrowth on a tree. It can be cut across to show very twisted grain. It is valued for its decoration when cut into veneers.

burlap—Coarse jute cloth used in upholstery. Also called *hessian*.

buttoning—Using buttons threaded with twine on

the surface of upholstery to retain the stuffing and to improve appearance.

cabriole leg—Furniture leg that curves out from a corner in a stylized form of an animal's leg. It may finish in a ball foot.

carcase—The main assembly parts that make up the skeleton of a piece of furniture, such as the framework of a cabinet or chest of drawers.

cast—Twisting of a surface that should be flat.

chamfer—An angle or bevel planed on an edge.

check—Split in wood in direction of the grain.

clamp—A device for drawing parts together, particularly when closing joints. Also called *cramp* or *cleat*.

cleat—Strip of wood joining other parts together, particularly as a support or brace across other boards to hold them together and prevent warping.

clench nailing—Using nails long enough to go right through so the projecting ends can be hammered over.

coniferous—Cone-bearing. Most softwood trees are coniferous.

contact adhesive—An impact adhesive that adheres as soon as the parts are brought together.

conversion—Cutting a log into boards and smaller sections of wood.

core—Base wood on which veneer is laid.

cornice—A molding above eye level that projects around the top of a cabinet.

cotton—Natural material woven in many ways for upholstery covering and loosely compounded for stuffing.

cotton batting—Cotton upholstery padding material.

counterbore—To drill a large hole over a smaller one so a screw head can be driven below the surface and then be covered with a plug.

countersink—To bevel the top of a hole so a flathead screw can be driven level with the surface.

crossbanding—Decorative veneering that uses narrow strips cut across the grain.

cup shake—A crack that develops in the growing tree and follows the line of an annual ring.

curly grain—A pattern on the wood surface caused by cutting across uneven grain lines.

dado joint—A groove in wood cut across the surface to take the end of a shelf or other part.

dead pin—A wedge or dowel.

deal—Tradename for some softwoods, such as pine and fir, but now less commonly used. Can also mean a plank or board.

deciduous—A leaf-shedding tree. Nearly all hardwoods are from deciduous trees.

dovetail—The fan-shaped piece that projects between pins in the other part of a dovetail joint. It is cut that way to resist pulling out.

dovetail nailing—Driving nails so they slope slightly at opposite angles to give an increased resistance to pieces being pulled apart.

dowel—A cylindrical piece of wood used as a peg when making joints. Dowel rods, produced in long lengths, may be cut into dowels for joints, but they have other uses where spindles are required.

draw bore (draw pin)—A peg or dowel across a mortise and tenon joint that pulls the parts together.

escutcheon—A key hole or the plate covering it.

face marks—Marks put on the planed side and edge when first prepared to indicate that further measuring and marking should be from them.

fall front—A flap that lets down to be supported in a horizontal position, such as the writing surface of some desks or bureaus.

fastenings (fasteners)—Metal nails or screws used to join parts.

feather edge—A wide, smooth bevel; taking the edge of a board to a very thin line.

figure—Decorative grain pattern, such as the medullary rays prominent in quarter-sawn wood; most often seen in oak.

fillet—A narrow strip of wood; e.g., to hold a mirror in its frame.

fillister—A rabbet plane with fences to control depth and width of cut. Not to be confused with a plow plane, which is used for cutting grooves.

firmer chisel—A heavy-duty, general-purpose chisel.

folding wedges—Two similar wedges that overlap each other in opposite directions to provide pressure when driven.

foxiness—First signs of rot. The color and effect may be regarded as decoration.

foxtail wedging—Wedges arranged in cuts in the end of a tenon that is spread when driven into a blind hole.

framed construction—Making an assembly of wood strips with the spaces filled by panels.

gateleg table—A table with drop leaves that is held up by swinging legs outward like gates.

gauge—A marking tool that tests for sizes, such as the thickness of wire or sheet metal, by a system of numbers.

gouge—A chisel with a rounded cross section.

haft—Long handle of a hammer or similar tool.

half-lap joint—Two crossing pieces notched into each other, usually to bring their surfaces level.

handed—Made as a pair.

hand screw—A clamp usually made entirely of wood.

hanging stile—The stile on which the hinges are attached.

hardwood—Wood from a deciduous tree that is usually, but not always, harder than softwoods.

haunch—The short piece of a tenon that is cut back where it joins another piece near its end.

heartwood—The mature wood near the center of a tree.

hessian—Another name for burlap.

housing joint—Another name for a dado joint.

impact adhesive—Another name for contact adhesive.

inlaying—Setting one piece of wood in another, either solid pieces or veneers.

jointing—The making of any joint; planing edges straight to make close, glued joints.

kerf—The slot made by a saw.

keying—Fitting pieces of veneer into kerfs. Used particularly across a miter joint to strengthen it.

knot—A flaw in wood where a branch was removed from the trunk. A method of joining cords.

laminate—Building up layers with several pieces of wood glued together. Used to make up curved parts.

laying out—Setting out details of design and construction.

lineal—Length only. It is sometimes used when pricing quantities of wood.

locking stile—The upright against which a door shuts.

marquetry—A system of inlaying that uses many woods, solids or veneers, to produce a pattern or picture.

matched boarding—Joining boards edge to edge with matching tongues and grooves.

medullary rays—Radiating lines from the center of a log that can be seen in some woods when radially cut. The markings are most prominent in oak.

miter—A joint where the meeting angle of the surfaces is divided or bisected, as in the corner of a picture frame.

molding—Decorative edge or border.

mortise—The rectangular socket cut to take a tenon.

mortise and tenon joint—One of the most common joints; the tenon on the end of one piece projects into the mortise cut in the other.

mullion—Vertical division of a window.

nosing—Semicircular molding.

oil slip—A shaped oilstone used on the insides of gouges and carving tools.

oil stain—Wood coloring with the pigment dissolved in oil.

oilstone—A sharpening stone for edge tools that is used with oil. Sometimes called a whetstone.

parquetry—Wood block flooring laid in geometric designs. Not to be confused with marquetry.

patina—Surface texture that is due to old age.

peck marks—Pencil marks used to transfer points on one thing to another.

pedestal—In furniture, a supporting post.

peen—The face of a hammer head. To turn over, as in riveting.

pigeon hole—A storage compartment that is often built into a bureau.

pinking shears—Scissors used in upholstery to cut a serrated edge on cloth.

plain sawed—Boards cut straight across a log.

planted—Applied instead of cut in the solid. Molding attached to a surface is planted, but if it is cut in the solid wood, it is stuck.

plinth—The base part of a piece of furniture.

plow—A plane for cutting grooves. It has guides to control depth and distance from an edge.

quartered (quartersawn)—Boards cut radially from a log to minimize shrinking and warping or to show the medullary rays in oak and some other woods.

quirk—A narrow or V-shaped groove beside a bead. A raised part between patterns in turned work.

rabbet (rebate)—Angular cutout section at an edge, as in the back of a picture frame.

rail—A horizontal member in framing.

rake—Incline to the horizontal.

rift sawn—Another name for plain sawn.

rive (riven)—To split boards from a log instead of sawing them.

rod—Strip of wood marked with distances of construction details; used for comparing parts instead of measuring with a rule.

router—Hand or power tool for leveling the bottom of a groove or recessed surface.

rule—Measuring rod. A craftsman does not spell it "ruler."

run—In a long length. Lumber quantities can be quoted as so many feet run.

sapwood—The wood nearer the outside of a tree. It is not as strong or durable as the heartwood in most trees.

seasoning—Drying lumber to a controlled moisture content.

secret dovetail joints—Joints in which the dovetail formation is hidden by mitered parts cut outside them.

selvage—The manufactured edge of a piece of cloth where the threads turn back in the weaving and the edge does not fray.

set—To punch a nail head below the surface. The bending of saw teeth in opposite directions to cut a kerf wider than the thickness of the saw metal.

setting out—Another name for laying out.

shake—A defect or crack in the growing tree that might not be apparent until it has been cut into boards.

shot joint—Planed edges glued together.

slat—Narrow, thin wood.

softwood—The wood from a coniferous, needle-leaf tree.

splay—To spread out.

spline—A narrow strip of wood fitting into grooves, usually to strengthen two meeting surfaces that are glued.

star shake—A defect in a growing tree that shows cracks radiating from the center.

stile—Vertical member in a door frame.

stopped tenon—Another name for a stub tenon.

strap hinge—A hinge with long, narrow arms.

stretcher—A lengthwise rail between the lower parts of a table or chair.

stub tenon—A tenon engaging with a mortise that is not cut through the wood.

tabling—The turned-in edge of a piece of cloth to strengthen it or prevent fraying.

tang—Small tapered end on a tool, such as a file or chisel, that fits into its handle.

template (templet)—Shaped pattern to draw around when marking out parts.

tenon—The projecting tongue on the end of one piece of wood that fits into a mortise on another piece of wood.

tote—A tool handle, particularly on a plane.

trunnel (treenail)—Peg or dowel driven through a joint.

tusk tenon—A tenon that goes through its mortise and projects on the other side where it may be secured with a wedge.

underbracing (underframing)—The arrangement of rails and stretchers to provide stiffness between the lower parts of table or chair legs.

varnish—A nearly transparent, paintlike finish that was once made from natural lacs and is now usually synthetic.

veneer—A thin piece of wood, usually decorative, intended to be glued to a backing.

veneer pin—Very fine nail with a small head.

wainscot—Usually refers to the lower paneling around a room. It also applies to quartersawn wood, such as oak, that shows figuring.

waney edge—The outer edge of a board that still has bark on it or is still showing the pattern of the outside of the tree.

warping—Distortion of a board by twisting or curving because of unequal shrinkage as moisture dries out.

winding—A board twisting in its length when sighted from one end.

working drawing—A drawing showing sizes, usually in elevations, plan, and sections, from which measurements can be taken to make the furniture. Not a pictorial view.

Index

Index

Other Bestsellers From TAB

☐ **ILLUSTRATED DICTIONARY OF BUILDING MATERIALS AND TECHNIQUES**

Here's a one-stop reference for do-it-yourselfers and professionals that gives you clear, straightforward definitions for all of the tools, terms, materials, and techniques used by builders, contractors, architects, and other building professionals. It includes almost 4,000 terms and abbreviations from the simple to the complex, from slang to the latest technical information. 272 pp., 172 illus. 7″ × 10″.

Paper $14.95   **Hard $22.95**
Book No. 2681

☐ **ALL ABOUT LAMPS: CONSTRUCTION, REPAIR AND RESTORATION—Coggins**

If the lamps and lighting fixtures in your home look worn, out of date, and generally unattractive . . . if you're stunned by the prices furniture stores and decorator shops charge for even the simplest new lamps . . . if you've admired the unique lamps made from old crocks, bottles, vases, and other "salvage" items that appear so often in home decorating magazines . . . then this is a book you really can't afford to miss! It's a complete sourcebook of ideas and plans for repairing, restoring, converting, and creating exciting lamps and lighting fixtures at costs even the tightest budget can handle. 256 pp., 196 illus. 8 full-color pages. (7″ × 10″).

Paper $16.95   **Hard $24.95**
Book No. 2658

☐ **PLANNING AND BUILDING FENCES AND GATES**

This colorfully illustrated guide gives you all the expert, step-by-step guidelines and instructions you need to plan and build durable, cost-effective fences and gates. You will be able to design and construct just about any kind of fence you can think of—barbed wire, woven wire, cable wire, mesh wire, board fences, electric fences, gates, and much more! 192 pp., 356 illus., 8 1/2″ × 11″. 2-Color Throughout.

Paper $14.95   **Hard $22.95**
Book No. 2643

☐ **CABINETS AND VANITIES—A BUILDER'S HANDBOOK—Godley**

Here in easy-to-follow, step-by-step detail is everything you need to know to design, build, and install your own customized kitchen cabinets and bathroom vanities and cabinets for a fraction of the price charged by professional cabinetmakers or kitchen remodelers . . . and for less than a third of what you'd spend for the most cheaply made ready-made cabinets and vanities! 142 pp., 126 illus. 7″ × 10″.

Paper $12.95   **Hard $19.95**
Book No. 1982

☐ **HOME ELECTRICAL WIRING AND MAINTENANCE MADE EASY**

With this exceptional sourcebook as your guide, you'll be amazed at how simple it is to learn professional wiring techniques that are in compliance with the most recent National Electrical Code requirements—whether you want to install a light dimmer, inspect your home's wiring system or install a complete wiring system from scratch! 272 pp., 550 illus. 4-Color throughout, packed with color illustrations. 8 1/2″ × 11″.

Paper $19.95   **Hard $28.95**
Book No. 2673

☐ **111 YARD AND GARDEN PROJECTS—From Boxes and Bins to Tables and Tools—Blandford**

Save $100's . . . even $1,000's . . . on more than 100 practical and exciting projects for your lawn and garden! Projects include: plant stands, storage shelves, climbing plant supports, benches, tables, window boxes, hanging planters and cold frames, gardening tools, fences and gates, garden carts, trolleys, wheelbarrows, and more! 416 pp., 301 illus. 7″ × 10″.

Paper $16.95   **Hard $25.95**
Book No. 2644

☐ **UPHOLSTERY TECHNIQUES ILLUSTRATED—Gheen**

Here's an easy-to-follow, step-by-step guide to modern upholstery techniques that covers everything from stripping off old covers and padding to restoring and installing new foundations, stuffing, cushions, and covers. All the most up-to-date pro techniques are included along with lots of time- and money-saving "tricks-of-the-trade" not usually shared by professional upholsterers. 352 pp., 549 illus. 7″ × 10″.

Paper $16.95   **Hard $27.95**
Book No. 2602

☐ **BUILDING OUTDOOR PLAYTHINGS FOR KIDS, WITH PROJECT PLANS—Barnes**

Imagine the delight of your youngsters—children or grandchildren—when you build them their own special backyard play area! Best of all, discover how you can make exciting, custom-designed play equipment at a fraction of the cost of ordinary, ready-made swing sets or sandbox units! It's all here in this step-by-step guide to planning and building safe, sturdy outdoor play equipment! 240 pp., 213 illus. 7″ × 10″.

Paper $12.95   **Hard $21.95**
Book No. 1971

Other Bestsellers From TAB